Fast As White Lightning

Also by Kim Chapin

The Road to Wembley
Dogwood Afternoons
The Beauty of Running (coauthor with Gayle Barron)
Billie Jean (coauthor with Billie Jean King)
Tennis to Win (coauthor with Billie Jean King)

4/2007

Fast As White Lightning

The Story of Stock Car Racing

by

KIM CHAPIN

Three Rivers Press • New York

Published by
Three Rivers Press, a division of Crown Publishers, Inc.,
201 East 50th Street, New York, New York 10022.
Member of the Crown Publishing Group.

Random House, Inc. New York, Toronto, London, Sydney, Auckland
www.randomhouse.com

Portions of this book previously appeared in *Sports Illustrated*, *Atlanta Weekly*, and *AutoWeek*

Printed in the United States of America

Library of Congress Cataloging in Publication Data

Chapin, Kim.
Fast as white lightning : the story of stock car racing / by Kim Chapin — 1st ed.
p. cm.
1. Stock car racing—Southern States—History. 2. Automobile racing drivers—United States—Biography. I. Title.
GV1029.9.S74C44 1998
792.72'0973—dc21 97-44926
CIP

ISBN 0-609-80108-2

10 9 8 7 6 5 4 3 2 1

Updated Edition

Every effort has been made to obtain permission from the appropriate parties for the photographs cited below, but if any errors have been made we will be happy to correct them for future printings.

Black & White Photo Credits: 1, 13, 61: *Southern Living* magazine; 2, 3, 4, 6, 9, 14, 24, 25, 34, 43, 45, 48, 51, 53, 54, 56, 57, 58, 59, 60, 62: Don Hunter; 5, 10, 18, 22, 32(a), 38, 41, 42, 46, 52: Darlington Raceway; 7, 8, 11, 12, 15, 16, 17, 19, 20, 21, 23(a), 31, 32(b), 36, 37, 67: International Speedway Corporation (Daytona International Speedway, Darlington Raceway, and Talladega Superspeedway); 19, 20, 23a, 31, 37: by Jack Jesse, courtesy Daytona News-Journal Corporation; 26, 27, 28, 39: courtesy Doris Roberts; 29, 33: Atlanta Newspapers; 30: Tom Morrison; 35: Mercury Marine; 40: Wide World Photo; 44, 47, 50: Charlotte Motor Speedway; 63: *Berkeley* (S.C.) *Democrat;* 64: Charlie Powell; 65, 66: Dozier Mobley.

Color Photo Credits: 1, 5, 9, 15, 16: courtesy of Goodyear Tire and Rubber Company; 2, 3: John C. Meyers; 4, 10, 11, 12, 13: courtesy of RJR Photography; 6, 7: courtesy of CMS Photography; 8: Jon Soohoo for the California Speedway; 17: photo by KPC Photography for the Goodyear Tire and Rubber Company; 18: photo by Phil Cavali for the Goodyear Tire and Rubber Company.

FOR MY FATHER,
Wendell P. Chapin

Contents

Fast As White Lightning

Prologue:

Tiny Lund Blows Their Doors Off on Dirt

Part I: August 19, 1975

People in the rural South don't bother much with road maps. What they do is, they happen upon an old barn, or a big produce stand, or a tobacco shed with a corrugated metal roof, or a mill warehouse, and they scratch their heads and say, "This seems about right," and pretty soon they're where they want to be. And so, following Tiny Lund's instructions for the second time in a week, I got off Interstate 26 at the St. Matthews exit and slowly headed east for a while on South Carolina Highway 6, and then south. On either side of the road there were fields of burned, dry corn, fields of green tobacco turning to gold, fields of beans and peanuts, and the occasional field of cotton. There were several neat, white wood houses along the way, a few old stone houses giving way to kudzu, one sharecropper's weather-worn shack. A dark face was dimly framed by an upstairs window of the shack; an old man sat quietly on the porch in a straightback chair. I drove through St. Matthews and Creston and Elloree and Parler and Santee and Eutawville and Eutaw Springs, small towns with wide streets that stood empty beneath the punishing midday sun. The dead dog still lay beside the road near Eutawville, bloated now. Dead, dry leaves lay everywhere, scattered and still. Soft clouds gave hint of later thundershowers.

Near Cross, Tiny's hometown, I pulled off the road and

stopped in front of Tiny's garage. Next to the garage was the house trailer where his mechanic, Roger Byers, lived. By the side of the garage Tiny's Sportsman racer, a battered, powder-blue Chevelle, No. 55, sat on the bed of its tow truck. The garage door was padlocked. Hanging from the padlock was a steering wheel wrapped with black electrician's tape. A small bouquet of white flowers and green leaves decorated the upper-left quadrant. There was no one around.

I left the garage and drove past Tommy Sweatman's Gulf service station and general store, which marked the turn-off to the Tiny Lund Fishing Camp, and for perhaps another fifteen minutes followed the pleasant contours of Lake Moultrie. On the northern outskirts of Moncks Corner I passed the Berkeley Memorial Gardens, deserted save for two black gravediggers who rested in the shade of a large and gnarled oak tree. I saw the green canopy, and the hole in the ground with the mound of earth piled in readiness beside it. One mile beyond was the Saint Michael Lutheran Church of Moncks Corner.

Six days earlier I had visited Tiny Lund in his idyllic world and watched him win a Sportsman race on dirt; now he was dead, having been killed on the seventh lap of the Talladega 500, a keystone event of the Grand National late-model stock car racing circuit, not forty-eight hours before.

Earlier that season, Grand National driver Bobby Allison had described a lap of the monstrous, 2.66-mile tri-oval at Talladega, which was located precisely fifty miles east of downtown Birmingham and was officially called the Alabama International Motor Speedway. "We'll start at the flagstand," he said. "You're out against the wall—within about six inches at the closest point—and you just kind of taper away into the first turn. The turn is the smoothest one lane up from the bottom, so you aim for that spot. But as you run through the bumps—waves in the track—they kind of move the car over just a little bit. At let's say 100 mph, the bumps are almost nonexistent, but at 200 mph, they become a series of *whomp-whomp-whomps* on the car and it's pretty much different. You take that arc through the corner and maybe pinch just a little before you get out into turn two. Then, as you blend out onto the back straightaway, you go out near the wall. It's comfortable to run close to the wall—about a car's width off the wall—but the design of this track is so perfect, especially for our speeds and all, that you can run anywhere you want to. About where some gates cross the straightaway at the entrance to turn three, you blend down into the corner and you go right into the bottom and just let the pressure of the car push you up a little bit. You swing on through the turn, and as you get off of turn four, you kind of blend out to the wall again for the short chute between turn four and the tri-oval. There's a bump coming off of four that's similar to the tunnel bump at Daytona, but much less severe. It does exist, though, so I mention it. Then you go all the way to the bottom in the tri-oval, and then you're through the tri-oval and back out toward the flagstand, where you blend back out to the outside wall.

"The track is good all the way, and it's easy to drive as long as nothing's going wrong. But it's very difficult to drive if you have any kind of a problem with the car, and also if you're suffering from a shortage of horsepower. It doesn't take much handling to go fast, but it does take a little to drive in traffic. And the track is pretty unforgiving if something does happen."

Question: You told a friend of yours recently that you feel uncomfortable on superspeedways.

Lund: I don't feel comfortable. . . . Well, I won't say that exactly. The thing about it is, there's not that many cars that handle well. You get in a car that really handles, then it's another thing. But just to go down there and have to brave one lap after another like I've had to do so long, it's uncomfortable.

Question: What form does the uncomfortableness take? Do you start thinking about things? Or . . .

Lund: Well, you know damned well if you extend yourself and go as hard as you want to, you're gonna get out of shape, or wreck yourself, or wreck somebody else. You can go on in there and forget about it, or you can just try to drive as good as you can under the circumstances.

Question: Have you ever been scared in a race car?

Lund: Oh, hell. Anybody that's human can get scared. It's not really a scared feeling. It's just . . . when you *know* you're in a tight spot, it's just a feeling that right there you're really down to the nitty-gritty.

Question: What does the fear feel like?

Lund: How about a feeling like if you're walking at night and you thought there was a rattlesnake ten feet from you—or two feet from you? You couldn't see him; you didn't know if you should move or otherwise. The instant that hits you, how would your feeling be?

Question: I asked you.

Lund: Well, how would *you* describe *that*?

Question: I'm asking for a physical description of fear. For example, if I'm going down the highway and something happens, I feel . . .

Lund: I'm giving you an example, in a different sense. I was just trying to give you a cross-example. If you were walking down around my landing there at my fishing camp at night and you heard a snake rattle—and there are a lot of snakes—and you didn't have no flashlight, and you was barefooted and with nothing in your hand, and you figured he was two feet from you, what kind of feeling would you have initially? Just like that?

Question: My stomach would probably go up in my throat and my legs would go cold.

Lund: Well, that's kind of like the feeling. For instance, I lost my steering once at Daytona Beach several years ago, and from the time I realized that there's no steering and I was gonna hit the wall, to the time I hit—that's a measurement of a few thousandths of a second. Well, then this feeling, or flash, is what you get. It's not really a thing of fear, I'd say. It's just a feeling that you know you're in goddamned bad trouble and . . . what are you gonna do? That particular time there wadn't a damned thing I could do but hang on the steering well, and it happened I was running real high on the race track and that saved me.

But as far as spinning a race car out on a superspeedway, I don't get scared or nothing. You're driving, you're

> shifting, you're turning, you're trying to get the car straightened out to keep going. And if you're spinning you're thinking: *Is there a guy coming gonna hit me broadside?* Y'know? *Should I keep backing? Should I try to make the car go down off the track? Should I shift gears?* All that stuff is going through your mind—*click!*—like that, just as fast as you can think.
>
> Many a-time I've been spinning and locked the wheels up momentarily and throwed the car in reverse and revved the engine up as high as it'll go and popped the clutch to make the tail come back around and then shifted to catch second or third to pull it forward and keep it straight. I don't know if you ever talked to anybody else, but I've done this my whole life. Many times I've spun it and caught it and kept on going. Which a lot of other drivers have, too, but some guys develop a knack for things like this more than others. Some guys, it just seems like they're always in the right spot at the wrong time to be in accidents even if it wasn't anything they could help. There are some guys that way. All my life I haven't been one. I've been rough and tumble—I might have wrecked sheet metal as far as roughness—but I really haven't been a guy that wrecked a lot of cars. I've really been pretty lucky to stay out of accidents.

Ralph Moody, a dour New Englander by birth who was one of the best mechanics and crew chiefs in the South, said, "Racing's dangerous if you're unused to it—like driving a motorcycle feels dangerous if you haven't driven motorcycles much. But when a driver says, 'I scared myself out there,' he's lying. What he really means is that he's afraid of damaging the car. If a driver feels he's going to get hurt, he'd be a fool to race."

The accident involved several cars, nearly all of them backmarkers, including one driven by Walter Ballard, a pleasant journeyman resigned with good grace to his position in racing.

"I should have never been back there myself," he said, "but I was just trying to play it safe. Red Farmer had blowed a piston on the second lap. He was really smoking and I thought he was going to blow his engine all to pieces. So I backed way off—just got scared of it and said I'm not going to go up there and wreck my car—and all those guys got ahead of me. And then I seen Red Farmer go to the pits, one lap before the wreck, I guess, and I just put my foot on the floor and never lifted. Elmo Langley was way up in front of me and I caught him in turn one and two. I was running about 15 mph more than him, it seemed like, because I was drafting him. I was setting him up coming off the second corner, fixing to pass him, when I saw the wreck. Well, I passed Elmo on the brakes—I'm *sliding* on the brakes passing him. Elmo said he heard them tires squealing and just knew I was going to run all over him. Elmo came down off the banking, and when he came down, I came down. We was side by side, with the brakes on. It was kind of dusty down there, and my car went sideways on me. There was a hole there, and Elmo got through it. I done got off in the grass and I just went sliding through the grass. And hit that inside cement wall.

"The deal was, Tiny was trying to get around J.D. McDuffie. Some other drivers said Tiny'd been running all over the race track and tried to go in between the wall and J.D. and there wasn't enough. . . . There was enough for about two-thirds of a car to get in there, they said. And Tiny went on down the track and spun around and Terry Link come through spinning and hit him.

"Terry Link got in the wreck before I got there. They said he drove right through the wreck and hit. . . . That's what they said. He was a rookie and drove right through the wreck and hit Tiny's car and hit him like *that.* I talked to Bill France, Jr. [the president of the National Association for Stock Car Auto Racing—NASCAR—which sanctioned the race], and he said he looked at the pictures. He said Link spun his car—just spun at least two or three times—before he hit Tiny.

"I helped get Link out and load him up because he was hurt pretty bad. His face was cut up and he was knocked completely out. I knew the other car was up there on the track, but I had no idea who it was until they brought Tiny into the field hospital. I was there in the hospital with him, but I was kind of dazed myself. Somebody told me it was Tiny and that it didn't look good. Then I knew they was working on him, on the table. I'm sure they announced him dead there, from what I understand. But in my own mind, I felt like he was still going to be all right, even when they hauled him away. That's the way I looked at it. At the time, you don't think about him being dead. I don't.

"It's kind of a weird feeling. I don't think you really can say what the heck happens to you. You know, I just talked to the man before we started racing, and it wadn't but fifteen, twenty minutes later he was dead. I imagine you can speak for yourself on something like that. But it's happened three or four different times and you're sure not going to let it just sit there and pry on your mind. It's like you see a lot of women—most of the women—they'll set there and cry and cry and won't get a-hold of theirself. The thing to do is to keep cool and not fuss about it, try not to think about it. Like it never happened."

So if the films and the newspaper accounts and the stories of Walter Ballard and other drivers were to be believed, and there was no reason to doubt any of them, then Tiny Lund was truly the instrument of his own destruction, having begun the accident that sent his car careening wildly down the back straight of that deceptive Talladega race track. For a few brief seconds, there was no problem. Lund's car came nearly to rest, sideways on the track, the driver's side exposed to the onrushing traffic. But there was no damage to Lund and little to his car. For a few brief seconds, it was just another long slide of the sort that happened often at a place like Talladega, usually with no more lasting result than the temporary embarrassment of the driver. But then the second car appeared through the dust, and Terry Link, spinning crazily himself, drove into Tiny's door and pushed it toward the middle of Tiny's car. In those few brief seconds—what? Was Tiny just trying to crank up his dead engine and get his car in gear, all the while chiding himself for the lost time? Or did Tiny Lund then know real fear? In those final milliseconds, did he see the coiled rattlesnake strike and send him into the abyss? An unsettling thought.

Lund was not hurt in any obvious way. He died of "massive internal injuries" ten minutes after he reached the field hospital as Walter Ballard looked on in disbelief and as a second team of medics worked to repair the cut-up face of Terry Link. However messy broken bones and bloody lacerations can be, they don't often kill. Even severe burns, as horrible as they will surely be later on, present at first only the most basic medical problems. But when one's heart and liver and kidneys are ripped loose from their delicate rest, there is precious little that can be done. Lund was a massive man who sat jammed and cramped in his contoured driving seat. A thinner, more flexible man would not have absorbed the punishment that Lund did and might well have survived.

The sanctuary of the Saint Michael Lutheran Church was filled to overflowing long before the funeral began. Loudspeakers were set up to broadcast the service to the latecomers, who milled about in the lobby and on the lush, green grass outside, some seeking refuge from the oppressive heat—the temperature was 97 degrees—beneath a single dying shade tree at the very back of the church grounds.

Among the last to arrive was Bill France, Sr., the founder of NASCAR and the president of the International Speedway Corporation, which owned the Talladega race track. A young usher failed to recognize him. He removed his light-blue sport coat and with the others in his party repaired to the shade tree. Within moments, however, his presence was noted and he returned to the church alone, looking very sad, very old, and in a rumpled sort of way, very dignified—like the patriarch of a well-blooded family no longer rich—and took a seat on one of the several folding chairs that had been set up in the rear of the church. The acolyte was summoned, and by entering the sanctuary announced that the service was shortly to begin.

Betty Jo Yarborough, the cute, perky, ex-cheerleader wife of Grand National driving star Cale Yarborough, wandered through the lobby, a look of shock and unease on her pretty face. It seemed obvious that this ceremony was forcing her to consider the mortality of her own husband, who now stood prominently at the end of a double line of drivers and friends outside the church as the casket was wheeled up a narrow sidewalk, then maneuvered through double glass doors and taken to the front of the sanctuary.

Tiny's wife, Wanda, whom he fondly called "Hillbilly" in reference to her upbringing in the mountains of western North Carolina, walked behind the casket holding the hand of their young son, Chrissie, who, too young to fully comprehend why he wasn't playing with his friends Tadpole and Shrimp down at his father's fishing camp, wore a poutish look on his dumpling face. (The chancel flowers, said the program notes, were given by Chris Lund "to the glory of God and in memory of his father.") Wanda wore a black skirt and a red, knitted vest. Her glistening eyes pleaded. But she remained composed, and one could almost hear Tiny saying, "Keep your act together, Hillbilly." Tiny's widowed mother followed, and then Tiny's sister, who wept openly.

The ceremony lasted nearly forty minutes. The minister was young and fair-haired and had skin the texture of bread dough, and he dwelt on the glory of death with a half-grin on his puffy face. If the purpose of the service was to give succor to the living, then it only half-succeeded, for although there was not a feeling of oppressive sadness, neither was there one of spiritual uplift. Mainly, there was boredom and a strange sense of discomfort. Several of the mourners became fidgety. Buddy Baker left the sanctuary, pleading the heat. Beyond the immediate family, Baker was outwardly the most affected by Lund's death. He had won the race in which Tiny had been killed—an important victory for him—but he was not told of his friend's death until his post-race press conference. Stunned, his triumph turned to brittle shards of ice, he needed several private minutes in which to compose himself. Several times in the lobby where Baker now stood my eye caught his, and each time he turned away. He, like the rest of us, was private in his grief and found little hope in this celebration of death.

At last it was over. The mourners filed out in haste. The

men, from the stars of the Grand National circuit to down-the-road friends, were variously dressed. Some wore suits, others wore sport coats open at the neck, still others wore only slacks and shirts. One of the last to leave was a man in bib overalls, a friend of the family. Also among the last to leave was Richard Petty, the most accomplished stock car driver of them all, resplendent in a vented, light-tan suit. From Petty and the other drivers there were no tears.

"We wadn't the greatest of friends or anything," Petty said, "but I could consider him a friend more so than a lot of the others because he worked for us for a pretty good while. Me and Dale and Maurice [Dale Inman, Richard's cousin and crew chief, and Maurice Petty, Richard's brother and engine builder] used to rassle with him. He was a big fella—he used to be a lot bigger—and he'd just throw us everywhere. I mean, we was like little ants on him. . . .

"When he had the wreck and I come back down the backstretch and seen him, I knowed that was it. I mean, some things you know, and that was just one of 'em, I guess. Dale and them always want to know what's going on, and so I told 'em on my radio. I said, 'Tiny's just crashed. He's backed up against the wall and it really don't look good.' And then when the green flag started the race back again, it was just all forgotten. I try to divorce all my thoughts when something like that happens. You knowed him when he was alive, and you just have to say, 'Well, it was just his time.' So we run along, 50 laps or something, and I called in and said, 'How's Tiny?' And Dale said, 'It's the worst,' just like that. I knew for sure, then. That was right in the middle of the race, and any thoughts that I had were gone by the time Dale told me about it. You know what I mean?"

Lund kept a busy schedule. The Talladega 500 had originally been scheduled for August 10, but an all-day rain had forced a week's postponement. Lund ran three Sportsman races in the interim. On Wednesday he won an outlaw race at Summerville, S.C., on Friday he blew an engine in Savannah, and on Saturday night he finished fifth at Hickory, N.C. Right after the Hickory race he hitched a ride to Talladega in Bobby Allison's twin-engine Aerostar.

"We talked just about all the way," said Allison, who did not attend the funeral. "About a lot of things—hunting and fishing and racing and good times and bad times and everything like that. The biggest thing was, he felt like he was better off than he'd been in a long, long time. He had his Sportsman deal going good, his fishing camp was going good, and he really felt he was making a mistake to go back to Talladega because his car wasn't an up-front car. He felt he was just gonna be another car at Talladega. Not that there was anything wrong with the car. He just wanted to be competitive, he wanted to win, and he knew the car wasn't quite in that group. But he'd promised the people who owned it that he would run. He didn't feel the car was unsafe. I don't feel it was, either. You can't get hit in the left door at Talladega in any car without being hurt.

"He was in excellent shape. He had worked all night Friday because he blew that engine, and he raced Saturday, but he actually slept in Sunday morning and was probably more rested than a lot of the regulars."

The sun and the soft wind played with Butch Lindley's hair as he stood in the double rank of drivers and intimates, which had formed a second time, and watched the casket being carried from the church to the waiting hearse. Lindley was a young Sportsman driver who had absolutely no inclination to compete on the big-time Grand National circuit, and he, like Allison, had raced with Lund on Saturday night at Hickory.

"When something like that happens," he said, "it makes everybody, from Richard Petty right on down, think of things you normally wouldn't think of. It made me think of superspeedway racing, and it made everybody think about it. If it didn't, they're not human and they're not real race drivers. Tiny wasn't in Grand National racing, he was in late-model Sportsman racing, and I personally feel he didn't have any business driving a Grand National car even though he was capable of doing it. I run right there with Tiny Saturday. I talked to him personally, and I saw that he was physically wore out, just really run down so bad that you wouldn't believe it was Tiny. I won the race and Tiny run fifth; I went home and went to bed and Tiny flew all night to Talladega. And the reason for that was, Tiny needed the money. He was down there at Talladega trying to make money to apply to his late-model Sportsman car and the national championship point battle. I tried to explain to Tiny all during the year not to run for the points because he couldn't afford to, but people just kindly get in a situation where they're so involved and so confused that they make the wrong decision, and I feel that's what Tiny done. He was a great champion, in his own way. He didn't have to prove nothing to nobody.

"Something way back caused the accident—like greediness in racing, the effort you have to put forth to make money, what you have to do to meet the obligations. Tiny extended himself so much. At Talladega, he knew he had to extend himself to be better than them other guys and it put him in trouble.

"Tiny was like a big child to me, even though he was older than me and I respected him in every kind of way. I would never have thought that he would get killed in a race car. I would have thought that he could of possibly got drowned—turn over in a boat or something—or eat up by a big shark, him trying to whip it out to sea. But I never would have dreamed that Tiny Lund would get in trouble in any kind of way in a race car. It was such a sorrow to me that I just couldn't hardly take it."

Such a sorrow. . . . Like it never happened. . . . It was just his time. . . . You know what I mean?

I was not at Talladega the day Tiny died. I was entertaining a friend in an apartment near Charlotte, N.C., I had taken for that summer and fall. I turned on the radio broadcast of the race and retired briefly to the bathroom. Then my friend pleaded through the door, "Tiny Lund's been killed." I returned to the living room only in time to hear the final words of a eulogy given by broadcaster Ken Squier.

And then, a strange thing. My friend and I adjourned to

a nearby lake for an afternoon of swimming and wine spritzers, and we brought along a portable radio, anxious for details. There were none—not in the ten-lap rundowns, not in the listings of the cars no longer running, not in the frequent recaps of the first part of the race—though mention was made of an accident involving several cars shortly after the start. It was as though Tiny Lund had never existed, or had ceased to exist, or at the very least, hadn't made it to Talladega that day. I began to entertain the crazy notion that perhaps my friend and I hadn't heard the radio right, that—ha!—the reports of his death were greatly exaggerated; that Lund was, in fact, down in Cross where I had left him just three days earlier, and with his mechanic, Roger Byers, and maybe Tommy Sweatman from the Gulf service station and general store, was working on that battered No. 55 Sportsman racer. Or maybe he was rock fishing out on Lake Moultrie, or playing with Chrissie, or doing any one of a number of other mundane things.

It was, of course, a false notion. NASCAR had notified Tiny's mother, Hazel Lund, of her son's death and had given Squier permission to broadcast the news. But it then became unclear whether his wife, Wanda, had been told, and rather than take the risk of her finding out by radio, Squier reluctantly acquiesced with the decision not to mention his name again.

His death was confirmed soon enough, though, and there was ample time for my own private thoughts and to wonder at the audacity of some of them. One in particular . . .

A small part of me was secretly pleased that Tiny Lund had been killed on my time. A harsh and selfish thought—even loathsome—but true. I certainly did not want Tiny, or any other driver, dead. I wished all of them long and prosperous lives burdened by the minimum of hospital visitations. But if Tiny was doomed by whatever capricious forces were at work out there, well then, maybe the tragedy of his death would help give focus to my current project.

Indeed, in the days and weeks to come, the death of Tiny Lund, this awesome intrusion into the violent but usually well-ordered world of Southern stock car racing, would become a set conversation piece on the Grand National circuit. Drivers who made jokes out of even their worst crashes, having survived them, were now confronted with the most basic evidence of their mortality. Reporters like myself, some of whom in moments of fancy considered racing a grand existential pursuit, could now ask the Great Question—"How can you race knowing that you might be seriously hurt, or even killed?"—with the hope of getting some revealing answers uncluttered by stories of how the ride to the infirmary was often more dangerous than the wreck itself. ("Slow down," Buddy Baker once told an ambulance driver who was carrying him to a hospital after the ambulance had jumped a curve and run through a half-dozen garbage cans, "I ain't hurt yet.") But the answers were not forthcoming, not really. The psychic distance between observer and participant was simply too great. Occasionally a spark would jump the gap, but that was all.

In the midst of one such dialogue with another reporter several years before, Richard Petty's father, Lee, the grizzled patriarch of the most successful racing family in Grand National history, suddenly asked his pesky questioner, "What sport do you play?"

"Tennis."

"Then," said the old man, walking away, "there's no point in me even talking to you."

I wondered at the cyclical nature of racing deaths. Automobile racing of all sorts had been relatively free of tragedy in the two or so years before that brutal Sunday in August, but even as Lund was being mourned, preparations were being made an Old World away to return home the body of Mark Donohue, an American road-racer who had crashed in practice for the Austrian Grand Prix the very morning of Lund's death. Donohue had been taken from his broken car, cut and dazed but apparently otherwise okay. He later complained of severe headaches, could not recognize close friends. He was rushed to a hospital in Graz, where a blood clot was found in his brain. He was operated on, there were complications, he died. (As an ironic aside, earlier in the month Donohue had set a world's closed-course speed record of 221.160 mph in a specially-prepared Porsche race car—at Talladega.) That made two, and one could almost predict a third before the year was out. There was a third, and in fact a fourth, though neither occurred on the race track. Jimmy Caruthers, a peppery Californian who campaigned on the United States Auto Club's Championship Car circuit, died of cancer of the aorta in late October. The next month, Graham Hill, the dapper Englishman who had twice won the world's Grand Prix driving championship, died in the crash of his private plane on a foggy golf course near London.

I remembered a story I had read about Dan Gurney, another American road-racer, who, when asked to name racing friends of his now dead, named fifty-seven and then stopped, his list unfinished. My own personal list was not nearly that long, and my relationship to each name on it, as in the case of Caruthers, Hill, and Donohue—and Lund, for that matter—was only that of a reporter to his subject, but it was long enough. My introduction to automobile racing was the 1964 Indianapolis 500, as a spectator who had come upon a good ticket in the grandstand on the outside of the fourth turn. We stood, all 250,000 of us, on a beautiful blue-sky day in May as the cars grumbled by in traditional three-abreast formation on the parade laps and then once more on the pace lap. We continued to stand as the cars again appeared in the fourth turn, shrieking now for the first time at full throttle as they sought the starter's green flag midway down the front straight. I felt a shiver of terror and shared excitement at this beginning, the same feeling I would have at the start of every other race I attended. There was silence, except for a distant hum, as the cars disappeared beyond the first turn; then there was the awful noise again, now separated into distinct units, as one by one the cars came by in a flash of noise and color, all of us still standing. Silence again, and again the building symphony of noise, pebble-grains of noise and flashes of bright color. Between and over the heads of those standing in front of me, before I could comprehend what was happening—my vision narrowed, my senses contracted, as with the onset of panic—I saw the burned-out shell of a car wander slowly (though it must have still been going quite fast) toward the outside wall, the driver slumped to his right, his head nestled on his right shoulder, his right arm dangling almost to the track. An orange bellow of flame, orange with Halloween twists of black, shot to the sky amidst a concussive *whump* as a second car hit the burned-out shell of the first. I felt a flush of heat, and like those around me I turned and sought escape toward the top of the grandstand. The panic was momentary; the race was stopped; my senses expanded. A fireman's asbestos sheet was placed over one of the cars, an ambulance hurried off, and even before the race was over there were newspapers circulating through the stands: SACHS, MACDONALD DIE AT INDY. It was my first race; Eddie Sachs and Dave MacDonald were my first two fatals.

I wondered at the memory of a short conversation I'd had in 1969 with a young and unknown Pete Hamilton. In February of that year there had been a particularly messy accident at Daytona Beach in the Sportsman race that traditionally preceded the Daytona 500. A car broke loose in the fourth turn and angled for the bottom of the track and safety. But the driver overcorrected and shot back up the banking and slammed into the outer wall almost head-on. His car was shorn in half directly in front of him. He sat there, slumped and exposed, looking like a limp puppet as his strange half-car wandered about and then came to rest facing back up toward the turn. There was an awful confusion as a half-dozen cars and more engaged in fearsome, spinning turmoil. Another car hit the funny car with the limp puppet in it—hit the puppet, actually, there being absolutely nothing in front of the doll-like thing to protect it. The safety crews rushed out and looked briefly at the puppet and moved on to the survivors, and Don MacTavish was dead.

A few weeks later I asked Hamilton, who was a close friend of MacTavish's and had raced against him often, "Pete, if you knew when you got in a race car that there was no way, *no way,* for you to ever get hurt, would you drive?"

Hamilton thought about that one for a long time. When the long time was over, he slammed down his fist and said, "No, dammit, I wouldn't. Putting your balls on the table—that's what racing's all about, isn't it?"

His answer was exceptional, and years later he revised it

drastically, citing the impetuousness of youth and false bravery as his excuses the first time around.

Still, a favored phrase around the race track was, "That's Racing," spoken with a capital "T" and a capital "R." It was used to indicate a benign acceptance of all the multitudinous ills that could befall a driver, from a too-long pit stop to the death of a fellow traveler, and it was invariably accompanied by a fatalistic shrug of the shoulders. Not long after Tiny Lund's funeral, Bobby Allison pointed out that one high school friend of his had been killed on a motorcycle while running from the cops, a second friend had suffered a fatal heart attack while watching television with his girl friend, a third had walked into a high-tension power line while carrying a steel rod around a grimy factory, and a fourth had met his end in the crash of a private airplane. Allison, who in his past had run cops, watched television with girl friends, worked in a factory, and flown his own airplane, said, "I don't like it, but we all have to go sometime. I guess I just block it out." And he shrugged his "That's Racing" shoulders and went about his business. I wondered at that, too.

Beneath the green canopy at the Berkeley Memorial Gardens, three rows of chairs had been set up for the immediate family. The rest of us wandered uncomfortably. Darel Dieringer, who on the afternoon of Tiny's death had backed his own race car into the wall at Talladega with sufficient impact to force his gas tank into his rear seat—though he got out with nothing worse than a stiff neck—nervously fingered the shrouds of the canopy and looked blankly into the void. Marvin Panch, whom Lund had rescued from the flaming wreck of a race car at Daytona in 1963, stood off from the crowd, most eloquent in his grief; next to him was Betty Jo Yarborough, still uneasy in hers. There were others, many others, all joined together in this final communion, and alone. Clouds gathered as the promised thundershower drew nearer. At times, the sun broke through the clouds, but weakly, without the full theatrical effect that a strong and brilliant shaft of light would have produced. There were scores of wreaths.

The minister with skin the texture of bread dough threw a small handful of moist earth into the hole. Two officials from the Dial Funeral Home of Moncks Corner, brightly dressed in suits of forest-green, removed an American flag from the casket, folded it into a small triangle, and presented it to Wanda Lund with practiced solemnity. The minister whispered to her his final, private condolences. "Where are we going now?" young Chrissie pouted, still unsure of what was taking place, as he and his mother and grandmother were led to a pair of silver-gray limousines, where they waited.

Cale Yarborough was the first. The 1975 season had not been a good one for him, and much of his natural exuberance had been muted by the cyclical frustrations of his trade. He even appeared vulnerable, a word one never before would have considered using in his description. Still, he was the first. He wiped his glistening, flushed forehead with a red handkerchief and walked over to where Wanda was seated in the open door of the first limousine. He kissed her warmly on the cheek and spoke words of insufficient comfort. Wanda reached up and hugged him around his neck.

The procession began. Buddy Baker, his square-jawed face twisted by indecision and pity, said over his shoulder, "I can't go over there." But he did, and the others followed, from Richard Petty to Tommy Sweatman to the man from the church in the bib overalls. Some were quick and decisive, others hung back in their awkwardness, but Wanda received them all. The pleading had not left her eyes, but perhaps in this last gathering of the friends of Tiny Lund she was able to find some small understanding.

I saw Roger Byers, shy and awkward in his tan sport coat, his head tilted one way, his body the other, as though they were not quite part of the same set. And I saw Johnny Holley, an occasional member of Tiny's entourage whom I had gotten to know a little bit.

"There are a lot of memories of that man," Holley said.

I had only one—of a night six days before when Tiny Lund had blown their doors off on dirt.

Part II: August 13–14, 1975

Tiny Lund's Sportsman racing operation, headquartered in that small, nondescript garage near Cross, was in no way exceptional. There were perhaps a hundred others like it in the Carolinas alone, a thousand more all across America. On the left of the work area was a Chevrolet Camaro, a dusty remembrance of things past but still a good source of parts; on the right was the scavenged shell of a car no *Dee*-troit automobile executive would recognize as one of his own; in the center was the car of the moment, a powder-blue Chevrolet Chevelle, *circa* 1965. On a workbench that ran the length of the back wall, and on the wall itself, there were scattered enough parts to assemble a dozen racers, at least in part: rusting flywheels, brake drums, and spindles; oiled crankshafts, camshafts, and gearboxes; a plethora of nuts, bolts, and washers in a score of sizes and configurations. Strewn about in kaleidoscopic disarray were oil rags and tool kits, parts catalogues and ice coolers, steering wheels and driving helmets. Off one corner of the work area was Tiny's office. It contained one telephone, one girlie calendar in the pinup style of the 1940s, one drafting board, one battered sofa, one overstuffed chair without legs. Off another corner, an L-shaped corridor led to the engine room. Outside, a jury-rig made from a garden hose, some copper tubing, and a timer served as an air conditioner. It periodically sprayed water on the corrugated-steel roof with a sound like that of driving sleet, but offered little respite from the hot and muggy summer afternoon.

The shop was a beehive of controlled chaos, for quite spontaneously, almost on a whim, Tiny had decided to go dirt-track racing that night at a little manicured bullring of a track near Summerville, not twenty miles down the road. There were just a couple of problems. His little battered and blue Chevelle, No. 55, was at the moment without a rear axle and an engine, serious omissions. Tiny moved from work area to office to engine room in no particular sequence, a look of bemusement on his massive face. The phone rang often. People wandered in and wandered out. There was little opportunity to talk.

Still, Tiny smiled. Tiny always smiled, a lopsided mouthful of a smile, childlike and gleeful, whether he was funnin' you or laying you out. He did the former often, the latter with determination—but rarely with malice. A fellow race driver would later say of him, "He was an 18-year-old boy who lived to be 100," and it was true. Although his brown hair was lighter and thinner than it once had been, and his weariness more apparent at the end of a long day, he still carried his 265 pounds on a 6 foot 5 inch frame with bearlike ease. The overall impression was that he had somehow confused time; that he was not lying when he reported himself to be 42 years old instead of the 45 he really was.

At the rear of the Chevelle, Tommy Sweatman, who ran the Gulf service station and general store just down the road, and his son, Tommy, Jr., helped assemble the rear axle, borrowed for this occasion from the dusty Camaro. In the engine room, Roger Byers, Tiny's only full-time employee, carefully dipped in cleaning solvent the dozens of rings, springs, cams and things of the engine he was piecing together on a portable chain hoist and air-hosed them dry. Byers worked at this tedious and time-consuming job with the patience of a watchmaker, for there would be little time to test his handiwork before the race.

Throughout the long afternoon, strangers and neighbors continued to wander in, either to work for a little bit or just to plunk themselves down on some fat racing tires for a few lazy minutes of easy conversation. Tiny's wife, Wanda, stopped by with sandwiches and drinks. She was a dark-skinned, dark-haired young woman with attractive features and sturdy convictions—she had been known to ring up surprised reporters and chew them out when she felt they had unfairly criticized her husband in their newspaper columns.

"I love dirt-track racing," she said, then bounced off to have her hair done, confirmation that Summerville would not be just a sporting occasion, but a social event as well.

"Meet Speedy Spears," Tiny said to me. "He went to school with 'Balls."

" 'Balls?"

"Fireball Roberts," said Spears, invoking the name of a

stock car racing hero from another era. "Nobody ever called him Fireball, just 'Balls. We left college together in '46. I've regretted it a hundred times since, but I don't guess Fireball ever did."

Speedy Spears was a lean and languid man who had almost died three weeks earlier when he forgot to take the pills he needed to keep his blood thin. He was a car owner, and that night his driver would be a rival of Tiny's, but right then he was at Tiny's place seeking help. The tow truck bringing his own race car up from Florida had broken down near Savannah, and he was in a quandary over the best way to get his driver, his crew, and his car to Summerville in time for the show. Long negotiations followed on Tiny's phone among Spears, his crew and driver, a truck mechanic in Savannah ("It's hopeless"), and finally the U-Haul people, who eventually gave deliverance.

Distractions. But work on the little blue Chevelle progressed steadily through all of them, and by 4:30 or so Tiny felt comfortable enough to leave the garage and adjourn to his fishing camp.

The Tiny Lund Fishing Camp, cut out of scrub pine on the western shore of Lake Moultrie, was an absolutely amazing place that at once suggested Arcadian tranquility and an almost primitive impermanence. There was a beach and a landing and a large clearing for camping. But of the more than half-dozen structures on the grounds, only one, a log building in size somewhere between a cabin and a house, was firmly anchored. The rest were mobile homes. Tiny, Wanda, and their son, Chrissie, lived in one, Tiny's mother lived in another, and the rest were for guests. The reason for the camp's curiously transitory character was that although Tiny had rented the land for years, he had never been able to purchase it or even secure a long-term lease. He was, in fact, preparing to move the camp to more permanent quarters nearby.

The camp was different things to different people. It was home to Tiny and his family, a pleasure cove for serious fishermen, a haven for the rest of Tiny's world—other drivers between races, journalists in need of a quiet place to dry out or escape domestic harassment, and just plain friends come down to enjoy Tiny's company. One pretty much had to be a fisherman to appreciate the place, though, for Tiny delighted in driving his nonfishing friends to sputtering fits of muttered oaths. Lake Moultrie was famous for its rock fish—freshwater striped bass—and rock fishing was an art Tiny understood well, having once landed a world's record catch of 55 pounds. (Thus his car number.) He pursued it with singular intensity. He would stand patiently at the wheel of his powerful cruiser, dead and quiet in the water, and with darting eyes search about for the telltale thrashing of water that signaled the presence of a lively school. Then he would speed in a frenzy to the appropriate spot and rapidly cast out as many as a half-dozen lines in succession, pulling back rhythmically on each one, the silver leader skipping on the surface, until the bait had been taken and the catch landed. Rock fish didn't stay in one place very long, and an afternoon filled with the promise of lazy, beer-guzzling calm could quickly become a maelstrom of frantic, demanding work. You had to love it to even like it.

Hazel Lund, Tiny's widowed mother, who claimed to be 72 although Tiny insisted she was 74, was the camp's straw boss, business manager, social director, and head conversationalist. Her base of operations was the one log building, a combination restaurant, living room, and general store, where a visitor could get anything from a home-cooked meal and a passel of racing gossip to a bucket of live worms. The world's record rock fish, as well as another of a mere 23 pounds, hung mounted on the back wall surrounded by perhaps a hundred plainly framed pictures of Tiny taken at the many tracks where he had run. Tiny estimated that he had raced stock cars of various sorts in at least forty states and a half-dozen foreign countries, including Japan, where his outsized bulk made him a lovable curiosity much as it had Frank Howard, the massive American baseball player who finished out his career there with the Taiheiyo Club Lions. Scores of Tiny's trophies were displayed at random on tables, shelves, and window sills. Racing helmets hung from rough-hewn ceiling beams, and fishing rods lay across them. In the corners sat boxes filled with yellowed newspaper clippings that Hazel promised she would someday collate for her son.

•

DeWayne Louis Lund was born in Harlan, Iowa, on November 14, 1929. He began racing motorcycles at 15, but being oversized even as a teenager, he broke four or five bones and lost pounds of flesh on the frisky bikes and wisely turned to stock cars. Over the next several years he built a fine reputation and a large following throughout the Midwest, and in 1956 he headed South to check out the Grand National circuit, then in its infancy.

Lund was a crowd-pleaser almost from the beginning. Being so physically imposing helped, of course, as did his equally outsized personality, but more important than either of these considerations was a basic sense of honor that often forced him into outrageous and bizarre personal confrontations. For example, there was the time in the late 1950s when Lund, poor and struggling for recognition, almost drowned Curtis Turner, one of the wealthiest and most successful drivers of that era:

> I was running a '57 Chevrolet; Turner was running a '58 Chevrolet. I was running second or third—I don't know—in a 150- or 200-lap race on the old Lakewood mile in Atlanta, dirt, and I could see them dollar signs. I'd slowed down, trying just to be conservative and finish. Turner was having trouble. He was way behind and he was driving like he always did—a yard and a half over his ass—and he come through there just a-flying and hit me and put me into the wall and about tore the front fenders off my car. I got out and looked at my car and I was so damned mad if I could have gotten a-hold of him I would have broken his belly. I tried to jump in his race car a couple of times and he threw me off on the ground. So I got some guys and we finished pulling off the fenders on my car and I got the damned thing fired up and took off after Turner, hard as I could go. I couldn't catch him. Then I stopped and waited for him on the front stretch. I'd turn right, he'd turn right; he'd turn left, I'd turn left. And we went like this around and around the entire race track at 15, 20, 30 mph. Finally the race finished and I went looking for him. He hid. I couldn't find him anyplace. I went down to the lake in the center of the race track, and there's Turner stooped over down by the lake washing. And I just made a damned run like a bull and grabbed him under

one arm and when I stopped running we was standing in water about up to my chest. But it was about over his head. Turner was praying. He was scared of water anyway, and I had him by the throat and he was praying. "Now Pops," he said, he called everybody Pops—"now what are you getting mad at me for? You know I wouldn't wreck you purposely. You got in my way." And I said, "You son of a bitch. I didn't get in the way. Goddamn you. You think you can run over everybody. I want you to understand you don't ever run over me on no damned race track." He said, "You know I don't run over you. We're buddies. We party together. We race together." And I said, "Yeah, but you don't have to fix your goddamned race car. You don't depend on it for a living. That old raggedy race car is all I got. You done tore that son of a bitch up, and now I'm fixin' to drown your ass." He told me he'd give me first-place money—anything I wanted. Goddamn. It didn't matter what it was, just as long as he could get out of my hands. And he prayed a little bit and begged a little bit, and I guess if I hadn't looked up and seen all the people on the bank hollerin' and yellin' —part of 'em to drown him and part of 'em to save him—shit, I probably would have drowned him even to this day.

Then there was Tiny's altercation with Lee Petty, Richard's father, a man for whom he had little personal respect, though he had worked briefly for the Pettys shortly after his move South:

Lee was about the most greedy person I ever dealt with in my life. The whole family was. I think Richard and Maurice have changed some now, but it was all take and no give when I was connected with them. But anyway, we was racing at Greensboro, N.C., and I blew a head gasket. So I had to slow down and pull to the inside. But I was trying to run enough laps so I could get that $100 or so to get home on and eat on the next week. Lee was leading the race, and at that time Lee was real bad about wrecking everybody, just continually tearing the fucking cars up for no reason. He used to have door plates bolting the doors shut instead of welding, and he'd leave big ol' bolts sticking out the side. He had four of these goddamned things sticking out, and when he hit a car broadside it'd be just like a can opener. So anyway, he's lapping me and I'm down on the inside, over as far as I can go, and that son of a bitch hits me a couple times. My engine's hot and I can't run, so I go into the pits and fill my damned car up with water. I went out there and . . . Shit, I could outrun him easy. I'd put my bumper right against his door and run him pretty near crossways, but I wouldn't spin him. I'd just back off. Then I'd get hot again and run back in and get some more water and run him again. All the time I was doing this I didn't know he'd tore the whole goddamned side out of my car. So we're in line at the payoff getting our money and ol' Lee was standing right behind me. We're on a platform, oh, a good fifteen feet in the air. Old country fairgrounds track—you know how they have a platform where they held their entertainment? So Lee says, "Don't you know where to go when you're being lapped?" I said, "Hell yeah, Petty, but goddamn, you don't have to run over me just because you've got enough goddamn sheet metal and parts down there at your place to build more race cars than what there is on the race track. You like to tear everybody's car up, but you ain't gonna tear mine up no goddamn more." He knew I knew how much stuff he had and how big of a hog he was. So I reached down for my money and ol' Lee hauled off and man, he busted me; goddamn he hit me. I saw stars. I held onto the table for a second until I got my damned equilibrium back, and I turned and said, "Lee, you're gonna regret the day you done that." I got my money and stuck it in my pocket and I took after him. And he run. He run to the edge of the platform and then stopped, because it was a long way down. And when he stopped, I kicked him in the ass and I mean he took on off of there like a big damned bird, like a big damned eagle floating off of there. And he lay on the ground and looked up and says, "Is that the way you fight?" I said, "Hell, no. Stay there. I'm coming right down." I jumped off there right the fuck on top of him and I commenced to knocking the shit out of him—and I was doing a good job of it—and here comes ol' Maurice; Maurice and Dale and Richard. All three of them were together, just like they are now. And ol' Maurice—goddamn. He hit me with a goddamn screwdriver—tried to jab me—and I got him down across his old man. And here comes Richard. He had a pop bottle and I got *him* down across 'em. And then ol' Speedy Thompson—he jumped in there and was gonna help me, but he'd been frog hunting and shot a hole through his toe and he was on a cane and one of 'em hit him in the goddamned toe and he went hobbling off holding his foot. Jack Smith—he got in there to help me and ol' Maurice bit the shit outta Jack. I mean he bit him like a dog. And about then—goddamn. Something hit me in the back of the head and man, I seen butterflies and everything. It was ol' Liz Petty, Lee's wife. She had a pocketbook. I don't know what she had in it, but she was going *pow, pow, pow,* just wearing my damned head out. And this broke things up. I got up and said, "I can't lick the whole goddamned Petty family." To which Buck Baker come up and said, "Goddamn if you wadn't doing a purty damned good job of it."

At Daytona Beach in February of 1963, Lund watched in horror as a birdcage Maserati driven by Marvin Panch crashed, flipped, and burst into flames during practice for the Daytona Continental, the sports car race that was the traditional kickoff to Daytona's Speed Weeks. Lund and four other men raced to the accident, and in an act for which they later received the Carnegie Medal for Heroism, pulled the badly-burned Panch to safety. Panch was the regular driver for the famous Wood Brothers factory-supported Ford racing team. From his hospital bed—in a story that was only partly apocryphal—Panch asked owner Glen Wood to give his ride in the upcoming Daytona 500 to Tiny.

Lund won the race. It was the first Grand National victory of his career, and it should have been the beginning of a fairy tale. It wasn't. Lund started five more races for the Wood Brothers, but at North Wilkesboro, N.C., he lost the chance to win when a mechanic inadvertently rolled a tire beneath his car during a pit stop; at Martinsville, Va., he chased down Richard Petty, who was nearly unconscious from the heat and fumes, but just as he was about to challenge for the lead, a caution flag came out to slow the field and give Petty the necessary breathing room, as it were, to keep his lead. Lund figured that if he had won those two races, he would have been on his way.

There were other opportunities, one in particular a few years later with car owner Bud Moore. "Bud was a lot of fun," said Tiny. "He was one of the last ol' boys that really did believe in having a good time racing. But he was hardheaded. If he said he wanted something done his way, he was gonna do it no matter if he didn't ever go to another race. Any number of times we could have won the race if Bud wouldn't of been so hardheaded and had let the mechanics get the car handling.

Come close to winning some the way it was. The last race I ran for him, at Rockingham [N.C.], we were faster than anybody, but Richard Petty ended up winning and we run fourth or fifth just because Bud wouldn't change the chassis for me during the race. It was pushing so bad I had twenty-one blisters on my hands and they were bleeding and I had to go to the hospital to have them treated. If a car doesn't work right, I don't give a damn who you are or how you spell your name—Richard Petty, Cale Yarborough, David Pearson, or otherwise—you've got to have a good piece of equipment."

Whether it was circumstance or a perverse stubborn streak of his own that kept Lund from the good ride was never easy to figure out. Whatever it was, he won just two other Grand Nationals during his career, both minor events. He raced hard and often at other levels, however. He won scores of Sportsman races, and in 1968, when NASCAR established a Grand American circuit for "pony" cars—Chevrolet Camaros, Ford Mustangs, Pontiac Firebirds, and the like—Lund won that championship three years out of four. In one remarkable stretch during the 1970 season, he won ten races in a row.

Question: Are you bitter that you didn't get a better shake from the factories?

Lund: Bitter as a son of a bitch.

Question: What kind of a person do you think you'd be if you'd been a Grand National superstar?

Lund: Just like I am right now. I had a little success with it. I got to play the same role they play—having a good car and doing PR work and making appearances and all kinds of endorsements and shit. It just didn't last as long, is all. There ain't but very many guys that it has lasted long for, that really made anything.

Question: Have you ever figured out what it is that you like about racing?

Lund: The challenge. It's a challenge.

Question: What kind of a challenge?

Lund: Man over machine; man over time; man against a competitor. I like to feel that I'm master of the car. I like to feel the brink of speed—running on the ragged line of perfection and disaster, you might say. I have a strong desire to win, and when I can't win and don't run good I'm a miserable son of a bitch; I'm usually miserable to everyone around me. Every win, no matter if it's big or small, is great to me. I want to win seventy-five races next year, to set a record.

Question: You're kind of a throwback, aren't you?

Lund: I guess you might say so.

Tiny emerged from his house trailer wearing massive, white swimming trunks. He padded about his camp on varicose-veined legs bowed in at the knees from years of supporting his massive bulk, on ankles grotesquely deformed by too many broken bones, and on absolutely huge, flat feet. He checked on his chickens and roosters as they scratched in the sandy dirt, played with a brace of his prized hunting dogs, and unsuccessfully tried to introduce the camp's resident mare, Ginger, to the joys of swimming. Then Tiny waded into the warm waters of Lake Moultrie by himself, and like some friendly sea monster paddled about in languid rest from his day's labors. Chrissie, a chubby 6-year-old, and some other neighborhood kids joined him in his frolic, but only briefly. It was soon time to return to the garage.

At 6:20, the Chevelle was finally ready. While Tiny swept out the garage, Roger Byers started up the blue race car and twice gunned it up and down the deserted highway in front of the shop. Satisfied that it would run but still wary because there was no time for any real testing—practice at the Summerville track had already begun—Byers carefully drove it onto its tow truck, and in caravan the Lund entourage headed off. Wanda, Hazel, and some of Hazel's lady-friends were in one car; Speedy Spears, his wife, Betty, and I were in a second; Tiny and the night's pickup crew—Byers, Tommy Sweatman and his son, and Johnny Holley, a friend who lived down the road in Moncks Corner—were in a third.

•

Tiny Lund was a prisoner of time. Although he moved casually through it, and in some physiological way seemed to have reversed the flow of it, he nonetheless was totally defined by it. There were planes to catch and dogs to feed and parts to buy and people to meet and a hundred other things to do —on time. Nothing unusual there. Away from the race track, Lund had only the time problems of any family man and small-business entrepreneur. But at the race track, his successes and failures were measured by the tick of the clock. The sweep hand of a stopwatch was as important to Lund, and to every other race driver, as a calendar is to the historian: tick . . . tick, a good lap; tick . . . . . . tick, a bad lap. At most tracks, regardless of their configurations, drivers spoke of time, not speed, as, "I run a twenty-three-four," meaning a lap of 23.4 seconds. Speed was relative; time was absolute.

At Summerville, this was high irony, this relentless dependence on a sliver of time no wider than the bat-bat of an eyelash, for Summerville was without time, best viewed through a hazy filter and not to worry who was in the White House. On this particular night, it happened to be Gerald Ford, but just as easily it could have been Nixon or Johnson or Kennedy or Eisenhower or even Truman. Going to Summerville was like crossing a bridge to a loud and sweaty Brigadoon, where you could lose yourself in the swirling mists of time and imagine yourself at the beginning. Such was the feeling of having wandered into the past that it would have been no surprise to see Fireball Roberts and Curtis Turner and Joe Weatherly—all long-dead drivers against whom Lund had once raced—walk through the pits, their biceps bulging beneath tight T-shirts, and as they casually held their short-brimmed driving helmets by their chinstraps, acknowledge with slight nods the deference of their peers and the accolades of their fans. Indeed, in texture and style, the Tri-State 200, a race for late-model Sportsman cars held on the dry-slick dirt of the 1/3-mile Summerville Speedway on the night of August 13, 1975, was very much like Grand National racing itself had been in its infancy a quarter-century before.

Late-model Sportsman racing, in 1975, was to Grand National racing what minor league baseball was to the major leagues, what *The Charlotte Observer* was to *The New York Times,* what summer stock theater was to the bright lights of Broadway. It was, in short, a notch removed from the big time, a circuit (to dally gently in cliché) where young drivers on their way up avoided the stares of those on their way down, where drivers thwarted in their ambitions by lack of money or personality, or perhaps by having had one too many bad crashes, raced side-by-quarterpanel with drivers who were tickled pink with their station in life and could not have cared less about Grand National fame and glory. Late-model Sportsman cars were older than their sleek and massaged Grand National cousins, the tracks upon which they competed were usually smaller than those of the Grand National circuit, the crowds were diminished and the payouts shrunken. All of which was important to know; none of which made any difference at all, this night, to Tiny Lund.

Tiny and his caravan arrived predictably late, just as a sun the color of a juicy tangerine paused briefly beyond the third and fourth turns, then settled through suspended particles of fine, red clay to its sidereal rest. He quickly pitched camp at the far end of the pits, up near the fourth turn next to Speedy Spears's crew, and almost immediately took to the track. A great roar went up from the crowd of perhaps 5,500 people who packed the small grandstand along the front straightaway. Lund had been a local hero to these people for nearly two decades, but he had not raced at Summerville in almost two years and his presence was an unexpected bonus. Lund himself didn't know he was coming until that moment an hour or so earlier when Roger Byers had fired up the Chevelle and had seen that it worked. The size of the crowd surprised even Charlie Powell, the promoter; but even as Powell looked in awe at the packed house, he skittered up and down the pits looking to bum some axle grease, for he would also be driving.

By his own admission, Lund had never been a good qualifier. The two separately timed laps each driver made to determine his starting position were annoyances to be gotten over with as painlessly as possible. On Lund's first lap, he wiggled his car through turn four and almost came to grief against the cement wall that fronted the grandstand; on his second, he got a little too broadside in turn one and had to wrestle furiously with his Chevelle to keep it from going over the lip of the banking, there being no retaining wall anywhere except along the outside of the main straight. His fastest lap, 19.910 seconds (tick . . . tick), was only tenth best, giving promise of a good show when he would begin to work his way through the field at the start.

Tiny and his crew spent the brief minutes before the race making final adjustments on his car. Byers and Sweatman changed the gear ratio and softened the springs. Holley hammered the right-rear fender away from the bulging race tire. Tiny tied a wire-mesh screen over the front of his radiator as protection against the inevitable clumps of flying clay. As the track queen, a young, shy blonde named Anne Stone, was introduced, Lund climbed in through the window of his race car—the doors were welded shut—and fastened himself securely with a safety belt and a shoulder harness into the specially molded contours of his driving seat. He put on his helmet and goggles and hung a spare set of goggles on his rearview mirror. Lund's car and twenty-three others were pushed out onto the track. Crew members wiped windshields. The safety vehicle, a dune buggy, led the guttural, throbbing race cars through their parade laps. Finally, the Tri-State 200, this pleasant blend of racing past and racing present, began, and this is how Tiny Lund blew their doors off on dirt.

To begin, Lund nearly exited the race track on the very first turn of the very first lap. With his eyes on the nine cars in front of him, Lund drove deep into the corner—too deep to permit his tires, which would adhere best only after they had warmed up and become slightly gummy, to gain traction. But as he had done in qualifying, Lund manhandled his car and kept it from sliding off the edge, and at the end of the second lap he had already picked off three cars and was running seventh. Three laps and two cars later, he was fifth. Yellow caution flags then intervened. Billy Judd drove by, his left door hanging by a prayer inches from the ground, like a scythe. He ducked into the pits, had the door removed, and drove the rest of the race without it. Lund was now third, and that was where he stayed while another driver spun in turn three and still another stalled between one and two. Wayne Shugart, driving the car owned by Speedy Spears, clobbered the cement retaining wall just off turn four, severely wounding his right-front wheel assembly. That was Spears's reward for his hearty efforts to get his car, crew, and driver over from Savannah in time to make the show: 50 laps of racing and a $1,000 repair bill. Lund was still third, but after the restart following the crash of his friend's car, he quickly took second, then paused, like a bridge player who has just seen the dummy hand revealed, before going after the leader, Ernest Steifle. Lund tested Steifle for several laps, trying to worry him into an error, and when Steifle bobbled just slightly leaving turn three on the 76th lap, Lund slipped beneath him and into the lead. The pass was as precise as a razor cut made so fine it doesn't even draw blood. The crowd roared in appreciation.

The remaining laps of the first half of the race were pulsing, metronomic rhythms of sound and flashes of rich light, impressive to the ear, delightful to the eye, as Lund played his brakes and accelerator and steering wheel with the joy of a cathedral organist gone mad. Lap after lap the grains of sound whirred and whummed in the night air, sound now so familiar it blended easily with the dark and suffocating Carolina night. There were mountains of sound as Lund roared down the straightaways to his braking points, valleys of sound dotted with hamlets as he backed off and caressed his car into the corners and slid ever so softly up the gently banked turns, upward slopes of sound as he came out the other side of the turns and gathered power for the surge down the chutes. The light from the far-spaced light poles—imagine the nighttime glow at a very-small-town high school football game—had the texture of brown-melted butter and gave an eerie depth to the bright colors of the speeding cars, and to the hard and firm track itself, which had been buffed smooth by the marauding racers and now looked as though it had been layered with soft, yellow wax.

Question: Describe how you drive one lap at Summerville.

Lund: Well, to begin with, the track last night was a dry-slick race track and you drive it more like asphalt, but yet you gotta let your car drift and come loose a little bit. For instance, into the first turn the other guys were driving in and crossing their cars up, but I was driving straight into the corner—straight and neat—and then braking. I don't know if you noticed. I'd pick up on 'em real good going into the corner, but they were leaving me some coming off because I couldn't get on the throttle. I knew the minute my tires got buffed in—or I was hoping after they did—that I'd be able to get on the throttle better coming off, and as soon as I did, I knew I really had 'em. Anyway, you go into the corner and there's a lip up there in one and two that you want to let your car drift up and catch, but I wasn't having too much luck up there. Plus that, there's the fact that a lot of those guys are wild and I wasn't wanting to drive on the outside of 'em and give 'em the advantage where I couldn't get away if somebody made a pass at me or if they lost it. Then, when you drive off of two down the backstretch, there's no retaining wall, and it's a good place to tear up a race car. I knew I had to run this weekend on asphalt, so I wasn't letting it drift out as far as I would if I wasn't worried about the car. I had to wait a considerable time coming off the corner before I could get in the throttle. And I wouldn't just jump in and let it spin; I was trying to ease it in all the time. Then I couldn't get a-hold down there coming off of three and four—I was having a worse time there than I was in one and two, really. I started using the brake when I was giving it gas trying to help it get a-hold. Which would help me a little bit. For a while. When you come out of four, you want to drive right into the wall—just keep driving right towards the wall—which I was trying to do, but it's hard to judge that wall because there's some shadows in it, and there's some breaks in the wall that appear like there's something protruding out and you think you're gonna hit it. Which you don't, but that's an effect you've gotta take into consideration.

Question: How do you pass another car on dirt?

Lund: You try to run in deep enough to where you can judge where he's accelerating out, and then you try to get him to break his pattern just a little bit—like going high a couple laps and trying him, and going low trying to get up underneath him. You put a little pressure, just maybe touching him. You maybe try to push him gently down the chute, or just as you go in the turn, maybe touch him on the inside of the quarterpanel. If he screws up the least little bit, you've got him.

Question: Are you actually trying to move him out of the way when you touch him?

Lund: No, no. I'm trying to annoy him. It's sort of a constant thrashing; like harassing someone, having him constantly know you're there. Same difference. Getting him mad enough to where he goes in just a hair hard and screws up, or to where I can get under him or above him, either one. All you can do is continually put pressure on him to make a goddamn mistake. Find out his errors, then try to make him drive the track the way *you* want him to drive it and not let him drive it his way. That's the whole object of any race.

Question: If somebody's putting pressure on you, are there things you can do?

Lund: Yeah, you can break up his timing. You don't never go into the corner just exactly the same way. If you're going in the same way all the time, he figures you out. But say you go in deep one time, and then the next time you back off early. This way, he can't judge. You break his timing and he has to get off the throttle, and by the time he gets back in, *you're* on the throttle and going. Something like that, for instance.

Question: You like dirt-track racing a lot, don't you?

Lund: I love to run dirt. There's a feel to dirt—for me, anyway. Even when the car may look out of control and broadsliding, I feel more at ease than I am sitting in a boat, and I think I can run dirt as good as anybody that ever run. I'm not saying any better, but I think I'm as good.

The Tri-State 200 was a split event. That is, it was stopped briefly at the end of 100 laps to let crews give minor maintenance to the cars still running and try to repair those that had fallen out. Tiny emerged from his car bathed in sweat, his face grimy with dust except for two white circles around his eyes where his goggles had been. His driving suit was streaked with oil and dirt, and there was a great tear in the back of it just above his right kidney.

In a flash, the soft tranquility of the evening vanished. There had been a lot of fender-banging in the first 100 laps, and suddenly the members of two rival crews, their passions inflamed in equal measure by honest anger and beer, squared off jaw to jaw and belly to belly. One man in particular, slack-jawed and corpulent, stood quivering, the pupils of his eyes dilated with unblinking rage. But before he could act, three sheriff's deputies appeared from the shadows, hands on their holstered guns, and stepped boldly in front of him. It was over in a minute. Tiny never let on he was even aware of the incipient altercation. He gulped down soft drinks purchased from a small, neon-lit concession stand in the middle of the pits and watched as Roger Byers gassed up the Chevelle and replaced a fan belt—there were two on his car—that had snapped during the first half of the race.

Tiny began the second 100 laps in first place, and by all outward appearances the rest of the race was a cakewalk. There was little obvious pressure from the other drivers, three of whom in particular, including Charlie Powell, the promoter, acknowledged Lund's obvious superiority by laying off his pace and racing each other for second. Lund's only concern was another succession of yellow caution flags that broke the rhythm of the race and kept him from maintaining a comfortable lead. Billy Judd, driving the car without the door, looped in turn four and needed a push from the dune buggy to get restarted. Arnold Hutto retired from the race, his engine steaming; Mike McWhirter spun in turn one; Kenneth Butler called it quits when his left-rear tire shredded; Walter Chubb stayed a one-car traffic jam as he ran slowly around the lowest part of the track, trying only to complete enough laps to finish in the top ten. But as it turned out, all these enforced slowdowns were essential to Lund's success. Without them, it is unlikely that he would even have finished the race, let alone won it.

It was an axiom of the race track that a car was never ready to race. Give a mechanic a month to prepare a car and he'd ask for five weeks. Give him a week and he'd beg for eight days. Tiny Lund had given Roger Byers one afternoon to rebuild an engine and Roger had crossed his fingers a lot.

Lund's problem was an overheating engine. In the first 100 laps, his oil temperature had soared dangerously high, even with the backup fan belt, and he had had to resort to an old trick of his trade just to keep running. What he had done was back off the throttle earlier than normal as he entered the turns, then shut off his ignition while he coasted through them, allowing raw gasoline to circulate through his engine. "You can cool your engine by as much as 15 degrees in a lap," Tiny said. "In my life I'd say I've won a hundred races doing that." With both his fan belts working the second 100 laps, Lund depended less on that device, but neither was he unhappy with the many interruptions. They kept his engine cool, just cool enough for him to win in a breeze.

Lund took the checkered flag. He made his victory lap and waved to the appreciative crowd, grinning his lopsided grin. He stopped at the start-finish line, tired and dirty and sweaty, but even before he could take a grateful swig of Budweiser and begin to relax, a half-dozen kids, part of a throng that had squeezed through a tiny gate in the fence, scrambled into his Chevelle. Tiny fired it up and took them on a lap, sliding politely and safely through the waxen corners. When he returned, a line had formed, of sorts—thrilled kids and giggly teenagers and shy, happy adults—and Tiny obliged them all. He loved every bit of it, seemed almost to prolong the moment even as the fine, red dust began to settle in the still, night air.

Finally, though, the crowd began to thin out. Tiny changed out of his driving uniform. Wanda, Hazel, and Hazel's lady-friends drove into the pits and watched Tiny's crew put away their tools and load the Chevelle onto the tow truck. Everybody commiserated with Speedy Spears on his frustrating day. There was much horseplay and storytelling, and much sipping of beer, and of V.O. with Pepsi, as Tiny unwound from the long day and waited for the payoff. His words became slurred, whether from booze or fatigue or emotional release was hard to tell. Well after midnight, after Tiny had collected his prize money—$1,600 for winning the race and $375 for leading the last 125 laps—he and his entourage took off for an all-night restaurant in Goose Creek. The conversation was subdued. Johnny Holley said, apropos of nothing in particular, "They'll remember Tiny around here for a long time," and asked the waitress to stick out her tongue. Tommy Sweatman allowed as how you never knew about Tiny. "Once, I packed a clean shirt to go racing with him for one night and didn't get back until four days later," he said. Speedy Spears decided not to stay the night at Tiny's place. He said he and his wife had better drive on down to Savannah and rescue his tow truck. When Tiny pulled into his fishing camp, the sky was already gray with the first light of dawn.

1

Scrapbooks and Conversations

TIM FLOCK LIVED IN A QUIET, SEMIRURAL SECTION OF Charlotte, N.C. In the front yard of his little bungalow, one of those 1950s tract houses that age quickly, sat a big, huge silver cucumber of a Crown Imperial Streamline house trailer, an indication that he would soon be on the move again, for the eleventh time, he reckoned, in the past ten years. The house sale had just been completed, and friends and neighbors, as well as two of Tim's sons and one of his daughters, passed in and out, taking with them the items of their particular purchase. Within the hour, Tim's wife, Frances, and Tim's mother-in-law would be left sitting on lawn chairs where the living room suite had been; within days, after the next race at the Charlotte Motor Speedway, where Tim worked as an advertising salesman, he and Frances would follow West the promise of a better job. Everything had been sold except the dozens of racing trophies, the model airplanes Tim had begun to build for relaxation three years before, and, of course, the scrapbooks. Those would be taken to Atlanta, where Tim still had some family, and put in storage.

Tim Flock's scrapbooks were famous. Though highly personal and often impressionistic, they were a reasonably complete record of Southern stock car racing in its first great flowering during the decade or so immediately after World War II. Frances in particular was very protective of this mother lode, and with good reason. There were eleven volumes in all, all of them neatly done, but the glue was brittle and the bindings were broken and the pages were torn, and as Tim sat in the master bedroom (the only room still with any furniture in it) and leafed through his memories, an occasional yellowed newspaper clipping, or a photograph, or a telegram or letter would break loose from its delicate mooring and flutter to the floor. Tim didn't seem to mind.

Flock, unlike his scrapbooks, had reached middle age with a minimum of difficulty. His hair was white and his cheeks were filled out just enough to blunt the hatchet-jawed profile he had once shown, and when he dressed in a vented suit, or even a sporty shirt open at the collar, he could easily have passed for a somewhat successful small businessman. There was, however, a faint aura of failure about him. His eyes suggested a slight confusion and a great need to be understood. It could have been only the real confusion of the moment, but one suspected there was something else: conceivably, the growing awareness of his own mortality. He had reached that age when the first thing people do in the morning is check the obituary columns for any surprises, and coincidentally, he had just learned that one of his first racing mechanics, Buckshot Morris, had died in Atlanta only a few days earlier. Although Flock was not yet 50, his father, one of his sisters, and his two racing brothers, Bob and Fonty, had all died young, and perhaps Tim was thinking that the Flocks were just not destined to receive the wisdom of old age.

But all this was conjecture and quite beside the point. Indeed, as Flock began to turn the pages, he seemed to gain reassurance from the old volumes and to put out of his mind whatever it was that troubled him.

CURTIS TURNER WAS AN OUTRAGEOUS MAN WHO LIVED AN outrageous life. He won 357 stock car races, a figure he compiled with the help of a friend not many years before he was killed in 1970 in the crash of his private airplane. He won his races in a variety of cars, on all kinds of tracks and surfaces, and at every distance imaginable. Everybody called him "Pops" because of the way he banged into the side of another car on dirt—popped it—and he, in turn, called everyone around him

"Pops." In his later years, he wore a big Stetson to cover an unruly shock of brown hair, and dark sunglasses to hide his weary eyes. If he liked you, which was nearly always, he offered you a tap of Canadian Club and Coke and then a doll-baby, of whom there were many. He did not speak from his mouth or throat; rather, his soft, Appalachian words rumbled up from somewhere deep in his belly, sounding like those of a sad growly-bear. He started racing when drivers wore bib overalls to the track and raced whiskey cars on them, and he ended his career in the best equipment Detroit money could buy. Throughout, his personal tastes ran to silk suits and Lincoln Continentals, setting him apart.

He raced not to win, but for the glory and the fun. One afternoon when a race at Lakewood, the one-mile dirt track in Atlanta, was rained out, Turner and his doll-baby got in his street car and slopped around in the muck just for the joy of it. On another occasion, he and his stubby, pugnacious sidekick, Joe Weatherly, showed up at a track too late for qualifying but wanting to race anyway. The other drivers did not think kindly of this until Turner explained that he and Little Joe didn't want any part of the purse. "Don't pay us no money," he said. "Just let us race." And so they did, beating and banging on each other until they both dropped out, their cars exhausted.

Turner was difficult to write about. The line between the facts of his life and the fiction was often so thin as to be indecipherable. Even when the words were Turner's own, the threat of apocryphalness was everywhere. What was to be done? For the most part, nothing. The rich stories were improbable, but true or not they carried the seeds of truth, and that was enough.

• In a genteel sports car race that Turner had somehow contrived to enter, he so infuriated Lance Reventlow with his dirt-track fender banging that the silk-scarved playboy driver announced, "Curtis Turner is a ruffian. And, I might add, a common ruffian."

• In a motel parking lot one night, an acquaintance saw Turner emerge about half-tuned from his Lincoln Continental, a doll-baby securely under each arm. "How're you doing, Pops?" asked the friend.

"Pops," said Pops, "if I felt any better, I'd come."

• Turner once explained to a West Coast journalist the intricacies of the bootlegger's turn, in which a speeding whiskey car was spun 180 degrees practically in its own tire tracks in order to quickly get it headed in the opposite direction. The journalist was skeptical about Pops's ability to perform this feat, and so Pops did—in the middle of a Los Angeles freeway. Not unexpectedly, a California state trooper pulled Turner off the road and a long conversation ensued. The result was that Turner again demonstrated the turn, this time for the benefit of the disbelieving state trooper.

• Turner himself told about a race at Columbia, S.C., a story that others repeated often, although the location of the track changed mysteriously with each retelling. "I was about half-tuned when I got to the race and didn't even have time to change my clothes," Turner said, "so I just got in the car with my suit and tie on and took off runnin'. Blew a tire and finished fourth. I told my sponsors they ought to want their drivers to dress like gentlemen."

• Pete Waldmeir of *The Detroit News* reported that a North Carolina state trooper, happening upon a car turned upside down in a ditch, its driver suspended helplessly by his seat belt, took a deep whiff of obviously alcoholic fumes and asked, "Say, mister, you drunk?"

"Of course," said Turner. "What the hell you think I am, a stunt driver?"

TO VISUALIZE TIM FLOCK'S SPEECH PATTERNS, IMAGINE a painting by a favored cubist in which a single, sharp edge of a line or a splash of brilliant color, though complete in itself, reveals nothing of the whole. Flock spoke the way most people think. In fragments. His words were a staple gun of phrases that gushed out unhampered by the conventional rhetorical filters of syntax and grammar. A half-dozen ideas, moods, descriptions, and anecdotes competed for space in the same sentence, each fragment tumbling out in a crispy Georgia twang to lie in the air like so many slices of pan-fried okra. He spoke as a thespian, often embellishing his words with sound effects and sudden gestures as he moved about the room and offered comment on the torn and brittle pages of his life, and of an era:

The beginning? Well, when I was four years old, my dad died. Had cancer. My mother worked in a hosiery mill for nine dollars a week, and they was eight little Flocks starvin' to death in Fort Payne, Alabama. So as each one of us got big enough to hep momma, we'd go to work, you know, to stay out of orphans' homes. Finally, the oldest brother, Carl, he moved to Atlanta. This was during Depression times. We had an uncle named Peachtree Williams, one of the biggest bootleggers that Georgia's ever known, so Carl went to work driving and hauling liquor for him. After two or three years, Carl said the kids need to get an education, and he got me, Fonty, and Bob and moved us into his house out in Atlanta and put us in school. And I'll never forget. He'd make us crawl through the woods leaving the house and make us slip back home to keep people from knowing where we lived 'cause we had a stash in the basement—this was government liquor, bonded; it wadn't moonshine—and if anybody knew where they was a stash at back then, they'd bring trucks and break your door down and just take everything. That's why you had to hide. I know one time Carl built a stash that must have cost him $2,500. You'd go in the garage and the whole floor would go down and another floor would come up over it, and they'd keep all that liquor underneath. I bet you right now whoever bought that house in Atlanta don't know that thing's under that garage because no one ever found it. No one would know unless they dug it up or something.

So Carl more or less raised us up until Bob got to be about 18 years old, and then Carl put him in a car driving and hauling liquor. Then Fonty. Bob was the oldest. They was three years' difference in our age. Bob's been dead seven years; he was 47 years old. Fonty died nine months ago, in January '73; he had cancer in his throat. And I'm 49 now and I'm the youngest, out of the boys.

Everybody in the dinged family's done something really wild. My father was a tightrope walker and a bicycle racer. That's where it all comes from, I guess. You take Carl—you might'n even heard about Carl—he was a motorboat racer, hydroplanes, and he run all over the country before Bob and Fonty and me even started racing. Ethyl, my sister, she run Langhorne, Daytona, Atlanta; she run all the tracks. Reo, my other sister, she's the one I told you about making the parachute jumps. She died when she was 26 years old, real young. She contracted TB from her husband way back when they didn't know what it was. Millions of people died from it; her husband died three weeks after she did. We've got some of the funniest names. There's Coretta and Forrestine, which is real unusual, Ethyl was named after the gasoline, and Reo after the car. Robert Newman Flock—that was Bob. Fonty's name was Truman Fontell Flock. Mine is Julius Timothy Flock. There was another brother, Charles, but he died real young, four or five months old.

CURTIS TURNER WAS BORN IN 1924 ON A SMALL FARM IN the Blue Ridge Mountains of southwestern Virginia, the son of one of the biggest moonshine operators, among his other professions, in Floyd County. "Daddy ran it and made it," Turner said. "He'd buy a whole boxcar load of Oldsmobiles—unload 'em right at the railroad siding—convert 'em and run 'em in caravan five or six at a time. He figured somebody'd always get through. He was kind of quiet, but his partner was a mean son of a bitch. One time, they was makin' a run and got stopped at a roadblock and paid off the cops $100 to let 'em keep goin'. They got back in the car and kept goin' down the road, and everything was real quiet. Then daddy's partner got to fumin' and said, 'Let's go back and get that hundred.' So they did, and tied the two cops under the bridge with their own handcuffs."

Turner was 10 when he made his first run. "I'd just learned to drive," he said. "Fact is, this was the first time I'd ever driven alone. I got in my daddy's car to go to the warehouse and had the people workin' for us load it up. They put about a hundred gallons of liquor on and closed the car up and everything was goin' along all right, but comin' back up the road to the house—a nice, ol' country road—I come up behind a damned mail truck. And hell, I forgot which side I was supposed to pass on. I went around on the wrong side and run up a damned bank and wound up against a fence."

When Turner was 14, he dropped out of school to work as a waterboy, for ten cents an hour, in his father's sawmill; by 16, having learned to pass on the left, except in extenuating circumstances, he was transporting regularly; by 18, he had saved enough money to buy three sawmills of his own and several thousand dollars' worth of equipment. "In the mountains," said a friend of Turner's, "you grow up in a hurry. Eighteen's an old man."

From the beginning, Turner demonstrated a precocious business acumen. Other sawmill operators cut their timber and sold it immediately; Turner waited for the right price. "Everybody was wonderin' how I could cut so much without sellin'," Turner said. "Well, I had to make runs every night to make the payroll, but damn, I did."

Turner joined the Navy for World War II and switched from tripping whiskey to running tires from the naval air station at Norfolk back to his friends in the mountains. After the war, he went back to whiskey. On one run, he escaped a roadblock by switching on a siren and a fake revolving police light, but when he got home, he took serious note of three bullets embedded in the gas tank of his Ford coupe and a fourth lodged in the back of his driver's seat just below his neck. "Don't believe any of this stuff about how it was a game and all, and how everybody was real nice to everybody," he said. "They was playin' for keeps and shootin' real bullets.

"Runnin' was a lot of fun, though. You enjoyed it. Aside from the money you made, you felt like you got by with somethin'. You get a feelin' after you haul a load of liquor similar to what you do when you win a race. That's the whole thing."

TIM FLOCK:

Dahlonega was in the mountains, the north Georgia mountains, about sixty, seventy miles out of Atlanta, and they must of been a hundred stills all back through there. Georgia was a bigger bootleg state than any state in the union, at one time, and to get you back to where this really started, these whiskey cars, they'd go up to Dahlonega, Georgia, and put about 90 or 120 gallons of liquor on there and bring 'em back in. This was the way the guys made their living, and it'd take me three weeks to get to you some of the crazy things that these guys would do to try and get that liquor back. What made it so rough on us, the city of Atlanta put a bulletin out to all the sheriffs' departments that if you caught one of these bootleg cars, on Saturday morning they'd put it at auction in front of the courthouse, and the *po*-lice officer or the sheriff who caught the car got half the money. So man, they went crazy. They wadn't making no money anyway, and when one of these things was auctioned off, they might make 100 bucks apiece, or 200, 300—whatever it cost. It got so bad the guys would starve to death that was hauling the liquor. So we'd come up with every kind of gimmick. We done everything in the world to these cars to try and get that 90 or 120 gallons of liquor back because you didn't eat if you didn't bring a load in. You didn't get paid.

The first thing we done was to put the radiator in the trunk with air scoops on the side of it and run big, long hoses up to the engine and put a half-inch metal plate where the radiator was. This was an old '39 or '34 Ford—the '39 Fords, you'll see a hundred of 'em in these books here, modified, but I guess more liquor was hauled in a '34–'35 Ford than any other car I know of. The reason we had to do this, these old sheriffs could see a car go up to the mountains, and when it come back, they'd just stand on the side of the road before we put these plates in and just blow the radiator out. And then they'd put the shotgun real easy on the seat—they got no hurry—crank up their car, and come on down the road. They knew we couldn't go but about two miles—no water—and they could have the car towed in and they done made 'em $100. So we put these plates in and they'd shoot the radiator, but that big plate would stop all the pellets and we'd go on into Atlanta and unload, see. It took 'em a helluva long time to find out what was happening. But they finally did.

Then they got a deal that was known as a cowcatcher. Worked just like an ice tong. They could run up behind you on a hill and they'd bump you and it'd close. Then they'd put on the brakes; just keep ridin' the brakes. It'd stop you. You'd have to get out and run across the woods and get somebody to pick you up after you'd run about three miles. So to stop this, we put the bumper on with two coathanger wires. They'd run up behind us and they'd put on the brakes and they'd pull the bumper, and every time it'd fall off right in front of their front wheels. By the time they got that damned thing untangled, the bootleg car's going on into Atlanta—either that or turned off on a country road—and that worked real good. They was every kind of gimmick, and you never have seen none of this in none of these pictures they've made. That's what gets me. But you had to survive. It was dog-eat-dog, really, just like the animals right now. You know how they eat each other? That's what we was doing, just had to, to survive. But they wasn't no killin's. I never did know of any killin's. Some of the guys got sprayed when they'd shoot some of the radiators out—some of the bullets'd ricochet through the window—but they wasn't trying to kill us. The sheriffs was proud of us, really, but they had to catch us to exist themselves. All they wanted to do was stop that car.

I went with Bob and Fonty on quite a few runs. Whiskey back then came in gallon jars—quart jars, gallon jars. We'd put 'em in a fishnet to keep 'em from rolling around in the car. The car was stripped. There wasn't nothing but a bucket seat. The rest of it was full of liquor. I'd get on a Coca-Cola crate or anything I could sit on, and when they'd catch us on the top of a hill, my job was to take a gallon of liquor—I got real good at it; it's hard to hold a gallon of liquor out the window, in the wind—and let it go right through the damned windshield. And that would run 'em off the road.

This was the way the guys made their living. But on the weekend they didn't have anything to do, and the guys that owned these cars—these were the men I guess you'd call the kingpins of the bootlegging business—they would argue about who had the best and the fastest cars. So the original way stock car racing got started—I don't care what anyone else tells you—was in a cow pasture right outside Atlanta, Georgia. On Sundays, all these bootleg cars would line up. They didn't have no fences or nothing, and they had more or less cut a place around this field maybe a quarter of a mile, and they'd run these cars. And they'd be some of the biggest betting among these guys that had all the money—not the drivers, the guys that owned the cars. The purse might win $100 for the guys that was actually driving, so they'd pass hats or take their helmets, and people'd stuff dollars, 50 cents, quarters. They wadn't making a danged thing. The guy that was betting on him made all the money. So after about five or six weeks, more spectators started stopping and they'd get lined up all the way around the field. Right then, this is where Bill France come in. Bill, you know, run some stock cars, but he seen all these people, and he thought about putting up fences, putting up some ticket booths. And that's how stock car racing got started.

Bob and Fonty run whiskey, I would say, three years at the most—three or four—and then all of a sudden Bill France started promoting them races, and to make a living all you'd have to do is outrun these other cars. We were good drivers to start with, and we'd had the experience over them country roads. I would go with Bob to the races to help him change tires, put gas in the car. Pit crews, just like you see now, only it didn't take but one pit man back then. Somebody to dump some gas. And the way I started driving, one day a car come over from North Wilkesboro [N.C.]. It was owned by Speedy and Jimmy Thompson's daddy, Bruce Thompson, and Mr. Thompson come up to me and said, "Tim, would you like to drive this car?" Well, I never had drove one, but I'd been around with Bob and Fonty, and they'd spun me out and done everything to show me what to do when you get in trouble. I'd drive with 'em on the track. They wadn't no rules. Anytime they wanted to warm up, I was with 'em in the car. I'd put a helmet on and I thought I was something else. But they'd spin me out to try to scare me. They didn't never want to let me run because one guy was gonna get an education and not become a race driver. But that day that car come over from North Wilkesboro, I got in it—and a gear locked up about the second lap. Next week, we got it running. I started winning races that first year, and outrunning Bob and Fonty is what thrilled me to death. These were modifieds: 15-lap heats and 25-lap features; $200, $150 to win the feature, and you got 40 percent of that. So we was still starvin' to death by the time you traveled and got back home. We run those for three or four years. We'd go out and run and risk our life and have promoters give us I.O.U.'s after the race. Of course, you don't run into that now. They have to put the money up before the race starts. But they's so many stories you could talk for three weeks on the experiences you've seen and the things you've done.

WHEN TINY LUND CAME SOUTH FROM HARLAN, IOWA, THE first place he settled was Taylorsville, N.C., just the other side of the Brushy Mountains from North Wilkesboro, where a young Junior Johnson was beginning to gain a measure of recognition. Tiny kept his car at the same shop Junior did, and when Junior went off to spend ten months and three days in the federal penitentiary at Chillicothe, Ohio, having been caught at the Johnson family still, Tiny even drove Junior's car a little.

Slowly Lund learned the ways of his adopted land. The first time he went to the race track at Wilson, N.C., a mechanic for another driver asked him, "I gotta make a little run tonight. You want to go with me?"

Lund didn't know for sure what a run was, but he went along anyway and discovered that making a whiskey run wasn't always the "Thunder Road" adventure that Hollywood made it out to be. "It was quiet, sneaky," Lund said. "We took one load the second day I was there, and I couldn't hardly believe it. We went right downtown and stopped in front of the hardware store and carried these cases of jars in the store and set 'em in the front window. And that's where the guy stored it and sold it from. You're looking right through the plate-glass window at it: stacks of Mason jars in cardboard boxes that were full of white lightning. Damn."

JACK SMITH SAID HE WASN'T AS GREAT AS HE SHOULD have been. "In racing," he said, "it's like in football and it's like in baseball. The more publicity you get, the more money you're going to make and the better deal you're going to get. Some of the greatest baseball players in the world has never got the publicity that they deserved. Look at Roger Maris. I mean, he wanted to win them ball games, but he wadn't a spokesman and he didn't take the time with them reporters and the press and all—take 'em out like Mickey Mantle would and buy 'em a beer, buy 'em a steak. All he wanted to do was go out there and play baseball and go back home and see his wife and family.

"It was unfortunate that when I was young, with very little education, I thought about one thing: *What am I going to do about that car?* Maybe I'm on the pole, but it's not just exactly right. Now: *Am I messing up? Is the handling messing up?* I was too much mechanically inclined, and I wanted to win too bad to take time like I'm a-taking with you today to set down and explain these things. You could be my best friend and come up and start talking to me, and it'd go in one ear and out the other one. It took me years before I realized that it didn't matter how great you was. I was a hard-ass . . . I was a hard-ass."

By the summer of 1975, Jack Smith had mellowed considerably. From the office of his transmission shop in Spartanburg,

S.C., he easily recalled the earliest years of stock car racing, which he had observed from the same north Georgia vantage point so familiar to Tim Flock:

> It was rough and rowdy. It was a lots of boys just getting out of the service—they had been over there four or five years in them wars—and I would say that at least 70 percent of the men that was driving the cars in '46, '47, '48 and on up was involved, or had been involved, in what we called trippin' whiskey, haulin' whiskey, maybe makin' a little bit of whiskey. And not only the people that was racing, but the people that owned the race tracks. They was just as bad as the race drivers. They had made lots of money during the war sellin' whiskey and different things, and then they come in and build a nice race track where other people didn't have the money. Some of the best race tracks that there is today was built with that kind of money. And some of the promoters that's promoting today, that's how they got their money to get started into this thing. If you found a man that was in that kind of business, he was a gambler anyhow. He didn't mind taking a chance on his money.
>
> In my opinion, where I was raised and all, I didn't think it was any more difference for them to make it than it is for Hiram Walker's Distillery or some of them others to be makin' it. The only difference was that they wasn't payin' taxes. They didn't do nothing but make a living out of it anyway, the majority, and they didn't know that it was wrong to make some moonshine because they had never been taught no other way. Some of them people was just as fine a boys as you'd ever want to know—such as Bob Flock, Fonty Flock—but I think probably racing in lots of instances kept these people from doing things that, if they hadn't of been racing, they might have got involved in. Such as myself.
>
> You asked the question. I have to truthfully say, yes, I've transported whiskey. Not as much as some of the other boys did, but I did do some of it. It was fun. If it wasn't fun, you wouldn't be involved. Just like driving a race car. You had to really love it, especially then, to go racing six or eight times a week, and not only just for one week, but for maybe a month, two months. Now, to do them things, it wasn't the money involved, it was that you enjoyed the challenge. And this is the same thing about the boys that was trippin' and runnin' the moonshine. They enjoyed that challenge. And most of the *po*-lices that was running 'em was enjoying it just as much as they were. I know many, many of them

got just as big a kick out of jumping me and trying to catch me as I did trying to outrun them. And I've known of times when I would actually run six or eight hours and could have stopped twenty times, but I wouldn't do it until I'd get nearly out of gas. Then I'd park the car and go on about my business.

When you was on the highway back then—this is number 9-and-19 highway out of Atlanta to Dawsonville and Dahlonega—we didn't have no traffic situation. You would leave Dawsonville late at night, and if you seen one car, you about knew that it was a trip car. If it wadn't, it was the sheriff or the revenue man—either the federal or state revenue man. If they jumped you somewheres, well, you knew the roads just as well as you knew the streets around where you was born and raised. You knew where every hill was, where every curve was, and you knew where the dead-end streets was and where you didn't want to get hemmed up at. You had to study that just like you have to study to do anything, and if you didn't, then you're going to get hemmed up and get in a place that you cain't get out of. I've seen 'em block bridges—take their cars and pull 'em across a bridge. There'd be a man coming up behind you, and you'd drop over a hill and you'd have two things to do: either spin the car and go back, or you could try to push around that car on the bridge and get by him. A lots of times it'd knock the fender down on the tire and you didn't have a chance. Maybe in two or three miles you knew that you was going to blow a tire, so you had to jump out and get gone. We always called that bush-bond, when we had to leave the car. That was a bad situation. Maybe you had everything you had tied up in the car. You'd always have to get a lawyer to buy-bid it back for you, but most of the time it would be higher priced than you could go out and build you another car. Most of the time when you lost one, you forgot about that car because they done had all the numbers off it and everything else.

Most people thought it wadn't no work to it. But it's as hard a work as any human has ever done because when you're trying to put 120 gallons of whiskey on a car, then you've got to stack that whiskey in there just right before you leave out. Maybe there's two of you. You've got to carry that stuff from the stash a quarter of a mile across a hill, or across the bottoms, and at that time you'd carry 12 gallon. It was in cans, and they would be in orange sacks, and you would have six gallon on each shoulder. Well, if there happened to be a squirrel or a possum or something that run out of the woods, naturally, you thought it was The Man; every move that was made, you thought it might be The Man. And then when you got on into Atlanta, or wherever you was carrying it, every time somebody'd say, "Boo," you was ready to jump out of your pants and run. I pulled up many times at a red light and looked up in the mirror and there'd be the *po*-lice pulled right up beside of me. You're settin' there thinking: *Is he going to look over here in the back and see that stuff?* So you was under a nervous strain. It was a challenge at all times, and that was the reason that the people that done it, enjoyed it. It was dangerous. Some people I think likes to live dangerous. It's just a matter of not getting caught and getting caught. I was one of the fortunate ones that I never served a day, and never got caught.

Back then, we had '34 Fords, two doors and four doors, '35 Fords, '36 Fords—that was a bad one because the way the steering geometry and all was—and then you'd get '38 Fords. We put cross-springs under 'em; had lots of different ways we tried to fix 'em so we could carry that kind of load. You had to stop and think. When you put 120 gallon of whiskey at eight pounds to the gallon, you're adding some amount of weight to that car, and the more weight you add to it, the more horsepower you've got to have to pull that weight. That revenue man that's running you, or the state man, or the sheriff, or *po*-lice, he doesn't have that extra 1,000 pounds of weight on his car. So that means one thing. You've got to drive harder. You've got to take more chances than he's going to take because he's not going to get no time if he catches you. We had shops for years that never touched nothing except whiskey cars—and race cars. In them years back then—just say in 1946, '47, '48—to build a car to put out on the road, a good trip car, the garage bill's gonna run over $2,500 to $3,000. If it happened to be a car that didn't have hydraulic brakes, you put a booster on 'em. You rebuilt the engine. You used a different type transmission. You changed the gear in the rear end where it'd run just as fast in the mile as it would in ten miles.

Now, if it was what we call a setup car, that you used in Atlanta, well, you want it to run just as fast in two blocks as it'd run in twenty. A setup car, that's a car they used . . . Maybe somebody'd call up and say they want 15 gallon or 18 gallon or whatever, and then you'd put 15 or 18 gallon on that car, and you'd go to the bootlegger that sold it by the pint, half-pint, quart—any way that he could sell it. Some of 'em sold it by the drink, just like a bar. So you fixed a car where it would jump from block to block just as fast as it would run in twenty blocks because that was the i-*dee,* to outrun that man two or three blocks. They didn't have radios back at that time. They didn't have no picture machines—no radar—and your object was to get away from him before you happened to run up on two or three of them. If you could run and hide from him and unload it, there wasn't nothing he could do. So it was a challenge to build a car to try to outrun them people. It was about the same way it is in the type racing that they're doing today. Every man that builds a race car, it's a challenge for him to build that car better than his competitor.

CURTIS TURNER BEGAN TO RACE FOR REAL IN 1946, AT A little track in Mount Airy, N.C. The first time out he finished last, eighteenth in a field of eighteen. But he won his second race, and it wasn't much later that the "Blond Blizzard," as he came to be called, began to build a reputation as perhaps the best dirt-track driver of them all. In time, Curtis Turner came to be the touchstone of an era, not because he was so typical of it—Tim Flock and his brothers were that—but because others could point to him, this outrageous, charming man, and, forgetting the long nights on the road, the blown engines, the flatted tires, and the crashes, could say, "Let me tell you about Pops. That's the way it really was, back then." And because he was also so good, he was the standard by which other drivers of his generation, and of succeeding generations as well, chose to measure themselves.

This self-comparison with Turner took many forms. Ned Jarrett, an excellent short-track driver himself, said, "I'd sort of write him off even before we got started. He outran me more times than I ever outran him, but I'd finish three times as many races. I never expected him to be there at the end." On the other hand, Freddy Lorenzen cried when he beat Turner in 1961 to win the first major race of his own magnificent career because, he said, he knew he had beaten the master.

Although Turner was 6 feet 2 inches and weighed about 220 pounds, he was not a violent man except when he was behind the wheel of a race car. In nearly all the stories about Turner that contained the seeds of wrath and anger, it was he who backed down, avoided the confrontation, defused the crisis.

Ralph Moody, the transplanted New Englander, remembered the first time *he* met Turner. The introduction was blustery.

"You'd better watch out," said Turner. "When we get racin', we race around here."

"You just haven't been where I've been," said Moody. "If something goes wrong, you'll be with me."

On this particular day, Moody and Fireball Roberts were driving nearly identical cars as teammates, as were Turner and Weatherly. Moody, for reasons clouded by time, shoved Weatherly off the edge of the track. Turner tried to reciprocate against Roberts, an action Moody did not appreciate.

"So I got right behind Turner going down the backstretch," Moody said. "He whupped that thing all out of shape to slide it into the corner, and I drove down under him and was gone. We get down to number one when I see him in the mirror. He's chopped it clear into the infield, and he's going to beat me about halfway through that corner and stuff me out into the woods somewhere. And when I see what he's doing, I just *whoaed* that dude, boy, and I caught him when he was coming out of there and got him crossways and run him back in the infield. There was a ditch in there and a old piece of barbed-wire fence and an old shithouse over in back—one of these little ol' crappers, y'know? I pushed him right straight through that thing. Just never shut it down. It bent his wheels all out of shape, and he run a couple laps and went in to pit."

Moody was still fuming when the race ended. "I walked up to the door of his car," he said, "and I snatched him right out of there. I told him, 'Look, big, tall man, if that's the way you're going to race, we'll do it like this: First, I'm going to whale the hell out of you before the race, and then I'll ride over you during the race, and then I'll whale the hell out of you after the race. You ain't going to do that to me.' He sat back down in the car and says, 'No, no, no, no.' He wouldn't have got into a fight anyway, but I didn't know that at the time. He was something else. He didn't give a damn for nothing."

And more than likely Turner said, "Now Pops, everything's gonna be all right. Let's have a party. 'Nother party's startin' in 'bout fifteen minutes." Because Pops always said that and everything usually was all right—and another party usually did start, in about fifteen minutes.

Bobby Allison's first altercation with Turner took place on a quarter-mile paved track in Winston-Salem, N.C., in 1966. Allison was in his first full season of Grand National racing and still a little unsure of what the big time was all about. "Turner was on up in years then," Allison said, "but he was still a tremendously competitive guy. He didn't run for 50 miles and then rest for 50 and run for 50 more, he'd run for 500. But he was also a guy that might show up so drunk he didn't know his own name, or be up all night partying and sleep on a creeper in the garage area for an hour before the race.

"He was driving for Junior Johnson, and Junior had to qualify the car at Winston-Salem because Turner showed up late. He obviously had been enjoying himself and was a little bit wild. I started in front of him, and while I was in traffic, just waiting on the guy in front of me and unable to push my car full speed, he ran over me from the back and spun me out. I ran him down. It took over 100 laps to do it, and by then, I'd worked myself into a little bit of a frenzy. When I caught him, I tried to pass him. He cut me off, and when he did, I spun him.

"I can still remember very clearly that it was quite a serious decision for me to make—whether to follow him or go ahead and spin him out. I decided that if I was ever gonna race and be respected, then I was gonna have to give him what he had already given me; I was gonna have to show him that he couldn't run over me.

"I went on and took the lead, and he got going again trying to catch me. And when he couldn't, he slowed down and waited a lap and ran into me. Then I ran into him, and he ran into me, and I ran into him, and pretty soon neither car would go anywhere. My car ended up parked in the infield grass, badly battered, and my crew and I took it home and worked night and day to get it ready to go to the next race."

For Allison, the incident was an initiation of sorts; for Turner, it was just another day's work. "At the next race," Allison continued, "I came walking in and he says, 'Hi, Bobby, old friend. How're you doing?' And from then on, we were friends right up till he got killed in the airplane crash. He was an unusual character—which racing is full of unusual characters—but he really was something special."

IN THE SCRAPBOOKS THERE WAS A PROGRAM FOR AN afternoon of racing at the Greensboro, N.C., fairgrounds on August 23, 1947, a Sunday. The promoter was Bill France, and race headquarters were at the King Cotton Hotel. First prize for the 50-lap feature was $500, part of the overall guaranteed purse of $2,000. The complete specifications for the cars were as follows:

All cars must have full windshield in place, and used as windshield.

CARS ELIGIBLE—1937 models and up.

Any model V8 Ford or Mercury or Ford 6 motor will be allowed to be interchanged in any model Ford.

Motors can be oversize.

All cars must have hydraulic brakes or, that is, have 4-wheel mechanical brakes in good order and must stand test.

Cars may be run with or without fan or generator.

Any Ford or Mercury carburetor may be interchanged.

Water pump impellors may be cut down.

Machined fly wheel will be permitted.

Any gear ratio may be used. And differential locked.

Any steering parts may be reinforced.

Any interchangeable wheel or tire size may be used.

Any radiator may be used, provided the same can be used without special fittings for the shell or hood.

Stock fuel and oil-tanks and capacities must be used.

Stock Ignition and Coil must be used.

Extra breakerpoint springs will be permitted.

Any type of manufactured spark plug may be used.

Any model manufactured flat type cylinder heads may be used. Cylinder heads may be machined to increase compression.

Springs may be reinforced.

Any valve springs may be used.

Multiple carburetors will be permitted.

All cars must have fenders if so equipped when new, and not abbreviated.

Altered camshafts will be permitted.

If a car is a convertible type, it will be permissible to construct a hood over the driver's head to protect driver in event of upset.

Shock absorbers, any type, will be permitted.

Wheels may be reinforced for safety.

All drivers must be strapped in and must wear safety helmets.

Bumpers and mufflers must be removed.

All cars must have Full Fenders.

All cars must have Running Boards if so equipped when new.

Also, the program noted, "No driver will be permitted to race if he shows any evidence of the use of any alcoholic beverages whatever. Absolutely no exceptions to these rules." If a driver chipped in a buck and a half, he was eligible for up to $500 in hospital and medical benefits.

THE EVOLUTION OF THE RACING STOCK CAR WAS HURried along by considerations of safety and performance, not always in that order. In the beginning there was the modified, although it did not necessarily go by that or any other name, and it was fast. A modified racer, more often than not, was a mid- to late-1930s Ford. (In the years immediately before and after World War II, the Ford Motor Company almost completely dominated what a later generation would call the performance market.) First, you rescued your rusting steed from the junk yard. Then you fine-tuned the engine, beefed up the rear axle, added heavy-duty shock absorbers and springs, fixed yourself a seat belt from a piece of rope, strapped the doors shut with a leather belt or chains, and maybe cut back the fenders. Whatever other modifications you made depended on how good a backyard mechanic you were. You might grind a special camshaft, add extra carburetors, or use different gears to suit the peculiarities of the different tracks. But whatever you did, you could build a car with all the stuff they had for $1,000, maybe $2,000.

Then late-model racing came along. At first, the cars were

simply called "strictly stock"; later, they were known as Grand Nationals. The idea was to race cars no more than three model-years old just as they were when they left the dealer's showroom. This presented problems, for the automobiles that left Detroit's assembly lines were not often suited for the rigors of the race track. If you hit a pothole, your battery would fall out; if you went through a turn too fast, your car would flex so much that your windshield would pop loose or a spindle would break, sending your right-front wheel, and maybe you, hurtling over the edge of the track. Or your car would simply overheat. The tires you used were plain old street tires, or recaps that were called "maypops" because you felt they just might. You looked for tires with a diamond tread and maybe a zigzag design on the sidewalls because you figured they would grab hold of the dirt better. As race cars, in short, the late-model automobiles were distinctly inferior to their hot rod cousins, the modifieds. Bruton Smith, a promoter, had the weird thought that some afternoon during a late-model show he would look out onto his track and find it empty; that with 50 or so laps to go, every car in the field would have overheated, crashed, or otherwise been eliminated. "What would I have done then?" he asked. "Just say, 'Okay folks, let's go home'?"

Of course, country engineering did provide some ways to help keep the cars running. By using their ingenuity and stretching the rules, backyard mechanics figured out how to cool engines and keep batteries in place. They discovered that the rear-end assembly from a three-quarter-ton pickup truck tended to twist less than did the stock rear axle provided by the manufacturer. They learned how to mess with a car's suspension parts so its frame wouldn't bend when it went broad-sliding through the turns, and how to redistribute a car's weight so its right-front wheel, which took the most punishment on the counterclockwise ovals, wouldn't go sailing out into the boondocks quite so often.

Everybody, naturally enough, sought access to the parts and ideas that improved performance, and few speed secrets remained secret for very long. There was considerably less enthusiasm for the safety of the driver. Safety items rarely made a car go fast, many added unwanted weight to a car, and most added to its cost. All were resisted. Take roll bars, for example. At first, the rules said only that a car had to have them, but since they didn't specify the kind of metal to be used or its thickness, the drivers showed up with roll bars made from electrical conduit piping, the kind of soft copper tubing a fellow could twist in his hands. Next, the rules said the piping had to be of a certain thickness—no more copper tubing. And no problem. The drivers turned to aluminum. That was plenty thick enough, but it did tend to shear on impact. Finally, the rules got tough. The roll bars had to be made of thick steel. Even then, some drivers who couldn't afford the extra cost or didn't want the added weight came to races with aluminum piping painted the color of steel. It took a lot of flatted-down race cars and not a few deaths to get everybody squared away on that one.

BILL FRANCE DIDN'T INVENT LATE-MODEL STOCK CAR racing, he just took the best advantage of a prevailing situation. The first Grand National, France's chosen name for his strictly stock promotions, was held at the old Charlotte Speedway on June 19, 1949, and was won on the track by Glen Dunnaway. It was won in the record book by an obscure Kansan, Jim Roper, when Dunnaway was disqualified. Two brackets were found attached to the springs of his car to help keep it from swaying through the turns. France ruled that this slight modification was illegal, and thus the official order of finish was: Roper, Fonty Flock, Red Byron, Sam Rice, and Tim Flock.

Grand National racing found an eager audience in the South almost immediately, and several theories sought to explain the sudden acceptance of this strange new sport that depended for its success on the willingness of people to pay hard-earned dollars to watch *passenger* cars, for Chrissakes, beat and bang on each other through long and dusty dogwood afternoons. (For several years, there was even a special circuit for convertibles.) One theory suggested that the popularity of Grand National racing was a natural outgrowth of the secret admiration Southerners had for the good old boys who drove the trip cars. That had a nice romantic tinge, but it didn't really wash because outside their communities, and often within them, the whiskey runners weren't necessarily thought of all that highly. France himself did the best he could to discourage their participation, especially if they had served time. Another theory maintained that Southern sports fans didn't have all that much to do except follow the Grand Nationals. This was closer to the mark, but it didn't explain why Southern newspapers gave the stockers only passing notice, with the notable exception of one or two major races each year. (Well into the 1970s, Grand National racing was not covered with nearly the same passion and intensity, for example, as college football and the professional golf tour.) The most nearly complete theory rested on the premise that Southerners depended on the automobile much more than people in other parts of the country. The postwar South was still very much a rural society, its hundreds upon hundreds of small towns and hamlets connected by a delicate latticework of lovely country roads. The only form of transportation available to the overwhelming majority of Southerners was the automobile, and Southerners, much more than urban Easterners and Midwesterners, could easily understand and respect what was involved in the preparation and driving of a hunk of iron that resembled, at least outwardly, the cars that sat in their own driveways. Southerners cared for the cars that raced nearly as much as they admired the men who drove them, and sometimes more.

Finally, there was the great man theory, which said that save for Bill France, there wouldn't have been any late-model stock car racing of significance in the country anywhere at all. At the time of his first Grand National, France was just one of many stock car racing promoters in the South, and the country, fighting to make a buck. His organization, the National Association for Stock Car Auto Racing, Inc. (NASCAR), was barely two years old, and he needed to use every carney-barker technique at his command to keep the sympathies of the fans, who cared only about the show, and the loyalties of the drivers, who cared only about the money. France was not popular with everybody all the time, for a variety of reasons, but he persevered and built an empire.

THE BEACH AT DAYTONA HAD BEEN A MECCA OF SPEED practically since the invention of the automobile. The first

Henry Ford came there dressed in black, his favorite color, to test an experimental car that never really ran very well; Barney Oldfield came there with the Winton Bullet and the Blitzen Benz, and a host of others came, all to run the measured mile on a sandy beach washed hard and flat by the gentle ocean tides. The last to arrive was Malcolm Campbell, in 1936. That year, his land speed car, "Bluebird," ran out of sand at 276 mph, and he headed West to find longer runouts on the salt flats of Utah, near Bonneville. To fill the void, and to help keep the garish, pink-stucco, Florida-land-boom hotels along Ocean Boulevard full, the city fathers of Daytona Beach sought to promote automobile races on their own. Their first venture was a financial disaster, and they were more than happy to give over their project to private entrepreneurs.

Bill France, born and raised to a height of 6 feet 4 inches near Washington, D.C., drove South two years before Malcolm Campbell headed West. He was a former motorcycle racer and a sometimes stock car driver with a burning desire to show his father he could make good, and he stopped in Daytona Beach (so goes the story) because that's where his money ran out. He opened a two-pump Standard Oil filling station on Atlantic Avenue, and in 1938 he entered one of the beach races. He flipped in the first turn of his first lap (so goes the story), and with a friend turned to promoting the races rather than driving in them. Within a year, the friend was gone and World War II was on its way. When automobile racing resumed in 1946, William Henry Getty "Big Bill" France was in this thing by himself.

France was given to loud sport shirts and had an uncontrollable shock of hair the color of his sand. He was, in fact, called "The Senator of Sand." He tacked up 3,000 posters single-handedly to advertise his race one year, but there were no fences at the track and many people scrambled through the palmettos to watch free—until (so goes the story) Big Bill tacked up some more signs that read: "Beware Rattlesnakes."

THE BEACH COURSE WAS ACTUALLY A BEACH-ROAD course, a two-mile stretch of beach and a two-mile stretch of Florida Highway A1A connected by two U-turns, the north turn and the south. The north turn was where a driver plowed through the heavy sands and somehow got his car up onto the highway; the south turn was where he left the highway and got back onto the beach. The south turn had a twelve-foot dropoff and was called "Speed's Junk Yard." Pictures from the scrapbooks showed that twelve, fifteen, sometimes twenty cars failed to negotiate the south turn in a single race and wound up at the bottom of the dropoff. The highway was bumpy and tightly bordered on both sides by palmettos; the beach was bordered on one side by the ocean.

Fireball Roberts told a reporter, "There is a hill on the road backstretch about a quarter of a mile from the south turn where you can't see ahead until you reach the top. My hair almost stands on end every time I hit that hill."

Banjo Matthews said, "I think this is the most dangerous track in the world."

Ralph Moody, who drove the beach course as well as anybody, said, "Going off the beach into the north corner, you had to run the car completely sideways because if you tried to go through there anywheres square, it would dig out the holes this big and the car would porpoise so bad that you'd just tear it up. But if you kept your foot in it and kept it sideways, it would go through there like a boat through the waves. Once in a while you'd flip one because you'd hit something wrong, but that was the easier way to get through. And you'd always hit the pavement all wound up in low gear, spin the wheels, bounce off of one another. . . . And, of course, that little old narrow road wasn't much wider than a room. Boy, going down that thing, it was so rough you just stayed off the ground, with the brush dragging on both sides and people sticking their heads out of the bushes. And some of those old cars that run down there, they'd run 130, 140 mile an hour—150 mile an hour, maybe, the last few years. Down at the end of that thing, the south turn, if you didn't pay attention, you'd just forget to stop and go right off over the end down a big gully. They used to pile a bunch of 'em up down there. And then you'd come out down there and just drift way out to the ocean and get on the wet sand.

"Things changed on the beach course real fast. They usually started the thing when the tide was out, but it don't take long for the tide to come in, and then you'd get where it'd leave wet spots—an acre here or a puddle there—and you'd duck those things. I don't know if you ever run through a big puddle of water, but it just *whoas* you. On the dry sand, you just lost so much traction you couldn't go. So when the tide got in, you'd be better off to run on the edge of the water. You'd run faster there."

Unless you drifted out too far, which was more or less what happened to Lee Petty, as Moody remembered events, in 1956. "It rained when we run that race," Moody said, "and it sandblasted everybody's windshield so bad it was like bathroom glass. Tim Flock was right in front of me, like a hundred yards ahead, and we were right down near the north end of the race track. All of a sudden, here comes somebody *this* way. [From the right, he gestured.] That was old man Petty. I guess he couldn't see where he was going, or didn't know where he was going. I don't know what the hell happened to him, but he'd been out in the ocean. So I thought I'd better turn it to the right to miss him and then make the corner. You'd *have* to go around the corner, or do something, because all they had was a string with some red and blue banners hanging off of it, and if you'd go down there straight, you'd kill a jillion people. So I missed Petty going *this* way and turned the *other* way, and in that rough sand I went side over side, upside down, all that crap. Knocked the windshield all out. The funny part of it is, when you stopped at the beach, they'd always throw a bucket of water on the windshield. It was the only way you could clean it. And here I come sailing into my pits, and the guy throws a bucket of water—right in the kisser. I had sand in the car and sand in the goggles and it knocked the goggles off and, oh, it was a mess."

IN 1933, HAROLD BRASINGTON, A LEAN AND LANKY SOUTH Carolinian from the small farming community of Darlington, went up north to see the most famous automobile race in America: the Indianapolis 500. Brasington was just another racing fan, but he came back home very much impressed with the 2½-mile Indianapolis Motor Speedway, as well as with the tens of thousands of spectators who, despite the Depression, turned out to watch the open-wheel, open-cockpit Roadsters compete in the Memorial Day extravaganza. "It hit me that if that many people liked Indianapolis-type cars," Brasington said, "then people down here would surely come out to see their own cars run."

By 1949, Brasington had built a successful heavy-contracting business and was able to sell his idea for a big, paved race track for late-model stock cars to a group of Darlington businessmen gathered for their weekly poker game. They raised $60,000 in seed money and let Harold have at it.

There were two problems. One was that Harold had never before built a race track. The only models he had to go by were the small dirt tracks on which stock car racing then conducted most of its business, and the mammoth Indianapolis facility, the only track in the country with a circumference greater than one mile. He borrowed a little from both. In overall size, he built his track to a distance of 1¼ miles, exactly half that of the Indy oval, and his turns were taken primarily from the dirt tracks. Whereas the Indy track had four separate and distinct corners, Brasington built just two huge U-turns at either end of his straightaways; whereas the turns at Indianapolis were nearly flat, Brasington banked his 16 degrees.

The other problem was Sherman Ramsey's minnow pond. Sherman Ramsey had donated seventy acres of his farm land for the track in return for shares in the raceway corporation. The anointed acreage held both a fish pond and a minnow pond. Ramsey said the fish pond could go, but the minnow pond, well, it had to stay. Thus, Brasington's oval turned out somewhat pear-shaped, with the east turn of significantly larger radius than the west. Barney Wallace, a peanut broker at the time and one of the investors, explained, "We built the track the way we did because that's the way it came out."

It came out weird.

The first race at the Darlington Raceway was held on Labor Day, 1950, and was 500 miles long. The wife of Strom Thurmond, the South Carolina governor, cut the ceremonial ribbon. The assumption was that no more than 5,000 or 6,000 people would show up; the 25,000 who poured through the gates surprised and delighted everybody. The winner was Johnny Mantz, a Californian who, while fighting a massive hangover, nursed the showroom Hudson Hornet that some friends had bought for him just that week to victory at an average speed of a tick over 76 mph. Seventy-five cars started the race and twenty-five finished it, and the first Southern 500, though it was not known by that name for several years, took over six and a half hours to run.

THE RACE ON THE BEACH AT DAYTONA IN FEBRUARY began the season, and the race on the strange new oval at Darlington on Labor Day climaxed it. In between was the dirt. In the 1950s, it seemed you couldn't drive more than fifty miles from any point in the Southeast without running across a dirt race track. There were scores of them, all the same but each with peculiarities that set it apart. They were quarter-milers and half-milers, rarely larger, and most of them were in the Piedmont, the crescent-shaped plateau that begins just above Richmond and stretches across the Carolinas and Georgia until it tickles eastern Alabama. The Piedmont separates the Appalachian foothills from the coastal plain and made for just about the best dirt-track racing there ever was. Further toward the mountains, the soil was too rocky; further toward the ocean, it became sandy and porous. But in the Piedmont, dead center in the Piedmont, that was the best. All you had to do was get yourself an earth grader and cut off the topsoil and there they were: the Charlotte Fairgrounds, Harris Speedway near Concord, Asheville-Weaverville, North Wilkesboro (in the foothills, but still an okay track), Mount Airy, Hickory, Greenville, High Point, Columbia, Gastonia, Wilson, Lakewood Speedway in Atlanta (one mile around and fast; a killer track), the Raleigh Fairgrounds, Richmond, and all the rest.

Not that there weren't some problems occasionally. The clay could get muckety-muck on you if you put too much water on, and then the broadsliding race cars would churn up huge roostertails of mud clumps and throw them right into the grandstand. Or if you didn't water your track enough and put down some calcium, it could get a little dusty. Sometimes the tracks just plain wore out. A clipping from the scrapbooks said of one particular oval: "The track was in such poor condition that engines were torn off their mountings, batteries split, springs twisted and frames pretzel-ized. Drivers swore they could have driven under their bounding competitors at times as they leapt from one hole to the next."

But if you did your homework—if you took a disc harrow and broke the surface of the clay to a depth of an inch, inch and a half, and raked it with a spike-tooth drag to break up the clumps, and then watered it, maybe 50,000 gallons in all for a half-mile track beginning four days before your show, and laid on the calcium—that red clay held together just perfect. You could sit back and let the cars buff off the loose stuff until what was underneath became as hard and as firm and as black as polished asphalt. Then your track was known as dry-slick, and it was pure ecstasy to watch the cars break traction and power slide into the turns two, sometimes three abreast in perfect harmony, a chorus line on wheels.

Tim Flock:

You gotta really know how to balance a car. We'd cross 'em up in the turns. It was more or less a controlled power slide, and I think balance is your main thing—knowing how far that rear end is coming around and correcting for it real easy without losing your speed. You just got to know right when to come back. I drove with my butt—my ass—and my dad, Carl Lee. . . . I'll give my dad credit. He was a tightrope walker, and I think the best race drivers, if you talk to every one of them, I believe they could balance themselves on a rope because they'd know when they were losing it. You can tell when a car's getting away from you.

The tracks we run were so dusty you couldn't see one car in front of another. You more or less had to guess. I'd count poles. . . . I'm serious. This sounds like a bunch of bull, but it ain't. . . . I'd count, "One, two, three, four, five, six"—and *turn.* And if you miscounted, you'd be over the bank. They didn't have no fences at half the tracks. . . . Lakewood was real dusty, and that thing was dangerous. *Loooong* straightaways and short turns. Real tough because you were going so damned fast out there. It killed forty, fifty drivers counting when the Indianapolis guys started running out there. . . . Let's see . . . Columbus, Georgia, was the dustiest track I ever run on. You'd run into somebody and back off. You'd turn a little bit and try to go by—and spin out. It was turrible. And the fans couldn't even see the race cars, it was so dusty. They was sitting up there *listening* to 'em. . . . But all your half-mile tracks all over the country was turrible. You'd be right on the inside of the race track at the start, and before it was over, you'd be hanging your back wheels off the top of the track to keep from hitting them big holes. Or you'd run through the infield. You just more or less made your own race track.

Jack Smith:

On dirt, you've always got more or less one groove, and that man's going to try to stay in the groove. And when he's trying to stay in the groove, you can keep diving under him. You're driving in the corner faster than he's driving in, and you're running down beside of him, and he's looking over there at you, and if it slides, you're going to slide up against him, and . . . Some drivers couldn't stand it. They just had to back out of it. It was one of the things that you really enjoyed, getting up beside of a man and seeing if you could make him move over a extra three inches and get one wheel up in the soft stuff by leaning on him. I won a lots of races that way, and this is the way Curtis Turner and Junior Johnson won a lot of races. But I cannot compare myself with a man like Curtis Turner or a man like Junior Johnson because most of the time that I was in the racing business, I worked on my car. That was my livelihood. Where Junior and Curtis Turner, as far as I know . . . I never knew of Curtis Turner putting any money in a car. When you're in somebody else's car, you can be rougher. It was better for me to let the man go on if he's going to keep banging around and tearing up $200, $300 worth of my equipment than it was to do like Turner.

Junior was rough. He was rough driving a car. But I never had as much trouble with Junior, on dirt tracks, as I did with Turner. I know there for a while that Turner got so bad that nobody wanted to put him in his car because, heck, they knew that when he come in that they was going to have to put new running boards and new fenders on it. He didn't care, just as long as he was leading the race. If he made $2, he was just as happy as if he made $200. I've had Turner when he just absolutely run over me. I remember one time, we was racing in Savannah—and I'd been down there four or five straight Sundays and won the race—and here comes Turner in with a car out of West Virginia. I'm leading the race, and the track—it'd been raining that night—the track down on the inside was just like glass. Turner kept diving underneath me, and the first thing you know, he just come right up over the front end of my car and just absolutely pushed me off the race track. And he won the race. And I go up to him after the race and I said, "Now, Turner, you got a lesson coming up. I'll be prepared the next time." So the next time, well, he started to do that, and when he did, I just mashed on my brakes as hard as I could and stood up. He slid up, and instead of having something to bank off of, well, he slides right on over the rim of the track. When that man started running underneath you, you had ways that you could eliminate him and not get involved. If you'd get smart.

Dirt-track racing, I think, was more fun. . . . Racing was more fun, back then, than it is today, and the further back you go, the more fun it was. One of the great race drivers that ever be, probably, was a boy from Atlanta named Gober Sosebee. Tiny Lund was as good a dirt track man as there was in the world. But Tiny and Gober, they was like Turner. They didn't worry about no part of the equipment. They'd tear a anvil up.

TO SAY THAT CURTIS TURNER WAS THE BEST EVER ON dirt would get an argument from the defenders of Junior Johnson, Tiny Lund, Jack Smith, and about a half-dozen other drivers—Gober Sosebee—but if a conversation about dirt-track racing ran long enough, Pops was generally the one driver that people talked about the most. Paul Sawyer, a stock car promoter from Richmond, and his partner, Kenneth Campbell, tried to explain why.

"He just had the technique," said Sawyer, "a technique of his own that he just knew how to get that automobile in and out of a corner."

"You can't describe it other than to say he was just the master of it," said Campbell, who proceeded to describe it. "It was just a smoothness. He knew exactly when to brake it—when I say brake it, I mean to cock it—and he could carry it right to the raw edge of where it was going to break loose and make it look smooth."

"He could put a car up on the rim," said Sawyer, "up in the loose stuff where nobody wouldn't even think about getting up there. . . ."

". . . In that loose, gravelly stuff up top. . . ." said Campbell.

". . . We'd call it the marbles," said Sawyer, "and he'd get a wheel hung up in that thing, and the first thing you know . . . Richard Petty reminds me of him some—picking a spot—although I don't think Richard was the daredevil type on dirt. But Richard's got the finesse for finding the groove in a race track, and this is what I'm talking about with Turner. If he was boxed, he could run down on the bottom, or he could run up on top. Either one."

"Turner had an inner sense of some kind," said Campbell, "that he knew what he could do with that car and where he could take it, and he was not afraid to try."

"Just an instinct built within," said Sawyer. "Mind, hands, and feet all together. He could make that automobile do just about what he wanted it to do. He was very smooth as far as engines, but he popped some sheet metal, man. I'll guarantee that."

ON THE LAST PAGE OF NEARLY EVERY ONE OF THE scrapbooks, there was a neat grid drawn in pen or ink. Each was a complete though cryptic account of one of Tim Flock's racing seasons. For 1949, each race was accorded one line. From left to right, the column headings indicated the prize money won by Tim's car, Tim's share of the total, the date of the race, the name of the track, the type gear he used, the size of his tires, his finishing position, and the number of points he collected toward the Grand National driving championship. There were also two other columns: "Trouble" and "Notes." At random, these read:

Trouble	*Notes*
Broke Crankshaft	–
Fowled 2 plugs	–
Turned Over	–

Broke Crankshaft	Jumped out of gear
Fowled Plugs	–
Drove a Dodge	Fast Race all the way
Running 2nd Got Hot	First race for new 90
Thought I won this	Starten in 26 place
Ed Samples push me in fence	bad night
Blowed up	exhaust came off
Coun't see for mud	windshield broke
To much mud on track	coun't get hold
Broke Jackshaft	–
Gearned a little to high	good race
Just right	good day
Just right	lot of wrecks
Skiping water pump	–

The figures indicated that in 1949 Tim Flock won $3,577 in prize money.

In another volume, Tim noted: "Got run over by a car at track; car ran over my head and body while I was asleep." That was in Spartanburg, S.C.

His comment for a race at the half-mile dirt track in Wilson, N.C.: "Track Dug up with big holes all over it."

Paul Sawyer:

I'll give you a little background on Wilson. With Joe Weatherly as a partner—he bought into the operation—we had Norfolk, Virginia; Richmond; and Wilson, North Carolina. The convertible circuit was strong at the time, so we ran the convertible races on Easter Sunday because nobody else wanted that date. But it was a good date down in Wilson, North Carolina, believe me. That thing was a dust bowl. We couldn't find clay anywhere. We hauled clay from all over the Wilson area trying to keep the dust down. We put calcium, and we wet it. We done everything under the sun, and them gals come out there in all that Easter finery, and boy, they didn't care because they'd see the durndest racing that was. There was so many stars that part of 'em drove the Grand National circuit and part of 'em—Weatherly and Fireball Roberts and Turner and Buck Baker—drove the convertible circuit. So we had a real nice show lined up for Easter Sunday in 1958. I had 2,000 seats that I moved from Norfolk to Wilson, North Carolina, and put 'em on the backstretch, and the race was scheduled for three o'clock in the afternoon.

It was an old fairgrounds, an old wooden stand that must have been there for about fifty years, with an exhibition hall that when they had their little county fairs, they had florist shops, or whatever they had, underneath it. And about two o'clock in the afternoon, the grandstand caught on fire. So I got a bucket of water and went up there and put it out. And about 2:15, it caught on fire again. So somebody else got a bucket of water and went up and put it out. Because this thing wasn't in the city. I mean, it's out on U.S. 301. You cain't miss it—it's right by the truck scales. So about twenty minutes of three—the cars are on the line and traffic's blocked up on 301 north *and* south and everybody's selling tickets and I'm trying to get all that mob in there—it caught on fire again. And some wise guy, he's going to find out where the fire is, so he goes down and he opens a set of them big doors under the bottom. Well, it was just like it was lit with gasoline. That thing just said *foosh,* and when it said *foosh,* that was it. Ray Melton was the announcer, and he done a beautiful job getting those people out of there. Nobody panicked, and nobody got hurt, not the first soul. I think we ruined two or three automobiles that were parked in the back. The insurance company had to pay for 'em.

That thing burned to the ground in twenty minutes. Completely. The cops out there on the highway, they're telling people to go on home, that there ain't gonna be no race. Joe and I found out about it, and we got everybody we could, and we stopped 'em, and we were out there selling tickets and stuffing money in our shirts and anywhere we can. It didn't make no difference as long as we got that four or five dollars. People went on over and filled up that 2,000 seats on the backstretch and stood up and down the fences. They didn't care. It was just first come, first served. Buy your ticket and get your best hold. We ran the race twenty minutes late. And that was a big crowd back in those days, 5,000 or 6,000. You put 5,000 or 6,000 people in a race track, we thought that was a big crowd as far as automobile racing was concerned.

THE FABULOUS FLOCKS

Fonty Flock Wins Spartanburg Feature	Tim Flock Wins Concord Car Race	Bob Flock Sets Record at Charlotte
Flocks Finish One, Two, Three	Fonty Flock Second In Charlotte Contest	Tim Flock Wins N. Carolina Race

As Tim guided his visitor through the scrapbooks, it was hard to believe that he and his two brothers were of the same blood. The only physical characteristic common to all was a pronounced jaw. Of personality and mood, there were no hints of any similarities whatever. Bob was of medium height and sturdy construction with a jaw that was hard, firm, and mean, a little like Kirk Douglas's but without the dimple. His eyes were unblinking steel nuggets, not at all those of a person with whom one would choose to be casual, let alone race against. A clipping said he was drafted by the Army in 1941 and continued to draw a 30 percent disability allowance for a nervous condition and a bad stomach following his discharge nineteen months later. Another story said: "It was the first race for the oldest of the Flock brothers since he broke his back at Spartanburg last July. Bob wore a special-type steel corset brace yesterday and his back was rubbed raw and bleeding when he climbed out of the car at the finish." Tim said that Bob was the best of the three, but that after he broke his back a second time, and then his neck, he got discouraged.

Fonty's jaw was equally pronounced, though its firmness was muted by round, full cheeks, a pencil-thin moustache, and a permanent smile. (Every picture of Fonty showed him smiling; every picture of Bob showed him not smiling.) When Fonty was a kid, he entered the Atlanta Soap Box Derby and added several bricks to his racer, bringing its illegal weight to 500 pounds. He crashed into a motorcycle cop at the end of one of his runs and broke both the cop's legs. Fonty also contemplated the ministry, changed his name from Fontell to Fontello for alliteration's sake, and won the Southern 500 at Darlington wearing Bermuda shorts. His shorts were later given to stock car racing's Hall of Fame.

Tim's jaw was thin and pointed, a classic hatchet jaw accentuated by thin cheeks, those sad eyes, and a generally emaciated physique. He looked not unlike an undernourished Robert Montgomery. A story from the beginning of Tim's career said: "A new meteor has flashed across the stock car racing skies, a meteor bright enough to cause even the most established stars considerable worry . . . He is Tim Flock, youngest brother to Fonty and Bob . . . The older brothers introduced Tim to the gentle art of smashing fenders and fences last season, and, under their careful (if sometimes rough) tutelage, he has blossomed forth into the big surprise of the year. In fact, veteran race observers have already selected him as 'the man most likely to succeed' in a sport where even the best do not hang around too long." The story reported that in a span of six races, Tim finished second, second, second, third, fourth, and went through a fence.

A newspaper writer handicapping a race in Atlanta wrote of Fonty: "Too frisky for clover, good stable and hungry, can do." He wrote about Tim: "Greatest win record of all, lightweighted and nervous, can take it all but tires in the stretch." This was later, and Bob had pretty much retired by then.

In one of the earliest scrapbooks, there were two sets of pictures of the Flock brothers, three pictures to the set. Beneath each picture, in Tim's handwriting, were penciled captions. Beneath Bob's two pictures Tim had written: "Shy Guy" and "All this guy needs is a *damn* good car for 1 time"; beneath Fonty's: "Womens Man" and "Second to none, first plenty"; beneath his own: "Still Trying" and "In the money most of the time."

Tim Flock:

Of course, we got outrun. Don't get me wrong. But we was after 'em, I'll tell you that. Wouldn't give up; wouldn't let up. To me, Bob Flock was the greatest. I know you've heard of Curtis Turner and I know you've heard of Buck Baker, about their power slides, but Bob Flock was the greatest power-slider that ever lived. I seen him slide a car half a block before he'd get to a turn, wide open and wheels spinning, and throw dirt clumps plumb into the grandstand going through the turn. He could not stand for nobody to pass him. He'd run over you, under you, or around you to get up front. If you tried to get by him in the first turn, he'd run you plumb up on the damned fence, or through the infield, and he'd run every race the same. He wouldn't lay back. He would *never* lay back. He'd go flat at the gun and blow the engine up. He had good equipment, and he won a lot of races by leading them all the way, but he could not stand nobody to pass him. I mean, he was this way his whole career, and that's why he had so damned many wrecks, too.

If you ever walked up to Bob and put your hand on him, he'd hit you. I mean, a fan or anybody he didn't know, if you just laid your hand on his shoulder, he'd pop you—and break his wrist. Bob run two races for [car owner] Carl Kiekhaefer, and—the funniest thing that ever happened—Kiekhaefer walked up to him one day and said, "Bobby, you didn't do right out there today," and just kind of shook Bob's chin a little bit. And he popped Kiekhaefer. Kiekhaefer fired him right there. . . . Imagine that. . . . Kiekhaefer should of never touched him, though. Bob was the most wonderful guy you'd ever met in your life. Quiet, humble—broke his arm twenty-two times a year hittin' people. And when he would get in a car before a race, he'd sit there and his eyes would change—he'd change all over—and he'd more or less kill you in a car.

I got a bad temper. I'm hard to get mad, but when I get mad, I'm . . . wild. I bumped a lot of guys, put a lot of guys in fences, but I never did get mad enough to try and kill somebody out there, like hit 'em in the driving door or something like that. But I spun 'em out, bumped 'em, shook the helmet off their head. You can bump a guy so bad you can see his head shake, and then the helmet'd come down over his eyes and he'd start looking.

If you ever met Fonty, you'd never forget him. He was a good chauffeur, a daredevil. I guess Fonty Flock tore up more cars than any driver I know of. He was a lot of fun cutting up, a jokester, and had more fans than anybody. He would talk to 'em in the pits. I always did, and Bobby, too. We took up a lot of time with the fans. But Fonty had that moustache, and he'd wear Bamooda shorts and just cut up. He was a clown, really. I guess Fonty had more fans going for him than anybody I've ever known. Still has, really. . . . Well, the younger generation don't even remember him now, but back then, he'd have an awful lot of followin'.

THE NAMES LEAPT OUT FROM THE WORN VOLUMES; marvelous names, good Southern names all suggesting darkness and the mists of time; guileless: Lloyd Seay . . . Pap White . . . Dink Widenhouse . . . Gober Sosebee . . . Possum Jones . . . Lonzo McGee . . . Rupert Cox . . . Peewee Jones . . . Coy Slate . . . Cullen Haddock.

Tim Flock:

Here's a true story.

If you drove or hauled liquor anywhere in Georgia, they's a city ordinance in the city of Atlanta you could not run on a city-of-Atlanta-owned race track, and the track, Lakewood Speedway, is in the city of Atlanta. So, Bob had a record, and everybody knew it, and they was several other drivers had a record. But this particular Sunday—it was right before the race—Bob had qualified up-front somewhere and was sitting up there in his car. He had a handkerchief on, and a helmet. All you could see was his eyes—those *eyes.* Somebody had told the police captain that Bob Flock was in the lineup, and the captain knew that Bob had a record of haulin' liquor for a number of years, so he walked up to the car and said, "Hey, Bob, I know that's you under that handkerchief. Get out of the car." So Bob looked around and seen that it was a *po*-lice captain, and he just jerked it in low gear and took off and went on down to the first turn . . . second turn . . . and stopped on the backstretch—a mile track. People just went crazy because they seen the *po*-lice walk up there, and they knew something was up. Everybody was watching. So the captain had these two motorcycle police sitting there, and he said, "*You* go around *this* way and hem him up, and *you* go around *that* way and hem him up." So the two motorcycle cops went all the way around, and they come down the backstretch, real close to Bob. When they got about twenty or thirty foot, he jerked that big modified in gear and you could hear it ten miles. He spun it right by one of 'em, went down in the third turn, and instead of turning on the track, he jumped over the bank out over a big ol' beautiful Cyclone fence—took it down—out onto Pryor Street and disappeared. With them two police cops after him. They didn't have a chance—against that souped-up car?—and he got away. They never did find him, but four days later he turned hisself in, and it cost him

$100. We got a picture of that, of him in court, in one of these books.

Indeed, there was. The picture, from left to right, showed Sgt. E. O. Mullen, the arresting officer; Fonty, looking terribly annoyed; and Bob, with those wild eyes. The accompanying stories said there had been a high-speed chase at up to 115 mph after Bob's exit from the track, and that he had gotten away and later turned himself in. One story explained: "Flock had been barred from participating in races at Lakewood . . . following passage of a city ordinance forbidding entries of racers who had criminal records. Flock has been in custody a number of times, Sergeant Mullen said; especially in connection with the illegal transportation and sale of whiskey." Bob was fined $136—$100 for violating the city ordinance that prohibited his racing and $36 for reckless driving, disorderly conduct, and disturbing the peace.

JOE WEATHERLY WAS THE PERFECT FOIL FOR CURTIS Turner. Pops emanated a great light that others sought out eagerly; Weatherly, from Norfolk, Va., was the most loyal of the seekers. He was a curly redhead with the face of an aging cherub, a bouncing chatterbox who, wrote one reporter, talked in shorthand, occasionally punctuating his staccato phrasings with streetcorner gibberish that made sense only to him. He was a practical joker without shame, as outrageous in his behavior as Turner was in his, and he was called the clown prince of stock car racing, though he hardly depended on the race track for his stage. Stopped by the police for reckless driving and asked to walk the traditional straight line, he did, perfectly, but on the return trip he hopped and skipped and sang with the merriment of a minstrel. He loved pigs and chickens, though he had a questionable understanding of how they worked. When the chicks on the farm he had bought for his retirement became ill, Weatherly gently forced fragments of aspirin tablets down their little throats, with predictably ghastly results. The chicks commenced to shit all over him.

Weatherly raced motorcycles—and was, in fact, a national champion—until 1951, when he turned to stock cars and met the fellow Virginian with whom he would wreak so much havoc during the next decade and beyond. Pops and Little Joe became the Gold Dust Twins, running and winning and raising Cain all through the South. They beat on each other like fond brothers, and protected each other, too. If a driver tangled with one, he invariably had to answer to the other.

Curtis Turner:

We flew in late to Elkhart Lake [a road course in Wisconsin] and didn't even get to time trial. We landed on the track, and they backed us up out of the way, and we had to start at the rear. It was pourin' down rain. They dropped the flag, and I looked down there and seen cars goin' every which way. Somebody up front had went into the first turn and spun, and everybody had piled into him. So I took off through a bunch of pine trees about four, five feet high—small, Christmas Tree size—and I thought I could see the road down the way 'cause I remembered flyin' over it. I come out on what I figured was the race track and took off, and sure enough, I *was* on the race track, leadin' the race. I looked in the damned mirror, and ol' Joe's comin' through the pine trees right behind me. Went from the last two positions to the first and second on the first lap, and we never had seen the track before.

Ol' Joe, he was forever cuttin' up. We was racin' at Wilkesboro, and he hit me real hard. Knocked me over in the boondocks; got by me. So I hit Joe—I hit him good—and when the race was over, Joe comes up and I knew somethin' was wrong 'cause instead of gettin' mad, he was jokin' and carryin' on. He had his motorcycle there, and he says, "Hey, Pops, jump on. Let's go get us a chaser." So I jumped on with him, and he got goin' on that thing. We was drivin' on them ol' dirt roads, slidin' sideways and every which way, and I'm beggin' him to slow down and tryin' to get off, and finally he says, "Pops, you promise you won't never hit me that hard again, and I'll stop and let you off." And I says, "Little Joe, I promise I never *will* hit you again."

He was always pullin' jokes. I remember one time he put mint julep in my damned water jug, and when ol' Buck Baker turned over and the yellow flag come out, I grabbed that hose to get me a drink. And I looked over, and there's ol' Joe just dyin' laughin'. He pulled up beside me and said, "Pops, gimme that hose." By the time the race was over, we was both about tuned.

> We run together quite a bit, got drunk together, partied together. One night after a race somewhere, we got two U-Drive-Its. So Joe and I are goin' down this four-lane road, and he just come over and hit me with that U-Drive-It—just stepped on the side of it—and when he did, I cut over, cut all the way over, and I come back and hit him. And then we'd spread apart and get on the shoulder, one on one and one on the other, and come back and hit just as hard as we could. Just tore those U-Drive-Its all to pieces. But they was still runnin', and when we got to the motel where we wanted to stay that night, Joe just kept his engine wide open and went straight into the swimming pool. The deep end. Got him out—this was about midnight—and we didn't even have no room there, and we just started openin' doors and found one that was unlocked. I noticed a suitcase, and we went in there, and—gawdamn. About three o'clock in the mornin', somebody's beatin' on the door. We had it locked—night latch on the door—and the next morning, we got out of it. Never did know whose room it was. Haven't been able to rent a U-Drive-It down there since.

IN THE SPRING OF 1950, BRUTON SMITH, A PROMOTER NOT yet out of his teens, called Bill Holland, the winner of the 1949 Indianapolis 500, and invited him to drive in an upcoming modified stock car race at Harris Speedway, a half-mile dirt track just outside Concord, N.C. The Automobile Association of America, which then controlled Indianapolis-type racing and had little respect for Southern stock car racing, was indignant. "They had many coronaries over this," Smith said. "It was beyond their wildest dreams that an Indianapolis 500 winner would dare step outside of AAA and run in another race."

The AAA tried to telephone Holland and it sent him telegrams, but Holland refused them all. He came to Concord, sat on the pole, and finished fourth. The Associated Press wrote a story about Holland's participation in the race—the first time to Smith's knowledge that the AP had ever written about Southern stock car racing on its national wire—and the capacity crowd was enthralled.

"See, just a few people from down here had ever been to Indianapolis," Smith said. "They thought that an Indianapolis driver may have a halo around his head or something, and that he might descend upon this half-mile dirt track with little wings.

"Now, you can't possibly realize this one little thing, and I don't hardly know how to put it to you—this one *simple* thing: This man has a bag with him, and he brings the bag to the speedway because in this bag he has a racing outfit. He has coveralls—racing coveralls—he has a helmet; he has driving gloves. Well, we country bumpkins, you know, had never seen anything like this before. We didn't know what driving gloves were. We expected Curtis Turner to get in a race car with some kind of bowl-type helmet on with a little brim on the front and a little leather around the neck and jump in that race car and go. But here, this man gets out and actually puts on a racing uniform. And, of course, people were pointing—'Look at him,' you know, 'Can you believe this?'—and possibly thinking that this man is some type of a sissy that he would *dare* come out there with something special to wear to a race, because we were not past the bib overall stage at that time. You can't possibly, I know, understand how different that was, and what a stir it was, when that man actually broke out his uniform."

It is perhaps not beside the point to report that twenty years later, in 1970, a mechanic for a well-known driver was heard to mutter, "Driving with gloves on is like fucking with a rubber."

THE SCRAPBOOKS REVEALED THAT THE FLOCKS, LIKE most race drivers, were a superstitious lot. Tim tried to wear the same shirt to every race. Whenever he saw a white horse, he spit on his right thumb, touched the thumb to his left index finger and then to his left elbow, and smacked his right fist into his left palm. Bob always touched dirt before a race, and one time when he didn't was the time he broke his neck. Fonty once tried reverse superstition. The color green and the presence of peanut shells were considered unlucky at the race track, and in the midst of a so-so season, he painted his car green, outfitted his crew in green uniforms, and scattered peanut shells on the floor of his car. He didn't win a race for six months. Then he painted his car black, swept out the peanut shells, and won the Southern 500—wearing "Bamooda" shorts.

Bob, Fonty, and Tim often raced against each other, and occasionally they entered separate races on the same day. Either circumstance presented a problem for their mother, Maudie, a stout, gray-haired, superstitious grannie.

Tim Flock:

Momma, my mother, she'd cross her fingers on her left hand when I was racing. If Bob was running, she'd cross her right fingers. And cross her ankles if Fonty was running. That's the way she'd sit for years, on the front porch or in the living room, from two o'clock until we called home and tell her what we'd done, and when we called, she'd uncross whoever called. [Demonstrating this, Tim looked a bit like a gray-haired pretzel.] And this was the most unusual thing you ever heard of: I went to Langhorne, Pennsylvania; and Bob went to Birmingham, Alabama; and Fonty went to Lakewood Speedway in Atlanta. I won Langhorne, Bob won Birmingham, and Fonty won Atlanta. That was really something —three brothers in three different states, you know, the same day —and momma sitting there with them fingers and ankles. The write-up's in here, in one of these books.

WHEN POPS AND LITTLE JOE WEREN'T MAKING A shambles of a race track or a motel, they often logged highly creative hours in their private airplanes. Both were excellent seat-of-the-pants pilots who had an awesome disdain for navigational aids. Such as compasses. They would start out for somewhere and simply follow the Iron Beam—railroad tracks —or a river, or they would pull out a road map and follow the highway. Pops recalled a time he and Weatherly were flying from Winston-Salem, N.C., to Roanoke in separate planes. Turner landed on schedule, but began to worry when, after a couple of hours, there was no sign of Little Joe. Just about the time the Civil Air Patrol was going searching, Weatherly sputtered in.

"Where you been?" asked Turner.

"Damn, Pops," said Little Joe. "I was just followin' Highway 221 when I come to a detour. Took the detour and got lost."

On a dare, Turner once set down his twin-engine Aero-Commander on the backstretch of the Darlington Raceway. Incredulous onlookers, Weatherly foremost among them, were certain the backstretch wasn't nearly long enough to take off from—or was it? Turner placed a marker up near the third turn at the point where he figured he had to be airborne in order to clear the guard rail and bet Weatherly he could make it. Joe jumped in the Aero-Commander beside Turner, who gunned the plane prayerfully. When it reached the marker, Weatherly reached over and yanked up the wheels. "If we ain't flying," said Joe, "you lose."

One Sunday afternoon, Turner and another friend were flying from Atlanta to Charlotte and discovered, sadly, there was no whiskey on board. However, the friend allowed as to how he had a bottle or two in his home in Easley, S.C., a small town that they just happened to be flying over. Turner landed on the highway, but as he taxied to his friend's house, he saw that it was right next to two churches just letting out from morning services.

"About then I got to decidin' I'd made a mistake," Turner said.

He wheeled his plane back onto the highway and prepared to take off. He hedgehopped several cars, clipping at least one aerial and panicking a deputy sheriff who later told an investigator from the Federal Aviation Administration, "I was just driving along minding my own business when I looked up and here comes a gawdamned *air*plane."

Then came the intersection.

It was a nice enough intersection, but right in the middle of it was a stop light suspended by heavy wires that stretched across what was now Turner's runway. Furthermore, since his Aero-Commander's third wheel was in the front, its tail stood tall. To accommodate this unfortunate situation, as Turner explained in one of the grand quotes of aviation history, "I had to raise my wheels so's I could fly low enough to get under it."

He finally did get his plane up, but he severed a telephone line, and phone service to much of Easley, along the way, and when he landed at Charlotte, his license was as good as gone.

As Paul Sawyer, a reluctant passenger with both men, said, "I'm telling you, I've flown some miles with them that if I had it to do over again, I wouldn't."

•

IN THE MID-1950S, GRAND NATIONAL RACING WAS BRIEFLY dominated by a fleet of huge, white, ghostly Chryslers owned by Carl Kiekhaefer, a Wisconsin businessman who had made a fortune as the founder and president of the company that manufactured Mercury marine motors. Kiekhaefer was stern and unyielding with all his employees no matter what their stature, as Tim Flock learned firsthand a few years after he won his first Grand National driving championship in 1952:

We didn't win much money, but we made a living. The biggest year I had was $55,000. That was 1955: Kiekhaefer. It's a storybook finish.

In 1954, a gentleman by the name of Mr. Woods from Kentucky called me up and says, "Tim, I got a brand new Oldsmobile, and I don't have no chauffeur. Would you like to drive my car at Daytona?" I says, "I sure will." I didn't have no car. I went to Daytona and we sit the car on the pole, a '54 Oldsmobile, and they dropped the flag and I led it all the way, from start to finish. After the race, they started tearing the cars down, and two days later, NASCAR come up with a deal that the butterfly shaft had been soldered. Chrysler Corporation had finished second behind me. Lee Petty was the guy. They disqualified my car and give Petty the race, and I'll go to my grave knowing that that car was disqualified on account of Chrysler had something to do with it. It made me so mad I went over to Bill France's house and I said, "Bill, did you really disqualify my car?" He said he sure did. He had one of these storm winders in his front door, and I slammed that damn thing so hard that the glass went all the way up into his kitchen. I said, "I'm through. I'll never run for you again." And this was the first race of the year, and I was the 1952 champion, one of his good drawing cards.

So I go back to Atlanta and bought me a Pure Oil service station, the biggest mistake of my life. This was in February, now, so February, March, April, May, June, July, August, September, October, November—all of 1954—I was on Piedmont Road in Atlanta, Georgia, starvin' to death pumping gas.

So around January, some friends of mine came by the station and said they're all going to Daytona and did I want to ride down and see it. I said, "Man, I wouldn't go see that damned race somebody give me $500." So they forgot about it. The race was real close to that February 14. About the 8th or 9th, they come back and said they'd like for me to go down with them. I was disgusted with the station and I knew I'd have a lot of fun down there, so we all get in the car and go down to Daytona. And we're down on the beach, just watching the cars go by, and all of a sudden here comes this big ol' white Chrysler—*wheecheeho.* I'd never seen a car run that fast on the measured mile—they'd run 'em back and forth—and I made a statement to these guys. I said, "Man, if I had that car, I believe I could win this race." I made it out loud. I don't know why. And some guy standing behind me of which I'd never heard was Tommy Haygood, a Mercury marine motors dealer in Orlando, Florida, and he says, "Hey, buddy. What's that you say?" And I says, "If I have that car, I believe I can win this race." And he says, "Well, I know who owns that car and he ain't got no driver. What's your name?" And I says, "Tim Flock." He says, "You won the race last year." And I says, "I sure did." He says, "Would you like me to introduce you to Mr. Carl Kiekhaefer?" I says, "I sure would." And I didn't know he was talking about Mercury marine and $60 million.

We got in the car and drove all the way across the bridge over into Daytona. Here's a brand new filling station—another Pure Oil. Never had opened. This old man had rented it, and here's that big, beautiful white car in there and about six guys with beautiful white mechanics' suits just working all over it. So I walked in, with Tommy. He hadn't warned me about what this guy was like. He says, "Hey, Mr. Kiekhaefer, I got somebody here I'd like for you to meet." Kiekhaefer had a cigar in his mouth. He looked down and—*grrrgrrrgrrr*—and went on off. Real busy. So finally he walked back and says, "What you say, Tommy?" He says, "I'd like for you to meet the guy that won the race last year, *sir.*" You know: *"Sir."* He says, "What's your name?" I says, "Tim Flock," and he says—real hoarse, mean, German—"My name's Carl Kiekhaefer," and I says, "*Yessir.* I believe I can win the race for you if you hadn't got a driver."

He puffed on his cigar—he looked like a steam engine—and walked on off again. About four-five minutes, he comes back and says, "Uh, you *really* think you can win the race with my car?" I says, "Yessir, I really do, because I'm mad at NASCAR, I'm mad at the race, I'm mad at everybody." He says, "Fellers, let Flock get in the front seat of that car."

So I got in there and got it all adjusted up, and—*snap!*—I *know* that's my car. Prettiest thing you ever seen. Had roll bars. So they fixed the seat and bolted it down. I qualified on the pole about three or four miles an hour faster than any car—they give you a mile straightaway run to qualify—and this thrilled me to death. "The only thing, Mr. Kiekhaefer," I said, "we got one problem. This car is automatic transmission, and this ain't gonna work in the race." And he says, "What do you mean, Flock?" And I'm all wrong right then, you know? I said, "All we got is low and then drive. You go into these turns, and when you come off, you got to have a second gear to get up to about 110–115 mph and pull it back in high and go." He says, "Don't worry about that. This car will run." So I says, "Okay, *sir.*"

So the race starts, and I'm on the pole, and we go down into the first turn. Man, I've done pulled about six car lengths in front of second place, which was Fireball Roberts in a Buick. We come off the turn. I pulled it down in low—*waah*—and I kicked it up in drive and—*blaaugh*—it sputtered. Fireball just come on by me in second gear. Walked out. By the time we got to the south turn, two miles down, I had run up pretty close to him, but I couldn't get by him. Same thing. He'd just stretch it out like a rubber band. We run that way all afternoon. I'd catch him in every turn, but I could not get by him. He won, and I finished second.

So Kiekhaefer's all upset. I says, "Ain't nobody in the world could have won in that car with that transmission." He finally understood that. I'm disgusted. We go on back to the motel. We slept all night, got up the next morning, and we was eating breakfast. Kiekhaefer was still fussing. He said, "I'm gonna get Chrysler to build some transmissions, I don't care if it costs me half-a-million dollars." I was sitting there listening to him, and some guys walk up and says, "Hey, congratulations, Flock. You won the race." I says, "What are you talking about?" Ol' Kiekhaefer looked up, and these guys put up the headline: "Fireball Roberts Disqualified; Tim Flock Wins Daytona." The pushrods in Fireball's Buick were shortened. So Kiekhaefer jumps up and he orders champagne. We had a ball that night. Wasn't this great? Storybook finish, you know, from the year before. But it wasn't no flukey. In three months, we had straight-stick transmissions from Chrysler, and I went on and won seventeen more Grand Nationals that year. That was a record, and it stood for twelve years—Petty broke it, and he broke it good. [Richard Petty, with twenty-seven wins in 1967.] Won eighteen out of about forty-two races, which is really going.

Kiekhaefer wouldn't take a nickel off any of his drivers. If you won $5,000, you got $5,000. He did ask us if we wanted to give the pit crew something to keep 'em on the ball. I give 'em 10 percent.

But see, what he'd do—this would be in November, the year I won the championship again—he called me up and said, "Tim, get on the next plane to Oshkosh. We need you up here on a promotion. When you get here, check into the Oshkosh Hotel." I says, "*Yessir.*" I get on the plane, and I check into the Oshkosh Hotel. I couldn't leave the room—couldn't go to the show or nothing. He says don't leave. Four days later, he called me up and says, "You can go back to Atlanta. I'm not going to need you on this trip." He just wanted to know where I was at in the wintertime.

And the following year, we go back down to Daytona, and he rents this whole motel. I'm talking about sixty rooms. He puts the mechanics and drivers on *this* side and—he got this bad—all the wives down on *that* side. He gets a room in the middle, and he just dared a driver to walk by to try and get with one of them wives. No screwing. Couldn't do it. None of that stuff before a race. And five o'clock in the morning, he'd blow a bugle. He'd get out there and blow a damned bugle. Or have somebody blow it: Here we go, just like the Army. And—I want to get this in here for you, if you use any of this—I done this for a year and a half until I was throwing up blood.

We went on through '56, and I went down to 130 pounds. I gotta quit Kiekhaefer. We was running North Wilkesboro, and I had told Herb Thomas, who was running real good back then, that if I won the next race, I was going to quit. He said, "You're crazy, making the kind of money you're making." I said, "I'm either going to quit or die," because the doctors done told me my ulcers were getting worse and worse. *Nerrrves.* So I won the race at North Wilkesboro, and I walked up to him and I said, "Mr. Kiekhaefer, this was my last race for you." Oh, he went crazy. He was about to die. He says, "Come to my room." We was staying at the Barringer Hotel here in Charlotte. We all drove back. I took a shower and went up to his room. He had a beautiful table up there —big steak sitting on it. He says, "Sit down, Tim, and eat a steak. . . . We want to talk about this. . . . I don't want you to leave. . . . You've been my most valuable driver. . . ." All this kind of bullshit. So I say, "Nossir. I'm not even going to eat that steak. I told you in North Wilkesboro I was through. I am through." I pulled the door to and went down to my room and went to bed, and I haven't never seen the man again. That's how we got started, and that's how we ended.

THROUGHOUT HIS CAREER, CURTIS TURNER TREATED stock car racing as something of an indulgence. Around 1950, as he told the story, he bought a mountain for $30,000. Then he improved the mountain, by building a road up it, for $2,500. Finally, he sold the mountain for $85,000. "Easiest money I ever made," he said. From then on, he was lured by the promise of fast and easy money, and to have heard him tell it, he usually found some, in the timber business or elsewhere.

It was this part of Turner's life, however, where fact and fancy most often got confused. Without question, Turner lived the freewheeling life, of which his silk suits and Lincoln Continentals were only a part. Whose money he used to live it was a question never satisfactorily answered. No matter. In business as in racing, he loved the action more than he cared for the results. If he was a con artist, as several of his business acquaintances suggested, he was the sort whose victims sought him out just to watch him play the game, even at their own expense. For sure, Turner had a quick and diverse mind. He studied the law, more, one suspected, to give instruction to his own lawyers than anything else. He never tried to pass the bar. When the first satellites went streaking across the skies in 1957, Turner said he spent thousands of dollars attempting to persuade government officials to let him develop a private satellite-communications system. He said he once tried very hard and seriously to get permission from the Treasury Department to print advertising on the margins of dollar bills. He claimed to have bought and sold more than two million acres of timber in the South, the Midwest, and even in South America. He retired from racing whenever he consummated a big business deal, usually in timber, and just as quickly unretired whenever he went broke. He didn't care whether he was on the up side or the down. He was restless and always just a little short:

> I don't think I'd be happy if I wasn't in some sort of trouble, in timber, racin', or elsewhere. I've made several fortunes, I guess —even saved a little bit now and then—but it don't last long. It's just like drivin' a race or writin' a story or anything else. Once somethin's done, it's over. It's behind you, and you can't ever get it back. I get itchy and start lookin' for somethin' else. I got an

overhead of about $15,000 a month. My auditors went over that one time and figured where I could cut that down to $10,000 or so, but hell, man, that $5,000 or $6,000 is what I like to live on. Livin' ain't no fun unless you got that. A friend of mine keeps tellin' me I've pissed away more money than most men make in a lifetime and that if I make $100,000 today, it'll be gone tomorrow, and I guess he's about right. In the timber business, you get a payday only once, twice a year, but Lord, it's a good one: $50,000, $100,000, $200,000. But if you make $25,000, you need $50,000. If you make $50,000, you need $100,000. I always need more than I got. I never know where my money's comin' from next, but it always turns up. Maybe I could be a success in somethin' else, a broker or a lawyer or somethin'. I put two corporations through the Securities and Exchange Commission. I even went respectable for a couple of years—operated a jukebox business—but it didn't last long. I got too restless. Timber's all I really know, and those damned trees have always come through for me. Satisfied? No, I'm never really satisfied—are you? Oh, some things give you temporary satisfaction, and these are the things you can be proud of. The satellite thing—it was the first time on record a private citizen had ever thought of somethin' like that. President Kennedy stole it and now it's Telstar. Cost me $40,000. And I'm proud of the speedway, even though they kicked me out of it. It's mine, and they can't ever take that away from me.

THE SCRAPBOOKS WERE NOT ANTISEPTIC. OBVIOUSLY, THE dark side of the sport was never far from Tim Flock's mind. A newspaper article:

> William Edgar Justice, 21, Winston-Salem, Route 6, was burned to death last night when his car caught fire after a crash in the auto races at Bowman Gray Stadium.
>
> It was Justice's third race. He was in sixth place in a field of ten cars.
>
> If he had won the race, he would have received $55.
>
> The car skidded out of control on the south turn of the track, struck the guard rail, teetered for a moment and then burst into flames as it landed right-side-up on the track.
>
> The young driver was trapped inside the blazing coupe by straps used to keep the doors closed. The straps are regulation equipment used for the protection of the drivers.

Mr. Justice stayed in the flaming car approximately four minutes. Several spectators tried to pull him from the car but were forced back by the terrific heat of flames which at times leaped five to ten feet from the car. One man was burned and required treatment at City Hospital.

As mechanics rushed fire extinguishers to the car, the young driver either pushed the door open or fell against it dead. It opened, and he was pulled out on the ground and wrapped in a blanket.

He was taken to City Hospital in an ambulance kept on the field for emergencies. Ambulance attendants said they thought he was dead when they left the track but believed he started breathing en route to the hospital.

Doctors there, alerted by phone, had cleared the emergency room and had plasma ready. But it was too late.

Mr. Justice's wife arrived a few minutes later. She had seen the crash.

The fatality was the second on the track in four years of racing. Bernie Fox, a midget car driver, was killed in 1947.

Last night's crash came as Mr. Justice made the south turn and entered the home stretch in the second heat of the amateur races.

No other car was close to the 1940 Ford coupe as it skidded into the guard rail.

The fans, accustomed to what is usually referred to as the "thrills and spills," chuckled for a moment as the car balanced on two wheels—and then gasped as flames filled the car.

The race was stopped and several men rushed out of the stands to try to save the young driver. As people in the stands screamed, "Get him out!" one man after another tried to rescue him, only to be forced back by the flames.

Several women and at least one man fainted. The aisles were filled with others who wanted to get a closer look—and with fathers and mothers trying to get their children out of the stadium.

One man, said to be related to the man trapped in the blaze, had to be held back by officers who knew that it was too late for anyone to save Mr. Justice.

The young driver stuck his hand out of the blaze once. Someone grabbed it but couldn't pull him through the open window of the car. . . .

William Edgar Justice, the story continued, was born in Forsyth County, N.C., on November 11, 1928, served three years in the Marines, and until recently had been connected with the Taylor Oil Company. His survivors included his wife, the former Miss Lillian Smith, to whom he had been married for less than a year, his parents, and "others." Bill France said the fire was caused by a faulty gas tank placed just behind the driver's seat and that "nothing could have been done to save his life." Mr. Justice, said the story, was covered by a $1,000 insurance policy.

The scrapbooks were filled with little items such as those, and with pictures. One clipping said that Charles L. Parks was killed when another automobile struck him in a cloud of dust as he crawled from beneath the wreckage of his own overturned car. Jesse James Taylor, said another, was in serious condition suffering from a fractured skull and severe skin lacerations following a race at Lakewood. A third said that Bruce Baker of Macon, Ga., suffered a pierced jugular vein during a race and succumbed at a local hospital. There was a picture of a car literally exploding—its trunk, hood, and right-side door all had sprung open at the precise moment of impact—with a pair of legs protruding from the driver's door. A second picture, taken minutes after the first, showed the driver lying half-in and half-out of the car, his left arm limp. The cutline beneath both pictures read: "RACER DYING IN WRECKED CAR —James H. Brinkley (center), race driver of Hapeville, Ga., is dying as track attendants pull him from his wrecked stock car on the Lakewood Park track at Atlanta. The 24-year-old youth was making the third start of his racing career. His car hit a bank on the first turn, turned over several times and pinned him beneath it. Brinkley died in a hospital a few minutes later." Another picture showed John "Skimp" Hersey half-kneeling, half-standing in a pool of flaming gasoline, burning to death, dazed and in shock and unable to move. Hersey's death was the third at Lakewood in seven weeks, said the accompanying story, but a city councilman defended the track, claiming the deaths were caused by mechanical failures or driver carelessness.

Another story explained that a wheel had flown off a car driven by Bob Flock and broken the legs of an 11-year-old spectator. Bits and pieces of several stories said that Herb

Thomas was critically injured in a race at Shelby, N.C., that several weeks later Fonty Flock was given Thomas's car to drive in the Southern 500 at Darlington, and that Fonty started a chain-reaction accident in which Bobby Myers was fatally injured. An Atlanta newspaper quoted Tim: "You see your buddies killed, crushed, and burned, and you wonder when it will happen to you. You see, we drive every week. You stretch your luck so far, and you wonder how much further it will stretch." A reporter asked Tim whether he felt dirt-track racing was good, steady employment. "Yes, I do," he said, "but not for nervous people."

A picture showed a crash in which Frank Lueptow of Tampa, Fla., was thrown from his car and then crushed to death beneath it. Under the picture Tim had written: "He was a swell guy and a very good friend of mine."

In yet another story, Tim told a reporter: "I'm not scared. If I was scared, I wouldn't go on the track. But there's one thing that all drivers worry about, and that's catching fire. I've seen eight or nine of 'em get it like that—a crackup, a big blaze, and all you ever see are the hands reaching out the window. You never get over something like that. It's almost put me buggy a couple of times. One time after it happened my wife and me were sitting on the porch. It was a bright night, and I looked into the sky and I could swear I saw 'em. 'Honey, I see hands,' I told her. But she's a jewel, that girl of mine. She talked me back to my senses."

Tim Flock:

I'll bet I've seen twenty-five guys get killed in races—I mean, really watch 'em get killed. I seen one guy get killed at Greenville, South Carolina. They was seven cars, and he flipped in the turn and got out of the car and was trying to get off the track, but he was dazed and more or less wandering around right in the middle of the track. It was a real dusty race track. I seen that guy get cut in two, I know, four different places. Come in the pits, seven different cars had pieces of him. That was the worst one I've ever seen—about getting hit. I've seen 'em burn. This shakes you up while you're watching it, but you get right back out there and go again. I guess more or less it's something that's in your blood:

"Ain't never gonna happen to me," you know. I was real lucky. I never did get hurt real bad. The worst I ever got hurt was twenty-two stitches in my elbow. We was running one of the first races right out here at the old Charlotte Speedway—it's out by the airport. Red Byron was leading the race. Hit the fence. I hit him and went up in the air about as high as a telephone pole. Jimmy Lewallen come under me—he was rolling—and Fonty. All four of us turned over. But Lewallen, I hit on top of his car and it got me rolling again, and I went all the way down the backstretch. The car wadn't two foot high noplace, and I was up under there—with twenty-two stitches. But I wasn't hurt other than that.

A TELEGRAM FLUTTERED TO THE FLOOR. IT WAS SENT BY Tim's wife, Frances, to Tim on the morning of the 1955 Southern 500:

DARLING I TRIED TO REACH YOU BY PHONE SUNDAY NIGHT HAD TO SAY HELLO BEFORE YOU RACED WILL BE THINKING OF YOU CONSTANTLY TODAY DO NOT WORRY EVERYTHING AT HOME IS ALL RIGHT THE VERY BEST OF LUCK TODAY WITH ALL MY LOVE AND KISSES YOUR WIFE CALL ME AT MOTHERS THE MINUTE YOU GET THE CHECKED FLAG I LOVE YOU VERY MUCH MAY GOD BE WITH YOU

Tim Flock:

You would do anything for a promoter. Bob and Fonty and I was probably the three drivers that would help promoters more than anybody because they'd give us $100, or $200, to show up a couple days before a race. And any kind of gimmick that you could come up with, you'd get more money. So my car owner, Ted Chester—he owned Hudsons, then Oldsmobiles—and I, right off we got a monkey. Named him Jocko. We built him a perch up by the right side of the window where he could look out. He had two nylon safety belts, a little suit, goggles, and we put "Jocko Flocko" on his door. My name was on the other door: "Tim Flock." It really got the kids. After a race, all the families would come down around the car, we'd give autographs, and the promoters would eat it up. That monkey was took care of real good—got fed the best bananas and everything—but he run about six or seven races that I know of, and then he quit eating. So I put him in the hospital in Atlanta, a veterinary hospital, and he died after about five days. It worried me because I thought maybe he might of got skeered. In fact—I don't know whether you've heard this—I was running second behind Fonty on the mile asphalt at Raleigh, and there was a trap door on the floorboard where you'd pull a chain and you could see your right-front tire when it wore: You see a white streak, and you can come in to keep from blowing a tire, and hitting the fence. Well, Jocko had seen me pull that trap door numerous times. He got out from under both belts, went down, and opened that door, and that tire spun and must have throwed a rock and hit him on the forehead. He come screaming back up in the car and got on my shoulder. So I reached up with my left hand—kept my eyes in the race—and got him by the neck and slowed down coming through the fourth turn and went down pit road and held him out and give him to the mechanic. It was the only time I know of in NASCAR that the official pit stop was for a monkey being put out of the car. Unusual. Just a gimmick.

I had a ball. Racing was more fun, a hundred times more, than it is now, other than when you was with one of them kind of teams like Kiekhaefer. Man, we'd party all night before a race, get drunk, and then get in them ol' cars and put mixed drinks in a tank up behind us and get drunk during a race. We'd say, "We'll take it down the straightaway and let Lord Calvert take it through the turns." It was just party after party, really. There wasn't no rules like there are now. You'd win money and throw it away, on women. These ol' gals would see our cars—I shouldn't even tell you this—and they'd come beat your door down at two o'clock in the morning. And we wouldn't let 'em in, of course—like hell. But the good ol' days will never be back because these guys now, you know, they're doing pushups, chinups, running. Of course, they make a lot more money than we did. I would like to make as much money as them guys is making now, but I don't ever want to drive anymore. That's all I done for thirteen straight years, but when I quit, I never did go back like some of these guys.

In the late 1950s and early 1960s, stock car racing metamorphosed, dramatically. Big, fast, paved tracks sprang up at Daytona Beach, Charlotte, and Atlanta. They were soon joined by other big, fast, and paved tracks in such diverse locations as Rockingham, N.C., Talladega, Ala., Dover, Del., Ontario, Calif., and Bryant, Texas, as well as in the Irish Hills of southern Michigan and the Pocono Mountains of eastern Pennsylvania.

Together with Darlington, which had been around forever, these new superspeedways quickly overshadowed the small, clay bullrings that for so long had been the sport's main venue. At the same time, the Big Three automobile manufacturers—General Motors, Ford, and Chrysler—began to channel huge amounts of money and technology into racing. Stock cars got more sophisticated, and they got faster. Few drivers could make the transition or even bothered to try. Tim Flock did not; Curtis Turner more or less built the Charlotte Motor Speedway.

The construction of the track was an adventure, to say the least. It was built because Curtis Turner had become known as "the Millionaire Lumberman" and because Bruton Smith, the promoter, was young and naive. "Youth has a way of being blind," said Smith. "Youth creates a lot of things. Mainly, it creates a lot of mistakes, but youth sometimes has a way of making something happen because youth didn't know it couldn't happen in the first place."

So Bruton Smith, the youth—he was not yet thirty—called Turner, the millionaire lumberman, and suggested they build a $2 million race track. Turner said he thought that was a splendid idea, and negotiations ensued. Then one afternoon Smith picked up *The Charlotte News* and read that Turner planned to build the track all by himself. Smith hurried down to Charlotte's other newspaper, the *Observer,* and announced that *he* was going to build the track, supporting his claim with solid cost projections, artist's renderings, and construction timetables. More negotiations ensued. Turner and Smith agreed to a shaky marriage of convenience.

The track was built on a pay-as-you-go basis, and it was very underfinanced. It became even more underfinanced when construction crews hit granite. As Smith explained, "There is rock, and there is rock, and there is *rock.*" The *rock* boosted costs by $250,000. Turner said, "It cost $70,000 blasting through the first turn alone."

Turner was imaginative when it came to meeting the weekly payrolls. On Fridays, he said, he would calmly write $50,000 to $75,000 worth of absolutely worthless checks, then scramble through the weekend to round up some real money before the banks opened on Monday. Turner bought a small bank, he said, so small that it could loan no more than $12,000 to a single individual. Turner loaned himself $75,000. Another time, Turner said, he gathered together the track's various creditors and their lawyers and paraded before them a certified check for $250,000 drawn on the Bank of New York. Only there was no Bank of New York. "It was a purty check, though," said Pops.

Despite all this, the track neared completion. Paving machines slowly worked their way down the long backstretch of the 1½-mile oval. Then the contractors balked. They demanded a quick $75,000, and to back up their demand, they wheeled out sixteen pieces of heavy equipment in front of the paving machines. Turner and Smith, armed respectively with a shotgun and a pistol, confronted the workers, one of whom, fortified by whiskey, suddenly grabbed for Turner's gun. Smith didn't hesitate. "I ran over there with this pistol and stuck it way up in this guy's ribs and yelled at him to put his hands up or I'd blow him in two," Smith said. "I had no intention of doing anything, but the bluff worked—I always remember my dad said that a bluff game's all right, if it worked—and the man turned loose of that gun and backed out of there."

Cooler heads quickly prevailed. The heavy equipment was removed, allowing the paving machines to complete their work, and on June 19, 1960, the Charlotte Motor Speedway's first event, called the World 600, was run before a healthy crowd of 40,000. Turner dropped out after 231 miles, the victim of a blown head gasket.

The financial shell game could only run so long, however, and both Turner and Smith were soon ousted from their track in a series of power plays by an unhappy board of directors. Turner, very bitter, never returned. (But, to complete this unlikely story, Bruton Smith did. He left Charlotte to seek his fortune elsewhere, found it, and quietly bought up controlling shares in the speedway corporation. He was formally installed as the track's chairman of the board in late 1975.)

EVEN BEFORE HE WAS PURGED FROM THE SPEEDWAY, Turner was embroiled in another controversy. In the summer of 1961, he asked the Teamsters Union for a loan of $850,000. At the time, the Teamsters were attempting to organize all major sports through a group called the Federation of Professional Athletes. Turner said that the Teamsters agreed to give him the loan if he would organize the NASCAR drivers and mechanics. Aided by Tim Flock, Buck Baker, and Fireball Roberts, he had nearly every Grand National driver of significance signed up within a month and drew up a list of reforms that included everything from a pension fund for drivers to a more equitable purse distribution.

Everything was moving along just fine until NASCAR president Bill France, vehemently anti-union and no amateur at power plays, stepped in. He said race drivers did not need to join a union because they already belonged to an organization that looked after their needs—NASCAR. Further, he maintained that it was illegal for drivers and mechanics to join a union because they were independent contractors and not salaried employees. On August 9, 1961, France presided over a stormy meeting of the drivers and mechanics before a race at Winston-Salem. According to *The Charlotte Observer,* France said, "Gentlemen, before I have this union stuffed down my throat I will plow up my track at Daytona Beach. . . . After the race tonight, no known union members can compete in a NASCAR race."

Turner and Flock did not attend the meeting. "France let 'em all in to the meetin' but me and Flock 'cause we was doin' the organizin'," Turner said, "but they had a window open, and I stood there by the window listenin'. So they was all talkin', and France said, hell, he said, if it was as good as I pretended it was and had all the benefits I said it had, he'd join himself. So I was outside the window, and I raised it up and handed him a card through the window and said, 'Here's your application.' Then they closed the window on me. From that meeting on, it was just lawyers and lawsuits."

All the drivers backed down except Flock, who was ready to retire anyway, and Turner, and France barred them both. Turner filed for reinstatement under the right-to-work laws of Florida, where NASCAR was headquartered, but got nowhere and eventually dropped his suit. He expected France to reinstate him immediately. France refused.

Pops was in limbo. He had lost his race track and a considerable sum of money, and now he literally had no place to run. For the next four years, he drove on outlaw tracks, often promoting races of his own just so he could stay behind the wheel.

Turner suffered his most crushing blow on January 21, 1964, when Joe Weatherly was killed in a freak accident on the road course at Riverside, Calif. Weatherly was superstitious, particularly about the number 13. He arrived in California on Flight 13, qualified thirteenth fastest, and crashed on the leader's 113th lap. He himself had made a lengthy pit stop early in the race and had absolutely no prayer of a decent finish. Thirteen dollars were found in his wallet. More to the point, his shoulder harness was probably loosely fastened. Little Joe didn't much care for the things.

Several years later, Turner still had not fully accepted the death of his friend. "He wasn't doin' but about 60 miles an hour when he got killed," Pops said. "I was at Indy listenin' to the race, and I couldn't hardly believe it. He'd crashed before at 160 and nothing had happened. But when the car hit, it threw his head out the window, and his head hit the wall. Car wasn't tore up much. Ol' Joe was just about gettin' ready to quit racin'. He told me he planned to quit pretty soon."

Turner paused for a long time before continuing. "Damn," he said. "There's four hundred ways that little bastard could have made a livin', but I don't guess he'd of been happy doin' anything else."

Tim Flock:

You don't make comebacks in a race car. I've seen four or five try this and ain't never none of 'em come back. When you quit, you're through. I knew when to quit. My eye . . . I couldn't judge. . . . I was driving over . . . I'd drive into the turns way . . . I was driving in so far, I was getting the car crossed up. I wasn't scared of the speed. I still ain't scared of speed. I bet I can run right now at the Charlotte Motor Speedway within two or three miles of the record—I'm talking about one of those topnotch cars, now; they handle like a dream—and I hadn't been in one in years. They don't drive now like we did. We used to have to rassle 'em. You could take a bad driver back then, and in a bad car he'd just push it to the limit to try and make a living. You had to or you'd starve to death. You don't see that kind of driving anymore. It's more or less a parade. I hate to say that, but I don't even enjoy watching 'em no more. I don't go to none of 'em, except these two at Charlotte. But you miss the money, even what we was making. I don't think I'll ever be able to get a job that makes as much as I did in '55—ever. Fifty-five thousand dollars is a lot of money.

FRANCE RELENTED AND REINSTATED TURNER IN THE FALL of 1965. Pops was 41. He had not been in a good Grand National car in four years, and few people felt he could ever again be a contender in a major race. Almost immediately, he was—at the Charlotte Motor Speedway.

The 1965 National 400 at Charlotte was the best stock car race ever run anywhere. With perhaps ten laps to go, A. J. Foyt, Fred Lorenzen, and Dick Hutcherson hooked up and drove three-abreast around the tri-oval, lap after lap, nobody yielding anything, as the fans stood in awe. On the banked turns, where normally cars traveled single file, the three drivers could not have been separated with a photo-finish camera, and right there in fourth place was Pops, biding his time, trying to figure a way. However, with only one and a fraction laps remaining, Foyt, who was on the outside, got carried too deep into the third turn by Lorenzen, or maybe he went there all by himself. Suddenly he was up on the loose stuff, the marbles, headed for the outside guard rail. "I couldn't tell which way he was goin'," Turner said, "but he was headin' for the wall, and I knew in a minute he was gonna be comin' back down right at me, and rather than take a chance on tearin' the car up, I just slowed up. If I'd of stayed on it and could of missed Foyt, I could of still probably got to the flag."

Turner fell in behind Lorenzen and Hutcherson, and the yellow flag that came out for Foyt's mishap consigned Pops to third. It was a nice try by the old man, people felt, and everybody headed off to the North Carolina Motor Speedway in Rockingham, at the time the newest of the Southern speedways and perhaps the most demanding physically. Races there were for 500 miles and 500 laps, and they often lasted five hours. In the fall, the crisp Carolina sun absolutely blinded the drivers as they headed into the second turn late in a race. It was a test of endurance and nerve, and Pops won it. Just like that. When the race was over, he was so exhausted that he could barely crawl from his car, and he spoke in whispers. But in Victory Lane, he replaced his driving helmet with his Stetson and covered his tired eyes with those dark sunglasses, and as he mounted the steps to receive his trophy and his check and his kisses from the doll-babies, he smiled and said, "Let's have a party. 'Nother party's startin' in 'bout fifteen minutes."

Turner's improbable comeback continued. In January 1966, he went to Riverside to avenge the death of Little Joe. Turner's car was a tick slower than the one driven by Dan Gurney, who had won the race, the Riverside 500, the three previous years, but by thinking hard and driving harder, Turner moved up to second, tight behind the defending champion. On lap 39, Gurney led Turner into the esses, a series of three quick turns—right-left-right—that had to be made with absolute precision and delicacy. At the second wiggle, instead of turning left, Turner went straight—off the road, into a ditch, and up the other side of the ditch. He catapulted by Gurney and slammed back down on the track in first place. Gurney, amazed and amused, said, "It was the first time anybody ever passed me airborne." Turner led for another 90 miles, but he was black-flagged when a loosely fastened gas cap fell off, and the lost time in the pits cost him the race.

In February 1967, Turner began driving an experimental Chevrolet Chevelle built by a masterful mechanic named Smokey Yunick, and sat it on the pole for the Daytona 500. Two months later, however, Turner and his Chevelle had one of the most spectacular mishaps ever seen at a race track during practice for the Atlanta 500.

Curtis Turner:

I don't guess we ever will know what happened. I was comin' off the fourth turn and the car was handlin' perfect, and all of a sudden somethin' happened and it just turned to the right. Cale

> Yarborough—about the only thing we got to go on—was runnin' right behind me, and he said the car was settin' perfect, and all of a sudden, the right-rear corner dropped down almost to the pavement. I hit the concrete retaining wall and went up in the air—they estimated it was twenty foot high—and when the car come down, it come down on the nose and went end over end two or three times, then rolled. Rolled right over Cale and didn't touch him. And then it come down on top of the inside rail and rolled off the rail on into the pit road. How far? If you was playin' golf, I'd say it'd be about a par four. I helt onto that steering wheel. All you're thinking about is waitin' for it to stop. You know, there's a dead silence when the car's goin' through the air—the ignition's cut off—and you can hear a pin drop. And you got your eyes shut because of flyin' glass, so you don't know when your car is stopped or if it's still goin' through the air. Well, I heard that dead silence about thirteen times, and I'm still there bracin' and holdin' on with all my grip I got, thinkin' I'm still hittin', when I heard somebody say, "Get out. It's on fire." Then I opened my eyes, and I knew it'd stopped.

Turner got out of the car under his own power, but collapsed at the track infirmary and was taken by ambulance to a hospital in downtown Atlanta, bumming cigarettes from the driver en route. Turner's only injury was a broken rib, but Smokey Yunick said right then, more to keep Pops off the track than anything else, "I'm not going to build the car that kills Curtis Turner."

POPS SLIPPED UNEASILY INTO RETIREMENT. IT WAS NOT a particularly happy time. He was divorced from his first wife, and Little Joe wasn't around anymore. A reporter remembered stopping by Turner's house and seeing him at his desk, sipping his Canadian Club and Coke. "Gawdamn, where you been?" asked Pops. "It gets awful lonely around here."

Still, although he had been removed from his main arenas, his outsized personality remained intact. And there were always the parties, such as the one he threw in Charlotte a couple of nights before the 1967 National 500.

By Pops's standards, it was a small party, not like a decade earlier when he and Joe Weatherly and Paul Sawyer, the Richmond promoter, had their party pad at Daytona Beach in the green-frame house near the sea, the place where moonlighting bartenders from the restaurant across the street served until dawn and the bill during Daytona's Speed Weeks alone sometimes ran to $5,000 and Little Joe used a fire extinguisher to serve drinks into flower vases. ("That way, you don't have to pit so often," he would say.) Still, the affair was impressive enough. When the speedway closed down after practice on Friday, mechanics and drivers, friends of Turner's, hangers-on and friends of hangers-on, who were attracted like gnats to the noise and lights of the rambling ranch house set on fourteen acres of rough Carolina earth at 4000 Freedom Drive, started arriving just about the time the red-dust Carolina sun was giving up for the day.

A small party: 250 or 300 people, perhaps—people like Fred Lorenzen, who, although of a more immediate era, had just announced his own retirement; Mario Andretti, one of the most prominent of the Indianapolis racers who had won that year's Daytona 500 just to show he could; Bobby Allison and Cale Yarborough and other NASCAR youngsters coming to their maturity; and the ghosts of Little Joe and Fireball Roberts and Bob Flock, images from Turner's own past.

Some came for Pops's bonded whiskey, and others for lie-swapping. They mingled in his living room and in his den, where Rodin's *Thinker* sat brooding on one wall next to Turner's law books and racing trophies, then moved to the patio, where a jukebox blared Country and Western, and as a concession to the age, the Temptations and the Supremes.

Pops, whom they all had come to see, spent most of the night in his bar, where fluorescent lights made shirts and teeth stand out in a purple-white glow and bathed the pop-art bar girls on the wall behind the bar and the pictures of three sumptuous nudes. He sat on a barstool that was balanced on two legs, with his back against a wall, and looked down at the slight roll that was threatening to girdle his scrunched up stomach. "Gawdamn," he said. "*Gaw*damn, where did that come from? I ain't never seen that before. Looks like it's full of air, like I ought to be able to cut it open and let the air out."

He was undiminished by time, and his performance did

not disappoint the legend seekers. Around eleven, he came out on the patio, this gentle bear of a man, and finding his doll-baby, a cute, perk-nosed brunette named Bunny who would soon become his second wife, kissed her gently on her forehead, and someone shouted, "Pops, the booze is gone."

Pops turned away from Bunny and said, "Don't worry 'bout nothin'. 'Nother party's startin' in 'bout fifteen minutes." And, of course, one did, and it lasted right on up until the cops came by and suggested that maybe five in the morning was a bit late for so much noise.

"Gawdamn," said Pops after the cops had left. "That about makes me mad." And in a few minutes, where but one jukebox had been screaming to the bleary-eyed sun, now rising, there were two. At seven o'clock, the last of the legend seekers, sated, left for their motels and an hour's sleep before the track would again open.

TIM FLOCK TURNED THE PAGES QUICKLY. "THEY HAD THAT Fourth of July weekend," he said. "They was five races, and Bob won every one of 'em. Down in Greenville, Spartanburg—all through that area—Columbia . . . There's that old Lincoln I was winning Daytona in and the pit crew was drunk when I come in the pits. There's the car right there. That write-up's in here, too, somewhere. . . . That's Columbus, Georgia. Lookey here—dust. From here, you can see real good, but you're out there and run into it? You can't see nothing. . . . There's Bob and them wild eyes, right there. . . . Fonty. . . . There's Bob at Langhorne. . . . Lookey here at the crowd back then. Isn't that something? For a modified race? . . . Here is the three right here: 'Bob Flock Wins Three Auto Races in Two Days.' Here's three of 'em. . . . See these people dodging? They don't know what's happening. Look at this guy. I think he was running about eighty miles an hour, and it knocked all these people out of the way and killed that little kid. . . . There's Marshall Teague. Dead. . . . There's Bill France. Look how young he looks. . . . Buddy got suffocated. . . . Bill Blair. He's still around. Got a garage in High Point. . . . Here are some of the wins. See here? . . . This is Daytona. The Streamline Hotel. . . . My car. . . . Wadn't that tough? . . . That's tough, baby."

•

CURTIS TURNER WAS KILLED ON A SUNDAY AFTERNOON IN October 1970, when his Aero-Commander crashed into the side of a hill near Du Bois, Pa., twenty minutes after takeoff. None of Turner's friends believed he was flying the plane when it went down. For all his craziness in the air, they were convinced he could have set that thing down in a cabbage patch if he'd had to. What they figured happened was that he got the plane off the ground and turned it over to the only other passenger, a friend named Clarence King who was also killed, and jumped in the back seat to take a nap. Pops often did that sort of thing. Bruton Smith, Turner's old business partner and rival, didn't even believe Turner was dead. He had to call the coroner in Pennsylvania to satisfy himself that Pops hadn't somehow pulled the ultimate practical joke.

Turner's survivors included his first wife and their four children, and Bunny, his second wife. Their child, a son, was born within a month of his death.

Bunny looked at the glistening casket at the gravesite and could not help herself. "Curtis," she cried, "I love you," and then she was led away.

TIM FLOCK CLOSED HIS SCRAPBOOKS AND HEADED WEST in his silver cucumber of a Crown Imperial Streamline house trailer. Two months later, he mailed a postcard from Caesars Palace in Las Vegas:

> Dear ________,
>
> On the way home. Nothing here for old ex-race drivers. Without a wheel is like without a pocketbook. This covers all sports; football (the dam ball), baseball (the damn bat), ect ect ect. Still you have got to go on.
>
> (Tim)

2

Halcyon Days

FREDDY LORENZEN OF ELMHURST, ILL.—FREDERICK Christian Lorenzen, Jr., to give him his full name, although nobody ever called him anything but plain old Freddy—came South to race against the good old boys the first time in 1956. He didn't do very well. He found a whole different environment from the one he had known in the Chicago area while driving at tracks like O'Hare Stadium and Illiana Speedway and even Soldier Field, the place where two years earlier he had gotten his start, in a Demolition Derby. Stock car racing wasn't a way of life around Chicago, and there were only one or two local hot dogs for him to worry about at each track. But in the South, Lorenzen found 15-year-old kids and 70-year-old grandmothers who all they talked about was racing, racing, racing because it was in their blood, and on the Grand National circuit there might be ten or fifteen drivers swarming all over him everywhere he went. Lorenzen returned home, and when he came South again, four years later in 1960, having established himself as the best stock car racer in the Midwest, he was determined to do things right.

Lorenzen and some buddies, the Talarico brothers, Jake and Joe, built a 1960 Ford Starliner with money Lorenzen borrowed from his father, a carpenter, and from a currency exchange he learned was controlled by the mob when his father called him at the shop one day and said there were four men in a big, black Cadillac out front who had stopped by to check on their investment. It took Lorenzen two months to go broke, but by bumming and borrowing, and by towing the 900 miles from Chicago to the South so many times that he often didn't know in which direction he was driving, he stuck out the season and then quit a second time, $7,000 in debt. He was resigned to working as a carpenter's apprentice in order to get back to being financially even when he got a Christmas Eve phone call from Ralph Moody, who asked him whether he'd like to work the next season for a company in Charlotte called Holman-Moody. No promises, mind you, but maybe something could be worked out.

HOLMAN-MOODY TOOK FORD SHOWROOM SEDANS AND made race cars out of them. Although it was barely three years old, its brief history told much about how the Big Three automobile companies—Ford, Chrysler, and General Motors—had gotten into the business of partially subsidizing Grand National stock car racing.

The Ford Motor Company had dominated the Southern performance market for decades. There was a reason why the cars that hauled moonshine out of the north Georgia hills and the North Carolina mountains and raced on the red-clay tracks of the Piedmont were nearly all Fords: They were the best around. But in 1955, Chevrolet joined the battle for the performance dollar in a big way by introducing the first V-8 engine in its history. At the same time, Tim Flock and other drivers were powering their massive, ghostly Chryslers to victory almost everywhere they went. Bill Benton, the assistant regional sales manager for Ford in Charlotte, N.C., got a little panicky and conveyed a message to the Ford brass up in Dearborn, Mich., that they'd better do something.

At the time, Ford's embryonic national racing program was being run by Pete DePaolo Engineering, Pete DePaolo having won the 1926 Indianapolis 500. DePaolo was charming and gregarious, and a terrible manager. His chief mechanic was Red Vogt, who in the not too distant past had prepared whiskey cars and race cars with equal success, and was likewise a lousy manager. And so on May 25, 1956, the Charlotte office of DePaolo Engineering passed into the hands of a man named

John Holman. In Holman's preliminary talks with Ford, he had been brief and to the point. "I was pretty well advised that the Ford Motor Company was spending quite a lot of money here and not getting any success for it," he said. "I didn't know that I could be successful, but I was willing to try, providing they were willing to let me try on my terms. I would be the manager, my word was to be the law, there could be no shortage of money. If they didn't like what I was doing, they could give me reasonable severance and dismiss me immediately. But while I was in charge, I was in charge. I would do this for a reasonable amount of money—salary—and if the operation became successful, I would at that time put my hand in their pocket for more money. And it was all agreed."

DePaolo Engineering's first race under Holman's leadership was two weeks later on a 1½-mile dust bowl in West Memphis, Ark. Ralph Moody, a DePaolo driver, won it, although he crossed the finish line unconscious. His windshield had popped inward on the last turn of the last lap and knocked him cold.

The race was catalytic. Detroit money and technology had found their way South before, but in bits and dribbles. This was the first time any of the Big Three had made an overt and concentrated effort to win stock car races. Competing factory teams similar to DePaolo Engineering quickly sprang up to counter the Ford challenge, and the first era of factory-supported stock car racing was under way.

The new arrangement was not universally popular. Grand National racing was supposed to be stock, and it was supposed to be sport. Now, it was neither. Sandy Grady wrote in *The Charlotte Observer:* "As the stock car crowd knows, the sedans are now so fast that they are becoming strictly *race* cars—with all the dangers and potentialities." Carl Kiekhaefer, the crusty genius behind the success of the Chrysler fleet, abruptly pulled out. "There is no room for a man who races for the enjoyment of the sport," he told reporters. "It is a deadly serious business with the Detroit people."

The first factory era ended as suddenly as it had begun. By 1957, automobile safety had become an important styling and marketing consideration, and Detroit executives found it counterproductive to advertise the speed and other performance aspects of their products at the same time that 50,000 or so Americans were dying each year on the nation's highways. A ban on direct factory participation in racing, agreed to by the Big Three through the Automobile Manufacturers' Association, went into effect on June 4, 1957. There was just one tiny problem. The three car companies each had a ton of money tied up in a warehouse or two full of racing parts. What to do? Ford, for one, resolved matters simply. It conducted what it claimed was an open auction for the DePaolo Engineering racing operation. The high bidder was John Holman, who, for the princely sum of $10,000, give or take a rumor, found himself the proud owner of a factory racing team—minus the factory.

At the same time, Holman formed a partnership with one of his drivers: Ralph Moody. It was an unlikely alliance from the start, and years later it collapsed under a heavy shroud of bitterness and lawsuits. Neither man ever liked the other very much, but their abilities meshed so perfectly that in due time the Holman-Moody race cars with their *Competition Proven* logographs became the most cherished rides on the Grand National circuit, with or without direct aid from Ford corporate headquarters in Dearborn.

John Holman, stout and muscular and with a personality to match, was born in Tennessee and raised in California. He was the Holman-Moody administrator and front man. He hired and fired, fought his company's frequent battles with NASCAR president Bill France, and those of the Ford Motor Company's as well, and wined and dined the press. Hardly anyone outside the racing fraternity disliked him; nearly everybody in the immediate family of drivers and mechanics did. Ralph Moody, the phlegmatic New Englander, had been weaned on open-wheel racers in the Northeast and did not discover stock cars until he moved to Florida at the end of World War II. An accomplished driver, he was an even better mechanic. Though often difficult for outsiders to approach and possessed by a monumental ego, he quickly gained the respect and admiration of his contemporaries and peers.

•

IN FEBRUARY OF 1961, EVERYBODY WENT TO DAYTONA Beach for the Daytona 500 and the start of another Grand National racing season: John Holman and Ralph Moody, who had made a bunch of Ford race cars that anybody could buy for $4,595 apiece and which Tubby Gonzales, a portly driver from Houston, unfortunately did; Freddy Lorenzen, the new boy on the block, who was down there in the employ of Holman-Moody to kick tires and learn cars and try to figure out why drivers like Fireball Roberts and Joe Weatherly were going faster than anybody else, and who was hoping that perhaps he could sign on as a relief driver for Tubby, who didn't figure to last the race; and Jacque Passino, who had been the corporate head of the Ford racing team back in 1956 and 1957, and despite the AMA ban, if the truth were known, still was.

It was apparent during practice that Tubby Gonzales's Holman-Moody Ford was quite a spiffy little number, except that every other time Tubby came careening down the main straightaway, his spiffy little number tended to be pointing back up toward the fourth turn. On the other hand, every time Ralph Moody got the chance to sneak Lorenzen into the car, the kid from Elmhurst (or wherever he was from) worked miracles. Passino held a meeting. The obvious thing to do was get Gonzales out of the car and Lorenzen into it, for good. This was not something that Passino could arrange on his own, however, for he was in Daytona only as an interested observer and certainly not as an official representative of the Ford Motor Company. Passino mulled, then hit on the idea of approaching Bob Trasker, a Ford dealer from Providence, R.I., and having Trasker ask Gonzales what his price would be to turn his car over to Lorenzen. Gonzales's price was a station wagon.

Trasker quickly and quietly shuffled some papers and transferred a wagon from his dealership to one in Houston, with the promise that it would be delivered to Gonzales after he—Trasker—got compensated by Ford through Ford's sales promotion budget. Everything worked out fine. Gonzales got his station wagon, Lorenzen got his ride and finished third in the 500, and Ford unofficially breached the AMA ban.

•

THE AMA BAN, OF COURSE, DID NOT MEAN THE END OF Grand National racing. It continued to grow, but with one important difference. Before 1956, it was enough to have Lee Petty race against Buck Baker, or Curtis Turner take on Fireball Roberts, no matter what the machinery. Now, thanks to the factories, it was just as important for fans to see a Chevrolet race against a Ford, or a Pontiac challenge a Plymouth. This was just fine with Detroit executives, but only for as long as their particular cars were winning, and during the years of the AMA covenant, the winningest, most spectacular cars of all were General Motors products. Ford and Chrysler squirmed, particularly Ford, which was why Jacque Passino nosed around Daytona Beach in 1961, and why Henry Ford II, finally having had enough, ordered his company back into racing in the middle of 1962. Chrysler followed suit, and in its own peculiar way, so did General Motors.

The routes each of the Big Three took were instructive. Each company had a research and development department where new ideas were nurtured and tested long before they saw the light of a dealer's showroom. Ford went one step further and created a Special Vehicles department, an unsubtle euphemism for a place where race cars were built. It was headed by Passino, in fact if not always in title, and his mandate was to make Ford once again the performance leader, not just in the South, but throughout the world.

Chrysler took a slightly different tack. Like Ford, it willingly announced its return to racing, and like Ford, it made special racing parts in its own factories or had them fabricated by special subcontractors. Unlike Ford, Chrysler operated its racing program through its public relations and sales departments. Both companies sent swarms of executives, technicians, and public relations personnel to the South, but with one difference: Ford sought to impose its corporate will on its Southern minons from the outside; Chrysler worked from within, To stretch an analogy only slightly, the often aloof and occasionally overbearing Ford corporate executives slapped a coat of paint on the rough-hewn Grand National house and told people how pretty it was; the lower-keyed Chrysler executives attempted to carry out extensive renovations of the house itself, at least those rooms that they occupied.

General Motors never admitted there was a house. When the AMA covenant was signed, General Motors, like its rivals, sent its racing program underground. When the covenant was broken, General Motors kept it there. General Motors did this by simply announcing that it wasn't going to go racing again, and much to the annoyance of the people at Ford and Chrysler who knew better, nobody ever seriously challenged the remark. As Frank Wylie of Chrysler said, "The damned thing was obvious. God, anybody who had gone up to Junior Johnson's place in 1963, for example, and seen the big crates that had 'Chevrolet Motor Division' marked all over them had to know something was up." General Motors also used an internal accounting system to hide the special racing parts that it made. Jacque Passino said, "The classic example is connecting rods. Say in a given year General Motors makes two million V-8 engines. That's 16 million connecting rods. Okay, now they're gonna need some racing rods for Vince Piggins to spread around. [Piggins ran the General Motors racing effort from his position as a Chevrolet assistant engineer for product promotions.] How many do you think he needs? Two thousand? Fine. So they knock all these goddamned rods out—the 16 million —and *among* them a couple of thousand special rods. So they figure up the whole thing and ask, 'How much did connecting rods cost us this year?' Well, it cost so many millions of dollars. Divide that by the number of rods, and that's how much a single rod costs. So the goddamned racing rod, then, disappears. Whereas at Ford, every time we built one of these rods, it was decked against our budget. The rod became an $85 or $90 item. I couldn't afford to give you a set of rods, where Vince Piggins . . . 'Christ, here, take 'em. Put 'em in your car. Run fast.' It was a basic difference in management philosophy."

The idea was for General Motors to be able to say that any part it made was available to everyone through any General Motors dealer in the country. If a General Motors car ran fast, fine. If it didn't, that was okay, too, for General Motors wasn't in racing, and who's to holler?

•

FIREBALL ROBERTS DEFIED EASY DESCRIPTION. IN A SPORT where a cliché or a simple catchphrase was usually sufficient to give at least the hint of a driver's personality, none ever came to mind that adequately suggested his complex nature. The later impressions of him by his contemporaries were a jumble of contradictions. He was fearless; no, more than most drivers he acknowledged his fear. He was a loner; no, though he relished his privacy, he was part of a loyal coterie whose horseplay and revelries were legendary. He had no sense of humor; no, he had a marvelous wit, dry and acerbic. He did not care whether he won races, only that he led them; no, he was the worst loser stock car racing had ever known.

Nor was there anyone against whom his abilities could accurately be measured. Like the others of his era, he started out racing modifieds on the dirt, but he was remembered exclusively for his performances on the first generation of superspeedways, those at Darlington, Daytona Beach, Atlanta, and Charlotte. When the transition to the big tracks began, most of the best dirt-track drivers of the 1950s were already retired. Either that, or the demands of the new tracks made them think seriously about it. Fireball had those years all to himself.

Then there was the legend and the mystique: Fireball, the great Fireball, driving with consummate skill and winning with consummate ease and crashing with élan and finally dying in the most horrible way imaginable. Bits and fragments of the truth sometimes filtered through, but the whole cloth? That was something else.

Bob Myers, a reporter for *The Charlotte News,* said, "He was an idol in a different sort of way. I don't think Roberts ever went looking for attention. It was just a sort of magic. He was such a good race driver, such a successful race driver, that people simply looked up to him. Maybe they didn't like him, and Roberts didn't seem to be terribly upset whether anybody liked him or not, but they respected him. For those who didn't know him very well, he would often give a bad impression of himself, I guess. He would be cocky and aloof and just sort of unfriendly. But I think a lot of that had to do with the fact he was wrapped up very much with his racing and didn't want anything to interfere with it. He always wanted to be the very best at whatever he was doing."

Doris Roberts, Fireball's widow, remembered hearing stories from her in-laws that when the Roberts clan gathered on Sunday afternoons and all the aunts and uncles went around hugging and kissing their nieces and nephews, young Glenn Roberts—he was 5 or 6 years old—would go off by himself and say, "Don't speak to me. Don't even look at me."

EDWARD GLENN ROBERTS, JR., WAS BORN ON JANUARY 20, 1929, in the small central Florida town of Apopka. His father owned an orange grove and was the superintendent of a local crate mill. In 1945, the Roberts family moved to Daytona Beach, and Glenn entered Seabreeze High School. At the end of his junior year, he quit to join the Air Force but was discharged ninety days later because of asthma. He took his senior year of high school at Mary Carl Vocational in Daytona Beach but chose to graduate with his boyhood friends back in Apopka. Somewhere along the line, Glenn was pitching one afternoon in a pickup baseball game when, after one of his throws, another player remarked, "That sure was a fireball." The name stuck.

Glenn, now the Fireball, studied mechanical engineering for two years and a semester at the University of Florida in Gainesville before dropping out, in January of 1950, to go racing full time with his friend, Speedy Spears. Already he had acquired a certain notoriety. At Daytona's Speed Weeks in 1948, Bernard Kahn of the *Daytona Beach News-Sentinel* reported: "Roberts's showing in his first outing here won him praise along Gasoline Alley. The reckless Daytonan creased the curves at breakneck speed and gave the thrill-seeking audience a run for its money." It was a nice enough blurb for a driver not yet out of his teens, but later that year a series of events took place that could only have happened to a future star. At a modified race in North Wilkesboro, a woman leaped from the stands and kissed Fireball firmly on the cheek before the start of a consolation race. Roberts's car broke down during the race, and he turned it over to Marshall Teague, a fellow

Daytonan, for the feature. Teague crashed and broke his collarbone. The next Sunday, at Greensboro, N.C., the woman, by now identified as "a blond aviatrix from Charlotte," again kissed Roberts. Again Roberts's car crashed, this time with him in it. Two weeks later, the mystery woman tried for a triple at Lexington, N.C. Fireball's car did a dramatic rollover, and he was taken to the hospital with a broken rib.

"From that day on," Fireball told reporters, "I decided no woman would ever kiss me before a race—including my wife."

FIREBALL ROBERTS MET DORIS MC CONNELL, A DARK-haired beauty from Kannapolis, N.C., at a race track in Charlotte early in the summer of 1950. On their first date, Doris watched while Fireball changed the engine in his modified race car. On their second date, they went to a race in Hendersonville, N.C., and on the way back home, Fireball said, "I think it's time that I get married."

"I think it is, too," said Doris. "Is it a girl from Daytona?"

"I'm asking you."

"You've got to be kidding. You must be out of your mind."

Three weeks later, Fireball ran a race in Charlotte, then he and Doris drove across the state line to York, S.C., where they were married in the wee hours of July 22, 1950. A daughter, Pamela, their only child, was born the next year.

Doris Roberts:

He came to my house several times before we were married, and of course I introduced him to my parents as Glenn Roberts—in case you wonder why I say "Glenn" all the time instead of "Fireball"—because I couldn't quite see my parents accepting the fact that I was dating someone named "Fireball."

He was an introvert. His mother said that she was surprised that Glenn ever got married because he was such an introvert. She didn't think that he would ever feel strongly enough about anyone to marry her. He was a very moody person. I learned, when we were first married, to speak when spoken to. Not that he was so overpowering, or so domineering, but when he was preoccupied or deep in thought about something, you didn't want to bother him about trivial things. You know, "The roof leaks," or something like that. You learned when to talk and when not to talk, and the best thing to do was just to be there and listen.

I could probably make him out as the champion son of a bitch of the twentieth century or an unheralded saint, and he was neither. He had his faults and he had his good points, which is true of anyone. I'll say this, there was never a dull moment. I think he had a very contradictory personality. I think Glenn's whole life was very contradictory—what he said today and what he did tomorrow—in a lot of things. Maybe he hit a happy medium.

There is one classic example. Glenn was a professed agnostic, and he didn't care who knew it because he would argue religion at the drop of a hat. He did not go to church. In fact, he was hardly ever in a church in the fourteen years we were married. But yet, in 1962, when he won the Daytona 500, when I got home from the track, he said, "I told God during that race that if he would let me win, I would go to church Sunday." For whatever reason, I was glad that he was going, but to me that's very contradictory. If you don't believe in God, how can you pray to Him? We went to an interdenominational church.

He had a temper, but he had tremendous control. And a fistfight? Glenn was never involved in a fistfight, anywhere. He didn't believe in that. His one very intellectual friend—his name was Robert—was also a great fighter. If someone, you know, set his beer down wrong, Robert would take a poke at him. And Glenn would let him fight. Robert would get so aggravated. He'd say, "Fireball, I would do anything for you, and you sit there and let this guy beat me up." And Glenn would say, "Come Sunday, I've got to drive a race car. I can't do it with a broken fist or a broken arm."

THERE WAS NO SUCH THING AS AN OVERNIGHT SENsation in any form of automobile racing. There were too many variables—the car, the engine, the mechanic, the driver—that had to be fit together before a driver could achieve even a small measure of success. By 1953, it was clear that Roberts knew how to go fast. According to his own journal, he started an even 100 races that year, most of them modified events. He sat on the pole in 26 of them, but won just 12. By 1955, however, certain other parts of the racing puzzle had fallen into place. He entered 36 races and won 20 that year, a phenomenally high ratio of success. Three years later, Fireball Roberts became a star. In April of 1958, he won the Rebel 300 at

Darlington; in September, he won the Southern 500 at Darlington. In one 14-race stretch that season, he had eight wins, three seconds, one fifth, and only two nonfinishes. He was magnanimous in victory. When Curtis Turner and Joe Weatherly, his two most prominent rivals in the Southern 500, fell out with mechanical problems, Roberts saluted both as he charged to the checkered flag. "I hated to see them go out," he told reporters. "I wanted to win it with both of them running all the way."

At the end of the 1958 season, a brief note in the NASCAR newsletter reported that Roberts and master mechanic Smokey Yunick would join forces the following season to campaign a new Pontiac. The timing couldn't have been better. In 1959, the 2½-mile speedway at Daytona opened, replacing the venerable beach course, and the following year the first races were held at the new 1½-mile tracks at Charlotte and Atlanta. With two races per year at each of these tracks, plus two more at Darlington, this gave the Grand National season eight races that stood out from the rest. If the pressures were greater at those eight superspeedway races, and they were, so were the rewards. The Fireball Roberts-Smokey Yunick era began in February of 1959 and ended in March of 1963. There were thirty superspeedway races during that period. Roberts won five, not a particularly impressive number except that no other driver won more than three. In qualifying, nobody was even close. Roberts posted the fastest qualifying time in fifteen of those races; no other driver was able to qualify fastest more than three times. The public relations advantages of those performances to Roberts, Yunick, and the Pontiac Division of General Motors were tremendous. The pole position was usually determined on the Wednesday or Thursday before a Sunday race, and thus the fastest qualifier and his car received three or four days of free publicity. The winner of the race often had to be content with just one.

Doris Roberts:

> He was very, very smooth. I loved to watch him on a track because it always seemed that he knew exactly what he was doing.

I always felt that he was in complete control, which, of course, is not true—it's not true of anyone—but this was the impression I got. He didn't just slam-bang, not to the extent that other drivers did. His style on the big tracks was his own, because there was no one to follow.

When I go to a race today and the cars come around on the pace lap, I still expect Glenn to be on the pole because that's where he always was.

IN SHORT-TRACK RACING, A DRIVER DIDN'T EXPECT TO get hurt, though many did. A driver simply didn't often go fast enough for a long enough time to experience even the illusion of danger for more than a few seconds. The big tracks were different, and Roberts had both a strong sense of self-preservation and the intelligence to imagine the dark possibilities of his trade.

Marshall Teague, an early patron of Roberts's, was killed at Daytona Beach in 1959 in the crash of an experimental open-cockpit race car called the Sumar Special. Teague and his driving seat were thrown 150 feet from his wrecked car. His watch, undamaged, was later given to his widow. Roberts, who saw the accident from pit road, buried his head in his hands and cried.

Doris Roberts:

Glenn found it very hard to accept the fact that Marshall was killed. I think this was something that he really did not want to face. I remember the family called and asked Glenn if he would be a pallbearer. Glenn said, "Yes." The morning of the funeral, I awakened Glenn and told him it was time to get up and get dressed. He said, "I'm not going. I'm sick." And I said, "You are not sick. It's time to get up." And he just looked at me as only he could and said, *"I am sick."* And he was. Not physically—not that kind of sick—but he was sick. I think I had not realized before then that no one had ever died who was this close to Glenn. He didn't want to go because if he didn't go, he didn't have to accept it quite so . . . You know. If you don't think about it, and if you don't see it, then it's not quite so vivid to you.

We didn't talk about deaths on race tracks. That was one of the things that we didn't talk about.

IN 1962 WHEN THE FACTORIES OPENLY RETURNED TO racing, each in its own way, Freddy Lorenzen was already a star, riding the crest of the new wave. More than that, he *was* the new wave.

In the spring of 1961, Lorenzen won his first Grand National, at Martinsville, Va. The next race was the Rebel 300, the spring event at the Darlington Raceway, a track Lorenzen had fantasized about as a teenager when he would listen to broadcasts of the Southern 500 from the coziness of a tent pitched in his backyard.

"That's a true story," Lorenzen said. "Jeez, you got it right down pat. I was a tent nut all my life. The only race I really knew about was the Southern 500. The big names then were Fonty Flock, Curtis Turner, Joe Weatherly, and then the youngster, Fireball Roberts. That's how long ago. He was just starting to come up when I used to listen, and I thought, *Jeez, someday I'd love to go down there and go racing. Someday I'm gonna go to Darlington.*"

Lorenzen qualified on the pole for the Rebel, edging out Roberts. He led until a blown tire forced him back in the pack, allowing Roberts and Turner to move up and duel for the lead. But with 25 laps to go, Roberts unexpectedly pitted for a change of tires and dropped from contention. Now it was Turner in front, with Lorenzen, this young, fair-haired kid who was so handsome he looked like he should have a silk scarf tied around his neck, moving up close on Pops's bumper while Ralph Moody, Lorenzen's Holman-Moody crew chief, watched from the pits.

Fred Lorenzen:

And I beat him. And I probably wouldn't have except he made me mad at the end, y'know? I had him beat fair and square, just flat-out running, but he wouldn't move over. He kept chopping me. Every time I'd go to the outside, he'd chop me off into the wall. So, I thought, *I'll bluff him.* I had preplanned it. . . .

Ralph Moody:

I'd been telling him, one of the things you've gotta remember at the end of the race if you're behind Turner, he ain't going to let you by. He's going to shut the door on you no matter where the hell you go, and he'll crash you if there's any way he can. That's just what it's all about. The thing you have to do with him is, you just keep trying him, one direction. Just keep trying to pass him on the outside. And never change. If you have to do it for 20 laps, or 50 laps, or whatever, and you can outrun him, just try to pass him that one way. Don't try any other way because if you do, he'll watch for you no matter where the hell you go. But if he thinks you're stupid enough to keep passing him running just one way, he's gonna say, "That jerk kid. He don't know any goddamned different." That's when you're gonna have him. You wait till right near the end of the race, like the last lap or two, and you keep tryin' him.

Well, Lorenzen didn't, to start with. He tried Turner this way and that way, and I'm out there with my goddamned hands trying to tell him, *Outside,* just one way. And he ain't paying any attention. He's mad because Turner's shutting him off wherever he goes. Finally, I get our crew to put that sign up: "W.H.M." "What the Hell's the Matter?" He knew what that meant. *Think.* So finally he gets his head straightened out. He'd get Pops way up there, and Turner would squeeze him over, and he'd dust some paint along that cement wall down there and everything. And he just kept doing it, just kept doing it.

Fred Lorenzen:

. . . So I had preplanned it coming off three and four to build up my speed and pretend I'm going outside, and when he goes to move up to close the gate on me, I'll dive underneath him. So that's what I did. And when he saw me, he dove down and he nailed me, and I just didn't move and I just turned right—I nailed him back—and I got him up into the fence. Then I came around and won the race and got the checkered flag.

Ralph Moody:

And the funny part of it was—and it was plain as day, too—when Lorenzen made that pass for the outside, Turner closed it off and he's like *this,* looking to the right, and Lorenzen was clear by him on the other side, almost completely by him, before Turner ever knew it. And Turner was so goddamned mad, boy, he could eat nails. He come in the pits and ran into our car, and he was some kind of hot. He come over to me, and he says, "If you'd tend your own goddamned business, you wouldn't have this kind of trouble." I says, "I ain't got no kind of trouble. The car I had won the race."

Fred Lorenzen:

He was just mad because he had gotten beat by a nobody. And I would probably feel upset, too, if some young, punk kid—a Yankee—comes down and beats me and I'm king of the South. He had very hurt feelings. But that's something you always gotta remember. You're never the best because there's always somebody better, no matter what you do or where you're at in the whole world. That's why the world keeps going.

That was my biggest stock car race I ever won, my biggest feeling, bigger than Daytona or anything, because it was my first big one, and I beat . . . There's not a greater feeling in the world than beating whoever's the best, and Turner was by far the king of racing. In fact, I have a picture upstairs of me in Victory Lane, and I'm gonna show it to you and you can see it. There was just tears in my eyes—other people have caught it—the eyes are just watering.

WHEN LORENZEN CAME SOUTH TO STAY, HE WAS A 26-year-old bachelor and a cocky, hotheaded perfectionist, but by some strange chemistry, he and the officious, egoistic Moody formed an ideal partnership of the mind.

"He was quite a different guy to get along with," Moody said. "He lived with us, me and my wife, for two years, but I've gone home from race tracks when he'd be so hostile you couldn't believe it. He'd talk to my wife, but not to me. He was on high G all the time: This had to be this way, that had to be that way; do this, do that. If he'd pit stop, he wanted to leave before everything was half done. A drink of water wasn't nothing. Hell, he didn't need a drink of water, just, *Get out of here.* So you had to settle him down to the point . . . Y'know, it took fifteen, eighteen seconds to get done what you were doing in a pit stop. You have a drink of water, you hold your foot to the brake, you keep the engine running, you wait until somebody says, 'Go,' and then you go. You don't set there hollering and screaming and raising hell and throwing stuff at people and cussing them out. After the first race we went to, I told him, 'Hey, I run the race car. I'll fix it. You just drive it, and most of the time I'll tell you how to do that, too.' "

"He knew me like the back of his hand," Lorenzen said of Moody. "He probably knew me better than my own father did at times."

It was no exaggeration to say that Lorenzen changed the image of Southern stock car racing as no single driver had before him. Certainly he was aided by circumstances, particularly the sudden presence of four superspeedways where a couple of years earlier there had been but one, and the reappearance of the factory teams.

He was the first successful superspeedway driver who had not learned to drive on dirt. Indeed, his success was due in part *because* he hadn't raced on dirt. Lorenzen had run his share of short tracks, but in the Midwest they were layered with asphalt and several were at least one mile around. Thus, he started no worse than even with the Southerners on the big tracks, and in one respect was actually ahead of them because he had no bad dirt-track habits to unlearn.

The factories often sought drivers who were not only talented but who possessed personality—drivers who would be a credit to their companies—and Lorenzen was a public relations man's dream. Russ Catlin, the publicity director at Darlington, was among the first to sense Lorenzen's possibilities. Humpy Wheeler, at the time the Southern field representative for the Firestone Tire & Rubber Company and later the general manager of the Charlotte Motor Speedway, said, "Catlin was a master at getting baseball-oriented sports writers down to see stock car races and filling them up with booze and everything else and taking them over and introducing them to the drivers, and he saw in Lorenzen a potentially tremendous gate-drawer. Lorenzen was a Yankee at a time when Yankee still meant something bad, and he was good-looking. Catlin built him up big, and when some slew-footed reporter from Winston-Salem would come to Darlington and not know what the hell to write about, Catlin would say, 'We got a guy down here from Elmhurst, Illinois, who's going to be a great race driver.' So the guy would go over and interview him."

Lorenzen was a good interview. He talked intelligently, didn't say "ain't" very often, and spoke in complete sentences. He was different. He was not like Roberts, talented as hell but cold as ice before a race and sometimes after; or Joe Weatherly, the practical joker who wasn't really all that good behind the wheel; or Junior Johnson, the mountain iconoclast who often didn't talk to anybody at all. Best of all, when Freddy won a race, he went bananas. He acted like he'd won a million dollars, and he would shake hands and sign autographs and stay up in the press box until sunset.

Most important of all, Lorenzen drove in a manner that was radically different from that of his rivals. Time and again he would come from behind to win on the last lap or two, the way he had done the first time at Darlington in 1961, and often there were comments about how "Lucky Freddy" had pulled out another one. But it wasn't true. "You make your own luck," said Lorenzen, and he made his by lurking in the middle of the pack and pacing himself while the hot dogs up front wore out their cars or themselves, and sometimes both.

"Why should I race fifteen or eighteen different Fireballs or Junior Johnsons when after 200 miles there's only two of each left?" Lorenzen said. "Why should I race everybody and wear my machine out? A machine's like a human. It can only take so much. Sure, once in a while you can run it to death and it'll stay together, but 90 percent of the time, it's not going to. You gotta treat a car like it's life."

With unending patience, he would wait. Then, hunched over his steering wheel, his head resting on his left shoulder in the turns, he would make a spectacular, come-from-behind charge to victory. His style was partly an illusion, for it was much safer and much more logical to make a run at one or two cars at the end of a race rather than blunderbuss to the front at the start and try to stay there, but it worked, practically and esthetically, and the fans came to love and expect it.

Lorenzen's memories of his earlier failures were a constant goad. "Racing down South wasn't just glory, you know," he said. "When I got in a race car saying, *I'm Freddy Lorenzen, and I'm gonna win the race. . . .* Big deal. After working all your life and saving money and losing it all, you learn what a penny is. I treated racing as a business: Nine o'clock, 9:30, I'd go to bed. . . . Mechanics? It had to be the same way. . . . Race track every morning . . . 8:01, had to be there . . . Weren't there? . . . Fired . . . Get rid of them. . . . Get new ones. You go down by the pit gate and watch the first three pit crews that come in. Those are the dedicated racers. I did want to race and I loved it, but I felt that the only way I could be the best was to be very strict. When I'd get done with the race, I would party and go out and have beers and stay up late and do a lot of crazy things like anybody else. But when it was race time, it was all business, the entire week. My car was waxed four times a day, always by me. I never wanted anybody to do my dirty stuff. Every little nut and bolt on it was shined. The tires were always washed with lacquer so they'd look pitch black, and then the Firestone or Goodyear insignia—whichever tires I was running—I'd fill that in just to make the car look extra sharp. Everything had to be perfect."

As Lorenzen, for his time and place, was perfect.

JACQUE PASSINO WAS THE FINAL ARBITER OF WHO among the many candidates got Ford factory rides and how long they kept them.

His criteria were somewhat prejudiced by certain events that took place shortly before the 1957 Rebel 300 at Darlington. The town, to use Passino's phrase, was not a particularly swinging place, and the Ford team commuted daily by private plane from DePaolo Engineering headquarters in Charlotte. On race-day morning, Passino drove to the DePaolo garage and was stunned to find assembled in front of him the largest collective hangover he had ever seen. There had been a monumental party the night before, and now Passino's drivers stood before him, in the bag to a man, and Passino thought, *Gee, these are our troops?* Fortunately, the race was postponed by rain. "Honest to God," Passino said, "if they had had to run the race that day, I don't know how these guys would have made it."

•

Jacque Passino:

The level of humanity, if you will, changed dramatically with Lorenzen. Some of the drivers that everyone thought were classy guys you really had to say were just classy barbarians. I don't say it with disrespect. Some of the ones that you had on a given day you couldn't be happier about, but by the same token you agonized over the fact that there you are, you put this dumb bastard in your car and kind of sit back figuring, *Well, I hope it comes out all right.* You could go to the race with Curtis Turner and Joe Weatherly and you never knew what the Christ was gonna happen. You knew that on balance you had a better car than anybody else, and you knew that on balance they could drive better than anybody else, but whether the two jerks were gonna get it all collected and let one another win was beyond you. Once the race started, it was, "Katie, bar the door." Forget it. They were just out having fun. I never really put too much faith in either of those guys because you never knew how long you were gonna have them running. And when you had these guys out at an all-night party before a race at Darlington, which is one of the bigger races, you had the prospect of having to go back and tell your boss what happened. If you tell him it really didn't work out as well as we thought it would because all these guys were at an all-night party . . .

"You dumb bastard. Where'd you get these guys?"

"Well, they swung out of a tree."

Which is what the name of the game was. So when you found a guy like a Lorenzen, you said, "Jeezuz, man, let's take him." Here's a guy that went to bed before the race, that got up and was ready to go. He was such a different brand of man from anybody that had been around the business. He was a neat, young, personable, strong, clean-living, handsome, smart, brave, very clever race driver, and all you had to do was meet him and you fell in love with the kid.

THE AUTOMOBILE FACTORIES AS WELL AS GOODYEAR AND Firestone, the two companies that supplied tires for Grand National racing, were capable of making quick engineering changes of the sort that under normal circumstances might have taken a year or more. If Plymouth had problems at one race because of an inefficient intake manifold, Chrysler engineers would design a new one within the fortnight. If Goodyear tires were a tick of the clock slower than Firestones at a major race in April, a new and improved batch would be ready by May.

During the factory era of the 1960s, a car's performance —as it always had been—was a function of the relationship among the engine, the chassis, and the tires. The chassis had to be strong enough to carry the power of the engine; the tires had to be durable enough to support the combined strength of the engine and the chassis. In a period of controlled development, this not-so-delicate balance was reasonably easy to maintain. But the factories' and tire companies' constant search for a mechanical advantage, however small, created a constant turmoil. No sooner was a parity of sorts reached, for example, than some genius would find a way to make his engine go faster, which required that somebody else build a stronger chassis, which in turn meant that somebody *else* would have to develop a more durable tire. By the time the new tire came along, however, another genius engine builder would have to come up with a new trick, and the whole cycle would need to be repeated. Everything mechanical was on the ragged edge, that fine line between maximum performance and disaster, as were the drivers who had to ride herd on it all.

DETROIT'S ABILITY TO MAKE QUICK ENGINEERING improvements had other ramifications. Suddenly, Bill France, the founder and president of NASCAR, found himself in a box. On the one hand, he professed a desire to keep stock car racing reasonably stock—after all, the name of his organization was the National Association for *Stock* Car Auto Racing—on the other, he was well aware that fans now came to his races as much to see the cars as they did to watch the drivers. It was fine that the factory public relations departments helped to create personalities such as Freddy Lorenzen, Junior Johnson, and Richard Petty, but it was also incumbent upon France to have as many different makes of cars on the track as he possibly could. This meant legislating equality. The factories' motto was, "Win on Sunday, Sell on Monday," and the Grand National circuit meant nothing to a factory if it wasn't able to win on Sunday. If one factory came to dominate the circuit, the others had to be made competitive. This was done by changing the rules to the advantage of the factories that weren't winning, which tended to annoy the factory that had created an advantage for itself in the first place. Equalizing the factories to the satisfaction of all parties required the wisdom of Solomon and the tact of a Japanese courtesan, for there was always the possibility that the factories would simply take their cars and go home. Worse than a massive withdrawal of all the factory teams would be if either Chrysler or Ford, the only two factories that openly acknowledged that they were racing, pulled out unilaterally. Would spectators stand for one make of car leading lap after lap and winning race after race, knowing that a competitive fleet stood idle on the sidelines? Hardly.

In 1956 and 1957, France maintained a balance with relative ease. The second time around, however, it was soon apparent that he had a tiger by the tail, and, to mix a metaphor, the tiger held all the aces.

This became obvious, for the first of many times, at the 1963 Daytona 500. France had a fine number of Chrysler and Ford entries that year, but he didn't have much in the way of anything from General Motors, the Pontiacs of Fireball Roberts and Smokey Yunick having begun to fall by the technological wayside. Chevrolet, however, had developed an experimental 427-cubic-inch engine called the "porcupine head" because of the way its valve stems and pushrods were angled, and had given some to Yunick to go racing with. As Paul Van Valkenburgh reported in his book, *Chevrolet = Racing . . . ?*: "They were not exactly the same 427 engine that was being marketed in the showrooms, but Bill France allowed them to be weasled into the Daytona 500 to create a little excitement. And indeed they did."

Long before the race, in fact.

Every kind of engine used in Grand National racing was supposed to be available to the public. "So, okay, I want the engine," said John Holman, who, of course, campaigned Fords. "France told Bunkie Knudsen [the general manager of Chevrolet and a General Motors vice-president], 'Look, if Holman can't buy the goddamn engine, they can't race.' So Smokey had to work all night getting an engine, which later proved to be made of secondary and thirdiary—you know, no raceable—parts. The paint was wet when we got it the next morning. Later on, when the engine had no value to us at all, Junior Johnson, who had one in his car, came by, and he took one look at it and said, 'That ain't the one.'"

Jacque Passino added, "You just knew damned well that no matter what happened, they were going to run those cars, and all we could do was grab our best hold. France needed somebody to run against us. He needed somebody to run fast. He had the Plymouths and a lot of Fords, and then a couple of Chevrolets showed up, and they went like stink. God, they were terrifying, and there was nothing you could do about it."

In all, there were three Chevrolets with the experimental engine. All three fell out early, but the incident was instructive on several levels. Bill France knowingly allowed an illegal engine to be raced in a major Grand National event in order to generate controversy and ticket sales (not, coincidentally, at a track he owned). Ford protested the engine knowing that its protest would be disallowed. France forced Yunick to produce a duplicate engine, but one that all parties knew wasn't the real thing. Chevrolet got a lot of free publicity. Ford won the race. It was a game of mirrors, a little something for everybody and a little chicanery by everybody.

Further instruction. The biggest winner was Junior Johnson; the biggest loser was the Chrysler Corporation. Although the porcupine head engine was withdrawn from competition immediately after the Daytona 500, Johnson continued to drive a Chevrolet, one with a more nearly legal power plant, for the rest of the year. He went to the post thirty-three times and won seven races, including major events at Atlanta and Charlotte. Throughout the season, he was portrayed as the humble David doing lonely battle against the twin Goliaths of Chrysler and Ford. Johnson saw no long-term future with Chevrolet, however, and at the end of 1963, he announced that he would drive the following year for Dodge. Sensing a natural, Chrysler's public relations department in New York put a hip new writer named Tom Wolfe onto the Johnson saga. The result was a loving article by Wolfe for

Esquire called "Junior Johnson Is the Last American Hero. Yes," that nearly a quarter of a century after its publication still held up as the definitive piece on stock car racing. Alas, racing loyalties being what they were, Johnson again jumped rides, shortly after the 1964 season began. The definitive piece of stock car racing journalism, suggested by the Chrysler public relations department about one of its own, thus became the saga of an ex-Chevrolet driver who, at the time of the article's publication, was driving a Ford.

FIREBALL ROBERTS BECAME INVINCIBLE AT THE Charlotte Motor Speedway in October of 1961 on the 113th lap of the National 400. Entering turn three as the race leader in his black and gold Smokey Yunick Pontiac, Roberts blew his right-front tire and smashed into the outside guard rail. His car slammed the rail three more times as it moved through the three-four turn, then slowly slid off the banking until it reached the grassy part of the infield near the exit of the fourth turn. There his car dug in, then slithered back on the track with its right side exposed to oncoming traffic. As though it were a rifle bullet, the Ford of Bill Morgan took dead aim. Fireball grabbed his steering wheel with all his strength and hunched forward. Morgan was traveling at approximately 125 mph when he hit, and the crash caved in the entire right side of Fireball's Pontiac.

Humpy Wheeler saw the accident from the press box. "It was an unbelievable crash right out in front of everybody," he said, "and Fireball did not move. The caution flags went out and the cars slowed down, and every eye in the Charlotte Motor Speedway main grandstand was looking at that car. And everybody, you know, thought he was dead. The car was crushed. Nobody would run out to help him—this was before NASCAR really tightened its get-out-there-and-get-'em-quick attitude—because the cars were all coming down pit road for pit stops. But Roberts, after about three minutes, finally got his senses back, got out of the car, very slowly, and never in the history of Grand National racing has anybody gotten more of an ovation. He was dead one minute and very much alive the next."

Roberts shrugged off the accident. "When it's all over, there's not much point in being scared," he said, and called Doris at their home in Daytona Beach.

Doris Roberts: He called me as soon as he got his bearings and was all right, and I think he waited until he knew his voice wouldn't give him away. But he *was* afraid. I think that was the most frightening thing that had ever happened to him. When he came home on Monday, he said, "I want to take you over to Smokey's and show you that car." I wouldn't go. But a couple of days later, we were going somewhere, and he was driving, and he took me over to Smokey's and he said, "You *are* going to look at that car." I think he wanted me to realize that this could happen to him, too, for me to realize how close he came to . . . You know.

Question: Was it that, or was it to show you what a strong car Smokey built?

Doris Roberts: No, I think it was this other thing. I think he wanted me to *know* how badly that car was torn up because he told me that he looked down and there was this car that had come in. . . . The front of the other car was against his leg, and that's pretty close.

Question: According to newspaper clippings, he was one of the few drivers who ever admitted being afraid in a race car.

Doris Roberts: And I think when you read that, he was quoted as saying, "You're either afraid or you're a fool or a liar." How could you not have some fear? I mean, every time you get in a race car, there is the element . . . you might not come home. Of course, this is not the overriding thing. You could never let it be. You could certainly not be at your best if every time you went into the number one turn, you were afraid that you were going to crash.

I don't think that he feared what *he* would do. At all times, I think he felt that he was as much in control as you could be in control. But he had no control over what someone may do in front of him. This is what frightened me, not Glenn's speed, nor his style of driving or what have you. It was the other people involved, people with perhaps less experience or with less brains than he had.

I felt that he was so capable that if you could just leave him alone, he was fine. Glenn drove with his head as much as he did with his foot. He thought about it. And this, I think, was one of the things that separated Glenn from the . . . oh, the brains and the brawn.

Although Glenn was a fatalist, very much a fatalist—he felt that it was a here-today-and-gone-tomorrow thing—I think that he had a very strong sense of self-preservation. But—I don't know whether I feel this way about all race drivers or just about him—I also felt that he had a license to commit suicide. Not that he had a death wish or anything, but many times I'd say, you know, "Don't carry this thing too far."

Question: What was his answer to that?

Doris Roberts: Oh, he thought that was funny. I don't think *he* felt that way. I don't *think* he did.

THE RIVALRY THAT DEVELOPED BETWEEN FIREBALL Roberts and Freddy Lorenzen was a natural: the cold-eyed veteran on his way to becoming the centerpiece of a Southern legend versus the brash, fresh-faced interloper from the North. At first, they raced each other from opposite sides of the corporate fence—Lorenzen in his pristine-white Ford, No. 28, and Roberts in his black and gold Pontiac, No. 22—and later they were wary teammates. It didn't matter whether the venue was one of the four superspeedways or something smaller. Neither did much Grand National racing on dirt, but the several half-mile asphalt tracks that dotted the Grand National landscape often provided some of the most enjoyable and dramatic racing afternoons of the season.

Jacque Passino:

I think the most fun is the dirt-track race, and the second most fun is a half-mile race on asphalt. There's a lot of action and a lot of noise and they're all too long, but a lot of stuff goes on. . . . Jeezuz, one year at Martinsville, Fireball was driving the Pontiac and Freddy was in our Ford, and they were going, just ding-donging around, and finally, Lorenzen caught Fireball. . . .

Fred Lorenzen:

You gotta wait and know when to make your move. You gotta stay right up on 'em, within a foot away, and you just wait for the guy to make a mistake. And sooner or later, he's gonna. Your best way is to wait for traffic. He's gotta make a decision which way to go because he knows one way is quicker than the other and 90 percent of the time he's gonna pick the right way, but the one time he makes the wrong move . . . There's always a way to get around.

Jacque Passino:

. . . And you know, on a half-mile there's no chute, and the way you pass is in the corner. You slide the other guy up, and then you shoot under him. Well, if there's somebody really capable running ahead of you that isn't going to slide up—and they don't *have* to let you slide them—you're dead. You just cannot get around the son of a bitch. So the next thing you do, you keep tapping him until you get right in the right part of the corner, and then you punch him and you literally slide him up there. You spin him out. And if you're real slick, he'll go up toward the wall, and you'll go on under him and you're past. . . .

Fred Lorenzen:

I was running good, but I wasn't thinking. Sometimes I'd lose my head, and Moody couldn't get to me that day. I was still a little cocky, I suppose, and I felt that I was running so much faster than Fireball that, *Move, boy. I'm coming through.* Because I couldn't go around. It was too hard at Martinsville. But he wouldn't move, so I rapped him in the bumper a little bit.

Jacque Passino:

. . . Lorenzen kept tapping him, tapping him, trying to get around, and Fireball was glib enough that he wouldn't let him. But he finally got tired of it. So they're going into the goddamned third turn, and Fireball spiked the brakes. Now Christ, Lorenzen hit him a ton. He broke the gas tank in Roberts's car, but he broke his own radiator, too. So the both of them were out of the race. They thought that was the funniest thing that ever happened to them.

For Passino, the boss, the incident and others like it posed something of a problem. What did he say to a driver who had eliminated himself from a race, particularly when the malefactor wasn't a Curtis Turner or a Joe Weatherly, from whom he might have expected such nonsense, but the Golden Boy himself, brave and loyal and smart and all the rest?

"How can you really say anything?" Passino said. "You can tell him what you think—'You dumb bastard, you ran out of brains'—but you really didn't kid about it afterward. And once again, it'd get to the point where you'd have to go back to your boss and say, 'Well, we didn't win that race because our genius driver ran into the car he was trying to pass. Put the other guy out, but he put himself out, too.' And they say, 'Well, Jesus Christ, what kind of idiots are you dealing with?' "

ROBERTS AND LORENZEN BECAME HOLMAN-MOODY teammates in the spring of 1963. Lorenzen said they "got along good," but tensions were inevitable. "I think it was mainly because a younger kid, a Yankee, was outrunning the guy that was the king dog down there for years," Lorenzen said, "but teammates, I don't think, are too good, race-car-wise. I've never seen them work in my life, anywhere." Roberts was hardly over the hill when he switched rides. At 34, he was just six years older than Lorenzen and in the prime of his career. But for the first time, he did not have center stage to himself. Then, too, it was generally assumed that when Ford engineers came up with a new and better idea, Lorenzen was the first to get the benefit of it. The Ford people said this wasn't true. *Some*body, they said, had to try out a new speed part, and if it didn't work, they didn't want all their drivers victimized the same way on the same afternoon.

If Passino had had his way regarding race strategy, Lorenzen and Roberts, as well as the other drivers under contract to Ford, would have used the system favored by racing teams in Europe whereby one driver assumed the lead, often by prearrangement, and kept it until the race ended or his car broke while his teammates trailed at a respectable distance. The concept was very civilized, but it never could have worked in the South. Doris Roberts recalled that Fireball was, in fact, once told to let another Ford driver—not Lorenzen—win a particular race. "If he can beat me," he growled, "he can have it." And that was the prevailing ethic.

Even as their rivalry grew in intensity, there were moments of high comedy. Lorenzen beat Roberts at Bristol, Tenn., another of those half-mile paved tracks that were so entertaining, in the summer of 1963, and it was charged that the way he won was to intentionally knock off Fireball's gas cap, forcing Roberts to the pits for mandatory repairs. Lorenzen dismissed the accusation. "How the hell are you gonna aim at a gas cap running 100 miles an hour?" he asked rhetorically. "A gas cap's three inches around."

And the Rebel 400 at Darlington the following spring was the setting for a multilayered confrontation that involved not only the two Ford driving stars, but Ralph Moody, who ran the Holman-Moody pit operation; Moody's partner, John Holman; Lorenzen's chief mechanic, Herb Nab; and, of course, Jacque Passino.

Moody said, "We was pitting those two cars right together, and I'm the one that's saying what to do with 'em and all that. They come down near the end of the race running first [Lorenzen] and second [Roberts], and when they stopped to pit the last time, it come to the point if you put right-side tires on, period, you took a chance on left-side. And I looked at the tires, and I gotta make the decision. If *I* were driving the car, what the hell would *I* do? Would I take a chance on the tires, or would I change 'em and run second and third? So I made the decision we change just the outside tires on both cars. While they was in there, I look at both of their left rears a couple of times, back and forth. So afterward, somebody from Ford said, 'What's the matter with the left-rear tires?' I told him, 'Nothing. They're still on there.' I didn't want to tell him anything was going on, that we're taking a chance that we're going to finish on these things.

"So first thing you know, here comes Holman over: 'Bring Lorenzen in and change the left-rear tire. Passino says bring him in.' And I says, 'You tell Jacque Passino to bite me in the foot. When it's all over, he can run it, but right now, I'm running it.' You don't take somebody that runs an office up there in Detroit and tell me what the hell I'm doing on the race car, not in the middle of a race."

At this point, according to Moody, Holman told Herb Nab, Lorenzen's mechanic, to motion in Lorenzen. Nab refused. Then Holman tried to wave in Lorenzen himself. Lorenzen ignored him, knowing that if he pitted and Roberts didn't, Roberts would win. Holman then tried to wave in Roberts. Fireball also declined the invitation.

Lorenzen, meanwhile, was peering through a trap door that allowed him to view the wear on his left-rear tire. He liked what he saw. "It was gonna be close," Lorenzen said, "but I thought for sure I could make it. I wouldn't come in unless Moody gave me a firm commitment. He didn't give it, and so I didn't come in."

"Right then's when we all got fired," said Moody. "They fired the whole damn bunch of us. I said, 'Good. We all quit.' Just threw all the stuff on down and everybody started walking out. They only had like ten laps to go, or something. And Holman said, 'Hey, you guys have got to load up.' And I said, 'We ain't got to load nothing. We all got fired.' And by the time the hassle's got all over, Lorenzen wins the race, and Fireball run second."

GENE WHITE, A RACING FRIEND OF FIREBALL'S, SAID, "It was his attitude that made him an exceptional race driver. I would have to say that he was probably one of the first with a genuinely overall professional way of thinking towards stock car racing on the big tracks as far as you've gotta perform 100 percent all the time. He was one of the first ones with that total thinking. Fireball would tell you himself that as far as a natural talent—born ability as far as being a race driver—he'd name you three or four people he thought had more than he did. Junior Johnson and Curtis Turner were the two prime ones as far as saying natural. But he'd also say, 'I'll guarantee you I'll do anything they do. They might do it in one or two laps and it takes me ten, but I'll do it. I just have to work harder at it.' "

When Roberts switched to a Ford from his beloved Smokey Yunick Pontiac in 1963, the earth moved—at least that part that concerned itself with Southern stock car racing.

Fireball said he got five hundred letters telling him he was a fool and five hundred more asking what took him so long.

His Holman-Moody Ford was painted light purple, so went the story, because lavender was Jacque Passino's favorite color. Doris Roberts, however, told a slightly different story. Passino, she said, had asked Glenn to drive for him at the beginning of the 1963 season, but Glenn had turned him down. In March, when it was obvious that the Pontiac era had run its course, Glenn flew to Ford headquarters in Dearborn and applied for work. According to Doris, Passino told her husband, "We will give you a car, and we will paint it purple because I want people to know you are on the race track."

"Passino wanted Glenn because he felt Glenn was the best," said Doris, "but he thought he had to bring Glenn down a notch or two."

Roberts won just two major races in that lavender Ford, but the second became his monument. Indeed, his winning race at Darlington in the 1963 Southern 500 was considered the most nearly perfect performance by a stock car driver in the history of the sport.

The week did not start well. Roberts missed the first day of qualifying and crashed early on the morning of the second. Late that same afternoon, however, Roberts qualified his hastily repaired car at a record speed.

The early leader was Junior Johnson in a Chevrolet. Roberts made only occasional forays to the front, choosing instead to wait for the inevitable sorting out process at the Darlington track, whose nature was such that a driver did not race on it so much to win as he did not to lose. But for the first time in the history of the Southern 500, there was not a single caution flag. The yellow light did flicker once, when Billy Wade and Bob James tangled on the 60th lap coming off turn two, but the accident was shielded from the view of race officials, and the field never slowed. The race was flat out and belly to the ground for the entire 500 miles. Roberts gained the lead for good with 24 laps remaining and took the checkered flag 25 seconds ahead of the second-place finisher, Marvin Panch. The race was exhausting, exhilarating, and nearly perfect, and it was Fireball's last win anywhere.

•

UP TO A POINT, THE AWESOME TENSIONS CREATED BY THE presence of the factories improved performance, but often they did not. "If you get a guy in a race car, and you've got the pressure on him to run up front to win," said Ralph Moody, "you ain't going to keep him in there anyway because he'll tear up more damned stuff than you can put him in."

Chuck Blanchard, the Goodyear field representative in the South, said, "This might be an oversimplification, but what happened with rides was sort of like what happens with a baseball manager or a football coach. Since there was an awful lot of money and energy and effort being put behind the cars, when your factory team was not doing too well, it was the easiest thing in the world to say it's got to be the driver. So . . . Change drivers. They were the easiest commodity to get rid of because there were always more drivers around than there were good cars."

Ned Jarrett, who won two Grand National driving championships, in 1961 and 1965, added, "I don't think the average fan would realize the amount of pressure that was involved. There was always somebody that was trying to get your job, and certainly you were aware of it, but it was never anything that really bothered *me* to the point that I lost sleep over it. If I lost the job, well, fine. I was out there doing my best, and that's all I figured anyone could expect."

Darel Dieringer was not as tolerant. "You had all those factory executives in the garage area or up in the grandstand with spyglasses seein' what you do wrong," he said. "And, of course, they don't know how to drive a race car. All they can do is tell you how, and that makes a heckuva difference. There's a lot of difference in settin' in that car and standing in the pits and saying, 'I wonder how come he didn't do this or didn't do that?' If you run second, you just as well run last because they won't even come around and shake your hand."

There were pressures on the corporate side, too. "You get so goddamned involved," Jacque Passino said. "At any given day at any given place, you've got your six drivers in the race, and you've got probably sixty pit people down there, all of whom are involved with some degree of danger, and you built up this tension by virtue of the fact that you've got the management back in Detroit—they're looking to you to go out and win for old State U.—and the pressure just keeps building and building and building to the point where, Christ, you damn near cry. And you'd walk down and talk to all these guys before the race started, on the one hand to calm them, and on the other hand to calm yourself. . . . You sure got cranked up on this goddamned thing after a while."

It all made for good theater, and except for the occasional pauses for rules disputes and tragedy, it also made for good racing. In the best years, under the best circumstances, there were a dozen cars, maybe fifteen, that had an honest chance to win a given race. And because the money flowed so freely and the technology advanced so rapidly, even the independents, those drivers not directly supported by the factories, could, with their secondhand parts, put on a respectable show. The national economy, so important to the health and well-being of the factories, tire companies, and accessory firms, was booming. Linda Vaughn, a former Miss Atlanta International Raceway beauty queen, was in the employ of the Pure Oil Company, and as Miss Firebird she rode astride a huge, flame-red Pegasus on the parade lap of every race, her blond hair flowing, her fine bosom bursting, and became the symbol of an era. The times were good, and it seemed they would never end.

THE NATURE OF AUTOMOBILE RACING DID NOT OFTEN allow a driver to be remembered only for his accomplishments. There were too many things that could go wrong. In 1962, Fireball Roberts told Lee Callaway of the *Nashville Banner:* "There are fifty places you can finish in a race . . . and you'll hit all of them sooner or later. In this game, you don't win thirty-seven straight fights. It just doesn't happen that way. There are no unbeaten seasons in auto racing." Even the best drivers lost, and lost spectacularly, much more than they ever won. And, of course, they occasionally lost more than just a race.

During an 18-month period that began in January of 1964, eight prominent American race drivers lost their lives: Eddie Sachs, Dave MacDonald, and Bobby Marshman from the United States Auto Club's Championship Car circuit, and Joe

Weatherly, Fireball Roberts, Billy Wade, Jimmy Pardue, and Larry Thomas (who was killed in a highway accident) from the Grand National late-model stock car circuit. Roberts was fatally injured on the seventh lap of the World 600 at the Charlotte Motor Speedway on May 24, 1964.

Jack Smith:

I could see what was coming. I had said three months before my contract runs out, next year will be the roughest year that's ever been in racing history. My wife says, "Why?" And I explained to her why, that everybody's going to be running on the ragged edges. If anybody understood racing . . . See, in 1963, we had Pontiac in the racing business, we had Chevrolet in the racing business, we had Ford, we had Chrysler. And then it was some young drivers come up. Good drivers. Good boys trying to get a start, trying to make a name for theirselves. And they would get a halfway decent sponsor from the factory, or they may get Joe Blow Construction Company to come along and furnish them a truck and mechanics and all. They was getting the parts, and they got all the tires, and the other people was paying the bills. So then it got down to where them two factories was telling you, "Well now, mister, we got to win this or Ford's going to pull out." Or, "If we don't win something, Chrysler's going to pull out." And they was putting the pressure to everybody: "We got to do this. We got to do that." This way, everybody was running on the ragged edges. Real ragged edges. Plus, the cars was going. . . . Chrysler Corporation was coming out with a new engine that was going to be pulling at least 140 horsepower more than the engine that they had before, and Ford. That means it's going to be greater speed. What happens? A tire blows. Boom. A man is gone.

Billy Wade. He's running tire tests. Blows a tire. Bam. Straight into the wall . . . Jim Pardue in Charlotte. Running a tire test. Blows a tire. Boom . . . Joe Weatherly. It was a freak, and he got killed at Riverside. It was a freak . . . Fireball. He gets involved and boom. The car blows up. Burns him.

Humpy Wheeler:

The 40-lap syndrome didn't have anything to do with laps on the superspeedway. Here's a man—let's say the average rookie, not really the star that's been on the superspeedways for a while—and for six or seven years before he ever gets on a superspeedway, his whole racing life is consumed in running 10-lap heat races and 40-lap features. In either one of them, you've got to go all out. You don't let up once. There's no such thing as pacing. Well, this builds itself into the man. His whole reflex system, his whole brain, is geared to running flat out for 40 laps to win the short-track race. You put him on a superspeedway, and it becomes an endurance race. Instead of 20 miles on the half-mile track, it's 500 miles, and it's awfully difficult for a race driver to get this out of his system, to untrain himself. He's all psyched up before a race—tremendously excited to the point of being disturbed—the green flag drops, and the crowd goes wild. This guy's tremendously competitive, and it's hard for him to sit back in fourth or fifth place. He wants to run out front, particularly in the early stages of the race. Which is very dangerous. All kinds of things can happen. The track is green, it's filled with cars, things fall off cars. . . .

Fred Lorenzen:

Everybody picked me to win the race because I was running probably the strongest there, but the minute they dropped the flag, I dropped to fifth, sixth, or seventh—way back. It was a big show in front, and I was just sitting back watching. But then it got rough, a little fender-banging. Everybody was battling like it was two laps to go on a short track. There's four or five cars in the pack, and when you're running that close together and somebody makes a mistake, they're gonna take all five cars out. And if they're gonna take all five cars out and I'm the next car coming, they're gonna block the track, and I will have nowhere to go. It looked like trouble brewing. So I thought, *I gotta get out of here.* I decided to go like fire, and in three laps I looked in my pits and they're giving me the signal to slow down. I just waved them off because I wanted to get by. I didn't want to lead it, but I had to, to get out of trouble. I think I passed them on the front straightaway, and then as I came off turn two, I saw a bunch of cars behind me get sideways. When I got on the front stretch again, I saw smoke and fire on the backstretch. And the caution came out. Then I knew there was trouble. That's when Fireball . . . He was in trouble.

Darel Dieringer:

There was myself, Ned Jarrett, Junior Johnson, and Fireball. The four of us were running out front, and we come off of number two and I was running, I think, third. And Fireball come off of two down underneath me, and by that time, Junior and Ned tangled in front of me—I think Junior was pulling out to pass Ned—and when they tangled, there wasn't nothing Fireball and I could do. They started spinning, and I just locked up my brakes and I found a hole and I went through it, and then I looked in the mirror and everything was fire behind me.

Ned Jarrett:

It started going into the first turn, but the cars didn't actually spin until we started off the second turn. Junior Johnson was trying to pass me, and knowing Junior and his style of driving, I knew he was going to lead to the front. And I was willing to let him because it was a 600-mile race, and I didn't care to think about being up there leading the race right then. So I moved over going into the first turn and gave him room to pass. He was passing me on the inside. There's a bump between the first and second turn at Charlotte, and either when he hit that bump, or the turbulence from all the cars running that close together, it caused him to momentarily lose control, just enough that he just hit my left-rear quarter-panel. I was on the outside when it started and he was on the inside, but we crossed over in the spinning, and I spun to the inside of the track and Junior spun to the outside of the track. Fireball was directly behind us, and in trying to maneuver around us, he lost control of his car. Now, probably someone hit him because the cars were jammed together right there, you know, running that close together. He spun to the inside of the track. My car hit the inside retaining wall and burst the gas tank—of course, that was before the days of fuel cells—and as I slid down the wall, it created sparks and set the car on fire. Fireball hit the wall also, and hit me. Now, whether the impact of hitting the wall burst his gas tank, or hitting me and the fire on my car caused his car to catch fire, I don't know. There was an opening in the wall about halfway down the straightaway—they've closed it in now—and his car hit in that opening and it flipped upside down. He hit the opening backwards, and that burst the firewall open and could have burst the gas tank. I don't know when it was burst. But anyway, we had forty-four gallons of gasoline all over that place.

Both cars were demolished. I got out of my car and ran over to his car. His was upside down, but he was in the process of coming out of the car. He was not injured. He was as alert as you and I are right now. The first words he said was, he said, "Oh, my God, Ned, help me. I'm on fire."

He was wearing one of those tight-fitting uniforms, and it's extremely hard to get off when you're in a hurry. He and I together just literally tore it off. It was just a matter of less than a minute, I'm sure, that the rescue people were there, and then they took over and helped to get the clothes the rest of the way off.

Jacque Passino was escorting Leo Beebe, his new corporate boss, to Beebe's first automobile race. "We're all down there, and the goddamned race started, and they had this fantastic wreck and everything," Passino said. "And really, Junior Johnson started the whole goddamned thing. Junior, in a Ford, and Ned Jarrett, in a Ford, and Roberts, in a Ford—all involved in the goddamned accident. And I'll tell you, it was some kind of a goddamned fire. Beebe was out of his mind, y'know? *What kind of a deal is this?* And honest to God, by this time, I had been racing for seven years and I had never seen a race fire in my life. I said, 'Hey, chief, this doesn't happen very often.' "

John Holman was in the pits. He said he didn't remember much about the accident, only that Fireball "was in trouble over there, and there wasn't anything I could do about it."

Doris Roberts:

I was in Daytona, alone, and Pam had gone down to the inlet with some friends. I didn't listen to the radio. A friend called, and she said, "Glenn has had an accident." And I said, "How bad?" And she said, "It was a fire and we don't know." And, of course, before Pam came home, she did learn about it, and she came running in, and she said, "When are we going to Charlotte?" All of this time I could not believe that Glenn was hurt badly, and I could not believe that he would not be all right. Maybe this was something that I had conditioned myself to always think: *It will be somebody else. It will never be you.* And then we did go to Charlotte that night. I went in to see Glenn as soon as I got there, and he was conscious. And, of course, what can you say except, "I'm here"? He said, "Have you brought Pam?" I said, "Yes." And that was about all that was said that night.

ROBERTS WAS FLOWN BY HELICOPTER TO CHARLOTTE Memorial Hospital. The first medical reports said he was "very, very critical," and a rumor quickly spread that he was not expected to live through the night. That evening, over four hundred people called the hospital to ask about his condition. The hospital issued medical bulletins three times daily. The response to a call for blood was immediate and overwhelming. One hundred and nineteen pints were donated in Charlotte, and another fifty were donated to the Halifax Hospital blood bank in Daytona Beach. In the first seventy-two hours, Roberts needed 123.

Roberts was attended by three doctors around the clock. On the fourth day, he was taken off the critical list, and on the fifth, he was removed from intensive care. Still, said one of the doctors, "Things could go sour in a hurry." Under heavy sedation, he drifted in and out of consciousness without warning. In midweek, he asked for news of the Indianapolis 500 and was told that the Memorial Day race was still several days off. After the race was run, and Eddie Sachs and Dave MacDonald were dead from their own fiery crash, the doctors decided against telling Roberts what had happened.

Fireball Roberts was a doomed man. He had suffered first-degree burns over 40 percent of his body and second- and third-degree burns over another 40 percent. His worst burns were on his back, arms, hands, and legs. Grafting would be essential if he were to have any chance at all, but the only usable skin was on his abdomen, and there just wasn't enough.

"I think we all knew it," said Doris Roberts, "even the doctors. But it was something you didn't admit, not even to yourself. One reason I would not let *my*-self think that was because of Pam. She kept asking me, 'Mother, will he be all right?' Well, how can I tell a 13-year-old, 'No, Pamela, he's going to die'? You don't do this."

Still, Doris remembered that her husband, covered with a blanket, didn't look all that bad. His face was relatively untouched. Doris said that it looked as though he had spent too much time in the sun. His feet were not burned at all. He had unusually fine and tapered toes, a fact Doris mentioned to him one day. "Flattery will get you nowhere," he said.

Fireball Roberts was in Charlotte Memorial for thirty-nine days. The fingers of one hand were amputated in early June. Had he lived, it is likely that a leg would also have been amputated.

DORIS ROBERTS:

One of the things I questioned was, "Why?" Why should he suffer for almost six weeks? This is a terrible thing to say, but why didn't God just take him? My mother said there's a reason for everything, and that possibly one reason was that God was waiting for Glenn to come to Him. And this may have been true. At least I . . . Something good had to come out of it, or I would see no reason for him to lie there in a hospital bed for that long.

Was there any indication that he found God? His mother would like to think so, and I hope that he did. I would hate to think that he died with the deep feeling that there was no God. But I don't think so. There were many times that Glenn said, "My God," in the hospital, but I don't think that it was from a religious point of view.

During his stay in the hospital, and feeling about religion the way he did, we did not allow a minister to go into the room because we were afraid that it would have some adverse effect on Glenn, that if he saw a minister, he might think that he would die, or think that *we* thought that he would die. No one was allowed to see him except the family.

On June 30, a Tuesday, Roberts developed a high fever. By the next morning, he had contracted septicemia—blood poisoning—and a mild case of pneumonia, and he lapsed into a coma.

Fireball Roberts died at 7:15 A.M. on July 2, 1964. He was 35 years old. That afternoon, Max Muhleman, a friend and a reporter, wrote in *The Charlotte News:* "Fireball Roberts, perhaps the most nearly perfect of all stock car drivers, is dead and it is like awaking to find a mountain suddenly gone."

THE FUNERAL WAS ON JULY 5 AT THE FIRST BAPTIST Church of Daytona Beach, the church of Fireball's parents. It was held one day after the running of the Firecracker 400 at Daytona Beach, the tickets for which were imprinted with a smiling photograph of the race's defending champion: Fireball Roberts. As the bronze casket was carried from the church by six Daytona Beach motorcycle police officers, all friends of Fireball's, one of the handful of Grand National drivers that had stayed over for the services stood apart from the others. Two days earlier—one day after Fireball died—Freddy Lorenzen, his Holman-Moody teammate, had guessed wrong when a car in front of him blew an engine during a qualifying race for the Firecracker. Lorenzen crashed viciously and was hospitalized with cut tendons in his left wrist. Now, as the soft Florida breezes played with his golden hair, Lorenzen raised his right arm in a silent, nearly unnoticed final tribute to his fallen comrade.

A nice story, but true?

"I can't remember a lot of it," Lorenzen said. "I just can't. . . . I wasn't supposed to go. . . . The doctor said I shouldn't go out of the hospital . . . but I went. . . . Snuck out. . . . And I don't remember much. . . . I remember never in my life seeing so many flowers. . . . That's about all I remember. . . . I didn't go to the cemetery. . . . I went back to the hospital."

Doris Roberts:

We decided there would be absolutely no tears. No one was to cry. No matter what else you did, you were not to cry. I told Pam before we went. I said, "This is asking a lot of you, but your father would want you to be strong, and he would want you to be brave. He would not want you to cry over him." And there was not one tear in the family.

YEARS LATER, DORIS ROBERTS STILL HAD TWO RECURRING dreams. In the first dream, she and Glenn were picnicking beneath a shade tree beside a placid lake. Glenn grabbed hold of a strong vine hanging from a limb, and like a boy at a swimming hole, swung far out over the water. When he returned to shore, he showed Doris his hands. "See," he said. "They weren't burned as badly as everyone thought they were."

In the second dream, Doris and Glenn were dining alone at a favorite restaurant, a hangout for drivers and their mechanics. The owner came to their table and made pleasant conversation with her but ignored Glenn entirely. Other friends did the same. Doris was very annoyed. Why, she wondered, were these people treating her husband as though he wasn't there, as though he didn't exist?

"Maybe," Doris said, "I have never buried him."

Jacque Passino:

> What I was looking for was a guy that was brave and who would run the car capably and for whom you had some degree of respect and who you felt was gonna do what you wanted him to do. In some cases, it was kind of a tragedy: Lee Roy Yarbrough, who raced for us later. I was at a testimonial dinner where the governor of South Carolina assigned him a special license plate and all this kind of stuff because he'd won so many things, and today I can't even tell you where Lee Roy Yarbrough is. He just kind of disappeared into the wilderness. We put him up where he deserved to be by virtue of what he did [Yarbrough won seven superspeedway races in 1969, a record at the time], but he didn't grab the brass ring and hang on. Whereas, some of these other guys—Lorenzen—they made it. Obviously, they aren't all Ph.D.'s and they haven't gone to the best schools, but they had a chance to do something through a God-given talent, and by virtue of being brave enough to exercise it, they took what we did for them and got what they wanted out of the thing.

THE WAY A DRIVER GOT A FACTORY RIDE WAS OFTEN rather cold-blooded. In 1963, Ford was looking around for a young driver to add to its stable, and Passino, who wasn't usually directly involved until late in the selection process, pushed hard for a driver from Timmonsville, S.C., whom he had been eyeballing for a couple years. His name was Cale

Yarborough, and he was sharp, jumpy, eager, brave, smart—a roly-poly Freddy Lorenzen—and he had a cute little wife named *Betty* Jo besides. At the same time, Passino's spies up North were touting a driver from Detroit named Benny Parsons, who ran all through the Midwest and, according to Passino's spies, was going to be the next Fireball Roberts. Not one to take sides, Passino set up a match race, of sorts. He arranged for both the unknowns to enter a Grand National race on the half-mile paved oval at Asheville-Weaverville, N.C., driving the finest equipment Ford had, and whoever did the best would be the next Ford star. One roll of the dice and either Cale Yarborough, a semiprofessional football player for the Sumter (S.C.) Generals, or Benny Parsons, a taxi driver from Detroit, would be in and the other would be out.

When the green flag dropped, as Passino remembered, Parsons never made Red Gap. "This is not totally out of disrespect for Benny," he said. "Neither one of them did very well. It's just that he wasn't as slick as Cale. It was obvious that Cale was a helluva lot better driver than Benny that day. And that's when we picked up Cale. Benny never really did make the team."

"I think I led the race for a while and finally went out with a bad radiator," said Yarborough. "But I ran good, ran up front, ran strong. And Benny had some problems. And so when it was all over, they said I had the job.

"It was a little bit cruel, wadn't it, to bring two people down and say, 'All right. One of you is going to be on the Ford Motor Company racing team.' . . . I don't know. If I had lost, it would have been cruel as hell, I'll tell you that. I don't know whether I'd be in the racing business now or not. I might be driving a tractor on a farm in South Carolina."

Because Ford wouldn't have given him a second chance?

"They didn't give Benny one."

Although it took five years for Yarborough to make his breakthrough and begin winning races consistently, and although Parsons won a Grand National driving championship in 1973 and the Daytona 500 two years after that, it was Yarborough and not Parsons who became a star and who, along with Richard Petty, David Pearson, Bobby Allison, and Buddy

Baker, dominated Grand National racing throughout the 1970s. All because of what had happened many years earlier on the half-mile paved track at Asheville-Weaverville.

GENTLEMAN NED JARRETT, A FORD FACTORY DRIVER WHO was raised on a farm in the northwestern corner of Catawba County, N.C., Thomas Wolfe country, understood his strengths and limitations with rare objectivity. He realized from the beginning that whatever success he might have would not come in the flashy, prestigious superspeedway races, but from his ability to plug along day after day and week after week on the short tracks, which, despite the superspeedways, continued to make up the bulk of the Grand National schedule throughout the 1960s.

"I was not, and am not, a speed demon," Jarrett said. "I liked competition, but I wanted the car to feel comfortable, and if it didn't, I'd slow it down enough to where it did. I didn't try to be a hero. I knew for a fact that there were plenty of people who were as physically as capable as I, and maybe some more so, of turning that steering wheel and getting that car around the race track. And really, I was not sent out there to concentrate that heavily on the superspeedway races. Of course, Ford wanted me to run good on superspeedways, and they wanted me to win as many as I could, but as long as I won my share of the short-track races, I could keep a deal with them. Where if some of the other drivers . . . If Lorenzen had not won more superspeedway races than *I* did, I don't think he would have kept his job, because that's what he was sent out there to do.

"On a big track in particular, I was not as aggressive as some drivers in wanting to stick my nose in a hole somewhere just because there was an opening. I'd evaluate the thing. Because once you've committed yourself, sometimes it's hard to get out of. I really believe that I looked farther ahead than the average driver. I developed a habit of looking as far around a turn as I could while I was still on the straightaway, and it saved me many times. You see a lot of drivers, you know, that go on in, and you wonder: *Well, golly. They were over* here, *and the crash happened over* there, *and they ran into it. Why couldn't they get stopped?* Well, maybe they weren't looking far enough ahead. I think that for a given period of time, like 1960 through 1965, that I had the lowest ratio of accidents of any of the drivers that was running most of the races."

Jarrett's forte, like that of the generation of drivers before him, was dirt-track racing—that, and using his head. "I would much rather win a race by outthinking or outsmarting someone than by just physically outdriving them," he said. "It meant more to me. I remember a race at Valdosta, Georgia, that I was getting beat very badly. Jack Smith was in the race, and Joe Weatherly and Lee Petty, and they were just running away from me. As a matter of fact, they lapped me, and that was pretty unusual on dirt. I was having a heckuva time getting around the turns. The groove in the track was down low, and I just couldn't get around there. So the very first lap after they lapped me, I went into the first turn a little bit hard and I got into the loose stuff. But the thing dug in and it got a bite for me, and I came off that turn and went right up on their bumper. We hadn't run but 50 or 60 laps of a 200-lap race, so then I went to work building me a groove. It took me about 30 or 40 laps to get myself a groove worked to where I could run the outside tires. This was about two feet wide, and you had to be very careful not to get out of it, but if you stayed in there and got those right-side tires on that . . . Now, I could go. I caught 'em and blew 'em off on the outside. Came around, unlapped myself, and passed 'em, and won the race with no problems whatsoever. Being able to detect what it would take, right then, and then do it. . . . That was a real challenge to be able to do those kinds of things."

IN 1965, GENTLEMAN NED DID IT ALL. HE WON HIS SECOND Grand National driving championship, and he won the one race that he felt would make his career complete, the Southern 500. The parlay did not come easily.

The season began splendidly. Jarrett's dirt-track car was the best he'd ever driven, and by June he and Dick Hutcherson, another Ford driver, were well ahead of the field in the race for the driving title. But at a Saturday night race in Greenville, S.C., Jarrett's well-ordered world began to crumble.

Around the 60th lap, with Jarrett leading, the caution flag slowed the field, and Jarrett came into his pits to take on gas and change tires. Jarrett led on the restart and jammed his car into fourth gear as the closely bunched pack roared down on the start-finish line to again take the green flag. Suddenly, his engine died. He tried to pull to the inside, but Little Bud Moore (so named to distinguish him from Big Bud Moore, a Grand National car owner) had already committed himself to that line and hit Jarrett just hard enough to knock him back into the middle of the track. The field piled in on him. One car flew over him; another hit him a ton in the rear just as he slammed the outer guard rail. The twin impacts demolished his car with such finality that his driving seat was torn loose. Jarrett was taken to the hospital with a searing back pain, and he was convinced that he had, in fact, broken his back. If that were true, he promised his wife, he would retire.

Jarrett's back wasn't broken, but it might as well have been. Two vertebrae were compressed, and most of his lower back muscles were ripped. The doctor told him that he would be fine, after two or three weeks in the hospital and three months or so of therapy at home. Jarrett explained that he had a Grand National race to run the following Thursday night. The doctor said that would be physically impossible. But after four days of intense, doubled-up therapy, Jarrett did race five nights later, wearing a plastic brace that extended from his buttocks to his chest. He wore the brace for the next three months and remained at the top of the points standings.

Jarrett had a premonition about the Labor Day Southern 500. A deeply religious man, as were his fundamentalist Christian parents, Jarrett spoke to a Methodist Youth Fellowship group the night before the race and asked the kids for their prayers. "Not that I or any other particular driver might win it," Jarrett said, "but I went away from there with a genuine feeling that those kids were behind me, that they would say a prayer for me. It made me feel good."

On the way to the track on race day, Jarrett told his family of his strange confidence, which seemed misplaced considering that he had been trying to win at Darlington since 1953 and, in fact, had won just one superspeedway race in his career. And, Jarrett added, wouldn't it also be great if Hutcherson, whom he was still fighting for the championship, just happened to fall out early? Not to wish Hutch any bad luck, of course, but a victory coupled with an early retirement by Hutcherson would certainly give him breathing room.

Jarrett's second wish came true when Hutcherson retired with mechanical problems after barely 100 miles. Jarrett stayed among the race leaders for 300 miles, but then his car began to overheat, and he had to slacken his pace. Freddy Lorenzen in a Ford and Darel Dieringer in a Mercury moved to the front as the race neared its end, and Jarrett fell to third, a full lap behind. He had resigned himself to that position when he drove down the main straightaway and saw Lorenzen's car in the pits with its hood up. Lorenzen was out with a blown gasket. On the next lap, Jarrett saw Dieringer in the pits, the rear end of his car on fire. Jarrett had gone from a hopeless third to a comfortable first in the space of two laps, and went on to win by the definitive margin of 14 laps, his being the only factory car left on the track.

With two championships and one Southern 500 to his credit, Ned Jarrett retired. "I always vowed to myself that however far up the ladder I got, I was never going back down the other side," he said. "I set certain goals for myself. Maybe I didn't set the goals high enough, but I accomplished what I set out to do."

DAREL DIERINGER WAS PARTICULARLY AFFECTED BY THE deaths of Billy Wade and Jimmy Pardue. Both men were killed testing for Goodyear during a time when Goodyear was developing a race tire with a safety shield, a tire within a tire that in theory would prevent a sudden loss of control in the event of a high-speed blowout, and Dieringer was part of the same test program. In part, the testing required that the drivers intentionally blow out a tire by running over a sharp object at very high speeds. In one such test at Daytona, Dieringer crashed violently, breaking a collarbone and most of his ribs. A week later, Billy Wade also crashed. The only difference in the two accidents was that Wade was killed.

Dieringer: I started off at 50 mile an hour. I wouldn't be afraid to blow *any* tire at 50 mile an hour, but when you started getting up to 100 mile an hour, then 120—each time, I went up about five miles per hour—it'll make your pucker string get pretty tight. The Daytona deal . . . it throwed me for a long time. I crashed one week, and Billy came down to finish the test that I had crashed in, and we lost him.

Question: This was when you were both cutting tires intentionally?

Dieringer: I was, but he wasn't. We really to this day don't know what happened. Even the firemen that was on the race track didn't hear nothing until he hit the wall. We didn't hear no tire blow. We didn't hear anything.

Question: The engine didn't . . . ?

Dieringer: No. He just damned near went straight into the wall. But his accident was almost . . . Car for car, when we brought 'em back to the shop, you couldn't tell one damage from the other. But just the way he hit, and possibly that his safety belts maybe weren't as tight as mine . . . there had to be something. The Good Lord looked after me, and the Good Lord just said it was Billy's time. I really don't know how to explain it.

Question: It must be a strange feeling, knowing you're intentionally blowing tires.

Dieringer: It's something that you got paid good for. But at the same time, after you lose a driver, you felt like you didn't get paid enough.

Question: What did you get paid?

Dieringer: Well, that isn't to be discussed. I mean, I just don't discuss it.

Question: I assume that you got paid more than the usual testing fee.

Dieringer: Oh, yes. They had it set so much a lap regardless of what. If you was even warming the car up, you got paid because it was very strenuous and nervous.

Question: Was it at all similar to actually racing?

Dieringer: No, because in racing, you don't know when it's going to happen.

. The roll cage of Richard Petty's 1970 Plymouth. After every race ıe car is taken apart and nearly all of its moving pieces are checked ɔr damage and wear. The car is then reassembled, with gear ratios, ıspension settings, and other variables adjusted to the haracteristics of the next track the car will run on.

3

2. *Left, top:* The roll bars and fire extinguisher in Buddy Baker's 1967 Dodge Charger. In the early days of the sport, fire was a major cause of fatalities.

3. *Left, bottom:* Benny Parsons wearing an improvised neck brace just after escaping from a wrecked car.

4. *Below:* An oil fire in Baker's No. 6 Dodge. Talladega, 1971.

5. Eddie Pagan tearing up the guard rail at Darlington, 1958.

6. Richard Brooks being helped from what remains of his car in the same race in which Tiny Lund was killed.

7. Johnny Allen in a rollover.

8. *Right:* Victory Circle at the July Fourth Firecracker 400 run at Daytona Beach, Florida. The 1976 winner, Cale Yarborough, with his wife, Betty Jo, to his left, and one of his young daughters.

9. *Below:* Lee Roy Yarborough with trophy in hand after winning the '69 Southern 500 at Darlington. His Ford shows the famous Darlington Stripes as well as the scars of a run-in with Bobby Allison.

10. Darlington raceway. Inaugurated on Labor Day in 1950 with a 500-mile race won by Johnny Mantz, a Californian driving a Hudson Hornet for six and a half hours at an average speed of 76 mph. Seventy-five cars started the race and 25 finished. The local investors who built the track expected about 5,000 people but five times that number showed up.

11. Cale Yarborough and Donnie Allison collide in the third turn of the last lap of the '79 Daytona 500 while 26 million people watch this breathtaking finale on television.

12. One of the most dramatic finishes ever was the 1976 Daytona 500 in which Richard Petty, driving No. 43, and David Pearson, in No. 21, slid and crashed into the outside wall as they came off the fourth turn of the very *last* lap. Pearson crawled across the finish line to win, while Petty's car sat fifty feet from the flag.

GOODYEAR
CHAMPION

Baker
union 76
CHAMPION

13. *Opposite, top:* "King" Richard Petty waits for his qualifying run. A blanket is draped across his windshield to keep out the heat. The webbed screen, when lowered and locked in place, will help keep him inside if the car rolls. The undisputed champ, Petty won an even 200 races in a 35-year career that began in 1958.

14. *Opposite, bottom left:* David Pearson, "The Gray Fox," from Spartanburg, South Carolina. He was the second stock car driver to win one million dollars in prize money.

15. *Opposite, bottom right:* Buddy Baker smokes three packs a day, chews an unknown quantity of gum, and takes Tylenol during his pit stops, all perfectly normal for someone who works in a hostile environment at speeds up to 200 mph.

16. *Below, left:* Bobby Allison: "Second through last is losing."

17. *Below, right:* 1980 Grand National Champ Dale Earnhardt: "You can't think about *what* to do, you got to *know* what to do. By the time you think about what to do, it's done happened."

18. *Right:* During his long career Curtis Turner (here in the late 1940s) won 357 races. Many think he was the best ever. The son of one of the biggest moonshiners in the Blue Ridge Mountains, he first ran white lightning at the age of 10. By 18 he had saved enough money to buy 3 sawmills. His nickname, Pops, was due to his liking to "pop" the doors of other racers.

19. *Bottom:* The old beach course at Daytona.

20. *Below:* Coming through the north turn, they're about to leave the beach and go out onto Highway A1A.

21. A typical dirt track of the early days.

22. Racing convertibles became popular in the '50s. Here Curtis Turner (No. 26) and Joe Weatherly (No. 12) vie on the north turn at Daytona in the 1957 classic.

23. William Henry Getty France, better known as Big Bill, the founder of NASCAR, seen here monitoring one of the first races he promoted at Daytona, circa 1948.

24. Edward Glenn Roberts, Jr., circa 1955. Oddly enough, his famous nickname—Fireball—was given to him as a teenager because of his great pitching arm.

25. Fireball leads the pack at a dirt track, circa 1955–56.

26. Fireball Roberts at age 19 in his first race at Daytona, 1948.

27. Fireball and his fiancée, Doris McConnell (July 1950).

28. The top three finishers of the first Darlington 500 run in 1950. Left is Fireball Roberts, who finished second; then Red Byron, who ran third; and winner Johnny Mantz.

29. Fonty Flock and his brother Tim with their mother, Maudie, and the beginnings of their famous scrapbooks.

30. Fonty, Tim, and Bob Flock, circa 1950.

31. Fonty defied the common track superstition about peanuts and the color green by painting his car green, outfitting his crew in green uniforms, and scattering peanut shells all over the floor of his racer. He didn't win a race for six months.

32. After he won the Southern 500 in 1952, wearing "Bamooda" shorts, Fonty often wore them afterward.

33. *Left:* Tim Flock tried to wear the same shirt to every race for luck.

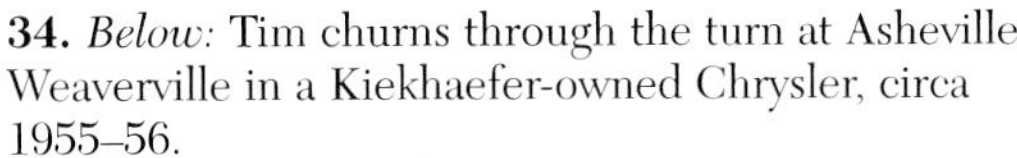

34. *Below:* Tim churns through the turn at Asheville-Weaverville in a Kiekhaefer-owned Chrysler, circa 1955–56.

35. In the '50s, millionaire Carl Kiekhaefer fielded a team of white Chryslers. While most drivers readily socialized, Kiekhaefer's teams were segregated from their wives and awakened at five A.M. with a bugle call. Here he is shown with Tim Flock after his second championship. Flock quit a few months later, unwilling to endure the stern rules.

36. Junior Johnson of North Wilkesboro (circa 1964), whose well-deserved fame was enhanced by a Tom Wolfe piece in *Esquire*. Caught at the family still, he had once served time in the federal penitentiary at Chillicothe, Ohio.

37. Smokey Yunick, chief mechanic for Fireball Roberts, Curtis Turner, and others. Track inspectors examined his cars like customs agents, trying to find the ingenious ways in which Yunick illegally improved his racers' chances. His were not the usual crude tricks like filling the tires with water to make the car meet weight requirements. After one particularly grueling inspection during which even the gas tank had been drained to check its capacity, Smokey was informed of an even dozen items the official wanted rectified. "Make it thirteen," Yunick replied and drove off in the car with the bone-dry gas tank.

38. *Top:* Fireball Roberts (*right*) after winning the 1959 Rebel 300 at Darlington.

39. *Top:* Fireball after winning the 1958 Southern 500 at Darlington. Between February 1959 and March 1963 he would win five superspeedway races and qualify as the fastest in fifteen. No other driver was able to qualify as the fastest more than three times. His win at Darlington in 1963's Southern 500 was considered the most nearly perfect performance in the history of the sport.

40. Roberts was fatally injured on the seventh lap of the World 600 at Charlotte Motor Speedway on May 24, 1964. He died at 7:15 A.M. on July 2. He was 35. Max Muhleman wrote in the *Charlotte News:* "It is like awaking to find a mountain suddenly gone." Fireball's car is engulfed in flames at the right. Ned Jarrett, who was also involved in the accident, is seen emerging from his racer at the left.

41. "Little Joe" Weatherly at Darlington.

42. Being interviewed by Bob Montgomery after winning. On January 21, 1964, Joe Weatherly was killed on the road course at Riverside, California. Superstitious about the number 13, he had arrived on flight 13, qualified 13th, and crashed on the leader's 113th lap. Thirteen dollars were found in his wallet.

43. Curtis "Pops" Turner—charming, outrageous, and the best, circa 1965.

44. Joe Lee Johnson (*left*) receives his trophy after winning the first race ever at the Charlotte Motor Speedway, the 1960 World 600. In the center is Bruton Smith and at right is Curtis Turner. Smith and Turner built the track, then were ousted from control by an unhappy board of directors.

45. Curtis Turner after winning the American 500 in 1965 at the North Carolina Motor Speedway at Rockingham. This was his comeback win after four years' suspension by NASCAR.

46. Freddy Lorenzen after his first major race, in which he beat Curtis Turner to the flag in the 1961 Rebel 300.

47. A. J. Foyt (No. 41), Freddy Lorenzen (No. 28), and Dick Hutcherson race three abreast for almost nine laps near the end of the 1965 National 400 at Charlotte. Lorenzen won what has become known as the best race ever.

48. Freddy Lorenzen, the driver from Elmhurst, Illinois, who changed stock car racing as no other driver before him. He was the first star driver who had not learned on dirt and one of the few stars who was not a southerner.

49. John Holman (*left*) with Jacque Passino, who ran the Ford factory racing effort from corporate headquarters in Dearborn. The Big Three automobile manufacturers—General Motors, Ford, and Chrysler—channeled huge financial and technical resources into racing.

50. Holman (*left*) with his driver, and later his partner, Ralph Moody, circa 1956.

51. Richard Petty with Miss Universe after winning the 1964 Daytona 500, the first major victory of his career.

52. Lee Petty with young Richard Petty, circa 1955.

3. Richard Petty with his only son, Kyle, circa 1967.

4. Lee Petty (*left*) helping service son Richard's car at a dirt track ace shortly after his retirement, 1961.

55. Petty cools down. In a 1973 test during a race the air temperature was measured at 90°F and the temperature inside the cars measured 130°F. Petty's weight dropped from 192 pounds at the beginning of the race to 181 pounds at the end.

56. Richard Petty, car owner Big Bud Moore, Buddy Baker, and Donnie Allison, 1975.

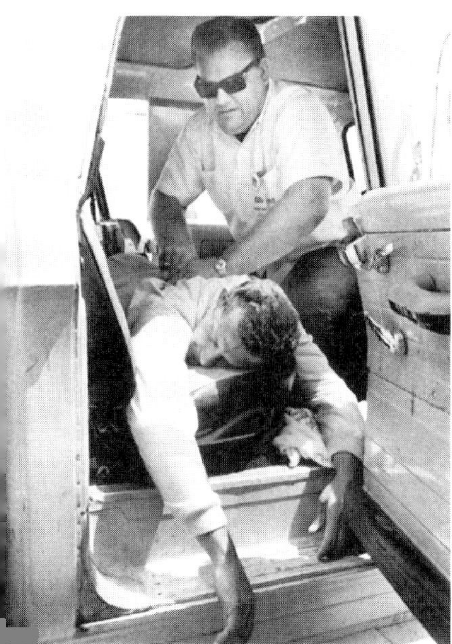

57. Getting a rubdown before a race.

58. Petty always sucks on a rag during a race to keep his mouth from drying out. In more than twenty years of driving he has finished in the top five nearly five hundred times and taken home nearly four million dollars in prize money.

59. Getting a drink from his father during practice, circa 1965.

60. After a long, hot afternoon of racing, it's not unusual for a driver to take oxygen to try to alleviate the heat and stress. On the average, heart rates double during a race.

61. Maurice Petty, Richard's brother and engine builder, prepares for a pit stop, holding a wire strung with lug nuts between his teeth.

62. Kyle Petty as he waits to get into a Grand National car of his own, which he did four years later in 1979.

63. Tiny Lund at his fishing camp. At Daytona Beach in 1963 Tiny Lund helped save a driver from a fiery wreck. The hospitalized driver asked that his car in the upcoming Daytona 500 be given to Lund to drive, and Tiny won his first Grand National race.

64. Tiny Lund after winning the Tri-State 200, with his wife, Wanda (*left*); his sister, Vi; and Roger Byers, his chief mechanic.

5. Tiny Lund, winner of the short-track Bulldog 400, Jefco, 1969.

6. A jam-up involving Tiny Lund and others at Lakewood, the ne-mile dirt track in Atlanta, circa 1959.

67. Everything mechanical is on the ragged edge, that fine line between maximum performance and disaster.

"I feel like I did *some*thing for racing by helping come up with that," Dieringer said, "because it's saved many an automobile and many a boy from being hurt, especially on the major race tracks. I would say that if you told the boys they had to run on tires like we used to run, that you'd have a heckuva time pouring about ten or twelve of those drivers in their cars. They'd just say, 'Forget it.' I'd be one of them."

DIERINGER WAS A WILLING CHARGER ON THE BIG TRACKS. This put him in perfect harmony with his Detroit bosses, but only to a point.

"I liked to run up front because if you run back in the pack, the only time you're going to get mentioned is when something happens in an accident," he said. "My theory of racing is, the public's got to know you're there. If you're not there, you're not doing the promoter any good, and you're definitely not doing yourself any good. The attitude was, 'Go or blow.' I mean, when you go out, you'd better go out up front. Don't fall out of the race running tenth. There's only one going to be leading, but they wanted you up there fender-banging and running to win. If you went out of the race leading—blew or crashed—they didn't think near as bad about you. But it's a helluva lot harder to lead than it is running second. You can run second and pick your nose. If you make a mistake, what the heck? You're still running second. But boy, if you're in the lead and have two or three guys hounding you and make a mistake, a guy could get around you. It's awful hard to do. The prestige of leading is great, but a lot of times it'll cost you a lot of races."

In 1966, Dieringer won the Southern 500 much the way Jarrett had the year before. Richard Petty, the leader for most of the afternoon, blew an engine with only ten laps to go, and Dieringer was home free.

"That last ten laps was the hardest laps of all," he said. "You can just hear everything going wrong with that car. You imagine you hear, or feel, vibrations, and you're looking at all your gauges and you *know* they're not like they're supposed to be. You know you've got the race won if you can just get through the next few laps—there's nobody even close to beating you—but still . . . It's a pressure deal that's hard to explain."

The race was the first, and only, big-track win of Dieringer's career. While a driver like Jarrett could keep a factory deal without winning on the big tracks, a driver like Dieringer couldn't, and one year later he was fired. His dismissal left him both bitter and philosophic.

"They said I wasn't pushing the button," Dieringer said. "We started about eighteen races that year—1967—and the car only finished four. We won one. We started on the pole at Wilkesboro and led every lap. We went from there to the next race track, and we started on the pole again. And what happened, during the parade lap, we run over something. The right-front tire went flat going into number one, and I crashed. And the next day I was fired. Because I wasn't pushing the button.

"I got the message over the telephone from the party I was driving for. He said, 'Well, I'm sorry to tell you, but you won't be driving.' He felt hard about doing it because he didn't feel like it was his place. He got orders from somebody in *Dee*-troit. It was just like anything else. They had somebody else in mind they wanted to put in the car.

"But that is water over the dam. I accepted it, and I went and got another ride. I drove for Cotton Owens. We started in Charlotte and qualified about sixth, and we took over the lead and we led till we blowed. We led until something happened to the car. So, I mean, I wasn't pushing the button there?"

LITTLE BUD MOORE WAS ONE OF THE BEST SHORT-TRACK drivers in the Carolinas. He won Sportsman race after Sportsman race in spectacular fashion, breaking his leg three times along the way. No matter. His future seemed limitless. "I don't know of anybody that was ever more aggressive than I was in a dirt race car," he said. "I always ran harder, I think, than anybody I raced with."

When the time came, however, Little Bud was not able to grab the brass ring. Beginning in 1965, he was an irregular regular on the Grand National circuit for eight years and never won a race. There were several reasons for his failure. He wore glasses, horn-rimmed glasses, and when he had the accidents that any young driver was bound to have, there was always the suggestion that Little Bud was "blind." He wore his hair long, which in the 1960s was not the thing to do in the eyes of the conservative and image-conscious racing establishment. He was from Charleston, which as any South Carolinian would tell you, was not really a part of South Carolina, let alone the South. More substantially, Little Bud had an acute understanding of his limitations as a driver and a unique willingness to accept them.

Moore: During the latter part of the 1960s, there was a lot of money in racing. Firestone was in racing at that time, and some of their people had watched me run a lot of short-track races and encouraged me to move to Charlotte. So I moved there—this was in 1967—and got the A. J. King car out of Tennessee, which was a '67 Dodge Charger. The car wadn't anything super—it wadn't a factory car—but it was right respectable, and the first couple of races I ran the car in, I finished real well. I ran fifth at Atlanta and fifth at Darlington and fifth, sixth—something like that—at Rockingham, and I looked real promising. In fact, the Dodge people gave us a factory deal for the next year. I was one of the few people that ever picked up a factory deal that quick. So I spent the first half of 1968 with a new factory car, but any time you step up to an operation where you've gotta produce, which we all felt like we had to do, there's a difference.

Question: The difference between running for fifth place and starting a race knowing you're expected to try to win it?

Moore: Right, right. The best way I know how to relate to you something like that is . . . I guess you can imagine the type of pressure a pro football player must go through knowing there's a guy standing in line for his job. This is pretty much the same situation in a race car. Man, I've never heard it said a lot, and I don't even think the news media people understand the amount of pressure that a person goes through in a race car. I don't think anybody understands, other than the man in the car.

In order to put a win together on a superspeedway, it

takes many things coming from many different places. I'd been around racing a long time, and I'd already run these couple of fifths and sixths, or whatever it was, but when this factory deal was offered to us, I told our people, "Look, don't think this is gonna mean we're gonna be heroes overnight. It's not. What you're gonna find is when we start putting this extra pressure on ourselves and I start punishing this car more, we're gonna have trouble. Things are gonna start happening that you didn't even know was gonna happen before." Because I drove the car to those fifth-place finishes using all the judgment and all the savvy that a man could use in order to make that car finish the race. There was times when I wanted to run a little harder, but I knew the kind of equipment we had, I knew the personnel we had, and I knew what that car would do. That car was a fifth-place car, and that's what it run. It run fifth place.

When this operation come along and these factory people got behind you, then things did change. Sure, the factories gave you some money and some equipment and all, but that was nothing compared to what had to be done on your part, on your sponsor's part, and it just created the situation where after a couple of races . . . To give you some idea of what I'm talking about, and to show you how unfair it might be, although I'm not criticizing the thing because I truly respect everybody in racing and I know how any kind of professional sport's got to be handled, we lost three engines prior to the '68 Daytona 500, and then we developed trouble right at the beginning of the race and fell out. And at Rockingham, and somewhere else I don't remember. The first three races of the year, it blew. All right. Atlanta was the next race. We went to Atlanta. And one of the factory people come to my people and told our chief mechanic that they thought it was time I stood on the car. Here was a case where the car blew up in every event we'd entered, and blew up early in the race, too, and here was a guy saying that he thought it was time for me to stand on the car.

The thing really disgusted me. I went to my people, and I said, "If you don't think I'm pushing the button, stick somebody else in it." I meant that, too. They said, "No. We know what's happening. You just go ahead and do what you gotta do." I said, "The car, from here on, it's gonna get raced. If it falls in the street, then it just falls in the street."

Question: What happened to you in the car when you started running to win?

Moore: I just became more aggressive, that's all. I took chances with the car. Dodge had a lot of pictures of Buddy Baker and myself running completely sideways in the World 600 at Charlotte. I remember people like Charlie Glotzbach said I scared him when I passed him. Now, coming from Glotzbach . . . I mean, Glotzbach scares me to look at him in the pit area. But that's what had to be done. That's what it took to lead the race. So this goes back to what I was trying to tell you—even sports writers and people that see racing week to week don't realize what goes on. I don't think they really understand what that guy's going through.

It didn't pay as good to lead the race and fall out as it did to run fifth, but in all honesty, I felt better about it from the standpoint that I was getting competitive. I was beginning to race with the people that I really wanted to race with. I look up on the scoreboard and I see number 1, my car number, in the number one position, and I felt good about it. So I drove the hell out of the car. I drove just the way I wanted to.

But there's a difference in superspeedway racing and other types of racing, and that is, the superspeedway racing will catch up with you. You can't keep doing that over and over and over. It'll catch you. I never felt like I knew what the car was gonna do from one minute to the next. My people just hadn't been doing that kind of racing long enough.

Question: Why weren't you turned on by the superspeedways?

Moore: Well, to be real honest with you—and, like, in all honesty, things that I never said to anyone else—man, like, they scared me. I'd been around racing to the point where I knew the kind of operation it took to be successful and to keep from getting hurt. I really was an aggressive type of person in short-track racing, and I got hurt a lot doing it, too. When I'd make some kind of a mistake, I'd make a good one. I've been in and out of hospitals all over this part of the country: Georgia, Florida, Virginia, North Carolina . . . I mean, that's nothing to brag about, that's just telling you like it is. And I really wanted to take care of myself.

The first superspeedway I went to was Darlington in '64, the Southern 500, and I was just a kid. I was running Sportsman cars three nights a week and I went to Darlington, which at that time was the hardest race track in the United States to get around. Old, single-lane Darlington. I'd just spent the weekend in the Myrtle Beach hospital when a accelerator hung up and run me off the race track, and I went to Darlington and started the race scared to death, man, I got to tell you.

Question: What scared you?

Moore: Just never having run that type of race track, and then running that fast, too, and being in a whole new environment. I was racing people that I'd been looking at since I was a kid.

Anyway, we qualified the car and the brakes were pulling to the left, and I kept telling the guy that owned it, "This needs to be fixed, man." But the fact that I'd never drove those speedways . . . They were just bypassing what I'd said.

I'll never forget the drivers' meeting. Johnny Brunner, Sr., the starter, said, "Now, we want everybody to be careful. We got a lot of factory cars. I know the way all of you feel. You want to win the race. But it can't be done on the first lap." I thought to myself, *These guys are mature enough that they're not gonna act like the people I've been running Sportsman cars with.* And look here, man, they dropped the green flag, and the first thing that happened, we went down into the first corner and Darel Dieringer did a number—spun—and all those cars making those moves? It was just like you was on a half-mile dirt.

I ran the first 50 laps of that race with my helmet unbuckled, I was so nervous, and when the strap started hitting me on the side of my face, I didn't want to believe what I felt: *God knows, this helmet's not even fastened.* I kept trying to get it fastened, and I couldn't, and I finally just had to drop down low one time to fasten the helmet. It was a good thing I did, too, because later on, I had my wreck with Junior.

Junior Johnson and some of them had spun off the second corner, and G. C. Spencer and myself had just gone under the caution light in the first turn before it come on, and we didn't have any way of knowing anything was going on. When we came off the corner, these cars were sitting in the middle of the race track, and we were still running flat out. Spencer reached up and grabbed the brake pedal, and I popped him in the back bumper and then reached up and put on my brakes. And my car, naturally, jerked to the left, just like it had been doing all along. And I mean to tell you, I hit Junior Johnson's car square in the back end. I pushed the bumper and the gas tank and all right up into Junior Johnson's seat. Later, I seen movies of the race, and my car hit so hard the whole car jumped off the ground, and my shoulder straps stretched so far that my head hit the windshield. And that meant another trip to the hospital to be checked out.

We did run good while we was in the race, exceptionally good for the type of car we had, but this took away from me. Everybody said, "That guy can't see anyway. You seen them glasses he wears?" And from that point on, everybody said I was blind.

Question: Are you sorry, or bitter, that you never really got your chance in the super ride?

Moore: No, not bitter at all. I'm not mad about it because I really deep down believe that if a man wants to do something bad enough, he'll do it. I overcame some things in racing that were just unbelievable to do what I really wanted to do. See, to start with, I never liked to work on the race car. I've done a lot of it, especially Sportsman cars, but I've watched people work and slave and do things that I wouldn't do, wasn't willing to do, and I guess that's the difference. I wasn't willing to sacrifice what some of them were. On a superspeedway, I never felt like the car I was in could be trusted or could win the race. I knew I was whipped before I started, and that's a bad way to be. I didn't have anything in common with a lot of the people that were in racing. I didn't spend a lot of time around them. They were so much different from myself. I used to go to the race track, and the inspectors and all would get down on me about my hair length, y'know, and just all kinds of things. And I think to be successful in anything, you've got to be a part of it. I didn't win any 500-mile races and I'm sorry I didn't, but that's just how it turned out. All those ifs doesn't make any difference.

I always made a deal with myself that if I ever got to the point where I wouldn't push the button as hard as I thought I ought to, then I'd get out of a race car. And, you see, this is something I couldn't do on a superspeedway. This was really baffling and discouraging, but I had enough sense to know that it was a good way to get killed. You follow what I'm trying to tell you?

Question: Have you talked with other drivers about the things you're talking about now?

Moore: Buddy Baker and Cale Yarborough and these people that I am close friends with, they understand how you feel whenever you know you don't have the equipment under you to do what you want to do. You don't just go charging off six car lengths more in the corner when it doesn't make any difference. What good is it to take the chance? That's what was so discouraging. Don't get me wrong. If six more car lengths would have made the difference of me leading the race, I would of went the six car lengths because that's what would have been important. And that's what you were getting paid to do, too. Anything less than that, you wouldn't have been doing yourself right because that's what you were doing for a living. That's what you were supposed to do.

"EVERYBODY IN STOCK CAR RACING, THEIR DREAM IS THE day they can get out of it," said Humpy Wheeler. "It's hard for people on the outside to understand. They think it's the most fantastic life in the world, that it's colorful, it's women, it's drinking, it's going to Daytona, it's going to Riverside. All of this is a bunch of crap. Stock car racing is a lot of travel, it's a lot of tremendous hours of work, there's the grease . . . just on and on. Everything's got to be done precisely, and the pressure is awful."

Race drivers did not often retire unexpectedly. Darel Dieringer quit at 43, having run out of good rides. Ned Jarrett stopped racing at 37, having attained all his career goals. Freddy Lorenzen's retirement was different. In February of 1967, he finished second to Mario Andretti in the Daytona 500, and there was talk that he could have won had he driven harder at the end. Two months later, he abruptly pulled his car behind the pit wall during the Atlanta 500 amidst speculation that his car was running perfectly. Lorenzen said he would run one more race, at Martinsville, but according to *The Dust and the Glory: A History of Ford in Racing* by Leo Levine, he was talked into quitting immediately by the Ford racing hierarchy. "I'll tell you what," Jacque Passino said to Lorenzen, "don't run Martinsville. If you're thinking about quitting, quit."

He did. He had won a record twelve superspeedway races, he was the only driver to have won on all of the five Southern superspeedways then in operation, and he had helped stock car racing make a successful transition to a new era. But he was only 32, an age when most drivers were just entering their prime.

"One thing I noticed several months before he quit was that he was highly agitated all the time," Wheeler said. "If everything didn't go letter perfect, he'd just get in an uproar. If his tires weren't mounted right, or if his spark plugs weren't gapped right—things that wouldn't bother a guy too much—he'd just go berserk. Things were getting to him. The reasons why things were getting to him, I don't know. He was an intensely emotional person, and I would suspect his emotions got misdirected. Not that retiring is a misdirection of emotion, but you've got to remember that for however many years it was, he had been totally involved in automobile racing. I think he just got tired of it. That, plus the fact that a lot of guys were getting hurt."

Lorenzen said, "I think everything just got to me. I wasn't feeling that great. I had a little stomach ulcer, but that wasn't the main reason. The main reason, the honest and true reason, was I was always gone from home. I was making good money—the government was getting a lot of it, but I still had more than the average guy—but I was never home to enjoy life. On the weekends, I was always gone racing. If I wasn't racing, I'd be gone making speeches for Ford all across the country. It's neat to be in the limelight, but after three or four years you just want to be home and take it easy."

John Holman said, "He did a fine job of driving. He looked good, he took a nice picture, he won a lot of races, and everything worked out fine. What's to holler?"

THE INFLUENCE OF THE FACTORIES ON STOCK CAR RACING was sublime, bold, and ridiculous, and occasionally all three at once. "Win on Sunday, Sell on Monday" was all-pervasive, and although nobody could calculate with real accuracy the number of Fords, Chevrolets, or Plymouths that left the showroom floor after a win by Freddy Lorenzen, Junior Johnson, or Richard Petty, the belief that race-track performance translated into corporate profit was sufficiently ingrained to keep everyone from the highest executive to the lowest tire buster motivated and jumpy.

At the center was the search for the Edge, not the kind that a driver created for himself during a race, but the sort that could be built into a car before the green flag ever dropped. A mechanical Edge. Kenneth Campbell, the Richmond promoter, suggested whimsically that the first time racing and engineering got mixed up was in the days of the chariots, when some Roman flunky spilled a pot of goat grease on an axle and observed that the wheel turned more easily. While it was true that the Edge was often obtained simply because one mechanic fine-tuned his engine better than the guy in the next garage stall, Detroit technology provided more. Dynanometers measured the horsepower and durability of an engine long before it was bolted into a race car. With space-age precision computer printouts told mechanics about spring ratios, caster, camber, anti-sway, anti-squat, and a plethora of other technically obtuse matters. Black-box instrumentation measured the stress on every minute part of a car, at speed. Indeed, there was the sense that one could learn infinitely more about the cars than about the men who drove them. All this was done with one idea in mind: to eliminate the variables and reduce the possibility of mechanical failure to zero. That would definitely be an Edge.

What Detroit technology and its technicians occasionally did not—could not—take into account was human ingenuity. What computer, for example, could have predicted the success of a mechanic such as Herb Nab, who used a ball peen hammer as precisely and daringly as a surgeon his scalpel? Or who could explain to a neophyte engineer from Detroit that the reason Ned Jarrett, after greasing the inside of his air cleaner, ran an intake hose to it from the *inside* of his car was because if he hadn't, the fine mist of red clay would have clogged up the air cleaner and rendered it useless? "The air from the inside of the car wasn't *much* cleaner," said Jarrett, "but it *was* cleaner."

THEN THERE WAS THE PECULIAR PHENOMENON KNOWN as cheating. Racing stock cars had to meet certain technical requirements regarding their weight, tire size, engine displacement, and the like, but there were always ways to circumvent even the most finely drawn specifications, particularly since NASCAR was rather lax about inspecting cars after a race had been run. NASCAR inspectors were diligent during practice and before qualifying, but if a driver could contrive to sneak an illegal car into the race itself, he was home free.

The cheating was often blatant and unimaginative. If a car didn't meet the minimum weight requirement, a simple solution was to fill up its tires with water before it was rolled, carefully, onto the scales. If a car was down on horsepower, an engine builder could bore out the engine block to obtain a few more cubic inches of displacement. If a car didn't meet the minimum ground clearance standards, the problem could be solved by wedging a pair of wood blocks beneath the front springs. When the car hit a bump on the track at racing speed, the blocks would fall out, and the car would suddenly be as raked and lowered as any hot-rod street racer in the country.

Cheating was an art rarely acknowledged openly, but its finest practitioners received the highest accolades because they, too, helped create the elusive Edge.

One year early in the 1960s, a NASCAR rule said that racing tires could measure no more than ten inches wide while inflated under 60 pounds of air pressure. At a race in North Wilkesboro, a batch of Goodyear tires exceeded this width. Working for Goodyear, however, was Crash Grant, a genius of a tire buster who told his field boss that if nobody asked too many questions, he'd get the tire past the NASCAR inspectors. The field boss was not inclined to ask any questions at all. He only found out much later what Crash Grant had done, which was take the inner tube out of the tire, tightly wrap it with electrician's tape, return it to the tire, and inflate the tire with the required 60 pounds of air. This effectively shrank the width of the tire. This also effectively created a bomb, one that Grant prayed would not go off until he had gotten the tire through inspection. Which, of course, he did.

The master was Smokey Yunick, the chief mechanic for Fireball Roberts and other General Motors drivers over the years. Smokey and NASCAR were always at odds about something, and on one occasion when NASCAR was particularly annoyed with him, for sins real and imagined, the inspectors went over his car with the tenacity and thoroughness of customs agents looking for smuggled dope. As the final step in their inspection, they drained Smokey's fuel tank bone dry in order to measure its fuel capacity. Having done that, they said, "Now, there are twelve things you've got to fix before we'll let you on the track."

Smokey, fuming, said, "Make that thirteen." Then he fired up his car with its "bone-dry" gas tank and drove off.

THE FACTORIES USED THEIR TREMENDOUS TECHNICAL and political clout most dramatically during a three-year period beginning in 1964. At that year's Daytona 500, Chrysler unveiled a 426-cubic-inch monster of an engine called the "hemi" because of its hemispherically shaped combustion chambers. The hemi was not a new engineering concept. It had been developed by Chrysler in 1951, then put on the shelf six years later because it was not economically feasible to market. It was, however, a super power plant, and at Daytona it blew everybody out of the tub. Paul Goldsmith qualified on the pole at 174 mph, five mph faster than the quickest Ford, and Richard Petty led a Plymouth parade to a one-two-three-four-six finish.

At Ford, there was predictable anguish. The hemi, argued Jacque Passino, was a racing engine, not a production-line item available to the general public. If Chrysler could use its racing engine, then Ford, which also had a racing engine, should be allowed to us one, too. NASCAR's Bill France said fine, if Passino could demonstrate that the Ford racing engine was a production-line item. No problem, said Passino, and invited France to Detroit to see the production line.

Ford's racing engine was a powerful, single overhead cam beauty that Special Vehicles had put together, sort of hurriedly. "We went through the drill and showed Bill France how we built those things," said Passino, "but Christ, the whole production line was the size of my living room."

Dividing the room was a screen. In the half of the room visible to France, partly assembled engines appeared on a conveyor belt in front of the screen. Workmen finished assembling the engines, which then disappeared behind the screen. On the other side of the screen, the finished engines were disassembled and hooked back onto the conveyor belt.

"France was counting the goddamned engines," said Passino, "but we only had about nine engines in the whole place. It wasn't an honest shot, and he knew it. What the hell. That was part of the game. He didn't buy it."

(In part, so goes a story that is probably apocryphal but too good not to pass on, he didn't buy it because a worker on the so-called production line was a deep-down Chevrolet loyalist and snitched.)

Still, with General Motors out of racing for real, the Pontiac of Fireball Roberts and the Chevrolet of Junior Johnson lost their edge, and France desperately needed to appease Ford. He did it by splitting hairs. In 1965, he said, the Ford single overhead cam engine would remain illegal, but the Chrysler hemi could be used only in the Plymouth Fury, a heavier and bulkier version of the Plymouth Satellite that had dominated Grand National racing in 1964. Chrysler officials were incensed. If the hemi was legal in 1964, they argued, not illogically, it should be legal in 1965, without restrictions. France was adamant, and Chrysler played its trump. It withdrew.

The Chrysler drivers scattered, most of them to the United States Auto Club stock car circuit, but one, Richard Petty, stayed behind to go drag racing, more to keep the Chrysler name alive in the South than anything else. Petty was doing just fine until one Sunday afternoon at a tiny drag strip near Dallas, Ga., when something broke on his car and sent it careening into an embankment and up over a fence into a crowd of spectators. Six people were hurt, and an 8-year-old boy was killed. Petty took to the sidelines and watched the Ford parade go by, in front of a lot of empty seats.

France had to relent. In the fall of 1965, he reinstated the hemi without restriction. In the spring of 1966, he legalized Ford's single overhead cam engine, but added a weight handicap of one pound per cubic inch of engine displacement.

Now it was Ford's turn to be upset. Ford never officially boycotted the Grand National circuit. Its cars and drivers simply didn't go racing very often. NASCAR, in 1966, turned into a Chrysler parade. There were more fights, more empty seats, and it wasn't until near the end of 1966 that a suitable compromise could be worked out. By then, it had been demonstrated conclusively that France needed the factories much more than the factories needed NASCAR, a situation that from NASCAR's point of view was untenable.

AS THE 1960S NEARED THEIR END, THERE WERE OTHER signs of unrest within the stock car racing fraternity, the most obvious being the drivers' boycott of the first race ever held at the Alabama International Motor Speedway near Talladega, the biggest and fastest superspeedway of them all, in September of 1969.

The boycott centered upon the fundamental labor issues of money and power. A driver's income was never what it seemed. If he drove for someone else, he received between 40 and 60 percent of the car's earnings. If he owned his own car, his overhead usually far exceeded his race earnings. Sometimes the difference was made up by sponsors willing to advertise their products on the side of a fast race car, sometimes it wasn't.

The peculiar financial structure pleased nobody. The drivers at the bottom were always broke, those in the middle struggled to break even, and the handful at the top never felt they earned enough. Three Grand National drivers earned $100,000 or more in 1969. By contrast, a score of professional golfers boasted of $100,000 incomes that same year, as did the stars of the National Basketball Association, and National Football League quarterbacks routinely pulled down $200,000 per year. And, as Buddy Baker said, "They don't have to hit walls at 190 miles an hour." A driver was also aware that if his career was ended suddenly, by a blown tire or a telephone call, he had precious little to fall back on.

The drivers were also upset by their utter lack of voice within NASCAR. Although NASCAR claimed to be an organization of, for, and by the drivers, as well as the mechanics, car owners, track promoters, and just about anyone else who wished to join (it had a membership in excess of 20,000), the drivers understood that Bill France, the founder and president of NASCAR, ran things his own way. His word was absolute in all matters ranging from the assignment of a track's racing dates and the technical specifications of the cars to the amount of money in the year-end point funds. However much the drivers respected France for having built up stock car racing, they complained often about the arbitrary and capricious way in which he administered it.

There had been challenges to France's power before, most notably in 1961 when Curtis Turner and Tim Flock attempted, with the aid of the Teamsters union, to organize the drivers and mechanics. But France always won easily, as he had on that occasion when he simply threatened to ban any driver who joined the union and everyone backed down.

In 1969, then, the drivers formed the Professional Drivers' Association and elected Richard Petty president. Rumors circulated that the PDA planned to boycott that year's Labor Day Southern 500 at Darlington just on general principles: more prize money, a better health insurance plan, a pension fund, bathrooms in the garage area. (It was true at several tracks that the drivers did not have showering or bathroom facilities.)

But the Darlington boycott never happened because the PDA realized that an even better showcase would be the inaugural race at Talladega. Bigger than Daytona by .16 of a mile, and faster, the Talladega facility was conceived and built by France as the final cornerstone of his empire, and he was determined that the first race, scheduled for September 14, 1969, go smoothly. At first, the PDA planned a show of unity based only on its laundry list of grievances. It was by accident that the organization was able to latch on to an issue that was both immediate and unquestionably legitimate.

On the first day of practice for the Talladega race, the tires on the fastest cars unexpectedly began to blister and chunk, a matter of no small concern. Nobody was sure precisely what the problem was, not even Goodyear, which had developed a special Talladega tire and supplied all the top cars in the wake of a decision several weeks earlier by its rival, Firestone, to withdraw from racing. The best guess was that the damage was being caused not by the absolute speed of the cars—nearly 200 mph—but by the movement of the cars across the rough seams that joined the parallel lanes of young asphalt. Goodyear flew in new batches of tires daily, but the result was the same. How dangerous the situation was depended on whom one talked to last, but the PDA had its issue, and the battle was joined.

The parties to the dispute were the factories, which controlled the top cars; Goodyear, which made the tires; Bill France, who ran NASCAR and owned the track; and the PDA, struggling for recognition and legitimacy.

France maintained that the tires and his track were safe, and besides, he said, nobody was forcing the drivers to go fast. He also said that he would drive in the race himself if the PDA membership pulled out.

Goodyear wanted France to postpone the race to give it more time to work on the Talladega tire. Failing that, Goodyear said that it would provide the tires as best it could, but suggested that the drivers keep their speed under 185 mph.

The factories, Ford and Chrysler, washed their hands of the whole affair. They did not demand that their drivers race, which displeased France, nor did they withdraw their cars, which displeased the drivers. The factories said they would keep the cars at the track and make them available to anybody who wanted to drive.

The PDA was in turmoil. Its membership was far from united on the question of a boycott. The race offered one of the largest paydays of the season whether or not the tires were safe. The drivers hoped that either the factories or Goodyear would withdraw. When neither did, the PDA called its boycott, and nearly all the top drivers went home.

France stood his ground. He said that any spectator who asked would get a rain check for the next race at either Talladega or Daytona, a gesture that cost him a reported $500,000, and that the race would be run as scheduled.

It was. The only name driver who showed up was Bobby Isaac. There were several yellow caution flags, ostensibly for "debris on the track," but their real purpose was to make it easy for the drivers to duck into the pits and change tires before they had run too many consecutive high-speed laps. There were no serious accidents. The winner was an unknown named Richard Brickhouse, who was never heard from again. The PDA, after wallowing in inactivity for six years, was formally disbanded in 1975.

It failed for several reasons. The top drivers, who had the most to lose in a prolonged fight with France, accepted the idea that they had a pretty good thing going, and their enthusiasm for the PDA waned. The backmarkers, the cannon fodder the stars passed on the way to the checkered flag and who stood to gain the most, could not hold the PDA together without vigorous support from the stars. And in general, the intense competition on the race track made it difficult for any two drivers ever to agree on anything for very long. The only issue that concerned every driver equally was safety, and despite its occasional tragedies, the Grand National circuit was by far the safest in the world. (In contrast, the Grand Prix Drivers' Association, a European-based group formed in 1966, had already become a powerful voice in the dangerous world of Formula One racing.) Finally, as the decade ended, so did the factory era, removing the two counterweights—Detroit money and Detroit power—that might have helped the drivers balance or even neutralize the power of Bill France.

THE FACTORY ERA ENDED QUICKLY. A DULLED ECONOMY forced the automobile companies to make massive cutbacks, and their racing programs were very nearly the first items to go. The national clear air crusade moved into high gear, forcing Detroit to turn its attention toward the Environmental Protection Agency's auto emissions standards. On the tire front, Firestone's withdrawal signaled the end of a costly war with Goodyear that over the years had seen both companies pour hundreds of thousands of dollars into the sport. Many accessory companies also retired, taking with them the free parts that often meant the difference between break-even and broke for the struggling independents. By 1972, there were few traces left of the factories.

SUCCESSFUL COMEBACKS IN SPORTS WERE RARE; IN automobile racing, they were so rare as to be nonexistent. But in 1970, Freddy Lorenzen tried to break the rules. He got sponsorship from Andy Granatelli and the STP Corporation and once again headed South, and with his old flair for showmanship even led the first race he entered, the World 600 at Charlotte. His car failed him halfway through, however, and over the next year or so, he never again led a race, much less come close to winning one. Why did he go back?

"Ego," said John Holman. "He used to delight in running down the halls at Chicago O'Hare—*Lorenzen's on his way*— and they'd hold the airplane for Lorenzen to get on to come to Charlotte. And I think too many times nobody knew who Freddy Lorenzen was in the North again, that's all."

"He had a lot of money when he retired," said Humpy Wheeler. "He wanted to lead the good life. He started loosening up and doing things. He went down to Fort Lauderdale, got his yacht, all the accoutrements, started finding there's another life. He had a big time. Matter of fact, he hardly ever came back to the race track. You'd see him two or three times a year and that was it."

"When I quit," said Lorenzen, "I decided just to be a thing

of leisure. Just do nothing. Then I think I got tired. It's just like anything else in the world. If you could play golf every day for a year, you'd be sick of it. I got sick of doing nothing—water skiing, flying my airplane, staying out all night, sleeping all day. It's neat to have money and just do nothing and be a bum, I suppose, but it really gets old. And the stock market took a big dive. I got tired of selling stocks to live off them. So I decided to go back. Plus, I missed racing so much."

After his year of little success, the opportunity came for Lorenzen to drive the Mercury Cyclone prepared by the Wood Brothers of Stuart, Va., one of the best racing teams on the circuit. He jumped at the chance. His first race for the Wood Brothers would be the Southern 500, at the same Darlington Raceway where he had scored his first major victory ten years earlier. Lorenzen was positively radiant. Indeed, his exuberance was a surprise to those who remembered his testy and nervous behavior in the months immediately preceding his retirement. On the Wednesday before the race, he told a friend bluntly, "I've got the best crew, the best car, and no excuses. This race will tell whether I've still got it." And even when he slapped the wall the first time in practice, a gentle tap in turn two, he shrugged his shoulders and said crisply, "You can't run here until you hit the wall one time at least. Now we're ready to go."

He then turned a practice lap of 147 mph, a good three mph faster than his closest competitor. But Lorenzen had felt the car bobble in turn four. Leonard Wood, the chief mechanic and the younger brother of car owner Glen Wood, suggested that they change the left-front spring first thing the next morning. Lorenzen said fine.

Early on that grim and overcast Thursday, Lorenzen nudged the wall a second time, his Cyclone leaving a streak of red and white paint on the harsh concrete barrier, again in turn two. There was no apparent damage, however, and shortly before 10:30, he was on the track again, checking the final adjustments the Wood Brothers' crew had made in preparation for the afternoon qualifying session that would determine the first twelve starting positions for the Labor Day race. In the pits, Glen Wood carefully noted Lorenzen's times, and after a half-dozen laps, he waved his driver in.

Either Lorenzen did not see the signal or he chose to ignore it. Lorenzen himself remembered nothing of that day, but later, in piecing together what happened, he said that Glen flashed "51+" on the pit board, indicating a lap of over 151 mph, and he guessed that he stayed out to try to hit 152 mph, a tick of the clock that would further confirm the presence of the Edge. Whatever the case, the next time Lorenzen came through the fourth turn, obviously with no intention of pitting, he started to broadslide toward the outside retaining wall. Richie Barsz, one of Buddy Baker's mechanics, heard the signs of trouble long before the crash. "I could hear his engine go *whuuup, whuuup, whuuup* as he worked the throttle," Barsz said. "He was working it right up until the time he hit." Had he found a spot of oil in the turn? Was he trying a new line through the corner? It was difficult to say for sure. Still, often the test of a race driver was his reaction in a crisis, and on this count, Lorenzen passed.

He hit the cement wall a tremendous blow. Both right-side wheels as well as the left front somehow briefly climbed the wall before the wounded car settled back on the narrow track and set out on a straight-line journey of 150 yards to its ultimate destruction at the hands of the inside pit wall. Amazingly, the first impact neither knocked Lorenzen out nor killed his engine. Hoping against hope in those agonizing moments before the second crash, Lorenzen kept the throttle to the floor and cranked the steering wheel hard right in an effort to spin the car away from the inside wall. It was what any driver would have done, but what Lorenzen did not know, could not know, was that his steering had been shattered by the first impact and that he was totally out of control.

Lorenzen hit the low pit wall at well over 150 mph. It was nearly a head-on crash, and the impact blasted a hole sixteen feet wide in the reinforced concrete and sent a grenade-blast of shrapnel, as well as the car's left-front wheel assembly, sailing through the pits. Here was where Lorenzen got lucky, and a lot of other people as well. The Mercury now tried to fly, and in so doing clipped a pair of aluminum light posts right at the start-finish line and sheared in half one wood telephone pole a good six feet from the ground. The car did a snap-barrel roll and landed on the track right-side up in its own ugly cloud of smoke and steam, pointed back toward the fourth turn. Had the poles not been where they were, Lorenzen would have slammed into a group of Goodyear tire busters who were working not fifty feet away.

The track's safety crews were caught unprepared. The first people to reach Lorenzen were three drivers and two Goodyear employees. They quickly put out an oil fire, then carefully removed Lorenzen from his broken machine and laid him on the track beside it to wait for the ambulance. Lorenzen was unconscious. A trickle of blood glistened on the left side of his gray-white face and neck.

Glen Wood did not immediately go to the hospital. "Lorenzen didn't have anything to prove," he said. "Not to us."

In the early afternoon, word came from the hospital that Lorenzen would be all right. He had a grotesquely dislocated left ankle, a concussion, several lacerations, and one deep gash on the left side of his neck that would temporarily mar his Golden Boy profile. But considering that two hours earlier he should have been dead, the report was good, and in the quiet garage area (the track was still under repair), you could almost feel the whoosh of air as the other drivers and their crews released their pent-up breath as one.

Lorenzen returned to racing later that season, but the damage was done. Not to him physically. It was just that he had taken a good race car and torn it all to hell. It wasn't the thing to do in the middle of a comeback.

"They say I got a good car and crashed it," said Lorenzen. "So what? Richard Petty crashed a car there. Same spot. The year before. Busted up just like I did. But I was on the hot seat, and I got into the car and made a mistake. It happened. I slipped. I don't know what happened. Maybe something broke, but I can't say something broke because I don't know. I don't think it did. I think I just flat lost it. I was trying to win the race practicing. Any other time, I could have been allowed the mistake, but the mistake came at a very critical time in my return to racing. It just happened that way, and I suppose it was meant to be."

•

ON A HOT SUMMER DAY IN 1975, FREDDY LORENZEN SAT on the screened patio of his pleasant Mediterranean-style house in Elmhurst. He was dressed in shorts and tennis shoes and a knit shirt, the perfect picture of suburban contentment. His wife, Nancy, whom he had married in 1972 after a courtship of several years, puttered about their expansive backyard while an intercom system helped both of them keep track of their napping two-year-old son, Christopher. A car sat in the front driveway with a vanity plate bearing his initials and his old Holman-Moody car number: "FL 28." He had turned 40 the previous December.

Earlier in the day, Lorenzen had driven a visitor past the Malibu Apartments in nearby Hillcrest. The Malibu had been his Chicago-area bachelor pad from 1962 through 1971, a lively party place, and he seemed mildly disappointed when he realized that it had apparently been taken over by families and older people. But only mildly. "I was the wildest guy that ever walked when I was single," he said. "Now, it's a complete turnaround. I am probably the quietest married man in the world. I know I am in this town. I love to sit here on the patio, with my wife and son, and anybody that comes over can't believe it's me. We don't go out hopping bars. We don't really entertain a lot—have tons of people come over—because I've done all that. I can just sit here and relax for hours and hours and hours."

He took his visitor on a tour of his house, ending in the trophy room that was a part of every race driver's home. He dismissed nearly everything—the Daytona 500 trophy, the three straight Atlanta 500 trophies, scores of other trophies, and autographed checkered flags—and pointed to the picture of him taken after his victory over Curtis Turner in the Rebel 300 at Darlington in 1961. In the picture, Lorenzen was wearing a white, short-sleeve driving uniform, and in his right hand he held the race trophy. His hair was tousled, and he was smiling. There were smudges on his cheeks. And when the visitor looked carefully, he could indeed see that Lorenzen's eyes were glistening. Truly.

3

The Southern 500

IN THE YEARS IMMEDIATELY FOLLOWING THE FACTORY pullout, stock car racing became polarized. The largesse of the automobile companies and accessory firms had been a great equalizer, and as the money supply in racing diminished, so in turn did the number of competitive racing teams. Success begat success, while the also-rans found themselves running farther and farther behind. During the five-year period that began in 1971, only five drivers were able to purchase the necessary technology and assemble the necessary personnel, or become associated with teams that could win races on their own: Richard Petty, David Pearson, Bobby Allison, Cale Yarborough, and Buddy Baker. Other drivers entered Victory Lane only when those five somehow found a way to lose. That did happen, of course, but rarely. Petty, Pearson, et al., won 140 of the 167 Grand National races during those years, including 86 of the 100 superspeedway events, and it was not uncommon for them to hold down the first five positions at the end of a given race.

Nor did any of them show any serious inclination toward retirement, although by 1975 their average age was well over 37, ancient by most sports standards. A series of rules changes designed to reduce costs, and once again, to legislate equality among the various makes of cars, had the salutary side effect of stopping cold the frightening rise in speeds that had characterized the 1960s. This, and the absence of the factories' "Go or blow" racing philosophy, gave the old warriors the sense of well-being they needed to continue driving even as they approached their athletic dotage. Which was fine for them, but in the process NASCAR lost an entire generation of drivers. There was simply no way for a young charger, however deserving, to get a good ride.

With the same drivers winning so frequently and predictably, one Grand National race tended to be very much like the next. The exception, as it had been since 1950, was the Southern 500 at Darlington, S.C., the traditional Labor Day climax of the Grand National season. In 1975 the race was held, for the twenty-sixth time, on Monday, September 1.

AS A VISITOR APPROACHED THE CITY OF DARLINGTON from the west along South Carolina Highway 151 on the last Tuesday in August, the bunkerlike structure of the Darlington Raceway suddenly appeared off to the right, low and ominous. All that could be seen from the road was the corrugated steel roof that covered the main grandstand, the grandstand itself having been built into a high mound of landscaped earth, and it was impossible to get a sense of the track's unusual dimensions. Bill Kiser, the public relations director for the track, was little help. He knew the track was exactly 1.366 miles in circumference, as measured ten feet out from the apron, and that it was vaguely egg-shaped, but in keeping with track president Barney Wallace's comment, "We built the track the way we did because that's the way it came out," Kiser honestly did not know the width of the track, the length of its straightaways, or the radii of its two very different turns. Nor, immediately, did any other track official. Kiser changed the subject and mentioned that after Cale Yarborough had blown an engine and coasted into the pits during a race at Talladega earlier in the season, a tanked-up wrecker driver had crunched his car pretty good while pushing it into the garage area—so good that Yarborough had felt compelled to go after the guy and grab him by the scruff of his neck.

The State, the Columbia, S.C., morning newspaper, carried an editorial blasting Jimmy Breslin, the newspaper columnist, for blaming New York City's fiscal problems on South

Carolina. Breslin had recently argued that New York was in a bind because South Carolina and other Southern states had historically refused to take care of their own, thus forcing the great postwar migrations to the Big Apple where "the official policy was to deny food or housing to no one." *The State* said that New York "is reaping a whirlwind sowed by its costly compassion and its lack of cost-consciousness." Breslin had concluded, "I detest the way [New Yorkers] must live . . . but we live this way because our city was compassionate, our official policy was that we would not be South Carolina, and for this forever I shall be proud to say that I live here." *The State* concluded, "Tell you what, Mr. Breslin: you stay in New York and we'll stay in South Carolina. Just call on us any time you need a scapegoat."

The State also reported that temperatures throughout South Carolina were in the high 90s, and that the heat wave would continue throughout the week.

The unofficial race headquarters was at the Sheraton Motor Inn. On Tuesday night, six days before the race, the bar, bathed in a purple light, was quiet and nearly deserted. The few patrons sipped draft beer or tried to enjoy highballs made from two-ounce miniatures, the latter a terrible compromise between the advocates of liquor by the drink and the forces of prohibition. A man, obviously from the neighborhood, said, "They ain't nobody but Yankees drink scotch," as another man, obviously from the North, ordered a J&B and water. A traveling salesman from Columbia said that few college graduates of his acquaintance were interested in stock cars. In his opinion, a person's interest in stock car racing was inversely proportional to his wealth, education, and social status. "Stock car racing," he said, "is a redneck sport."

ON WEDNESDAY MORNING, THE FIRST DAY OF PRACTICE, Richard Brooks, a journeyman driver from the logging community of Porterville, Calif., who had moved to Spartanburg, S.C., in 1969 to seek his fame and fortune, only to find little of either, walked into the Darlington garage area perspiring heavily. "Let's call this off right now," he pleaded.

Richard Petty, who had plenty of fame and fortune both,

chomped down on a cigar, and with a pearly white grin cackled, "I see Buddy done lost his pants," as Buddy Baker emerged from the drivers' lounge in a pair of incongruous powder-blue Bermuda shorts.

Brooks said somebody had recently given him a copper bracelet. He said he'd finished every race he'd run while wearing it, but that he hadn't had it on ten days earlier during a horrendous, end-over-end crash at Talladega exactly 66 laps after Tiny Lund's fatal accident. "After I got out of that car, I put that bracelet right back on," Brooks said. "It turns your arm green, but I don't give a good goddamn."

Of the heat, Petty said, "This is the way it used to be down here. It's going to bother a bunch of guys if it stays like this." The last time Petty had needed a relief driver was in the 1973 Southern 500. Before that, in either 1971 or 1972—he couldn't remember—he said there had been a stretch during the middle of the season when he needed relief in two races and nearly collapsed at the end of two others. He wasn't sure whether that had been from gas fumes leaking inside his car or from the heat. "Just going through a period, I guess," he chuckled.

Brooks said his Talladega accident started when Donnie Allison, Bobby Allison's younger brother, tapped him while trying to pull a draft off the second turn. Brooks started to slide toward the outside wall, but then the front end of his Ford dug into the pavement, and he was gone. He said films showed that he flipped backward two or three times before he ever hit the ground. Then he began bouncing. "I closed my eyes, lowered my head, and got a good grip on the steering wheel," he said. "I just wanted it to stop."

Petty pointed out there were fewer cars than usual on hand for the first day of practice because it was a sixteen-hour tow from Michigan, where the season's last race had been held the previous Sunday. Indeed, the schedule was becoming ridiculous. Because of rainouts earlier in the year, there had not been an open weekend for nearly a month, nor was one scheduled for another five weeks. Equipment was worn and tempers were short.

Brooks said that he'd had three accidents in the past six weeks. He had blown an engine in a Sportsman race at Metrolina Speedway in Charlotte and sailed out of the track during another Sportsman race in Beltsville, Md., and then he went to Talladega. "I got to stop doing that," he said.

Petty drew attention to the cement retaining wall in the third and fourth turns. It had been installed earlier in the year, on the eve of the spring Darlington race, the Rebel 500, to replace a worn section of metal guard rail. Petty said several drivers had complained during practice for the Rebel that they could not see the wall clearly because of the shadow it cast. He said the track management told the drivers there wouldn't be time to paint all of the wall before the race, but that a white stripe would be inscribed down the middle of it. Petty looked at the wall, which, four months later, still had only a stripe, and said, "This is the cheapest damned place in the world."

The pavement in the third and fourth turns of the track was covered with "bear grease," a Darlington euphemism for an oil-based asphalt sealant called Giminite that was supposed to help prevent the racing surface from breaking up under the heavy pounding of the cars. When the sun struck at just the right angle, this portion of the track had the appearance of a slippery, waxed, and polished table top. There was a yearly dispute over whether the parts of the track that had been treated with Giminite were, in fact, slicker than the rest of it. What few disputed was that the treated portions *looked* slicker, and thus the psychological damage was done.

SHORTLY BEFORE ONE O'CLOCK, CALE YARBOROUGH AND Dave Marcis engaged in a deep and animated conversation, the aftermath of a little bumping incident between the two at Michigan the previous Sunday in which Yarborough claimed that Marcis had intentionally driven into him near the end of the race. Marcis, who looked like Bob Newhart, the comedian, and even talked a little like him, his Wisconsin-bred voice always seeming to verge on hysteria, said that was certainly true, but only because Yarborough twice had roughed him up earlier in the day. Marcis said it had been more or less a spur of the moment thing, although he had told his crew chief on his two-way car radio that he was going to do something. "You've got to," Marcis said, "or they'll run all over you."

Unfortunately, when Marcis turned right, into Yarborough, Yarborough chose that moment to turn left, into Marcis. Both cars went spinning, and neither driver finished the race. "It was a helluva jolt," said Marcis. Their meeting at Darlington was to make sure the incident remained up North and would not carry over into the Southern 500.

The entire season had been one of frustration for Yarborough. The year before had been his best ever in terms of both wins and prize money, but so far in 1975 he had won only twice, neither victory a superspeedway race, "The ones that count, the ones that people really look at." There had been a series of misfortunes, mainly involving the engine of his white Chevrolet. Later, when the season was over, Yarborough would say that the marital problems of his engine builder were the cause of many of his difficulties, but at the moment all he could do was keep up a gentlemanly front and suffer the indignities of bumping duels, blown engines, careless wrecker drivers, and, as had been the case at Talladega earlier in the month, the ignominy of being a full 10 miles per hour off the pace.

At precisely one o'clock the mellifluous voice of Ray Melton floated through the public address system amidst the debilitating heat: "Attention in the pits, gentlemen. The track is now open for practice."

"Let's go, Cale," said Herb Nab, Yarborough's chief mechanic.

"I hear it's going to be cool later," Yarborough said, trying to demur.

Darrell Waltrip was the first driver onto the track. Benny Parsons was next, followed by Yarborough and Elmo Langley. All returned after just a few laps. In the second wave were Buddy Baker, Langley again, and, as the honeyed voice from the public address system said, "Sir Richard Petty."

Still, the drivers stayed out but a short time. Darlington was not a track for which a driver and his crew could prepare quickly. Yarborough explained that when things weren't working well at the start of practice, you really didn't know whether the problem was with the car's chassis, the track, the engine, or the driver. An hour or so later, he said he felt that the chassis was pretty close, but that the engine, as usual, was way off.

•

CALE YARBOROUGH GREW UP THIRTEEN MILES DOWN the road from the Darlington Raceway on a farm near the small town of Timmonsville. In 1957, when he was 17, he lied about his age and raced in the Southern 500 for the first time.

"That was quite an experience," he said. "I'd had a couple of years of dirt track under my belt, and I really thought I was a race driver. I thought I'd make Buck Baker and Fireball and all those boys stand back and take notice. I found out that I wadn't ready to carry their helmet bag."

Years passed. Yarborough, short, tough, roly-poly, and adventurous, kept up with his racing, but also dabbled in other pursuits. An all-state high school football player, he turned down several college scholarship offers to play for the semi-professional Sumter (S.C.) Generals. He took up sky diving and made 200 free falls before he found out about the static line. He tried turkey farming, but went broke when all his birds died on him one night.

Then Jacque Passino discovered him, and in 1968 Yarborough put it all together, winning a record four super-speedway events, including the first of three Southern 500s, for the Wood Brothers racing team. Two years later, he, like so many other drivers, got caught by the sudden factory pull-out. Faced with the prospect of a second-rate ride down South and needing ready cash to protect investments he had made during his years with Ford, Yarborough went North to race, unsuccessfully, on the United States Auto Club's Championship Car circuit. He returned South in 1973 and signed on with Junior Johnson, the former driver, who had become a successful Grand National car owner. Yarborough stumbled through that season, but in 1974 he won ten races and over $250,000 in prize money, and his star was once again in its ascendancy.

Yarborough's house, a pleasant, pillared mansion, was set on seven acres of land just outside the Timmonsville city limit. Right at the city limit was a sign that read: "Timmonsville, Home of Cale Yarborough, the World's Fastest Driver." The sign was usually in good repair, but one afternoon some six weeks before the Southern 500, it was askew and badly in need of a coat of paint. Somehow appropriate, given the circumstances of Yarborough's current season.

Question: What does the kind of year you're going through now do to your relationship with Herb Nab, your mechanic, and Junior Johnson, your car owner?

Yarborough: I don't think a whole lot. I know it's not their fault, and I hope they don't think it's my fault. They're spending a lot of sleepless nights and working twenty-four hours a day for several days at a time. They aren't just sitting down and giving up. Right now, it's just the circumstances. It's a terrible feeling. I still give it 120 percent —I haven't backed off of that yet—but it's not a real good feeling knowing that every Sunday morning when you go to the race track, that in order for you to win, somebody else has to have trouble. It's a bad feeling for a man that likes to win.

Question: Your relationship with Junior ought to be ideal, considering the reputation he had when he was driving, and yours now.

Yarborough: I like Junior. He's my kind of people. He's a down to earth type of person, and what he tells you, you can bank on it. As far as I know, he doesn't lie to me, and I don't lie to him. If he asks me something, he and Herb both, I try to tell 'em just like it is, and that's the kind of relationship you gotta have. You gotta work close, and you gotta lay everything on the line. The first year I ran with 'em, in '73, we didn't have a whole lot of success, and we bent up a lot of sheet metal. We ran up front almost everywhere we went, but it just seemed like everything that happened on the race track happened in front of me. I was always where the action was. Of course, I don't deny that I didn't get into somebody else a time or two, but Herb and Junior never said anything about it. And '74 came along, and sure enough, it clicked.

Question: People have said Junior doesn't like racing nowadays because you've got to stroke it a little bit. You can't go flat out from flag to flag, or until the car breaks, like you could in the factory days.

Yarborough: He's never told me to stroke it any, and I've never tried to stroke it any. He says that when the race starts, he runs the pits and I run the car, and that's the way we go after it. I can't say that I deliberately try to break an engine, but I have to run it to the breaking point in the situation we're in now. If I didn't, I'd be back there in fourth or fifth place. I don't want to run back there, and Junior Johnson don't want his cars to run back there. So that's the attitude we take. We run it until something breaks, as hard as we can.

Question: Do you feel you're a better driver now than you were, say, in 1968?

Yarborough: I know I am, in all respects. I think I'm in as good a physical condition as I've ever been in, and that I can drive a car with much more caution and finesse. Working traffic and stuff like that. I was more like a bull in a china shop in '68. Maybe now I'm more like a kitten in a china shop, but doing the same job. Like, back then I felt when I got to a car, I had to pass him when I got to him. Now I realize that I might wait until the next straightaway, wait till the coast is a little clearer and the traffic's not quite as bad. . . . Still get the job done, but do it without taking as many chances of tearing the car up.

One big thing that makes a man a better race driver is . . . I hope I don't have anything to prove anymore. I don't have to prove to Jacque Passino that I can get the job done. That makes a big difference. In '68 I still had a lot to learn. I was still in the proving stage.

Question: What was a driver expected to be then? Passino and other Detroit executives gave the impression that while a driver's ability, of course, was important, so was his public relations value.

Yarborough: Very definitely. They wanted you to represent their company off the race track as well as you did on the race track. They wanted you to be able to meet the public, and if you needed to go to a meeting at the Ford Motor Company with all the big brass, they didn't want to be ashamed of you. They wanted you to do a good job for them.

Question: Did you appreciate that attitude?

Yarborough: Yah, I did, because I was kind of brought up that way. I enjoyed working with different people, younger people, groups of people. And anything you enjoy, it makes it easy.

I'll tell you, I haven't seen Jacque Passino in a long time and I don't know what's happening or nothing, but I'll never forget that man. I feel like he's the man that put me here today. I can remember him telling me one day, "I don't care how many fenders is on that car, I don't care whether it's upside down, I don't care what kind of condition it's in—as long as you were in front when it happened." I never forgot that, and I made it a point to always run up front if there was any possible way. That's the way he wanted it, and that's the way he got it.

Question: Did you have that attitude before Jack . . . ?

Yarborough: I had it, yah, but I was glad that that was what he wanted. He just punched the fire and got it burning a little brighter.

Question: If you were a young driver coming up today with no factory telling you that it was okay to break a car as long as you were in front, what do you think your attitude would be?

Yarborough: I'm glad I came up when I did.

Question: What do you remember about your first Southern 500 win, in 1968?

Yarborough: It was a rough race. I think I hit every car and every wall on the race track. And still won the race. Tough competition . . . terribly hot. . . . I was so sick I couldn't stand it.

Question: During the race?

Yarborough: No. I've been tired and hot and sick at races, but it's never bothered me until the race was over. It's just like the Atlanta race last year, the Dixie 500. I am going to tell you, when that race was over, I almost died. I had a transmission that was leaking fluid inside the car, and smelling that ol' burnt oil all day. . . . When the race was over, I threw up two quarts of Valvoline. It was hard to be sick all the time, but it didn't bother me a bit until the race was over. When you roll to a stop, then everything stops.

It was that kind of a day in 1968. I remember very, very little about winning. I was so gone I can't remember any of the winner's circle activities, even though in years to come that will probably be my most prized win. That was before the race track was changed. It was the old Darlington then, and any race driver that has had a good opportunity to win when Darlington was in that condition, and didn't, will always go through life missing something. Because that was a challenge. That was the toughest race to win that there has ever been and ever will be.

Question: Do you keep a book on drivers?

Yarborough: In my head. Not a real book.

Question: Can you tell me what you think of the other top drivers?

Yarborough: Well, they all have different driving techniques and characteristics. It's really hard to tell you what they do.

Question: Because you don't want to, or . . . ?

Yarborough: Well . . . I know some things that Richard does and things that Pearson does and things that Baker does that I really wouldn't want them to know that I know, about their driving style and how you can put them in different situations. I'm sure they know the same about me.

Question: What *can* you say, for example, about Richard Petty?

Yarborough: The only thing that I can tell you is that he's a heckuva race driver. He's cool, he stands up under the pressure as good as any race driver that ever lived, I guess, and he's got as much talent as any race driver that ever lived.

Question: David Pearson?

Yarborough: David probably falls in the same category.

Question: Buddy Baker? If you say he's cool all the time, you're lying.

Yarborough: No, I can't put him in the same category. Buddy's not as cool a race driver as Richard or David. He's got a little temper, maybe—like me, a little. If you do the wrong thing to him on the race track, he'll get hot at you. And that's not good. It hurts you more than it does anybody else.

Question: Bobby Allison?

Yarborough: Bobby's a little different-type race driver than Richard or David. He's the kind of driver that . . . Y'know, I hate to say these things about these people. . . . Bobby's the kind of race driver that it don't make any difference how many times you lap him, when you get to him on the race track, he's going to fight you tooth and nail to keep you from going by. And *that's* not good.

If I had lost a lap other than being outrun—say I lost it in the pits—I'd race a man. He'd have to pass me on his own. But if I lap, say, Richard Petty on the race track, when I come up to lap him again, he'd let me go. And I'd do the same for him. Anytime a man is running fast enough to lap me fair and square, I'm going to get out of his way when he comes around. I'm not going to jeopardize him by trying to hold him back. But Bobby will, and in my book, just because he'll fight you doesn't make him that much a better race driver than anybody else.

Question: Of the four, whom do you most, or least, like to race against when it comes down to the last lap?

Yarborough: I couldn't answer that fair.

Question: Have you ever figured out why you're a good race driver?

Yarborough: The will to win . . . I don't really know what makes a good race driver. A lot of people are born with talents that maybe they can adapt to certain things easier than others, but I don't think anybody is a born race driver. I believe you have to develop into whatever you turn out to be. Some people do it easier than others. The ones that do end up being your superstars.

Question: What attracted you to racing? Why has racing kept your interest for so long?

Yarborough: I'm kind of an adventurous type, I guess. I love speed, I love the outside—I love everything that goes along with racing. I love anything that's competitive, where you've got to beat somebody else. Even though racing is a team sport, when that green flag drops, it's man and machine against man and machine and the race track. It's just as big a thrill for me to win any race today as it was the first one I won, and I think that's what keeps me going.

Question: Do you ever think about retiring?

Yarborough: *Noooo.* I really don't believe I'm in my peak yet. I think I'm a better race driver this year than I was last year, even though we aren't doing as good, and I think I'll be better next year than I was this year. If I didn't feel that way, I'd be going downhill.

Question: What *would* make you stop racing?

Yarborough: Not being able to drive a competitive car. If I didn't have a chance to win, I wouldn't race.

Question: A final question. Describe yourself.

Yarborough: I'm a kind of person that loves to do anything he does to the best of his ability. I like things done right when you do 'em. I like pretty things. I love hard work, physically hard work, I guess because I was born and raised on a farm. My goals in life are . . . No use to mention those because I'll never reach my goals. They're past the stars.

AT 2:30 ON WEDNESDAY AFTERNOON, DAVID PEARSON took out the white and maroon Wood Brothers Mercury for its first practice laps of the day. Bobby Allison, driving the red, white, and blue American Motors Matador owned by Roger Penske, had not yet arrived at the track. His bored crew sat in the garage area playing cards. Bill Champion, at 53 the oldest driver at the track—he and Joe Weatherly were racing motorcycles three decades earlier, before either one of them thought about stock cars—turned one lap and returned to the pits, his engine smoking. Darel Dieringer and Marvin Panch, old racing rivals, talked quietly in a corner of the track cafeteria, the social center of the raceway. Dieringer was in Darlington as a recently unretired driver. Panch, who retired in 1966 and stayed retired, was the field representative for Grey-Rock brake linings, an accessory firm.

At 3:15, suddenly gathered clouds spit rain, but not enough to break the oppressive heat or even wet the track. In the garage area there was a general air of levity, an indication that nobody was quite ready yet to take the race seriously. Tiny Lund, whose funeral had been eight days earlier in nearby Moncks Corner, was either forgotten or remembered fondly; Mark Donohue, who had been buried two days earlier in faraway New Jersey, they hardly knew.

Yarborough coasted into the garage area with a leaking valve-cover gasket. Herb Nab screwed it down and sent his driver back onto the track. Yarborough had the narrow ribbon of asphalt to himself, and from the pits Nab could hear the moan of Yarborough's engine bounce off the empty front grandstand long before Yarborough appeared to his sight, sliding gracefully up to the white stripe on the cement wall in turn four.

"RACE DRIVERS ARE SUPERMEN," SAID DR. NASEEB B. Baroody, Jr. "If you don't believe me, dress yourself from head to foot in a wool suit, put on a driving helmet, and on the hottest day of the year, drive with your foot to the floor from Rocky Mount, North Carolina, to Philadelphia and see how you feel."

Dr. Baroody said you wouldn't feel very good. He was an internist and cardiologist with a long-standing professional interest in the effects of stress on the human heart who lived and practiced in Florence, S.C., twelve miles to the east of Darlington. In 1972 he and two colleagues, Dr. John Thomason and Dr. E. Conyers O'Bryan, Jr., concluded that the Darlington Raceway was about the best laboratory they could ever hope to find in which to conduct a stress test, and in that year's Southern 500 they did. They hooked up six drivers to portable electrocardiogram scanners and sent them on their way. At the end of the race, one of their guinea pigs, Dave Marcis, slugged down four huge Cokes and collapsed. Marcis had a resting heart rate of 86, on the high side of average, and the doctors wondered whether there was a correlation between that and his sudden post-race faint. In 1973 Dr. Baroody and Dr. Thomason again hooked up six drivers and ran a more complete test that measured not only heart rate, but fluid and weight loss, changes in blood pressure and blood composition, and several other biochemical niceties.

The drivers tested were chosen to give the doctors a wide cross-section of age, from 26 to 50; ability, from Yarborough, Petty, and Pearson to noncontenders Bill Champion and Joe Frasson; and medical histories, from several "nothing unusual" to Marty Robbins, the Country and Western singer and part-time Grand National racer who in 1969 had undergone a triple coronary bypass. The findings from the two tests were somewhat predictable, but instructive nonetheless.

On an average, the heart rates of the drivers during competition were nearly double their resting rates. To take one driver, David Pearson, through the 1972 test: at rest, 72; moments before the start of the race, 120; at the precise start of the race, 136; during a wreck that he saw but was not involved in, 146; during a yellow-flag caution period, 136; at the finish of the race, 174. Pearson's numbers were not unusual. However, the heart rate of one driver, Richard Brooks, jumped to 214 during an accident in which he was gently but scarily T-boned on the driver's side by another car. "And that," said Dr. Baroody, "is about as high as you can get."

In 1973 the outside air temperature was 90 degrees, the track temperature was 150 degrees, and the temperature inside the race cars reached at least 130 degrees. The six drivers tested that year suffered an average weight loss of 3.6 percent. Richard Petty's weight dropped from 192 pounds to 181 pounds, a loss of 5.7 percent, and he was forced to seek a relief driver with the race two-thirds completed.

The drivers' blood pressures, measured in the driving position, fell dramatically during the three hours, forty minutes it took to run the 1973 race.

Dr. Baroody pointed out that it was impossible to separate the physiological causes of stress from the psychological. The increase in a driver's heart rate moments before a race, for example, was totally psychological in origin, while the increases during a race were a combination of physiological and psychological causes. In the September 1975 issue of *The Physician and Sportsmedicine,* Dr. Baroody and Dr. Thomason concluded, "The combination of these [psychological and physiological] stresses soon causes significant pathophysiologic changes, and impairs the driver's skill, alertness, judgment and accuracy."

ON THURSDAY MORNING AN INDECISIVE CLOUD COVER moved in over Darlington. The relief was slight, but welcome. Outside the track a few cars and several campers were already parked in the grassy fields along Highway 151 in early anticipation of the weekend festival. A gaggle of people were lined up at the raceway office to buy tickets. Next door, at the Joe Weatherly Stock Car Museum and Stock Car Hall of Fame, a trickle of people wandered casually through the aisles looking at an eclectic collection of memorabilia: the fire-red, winged Dodge, No. 6, with which Buddy Baker had set a closed-course speed record for stock cars of over 200 mph at Talladega in the last months of the factory era; those "Bamooda" shorts Fonty Flock had worn to victory in the 1952 Southern 500; the black and gold Ford that Curtis Turner had driven in 1956, when he won twenty-two races on the old convertible circuit, and after the car was converted into a hardtop, the Southern 500; various "cheater" components the backyard mechanics had tried to sneak past NASCAR inspectors over the years; the 1963 Chevrolet in which Junior Johnson had achieved his greatest fame.

In the pit area during the morning practice session, the last before the afternoon qualifying runs that would determine the pole winner and the first twelve starters, nearly every driver who was not on the track fondled a stopwatch and, *click*, checked the progress of his rivals. This ritual was very hierarchical. Hot dogs timed other hot dogs, drivers of the middle rank timed only each other, as though the hot dogs didn't exist, and backmarkers who would be competing for the last few places in the forty-car starting lineup checked only the times of other stragglers. Chief mechanics examined sets of spark plugs with the thoroughness of watchmakers, looking for telltale carbon deposits and hot spots that could inform them of an improperly firing engine. Crew members wheeled fat, treadless racing tires in little toy wagons from the garage area to the Goodyear service tent, then returned with a new set of fat, treadless tires that had been mounted and balanced by strong-armed tire busters. There was a certain tension in the air, but in all honesty, it did not begin to compare with the pressures of first-day qualifying in the best years of the factory era. Then there might have been a dozen or more cars competing for the first eight spaces on the starting grid, and qualifying was a big deal. But times had changed. At Darlington there were only five real contenders, and their qualification was fairly automatic. Winning the pole would be worth almost nothing in terms of money and prestige.

Shortly after eleven o'clock, Yarborough puked an engine in turn three. His oil pressure dropped suddenly to zero, which meant that his oil was no longer circulating through his engine but was gushing out onto the track directly beneath his rear wheels. For a brief, desperate second he slid through the turn sideways at a speed approaching 140 mph, then was able to gather up his car and ease it down off the turn and into the garage area. Yarborough emerged from his car in great distress, not even bothering to arrange his thinning, light-blond hair over a massive frontal bald spot. He recovered quickly, though, and engaged in brief repartee with Baker, Pearson, and other drivers who came over to commiserate. The quips that flew, however, could not hide the fact that Yarborough had no reserve engine on hand and would not be able to qualify the first day. It was just another burden of a season that was already overly long and frustrating.

The track was closed for thirty minutes while maintenance crews distributed a dusty absorbent called Quick-Dri to soak up Yarborough's oil. Almost immediately after the track reopened, there was an unnatural silence on the front straightaway. When a race car was running smoothly, either alone or in a pack, what was actually a very loud and throbbing roar, harsh pebbles of sound, became so much background noise, like piped-in music. If an onlooker's eyes were not on the track, it was easy to forget the car's presence entirely, until a slight change in the pitch of its engine, or worse yet, silence, signaled an untoward event. In this instance it was Joe Frasson, a Minnesotan with the face of a heavyweight and the body of an anvil, who was in trouble. As his car spun along the straight in front of the pits and came to rest in a cloud of white dust and smoke, it looked as though a small grenade had exploded somewhere beneath the driver's compartment. Frasson was unhurt, but a few minutes later he walked through the cafeteria in search of a beer and muttered, "Boy, that scared the hell out of me."

At the end of practice Bobby Allison removed his green-tinted, bubble-shaped driving goggles and his orange driving helmet and said he was going to race his Sportsman car that evening in Savannah, on Friday in Columbia, and on Saturday in Myrtle Beach. Allison enjoyed driving Sportsman races between Grand National events, but three extra races the week of the Southern 500 was, even for him, a hefty undertaking. Pearson changed into his civvies and left the track. Allison said his wife, Judy, wouldn't be in Darlington. "She's all raced out," he said, adding that she often wore down about this time every season. Baker changed into his powder-blue shorts again, looking for all the world like a car salesman on holiday. Allison agreed to a short radio interview in the track cafeteria. When it was over, the interviewer asked him a couple of technical questions about suspension, explaining that he was a part-time racer himself. Petty, who had practiced sparingly, was nowhere to be seen.

QUALIFYING WAS A SIMPLE PROCEDURE. A DRIVER LEFT the pits and had nearly a full lap to get his car up to speed. The first time he passed the start-finish line, the flagman, perched on a screened-in platform ten feet above the outside of the track, gave him the green flag. He made two laps, and the faster of those laps determined his starting position.

At the head of pit road, Don Wall, a dour, former Marine master sergeant, ran the show, connected by radio earphones to the NASCAR control booth above the grandstand. The cars were lined up in scraggly order, many with blankets over their windshields and radiators to help keep out the heat. Wall, bull-necked and dressed in white slacks and a white T-shirt, walked to the first car in line and said to its driver, Richard Childress, "All right. Put your helmet and glasses on. . . ." He paused dramatically as NASCAR voices crackled in his ear ". . . All right. . . ." He gestured dramatically with his beefy right arm, the ringmaster of a mechanized circus. ". . . Let 'er go."

Richard Childress made his run. Unimpressively.

Benny Parsons. His best lap was 151.184 mph, which would be fifth fastest for the day.

David Cisco. He qualified twelfth fastest.

Darrell Waltrip. "One of the next superstars of the Grand National division," said the public address announcer. The next superstar was a disappointing ninth.

G. C. Spencer, an old, old man, a veteran, "a great veteran," threw down a half-smoked cigarette. Spencer's first lap was 146.405 mph, eleventh best, but as he completed his second lap and drove past the pits into turn one to begin his cool-down lap, smoke was pouring from his car. He had obviously blown an engine. But where? A member of Richard Brooks's crew asked Wall whether Spencer's engine had been smoking all the way around the track. Wall's answer was a quick, "No." But just as quickly, the NASCAR radio reported that Spencer had blown while he was coming through turns three and four. The track was closed so Quick-Dri could be laid down at that end of the oval.

Now Buddy Baker's car owner, Big Bud Moore, came over to ask Wall questions of his own. Big Bud, a quiet and bespectacled man, was best described as a cross between a redneck and a hippie. He was one of the last of a generation of Grand National racers who, as they said, knew how to have a good time. Nonetheless, he was serious about his racing, and when drawn to anger, his temper easily matched that of his driver.

"They say he blew out of the groove," said Wall.

"The shit he did," said Big Bud. He stalked away to inform Baker, who was third in line and the first of the real contenders. Baker was not happy when he received Big Bud's message. Although the Quick-Dri did absorb oil, it was not pleasant to have to drive flat out through the dusty powder immediately after it had been laid down.

Tommy Gale failed to qualify.

H. B. Bailey, the stub of a cigar clenched in his teeth, made his run. Slowly.

Buddy Baker, his clenched teeth clenching nothing, his bulky 6 foot 4 inch, 220-pound body wedged as comfortably as was possible in the driving seat of his pearl-white Ford, sponsored by the U.S. Army, turned a fast lap of 152.663 mph. It was the best speed of the day to that point, but Baker said the oil from Spencer's blown engine had worried him and probably cost a tick or two of the clock.

Richard Brooks got in seventh fastest.

Walter Ballard, his red Chevrolet uncluttered by the many decals and signs that signified strong sponsor support, completed his laps and went to the cafeteria to sit with his wife, Katy, where he learned that he had been too slow and would have to requalify on Friday.

Randy Tissot . . . Lennie Pond . . . Jim Vandiver . . . Elmo Langley . . . James Hylton . . .

David Pearson was the first of four fast cars in a row. He had been the fastest throughout practice, driving with grace and precision while the other drivers struggled, and during his qualifying run he neither surprised nor disappointed his followers. His first lap, his faster, was 153.901 mph, a solid 1.6 mph faster than Baker's best.

Bobby Allison . . . Dave Marcis . . . Richard Petty . . .

None of these three nor anyone else came close to Pearson, and the pole was his. He won exactly $300.

Qualifying was over for the day. On Monday, Pearson would share the first row with Baker, Pearson on the inside and Baker on the outside. The contrast between the two in personality, driving style, and achievement was stark and bold. Both were among the five best stock car drivers in the country, but they could not have been more nearly opposite.

IF THIS BOOK WERE ONLY ABOUT DAVID PEARSON, ITS title would be *The Natural* and it would be very short. Unlike Petty, Pearson was not gregarious; unlike Baker, his sense of humor was meek; unlike Allison, he was not complex; unlike Yarborough, he was not particularly colorful. He was, simply, *there,* going about his business with the same professionalism and rectitude that he had demonstrated for most of his sixteen years in Grand National racing. His attitude was that if he had the best car he would win, and if he didn't he wouldn't, so what was the big deal? He, more than any of the other top drivers, was secure in the knowledge that his innate talent would get him through. Going by the record book, he was no worse than the second-best driver in the short history of Grand National racing, and by one standard, quite possibly the best. Although Richard Petty held an unsurpassable lead in total Grand National victories, 173 to 87, on the big tracks they were nearly even. Petty had won 34 superspeedway races; Pearson 33—with considerably fewer starts.

In 1960 Pearson was the Grand National Rookie of the Year, driving a year-old Chevrolet he had built with the financial support of several friends from his hometown of Spartanburg, S.C. In 1961 the intercession of two Spartanburg residents, Cotton Owens, former driver turned car owner, and Joe Littlejohn, a track promoter, got Pearson a ride in a factory Dodge prepared by Ray Fox. Their first race together was the World 600 at Charlotte, which Pearson won. He also won two more superspeedway races that year, nearly overshadowing the performance of another youngster by the name of Freddy Lorenzen and everyone else besides. Then there were six years of nothingness. He won his share of short-track races and even a Grand National driving championship, but he didn't win on a big track again until 1968. For much of that time he drove for Owens, his old benefactor.

"I knew he'd be good because he didn't freeze up on the track," Owens said. "One time, we went to a track he'd never seen before, a road course, and he outqualified everybody by two seconds. *Two seconds.* You can carry him to a long track, a short track, a road track, or a dirt track. It don't make any difference."

But why the long drought on the big tracks?

"Wildness," said Owens. "We were leading at Charlotte in '66 by six laps, and he put it into the wall. A wheel broke because he drove it too hard. Pearson was like all drivers, young and wild, and he thought he had to lead every lap. You only got to lead the last one, and it takes a long time to learn that."

Late in the 1967 season, Pearson switched from Cotton Owens, and Chrysler, to Holman-Moody, and Ford. The new alliance produced back-to-back driving titles in 1968 and 1969. Still, the glory went to other, more public-relations oriented drivers in the Ford stable, and it was something of a shock to Jacque Passino when Pearson once complained mildly, "Why are all those other guys getting the publicity? I've won more money than any of them." Passino had to look it up, but Pearson was right.

In 1970 Pearson had a falling out with John Holman over the driver's percentage of the race purse and left the Holman-Moody ride. For two seasons he languished in obscurity driving some perfectly awful purple Pontiacs owned by a mysterious Indiana entrepreneur named Chris Vallo. But in 1972, Pearson fell into the best deal of his life. Car owner Glen Wood, although without a solid sponsor following the factory pullout, had managed to race several times with A. J. Foyt as his driver. Foyt, of Indianapolis fame, introduced Glen Wood to the Purolator Corporation, and Purolator agreed to sponsor the Wood Brothers full time. Foyt, however, was committed to the United States Auto Club's Championship Car circuit and could only race in a handful of Grand National events. Wood picked up Pearson as a second driver. In 1972 Pearson won six major races in the Wood Brothers Mercury and Foyt won three. The following year Pearson drove for the Wood Brothers alone and won a record ten superspeedway races in just sixteen starts and became the second stock car driver in history, following Petty, to win $1 million in prize money.

Despite his success, Pearson remained in character. "I never wanted to be rich," he said in 1973. "I'm happy. I got enough to buy whatever I want. Some guys, the more they got, the more they want, but I don't know what I'd do if I had more money than I could spend."

Also in 1973, Spartanburg held a David Pearson Day. It was put together by Gene Granger, a Spartanburg journalist, and it was possibly the most terrifying event of Pearson's life.

"I went to Gene once to try and talk him out of it," Pearson said. "I was afraid it'd be a flop, that nobody'd show up."

Over three hundred people did. "I got up to speak," said Pearson. "I had a lot to say, but I wasn't gonna use any notes or anything, and when I got in front of that microphone and saw all those people, I forgot everything. It was a short speech."

And so David Pearson returned to the speedways, where he felt most comfortable, in a race car outfitted with a cigarette lighter to help support his three-packs-a-day habit, and by the eve of the 1975 Southern 500, he had built a most enviable record.

For all his success, the 1975 season had been most awkward for the driver who had come to be known deferentially as "The Gray Fox." He had won only three races, a satisfactory number for almost everyone else but Pearson, and he had lost two by making what most observers thought were grievous driving errors. He was leading the Daytona 500 by almost a full lap when he foolishly tried to pass Cale Yarborough, who was several laps in arrears, as the two headed down the back straight toward turn three. Pearson spun—whether the two cars touched was something their drivers could never agree upon—and crashed into the outside wall, allowing a rather startled Benny Parsons, who had long before resigned himself to second place, to coast home and take the checkers.

Yarborough was taking a shower in the drivers' lounge when he was told that Pearson had accused him of deliberately causing the spinout. Yarborough dressed in a fury and rushed into the center of a cluster of reporters that had gathered around Pearson.

Yarborough said, "I just waded through the crowd and said, 'David, you'd better tell the story like it is. Don't accuse me of doing something that I didn't do.' He didn't accuse me of a thing then, and kind of shook it off and said, 'Let's just forget about it.' I really feel like David knows what happened. I *know* he knows. If he was in his lane and I had turned into him deliberately, it would have been the damndest fight that you ever saw. He'd of had to fight over that."

Less than two months later, Pearson ran into Benny Parsons as the two drivers fought for the lead in the final laps of the Rebel 500 at Darlington and knocked both cars from contention.

Worse than either of those incidents was a third, over a year old, that involved Richard Petty. At the Firecracker 400 at Daytona Beach on July 4, 1974, Pearson had constructed a comfortable lead when a yellow flag allowed Petty to move up on his bumper with just a few laps remaining. On the green-flag restart, Pearson dived to the inside of the track and slowed slightly, apparently in trouble. But it was only a ruse designed to force Petty into the lead so that Pearson could slingshot past him to the checkered flag. Which Pearson did. Petty was furious at what, to his mind, was both a very dangerous maneuver and a devious breach of racing etiquette.

"There's some things you do on a race track and some you don't," said Petty, "and one thing you don't do is let off on the race track, not halfway down the straightaway. It's just a cardinal sin, more or less, and I lost a lot of confidence in him. I've told people before that if David and I were to go down to the corner and he'd make a right-hand turn through the fence, I'd follow him because I'd figure he knows what he's doing. That's how much confidence I had in him, but that took a lot of it away.

"We had a pretty big argument, heckling each other. I wadn't blaming the part of him winning the race, and I wadn't blaming the part of getting outsmarted. What I was getting at was, it was a very, very dangerous move in a very dangerous situation. If I'da happened to have touched him, there'da been two crashed cars there. And there'da been some tore-up heads. If they hadn'ta been tore up when we got out of the race car, there'da been some tore up after."

And so there were questions. Had Pearson lost his natural ability, finally, to age? Was he near the end of his career? He was, after all, 40 years old and a grandfather, and there was much talk of his impending retirement.

BUDDY BAKER'S REAL NAME WAS ELZIE WYLIE BAKER, JR. He was square of jaw, steely of eye, and he had a lilting, tippy-toe gait in the manner of Rod Steiger, the actor, playing the role of Napoleon Bonaparte. He smoked three packs of cigarettes per day, minimum, always filtered, usually mentholated. He chewed an unknown quantity of gum, and took Tylenol during his pit stops. He had a sharp intelligence, sometimes disjointed.

Once, early in his career, Baker was on his way to a race somewhere with Little Bud Moore, the driver, and Humpy Wheeler, of Firestone. An argument bubbled, over the existence of flying saucers. Wheeler loudly opined that they did. Little Bud heatedly asserted that they didn't. Baker was silent, pondering the weighty rhetoric.

Finally, he announced his verdict. Yes, he said, in his opinion flying saucers were for real.

Little Bud was livid. "How can you say that?" he shouted. "The people in them—they would have talked to us."

Baker paused. "Would you talk to an ant?" he cooed.

If David Pearson was a natural, then Buddy Baker could only be described as an unnatural. Pearson was impressive because he was so comfortable with his ability, and so unaware of it, that he did not act like a race driver at all. Baker was impressive because to others it appeared as though he acted the way he thought a race driver ought to act. It was as though he carried around with him a well-thumbed copy of *The Race Driver's Guide to Proper Deportment:* "Before a race, be grim, tense, aloof; during a race, be fierce and unyielding; after a race, be angry when you lose and tearful when you win." Which was strange because David Pearson's father spent too much of his life in a cotton mill while Buddy Baker's father, Elzie Wylie Baker, Sr.—Buck—was a hard-nosed bus driver for the Duke Power Company in North Carolina who became a fierce, naturally fierce, star of the dirt-track era, a contemporary and an equal of the Flock brothers, Curtis Turner, Joe Weatherly, Lee Petty, and all the rest, and won two Grand National driving championships.

Thus, Buddy Baker was born to racing. He entered a Grand National race for the first time in 1959, driving a second family car prepared by his father. The liaison didn't last long. Buddy crashed so often that he almost put his father in the poorhouse. "I don't know how I drove in races then," Buddy said. "I wasn't all that good on the highway." In the early 1960s, Baker drove a series of independent cars that were no match for the sleek and powerful automobiles being bankrolled by the factories, and it was not until 1967 that he won his first race, the National 500, in his hometown of Charlotte. Possibly because the wait had been so long, Baker said that in Victory Circle he uncharacteristically felt all the emotion of a Philadelphia lawyer. The wins came no more easily after that, though his cars were usually among the best, and whenever Baker did triumph, there was the sense that *he* felt he had just won his first race all over again. On the eve of the 1975 Southern 500, he had exactly ten career victories.

Baker's problem was certainly not a lack of courage. He and Yarborough were rated equal in that department. Nor was it a lack of talent, although most of his wins had come on the biggest tracks, where there was a premium on balls, and hardly any on the short tracks, where there was a decided emphasis on finesse. The problem, if he had one—and it was generally agreed that he did—was his awesome lack of judgment and sense of pace. These were faults of which he was well aware. Although he lost frequently, he made up for it by losing spectacularly, often in the waning moments of a race. During one particularly ghoulish stretch, when Baker crashed, cut tires, ran out of gas, and otherwise injured his car, always, it seemed, with victory in plain sight, Baker moaned, "If only these things were 20 laps shorter."

For years he was considered to be accident prone. That was not precisely true, although once he did eliminate himself from a race by crashing his car during a caution period. It was just that he could not judge accurately when his car was strong and when it was weakening.

Still, he was one of the more popular Grand National drivers, a hero to those who liked their favorites to go all out for the entire distance. Humpy Wheeler said, "When the green flag drops, Baker's eyes turn red. He's intense and headstrong, which are perfectly normal feelings for somebody who works in a hostile environment at speeds up to 200 mph. He's an absolute master of the unexpected. There's not one other driver out there who isn't scared absolutely crapless when Buddy's behind him. Nobody knows what he's going to do, probably including Baker. He is the only top driver down here who can sell tickets without winning races."

Baker's size gave him a certain presence, and his sense of humor was unfailing. He ripped off one-liners that were always on the mark. Of Darlington, he once said, "You got to be a genius just to drive into the pits here." Things like that.

Darlington was the track where Baker had achieved his greatest success, winning the 1970 Southern 500 and the following spring's Rebel 500 back to back. Partly because his father had won the Southern 500 three times, partly because his mother's family was from nearby Florence, the Southern 500 was the race he cherished the most and the Darlington Raceway the track whose history he could most appreciate.

"When I walk into this place," he said, "I feel I'm here to race. That happens at other tracks, too, of course, but here the tradition really gets to you."

Perhaps that was a little sentimental, even corny. But this was how he described his Southern 500 win: "In the last laps of the race, when I knew I was going to win, it just hit me. It was a dream come true. I had watched my daddy win for the first time here in 1953, and I had stood on the main straight after the race when all the people swarmed down on him. My kid vision was to win here, and then to know it was going to happen. . . . It was a difficult feeling to explain. It was like I was choking to death. I was excited to the point it almost took the fun out of it. I grabbed a large Coke in Victory Lane, which was the wrong thing to do, and almost went to my knees. I was sick for two days. But after those two days, I was a proud son of a gun. And the look of my kids . . . Even though they weren't that old, they knew I'd done something."

YARBOROUGH'S IMPORTED DRIVING SHOES WERE MADE OF soft red and black leather, and there was a neat row of metal studs along the sides and around the heels. Further, the heel of his right shoe was built up with Styrofoam and gray electrician's tape. The purpose of the studs and the Styrofoam-and-tape reinforcement was to protect his feet from the searing heat transmitted to the floorboard by the exhaust pipes that ran beneath his car. Yarborough's shoes were a ragged mess, being the oldest of three pairs he had once owned. The other two pairs had been ripped off, in Daytona Beach and Atlanta.

Baker's shoes were similar to Yarborough's, except they were newer and neater and had no external reinforcement.

Pearson wore plain black loafers.

Allison's shoes were suede and crepe-soled.

Petty wore black, beat-up cowboy boots. They would have been true shit-kickers except they were square-toed. The heel of his left boot was reinforced in a way similar to the heel of Yarborough's right.

BY LATE THURSDAY AFTERNOON YARBOROUGH'S BLOWN engine had been removed from his car, and it now hung suspended, like a wounded testicle, from a portable chain hoist. It was an awesome and frightening sight, this $15,000 engine just hanging there with a gaping, jagged hole the size of a man's fist in the left side of its oil pan, right where the oil pan joined with the engine block; right where a broken connecting rod had seized up and let loose. The phrase "a blown engine" meant exactly that. There was talk that Yarborough would have to borrow an engine for Friday's qualifying session from another team.

ON THURSDAY NIGHT THE UNION 76–DARLINGTON Record Club banquet was held at the Florence Country Club. A driver gained membership in the Record Club by qualifying his car faster than all the other cars of the same make that were entered in the Southern 500 in a given year. The club was of no particular significance, but its sponsor, the Union 76 Oil Company, gave a great deal of money and technical support to Grand National racing, and because of this the drivers attended the annual affair faithfully.

Cale Yarborough arrived in a white sport coat and talked about hair transplants. "I'm fixin' to have some more done this winter," he said. Hal Hamrick, a track promoter and radio announcer, stabbed a cold shrimp and said he knew a good guy in Atlanta for that sort of thing.

David Pearson arrived in a loud sport shirt that defied description and immediately sat down to await dinner at the first table he came to.

Richard Petty looked across the banquet hall to a far wall where large black and white pictures of each member were displayed, in order of their induction. Petty, who joined the club in 1963, said, "Go look at me when I was beautiful," and grinned his pearly white grin. The collection of flattop, burr-top, and greased-back hairstyles in the pictures made the wall look like a photographic reunion of the Class of '55. Junior Johnson looked for all the world like the Homecoming King of Wilkes County, N.C.

WALTER BALLARD ENTERED THE HALL AND SAT DOWN IN a straightback chair off by himself. He was 42 years old, slightly pudgy, and had curly hair and a tired, twinkling smile. A driver who also owned his own car, Ballard was from Charlotte by way of Houston. He was perhaps the most independent of the independents, and had been since 1971, the year he joined the Grand National circuit. That year he was named Grand National Rookie of the Year, and made the Record Club through something of a fluke, having driven a Ford in a year when none of the dozen or so Fords that were entered at Darlington was particularly fast. Ballard had failed to qualify his decal-free red Chevrolet that afternoon and would have to go to the line again Friday. In this respect, Ballard was in the same predicament as Yarborough. It was one of the few times when Ballard had something in common with Yarborough, or with any of the other top drivers.

Question: What were you doing in Houston before you joined the Grand National circuit full time in 1971?

Ballard: I'd run super-modifieds there ten or twelve years in all, I guess. I held the track record in Houston for three years and won a lots of features. Always was a front-runner. If I wasn't second or third, I was first. If I wasn't first, I was wrecked or either quit running.

Question: Why did you decide to run Grand Nationals?

Ballard: Just like everybody else, I'd set there and read books and all this stuff about Grand National, where they got this big, publicized deal up there. Actually, I'm more a fan than I am anything else. I enjoy racing with the big hot dogs and being associated with 'em. One reason I came was just to see if I *could* run, and how long I could run. I knew I didn't have the money or equipment. I had no intention of ever coming up and outrunning those guys. The hot dogs, they go there and they're worried about the pole. I'm worried about making the race.

Question: Did you have any hope, in 1971, of acquiring the sponsorship you knew you'd need to be competitive?

Ballard: We had several deals working. The lawyers stopped one man from doing it. He was a millionaire, and he was fixing to put in a bunch of money. But when it came down to his lawyers, his advisors, they wouldn't let him do it. They convinced him that if he had his name on the side of the car, he'd get sued if it ran up in the stands and killed people. So I quit messing with him.

As far as a sponsor, I've never had one. I'll pick up a sponsor for $300 or $400 for just the one race in different locations, but I'm not much of a salesman. Maybe I don't work hard enough at it, but I'm the kind of a guy that I hate like hell to go in and ask a man for money, and that's about what you're doing. I'll just take my two dollars and go on.

Question: What are the finances of an independent? What does it actually cost you to run a car for a season?

Ballard: It's costing me a minimum of $75,000 a year. That includes expenses and everything that's deductible on your taxes, which your motel bills and your food bills and your help—all of this stuff—is. There's nobody can come up here and run for less than that because that's doing most of the work yourself. I have a man that works for me full time, one man, but he doesn't mess with the engines or nothing like that. I build my own engines. I buy a lot of used tires. I might buy $1,000 or $2,000 worth of tires in one time, all used, from the hot dogs. I pay anywhere from $20 to $50 a tire, depending on how much they've been used, so you save a lot of money there. But you cain't run like you want to. I'm always running tires that's done been cooled off and got harder from being hot.

Anytime you take a piece of rubber and heat it and let it cool, it's gonna be harder, and they're not gonna run worth a damn, even though the tire might practically look like a new tire. That's the reason my car won't drive as good and handle as good as theirs.

Question: So, how do you get back that $75,000?

Ballard: Usually I end up breaking even for a year. I've usually won about $35,000 a year in money out of the purse. And then we're on what they call a research deal. If I'm in the top twenty-five in points, the following year I get show-up money. I get $500 extry money for a superspeedway, and I get $250 for a short track. Now, if I hit the wall, say, I can go up and see The Man—the promoter—and even though I'm on a $500 deal, he'll write me another check for a certain amount of money. If I had a good day, I don't go in and talk to him, but if you've had a bad day, you're always going in and talking to promoters. They've got some purty nice promoters, and there is some of them that won't give you anything. Your research money and the extry deals . . . You'll probably pick up, say, between $15,000 and $20,000 a year. Then you've got your point money at the end of the year. About the minimum I've got is $10,000. I have gotten up as high as $20,000.

Question: You're up to around $70,000. That leaves you $5,000 short.

Ballard: Right. This year I'm about $15,000 short, right now. The other years I've broken even.

Question: What do you think about on the race track?

Ballard: Probably the thing I'm most thinking about is I wish to hell my car'd run faster so I could run up there with those guys having all the fun. But other than that, I don't have much thought other than I hope to hell the thing stays together to finish the race. I'm trying to concentrate on what's happening. The guy like me has to drive harder than a guy up front because I have to drive with the rearview mirror as much as I do with my head. We have to look and make sure that we don't get in their way or nothing. We're actually more busy than they are.

Question: One would think that would get to you after a while.

Ballard: It does.

Question: In what way?

Ballard: Well, it just feels like you're less of a man, or something, because you can't do the things they do. But . . . you know in your own mind and heart that it's just because you didn't have the equipment to start with. I wish to hell every time I pit I could have a man slap me a new set of tires on. You can have all the horsepower in the world, but if you hadn't got good rubber on your car, the guy with the new tires is gonna beat the hell out of you.

Question: What is your general impression of the top drivers?

Ballard: I don't have no different impression of them than I do of any of the guys that runs in my class. They're the same kind of people. They're just running faster. Those guys have got a lot of pressure on them because they're driving somebody else's car, and they've got to go up front. If I'm driving my car and I don't feel like running as fast as it'll go, I don't have to. I ain't got nobody to answer to. But those guys do. They've got to be ready to go wide open all day long, so you'll find 'em in a deep trance a lot of times. And other times they're just like the rest of us. When they relax, there's no difference.

Question: How do the hot dogs feel about drivers like yourself, the independents?

Ballard: The way I look at it, they enjoy in getting along good with us because they know if they don't, that I can get in their damned way and stop 'em—slow 'em up, cost 'em a race, or whatever. So they'll come around and talk to you. They appreciate you moving over for them and giving them room to race. There has to be a certain amount of social deal there because the guys like myself, or any guy in the back . . . I feel like I'm just as much a man as they are, and if they start screwing around with me, I can screw around right back with them. And it's going to cost them more money than it's going to cost me.

Question: Have you ever been tempted?

Ballard: I've had some anger moments.

Question: How would you describe yourself, as a driver?

Ballard: I feel like I could drive just as good as they could if I had the equipment. Now, whether we know that to be a fact, it'll never be found out because I'm wise enough to know

I'll never have the equipment and stuff they've got. It would take time, just like everything else, but I do feel that way.

Question: Then why did you wait until you were 38 years old to try Grand National racing?

Ballard: Well, if I'da waited until I was 42, right now, I'da waited *way* too long, wouldn't I? But like I said, I came up here because I'm probably one of the number one fans. And I got a good seat.

I feel like this: I've accomplished a lot that a lot of people haven't accomplished up here, and with a helluva lot less money. I'm in my fifth year, and after the first two or three races I tried in the Grand National, I've missed one race in five years. I feel like it's a helluva accomplishment, that I've done damned good to make all the shows. And I've gotten in the Darlington Record Club, I've won Rookie of the Year, I've won a couple other awards. So it hasn't been all that disheartening to me, for a man my age.

Ten years ago, I could go like hell, but you get up to your forties, and then you'll slow down. I'm not near the man I was, and it aggravates the hell out of me.

Question: How do you notice that on the race track?

Ballard: On the race track, it doesn't bother you so much. Just like David Pearson. He's about the same age I am and it doesn't bother him, but all he has to do is come to the race track and concentrate on driving. Never touches the car. But I have to go out and work my butt off all damned week long. I get out to the race track, and I'm flat give out. Tired. I used to go all night long, twenty-four hours a day, and it'd never bother me. But I can't do it any more. I put in eight or ten hours out there in that shop working with that damned race car, my God, I'm beat. Ten years ago, if something hadn't been done I wanted done, I'm ready to go another eight or ten hours. But now, I'll walk over and look at the car and walk away.

ON FRIDAY THE TROUBLE BEGAN SHORTLY AFTER THE track opened for morning practice and continued throughout the afternoon qualifying session. The best drivers were safely in the race, all except Yarborough, but for those of lesser ability and without the best equipment, the pressure of attempting to make the race was greater than the demands would be of the race itself.

In practice, Dexter Price spun in turn one and flattened all four tires. Coo Coo Marlin slid into the wall, a minor shunt that scraped the paint from the entire right side of his Chevrolet and cracked its windshield. Carl Adams, a rookie, was next. As he later told the press, "I just flat got took. I knew I was flirting with danger by going into the first turn so hard, and all of a sudden I was skating on thin ice. The car just took off and kissed the wall real good." In the garage area, Adams looked at his crumpled racer with disgust.

The mishaps continued during qualifying. Grant Adcox, another rookie, backed into the wall in turn two. Earl Brooks, who was 46, spun out—the first time, he said, that he had done something like that during qualifying in twenty-eight years of racing. "I should have known better," he said. "I just got my face slapped." And finally, Bruce Jacobi, a 40-year-old veteran of other kinds of racing but a Grand National rookie, hit the outside wall in turn four, then continued on at an angle and hit the inside wall in front of the pits. It was a violent accident, both halves of it, but Jacobi was not injured. His car, however, was fairly battered on both sides, a prelude to Monday.

ALL THESE UNTOWARD INCIDENTS, THOUGH MINOR IN nature, were indications that the Darlington Raceway was once again beginning to work its devious magic. Indeed, the appeal of the Southern 500 was related directly to the unusual and demanding nature of the track. And to its long history as well. From the time it opened in 1950 until the first race at the Daytona International Speedway in 1959, Darlington was the only big track upon which the Grand National cars raced regularly, and thus the stories of its mysteries went back at least a decade farther than those of the second- and third-generation superspeedways, all of which were more gentle, more forgiving, more antiseptic. By 1975 the Southern 500 was neither the richest Grand National race nor the longest nor fastest, but its prestige remained unsurpassed.

The track had gone through four evolutionary changes

during its twenty-five-year history. It was built to a length of 1¼ miles with both its sweeping turns banked 16 degrees. In 1953 the one-two turn was pushed out a bit, increasing the track's length to roughly 1⅜ miles, and the banking of the turns was increased to 26 degrees. This was the configuration that lasted the longest. In 1969 the three-four turn was totally remodeled, with rather strange results. In 1974 more work was done in the three-four turn in a largely unsuccessful attempt to undo the results of the earlier remodeling.

Other changes were brought about by fears, not completely unfounded, of mass slaughter. The scoring stand originally had been placed on the outside of turn four to give the scorers a better view of the track. This was a fine idea, except that in 1960 Johnny Allen sailed out of the track and couldn't have hit the scorer's stand a fiercer blow if he had aimed for it. Fortunately, the day was chilly, the stand was half in the sun and half in the shade, and all the scorers were huddled together in the sun. Allen smashed into the shaded section of the stand and was the only person hurt. The next year, the stand was moved back to the inside of the turn.

Until 1966 the Darlington press box was precariously situated on thin stilts outside the guard rail in turn one, giving the nation's motor-sports writers a unique opportunity to flex their collective machismo and demonstrate their collective foolhardiness. The press box afforded the writers an absolutely superb head-on view of the cars as they barreled down the main straight, but being no more than twenty feet away from the guard rail, a pair of rubbery metal bands, it was also the only press box in the country that filled up from the back row first. Finally, it was an open-air structure, and with the swirling dust, dirt, and granular rubber, it was often difficult to tell writer from driver at the end of 500 miles of racing. The difference was made painfully clear on occasion by the press box's permanent residents, a swarm of hornets.

In 1966 things changed forever. One writer, having arrived late, was escorted to a lovely first-row seat. Midway through the race he lowered his head to scribble something on his note pad, and as he did, he sensed a menacing change of pitch in the sound of rolling thunder. Reacting quickly, he raised his head just in time to see the *under*side of a race car hurtle past at eye level. When he and his fellow writers were able to talk, they determined that Earl Balmer had mounted the guard rail after having been hit from behind and had come within a teeter of falling outside the track and at the very least collapsing the press box's meager supports.

Following that incident, Darlington's was the only press box in the country that didn't fill up at all. The guard rail in the one-two turn was replaced with more unyielding concrete, and two years later Balmer's Box, as the place had come to be known, was enclosed, moved back a few feet, and given stronger underpinnings. The hornets were evicted, too.

(Darel Dieringer, who won the 1966 Southern 500, much later said of Balmer, "He was a peculiar driver. His theory of driving a race car was if he drove it in the corner and made it, that meant the next time he could drive it in farther. It's not a very good theory.")

PERHAPS THE MOST ACCURATE REMARK ABOUT THE Darlington Raceway and the Southern 500 was made by Bobby Isaac. "I'd rather drive almost any other track," he said, "but I'd rather win this race more than any other on the circuit." Why? Simply because it had been there the longest and was the most demanding test, physically and mentally, that the drivers faced.

The reasons were technically precise. Because each straightaway was relatively short, 1,800 feet, and the fastest cars lapped the track in excess of 150 mph, there was little time to relax anywhere on the circuit. Rest & Relaxation on a race track was obviously relative, but at mammoth plants such as Daytona and Talladega, drivers' minds often wandered during the duller stages of a race even though their cars were traveling in excess of 200 mph. On the long chutes the drivers could enjoy a tight sweater and other race-track scenery, converse with each other by hand signals, exchange bawdy humor with their crew chiefs over two-way radios, and even, as David Pearson did, light up a cigarette.

There was no such respite at Darlington. A driver, it seemed, was always in traffic, and forever had to be aware of the cars with which he was racing, the cars he was about to pass, and the cars about to overtake him. He was on the front and back chutes for about six seconds each, but because the straights were slightly banked, he had to keep his car in a firm, right-hand bind.

Then there was the Darlington Trap to worry about. Six seconds was not quite enough time for one very fast car to cleanly pass another very fast car, and since Darlington had but one fast racing groove, six seconds was also not enough time for the car being overtaken to negotiate turn four, say, and pull down to the inside and let the faster car go by on the high side, which was the proper etiquette on nearly every other big track. Therefore, the driver making the pass often had to dive to the low side himself, praying all the while that the slightly slower car stayed high, then line up in front of the car he had passed before they both reached the next turn. It was a sophisticated game of chicken, and it was played on almost every lap.

The west, or one-two, turn was a problem because a split second after a driver flipped his steering wheel and began to drop low into the turn, he hit a series of ripples not unlike the ribs of a mammoth tuna. These ripples were delightful leftovers from the earliest years of the track when a stream, since diverted, ran beneath turn one and caused frequent cave-ins, which made necessary equally frequent repairs. In a passenger car, with its mushy suspension, a driver would not feel a thing; in a race car, however, this was like running over a washboard, or a series of finely spaced frost heaves. As the centrifugal force of the turn began to push his car up the rippled banking toward the outside concrete wall, a driver felt absolutely certain that he was without solid traction.

(A word about retaining walls. There were two ways to protect a driver who had run out of race track. One was with steel guard rails supported from behind by heavy wood pilings. The other was with concrete. The advantage of a guard rail was that if a driver bumped it gently, all it would do is give a little, scrape his car slightly, and send him on his way. The disadvantage was that if he clobbered it hard, it would occasionally break apart and perhaps even leave a hole big enough for him to sail out of the track through, which was not often pleasant either for him or for any spectators on the far side. Concrete, on the other hand, rarely broke up under even the most severe impact; under a slight impact, it didn't give at all. That, as it were, was the rub. If a driver even brushed a concrete wall, the chances were good that he would have to pit at least long enough for his crew to bend away a fender or two from a tire or two, perhaps longer.)

So. There was a moment during every lap about a third of the way through the west turn when a driver not only felt that his car was out of control, but knew for certain that he was going to drift out to within a foot or two of that concrete wall through absolutely no fault of his own. He wanted to be high exiting the turn, but he might have wished for a little more say in exactly how high.

If a driver successfully negotiated all that, and then the back straight, he then had to worry about the east, or three-four, turn. The east turn made the west turn seem a snap.

Before 1969, when the east turn got its face lifted the first time, that section of the track caused more heartache than all the rest put together. Right from the first race, when Red Byron put the two right-side wheels of his 1950 Cadillac high near the single guard rail, which was all that then stood between the drivers and disaster, the drivers realized that the fastest way through the turn was in a groove that carried them to within six inches or so of the top. This was not a tremendous margin for error, and whenever there was the slightest bobble, *wham,* into the rail a car would go. Although not considered good form at first, after some unintentional experimentation a few hardy souls began to slap the rail on purpose, ride it around for a bit, and then fall away from the fence and line up for the run down the main straight. Drivers discovered that hitting the barrier actually helped them get through the turn faster, if, of course, they didn't cut a tire or mess up their suspensions in the process. Fireball Roberts once remarked, "If I could put roller skates on the side of my car, this turn would be perfect."

The maneuver produced strange sights, for after only a few high-speed laps the lead cars in every Southern 500 would invariably show the telltale streaks where they had struck the wall. The "Darlington Stripe" was not only the mark of a fast car, but its driver's badge of courage as well.

"No one really *wanted* to hit the guard rail," said Pete Hamilton, "but you had to drive as though it wasn't there. You usually got it with the right rear first. You would hit and never get off the gas. It was so quick. Just a *whap.* Jeez, the first time for me, it sounded like the car had fallen apart. I thought I had destructed. It would go *blrrrp* because the sections of the rail overlapped, and it was like you'd run a stick across a wicket fence."

The additional 10 degrees of banking that were added in 1969 meant that the drivers no longer had to challenge the outer limit of the east turn quite so openly, but the remodeling also created another problem. There was still only one fast groove, and it was still as high up in the turn as a car could go, but now the groove literally ended long before the finish of the turn and there was no exit. Before 1969 a driver could stay in the topmost lane all the way through the turn in a reasonably constant-radius arc; if he tried that after 1969, he would wind up in Row Six of the Paddock grandstand. Drivers had to drift beautifully through the first part of the turn, then abruptly snap their steering wheels hard left long before they had exited the turn in order to get their cars off the wall and pointed down the main straight.

In the latest remodeling of the one-two turn, in 1974, the guard rail was replaced with concrete, and an attempt was made to make the turn wide enough for passing. Well, a driver could pass there, if he was very careful and very lucky, but all the new work really did was make the turn faster. This annoyed at least one driver no end, for it was in the east turn in 1970, between remodelings, that Richard Petty had the only serious accident of his career. He drove into the fourth turn too high and too far, just as Freddy Lorenzen would do the next year, and when he tried to cut down, his Plymouth slid up and clobbered the wall. The impact shattered his steering, and he came straight across the track and hit the inside wall. Petty was knocked cold, and while his left arm dangled out the window like a rag doll's, his car began to flip. Petty suffered only a dislocated shoulder, but retained bad memories of that day.

"I've lost some of my enthusiasm for Darlington," he said. "It was a driver's race track and I really liked it, and now . . . well, I haven't really liked it since they redone it in '69. It made the track a lot faster, and there wasn't room to make the track faster. I guess up till my accident I knew the track was dangerous, but maybe I didn't realize how dangerous. Now I know you can get your neck broke right quick if you're not careful."

Several years earlier, Petty had spoken more gently of Darlington. "At most tracks," he said, "the two turns are pretty much the same. But here, in the one-two turn you're loose, and in the three-four turn you're pushing. If you set up for one, you can't get through the other. Everything you do to your car is a compromise. You don't come close to using all your engine.

"I'll tell you, a lot more races are lost on this track than are ever won. On most tracks, you've got a margin for error; here, you're on the edge all the time. You slide just a little, and you watch the rest of the race from the pits. You can't relax. . . . Oh, maybe you can after a little while, but you can drive 50 laps perfect, and the next time around you'll be flat sideways and that wall will come out and grab you, and you'll swear somebody spit on the track. It's a tough one to figure out. If a cat finishes this race without running over nothin', he can sleep good that night. He don't have to win, and that might not be true at other tracks."

THE WEATHER ON FRIDAY WAS CLEAR AND DRY, BUT STILL oppressively hot, and there was a report that a hurricane moving through the Gulf of Mexico might well affect the race, now less than seventy-two hours away.

In the track cafeteria, a driver told Bob Myers of *The Charlotte News,* "I love racing, but it cost me my wife, it cost me my father, and it isn't going to cost me anything else until I get me some money."

In another part of the cafeteria, Walter Ballard talked with his wife, Katy, a blond and beautiful woman who played a race-track beauty queen in *The Last American Hero,* a film loosely based on the life of Junior Johnson. As Walter left to make his qualifying run, Katy said, "You stay off that wall, now. Don't come back here if you hurt that car."

A half-hour later Ballard returned, in his civvies, and plopped down at a table. "On the second lap I done messed up," he said. "I got all crooked." Still, he was the sixth fastest of the day's twelve qualifiers.

Cale Yarborough also made the show, using an engine his car owner, Junior Johnson, had borrowed for the occasion from Hoss Ellington, another Chevrolet owner. Although Yarborough was the day's fastest qualifier, he would have to start the race in thirteenth position.

ON SATURDAY THE FINAL SIXTEEN CARS OF THE FORTY-car field were qualified. One of them was not Joe Frasson's. The Minnesotan crashed again, nearly duplicating his mishap of Thursday. He was taken to the field hospital in an ambulance but was quickly released, sporting a limp and a sour disposition. He explained that on Thursday a "thin-walled" drive shaft had come undone and shattered into three pieces, which was why his car had looked as though a small bomb had gone off beneath it. On Saturday he substituted a "thick-walled" drive shaft, which also broke loose. Only this time it did not fragment. It punched a hole up through the floorboard and came into the driver's compartment, slamming Frasson's interior fire extinguisher into his right leg. Frasson also explained that the night before he had had to run the last 30 laps of a Sportsman race in Columbia on a soft tire, which had effectively removed him from contention.

"It's been a helluva week," a friend commiserated.

"I should have gone fishing," Frasson grumbled.

FOR THE TOP DRIVERS, THERE WAS NOTHING MUCH TO DO on Saturday. Yarborough's crew worked to install his race engine, which had arrived from Junior Johnson's shop in North Wilkesboro, 200 miles to the north, but activity around the other cars was minimal. It was a convenient time to pause and consider Richard Petty and Bobby Allison, the two drivers who were perhaps the most interesting of the five who had come to dominate stock car racing, and who would be starting side by side in row two, behind David Pearson and Buddy Baker.

As with Pearson and Baker, the contrasts between Petty and Allison were pronounced.

Petty, who had reigned supreme in the South for most of his career, had the facile intelligence of the confident insider. Allison, who had challenged that supremacy for nearly a decade, sometimes successfully, sometimes not, was the introspective outsider. Petty, who lived in Level Cross, N.C., had always had at his disposal the best Grand National cars money could buy. Allison, who was raised in Miami and lived in Hueytown, Ala., a suburb of Birmingham, came up through the ranks, racing modified and Sportsman cars for years before he joined the Grand National circuit. In background and personality, they were point and counterpoint, a fact that had often put them in violent conflict on the race track, particularly in 1971 and 1972. On no fewer than twenty occasions during those two years they finished one-two, and hardly a Sunday afternoon went by without a heated post-race discussion of each other's driving tactics.

Question: When you were growing up, did you get much encouragement from your family regarding your racing?

Allison: I got discouragement from my family. At the time, racing really hadn't cleaned up its act, so to speak. I knew guys that ran whiskey for a living and raced for a hobby, and my parents were sensitive to those kind of things. They wanted their son to be an upstanding young gentleman and all the other things that all parents want their children to be, and they tried to discourage me at first. But they found out I was serious about what I wanted to do, and they also, I think, recognized that racing was becoming more and more an American sport, a really bona fide, 100 percent American sport. As I went on, they became great supporters of mine.

When I was a senior in high school, me and a bunch of my buddies found one small, abandoned race track, and we'd drive our school cars around that thing as wide open as we could. Those guys would spin out and hit the fence and all those sort of things, but I never did because when the car started to slide, I did something to change it. I backed off the gas, or I got on the brakes, or I'd turn the steering wheel—something. I didn't wait until the thing was totally out of control. Another thing that we did that I always thought was a tremendous amount of fun was to purposely put the car out of control. I was raised in Miami, Florida, and the big arena in our area was the Westflagler Kennel Club, the dog-racing track, and their parking lots were these tremendous grass fields. Miami being almost a tropical climate, there were a lot of afternoon and evening showers, and what was fun was to come right down the main street at 40, 50, 60 miles an hour—whatever you could get away with—and turn out into one of those grass fields and see how many times you could spin around before the car stopped. I feel like even that gave me some experience at the feel of a car.

In 1959 I went to Alabama. I heard there was good racing in Alabama, and I just put the race car, a modified, behind the pickup truck and went to Dothan because that was the closest big city in Alabama to Miami. And I asked a guy there, "Hey, do you know where there's any race tracks?" And he said, "Yeah, up in Montgomery." So I went to Montgomery and I asked the guy, "Hey, where's the race track?" And he said, "C'mon, I'll show you. We're racing tomorrow night, but they're racing in Birmingham tonight. I know the promoter and I'll call him for you. He'll give you a place to work on your car, and he'll do this and he'll do that, and boy, just go have a big time." And so I did.

I knew I wanted to race, but by then Judy [Allison's girl friend] and I had been going together a long time, and I felt I was very much in love and that marriage was somewhere in the near future. And with marriage was responsibilities. I had to be serious about supporting her and whatever family came along. If I'da just struggled along and couldn't make a living, I know that I would have had to adjust my thinking to do something else as a career and maybe race as a hobby. But the second weekend I was in Alabama, I won my first professional feature race ever. That was a very timely situation.

Question: Was there ever any question about your driving a race car?

Petty: It wadn't no burning desire or anything, but I wanted to try it. When I got to be 18, I told daddy [his father, Lee] I wanted to drive a car and he said, "No. Wait until you're 21." When he said that, I said, "Okay," because I knew I wasn't going to drive until I was 21. I think parents were a little sterner then. And so when I got to be 21, I said, "Build me a Sportsman car, and in a couple of years I'll sort of learn how to drive." He said, "No. If you take a Sportsman car, it's going to take you two or three years to learn to drive it, and then when you get in the Grand National, it's going to take you two or three years to learn how to drive *it.* If you want to drive Grand Nationals, the best thing to do is to get in one. In two or three years, you'll know how to drive it." He wadn't too far off.

Question: Three prerequisites for good driving seem to be confidence in your own ability, confidence that your car won't hurt you, and smoothness. Would you agree?

Petty: That's three of 'em. I don't have any more. A lot of people win races that's not smooth and a lot of people run that really hadn't got that much confidence in their equipment, but they got enough confidence in theirselves that they can carry the load. Now, from my standpoint, I probably hit all three of 'em pretty close. I've got fair confidence in myself, I've got tremendous confidence in the car, and I try to drive smooth. Sometimes I just don't look like I do it, but I know that's the best way.

Question: When you say "smooth," do you mean the ability to clip off lap times that are within a tenth of a second of each other, or . . . ?

Petty: Well, that's part of it. But the overall deal is, we run so many long races, you've gotta be constant in whatever you do. Whether you run slow or fast, you need to be even at it, and that's what you call being smooth. Some people run erratic. They'll run real fast for a while, and then they'll slow up or loaf for a while, and then they'll run fast again. When you jerk a car around, you can use up any equipment, no matter how good it is. Especially in a long race. Basically, I might not run as fast to begin with, but I try to run the same speed the whole race. That's consistency just as much as anything. That's what makes a smooth driver.

Question: Did you always have confidence in your own ability?

Petty: Not really. When I first started driving a race car, my father was taking the same cars and winning races and championships and beatin' everybody. When I crashed the car or got outrun, I couldn't jump out and say it's the car's fault. I knew they was winnin' cars. I had to say I done the best I could: I'll have to do better the next time.

I knew I had to be able to beat some of the cats out there running, and the deal then was learning to beat the ones in the back. Once I got them beat, then I moved up to the middle crowd. And then I got to working on the cats up front. But even when I won a race, I wasn't constant. I'd run one good show and have two bad ones. Everybody has good nights. But once I could have more good nights than I had bad nights, I felt like I was on the right track. That builds confidence in you, and the more confidence you've got, the harder you can press yourself. Not particularly as far as being a careless driver or anything, but you just concentrate more on what you're doing. By 1960, my third season, I felt pretty confident about winning about anyplace we went, as far as the short tracks.

Question: In those early years, how did your father work with you? What did you and Lee talk about?

Petty: He didn't really tell me a whole lot. He tried to tell me the fastest way around some of the short tracks, but he just sort of let me go, on the long tracks. He didn't like them anyway. The main thing he helped me in was *not* telling me what I was doing wrong. If you make a mistake and run into somebody, or spin out, or can't get around the race track, you pretty well know what's going on. He knew there was no need to tell me I'd done wrong because there it was, all bent up. If I done a bad job, he just didn't say *nothin'*. So in doing that, he sort of just left it up to me to build my own confidence.

Question: Have you figured out why you're a good driver?

Allison: I think mostly because I enjoy it. I feel that somewhere I did have some natural talent. I think that everybody who is a really good race driver has to have some natural talent. It's a seat-of-the-pants feel. I tried to explain it once. It was in the Indianapolis-type car I ran last year, in '74. Y'know, I worked and worked and worked with the Indy cars because I wanted to win with those, too, if I was gonna drive 'em, and I got pretty disappointed in how we was doing. I came in one day and complained that the car wasn't handling, that I could feel the car slipping, but to the chief mechanic it looked like it was going in a perfect line. I told him I don't have to slide twenty feet to tell that I just slid, I can feel it when it slides a quarter of an inch. And I think that is a natural talent. A guy has gotta have that feel, and then he has to develop it, and he has to work.

I've always felt that I was a better mechanic than I was a driver, that I can figure out how they engineer a race car better than the next guy—sit down and sort the pieces out. That helped me become a good driver. I felt like I always drove more on confidence than I did on bravery. I always worked to where I was totally confident in the car, and what I could do with the car, rather than say, "Boy, Joe Blow went down to that third light pole before he backed off the gas, so I'm gonna do that, too."

Question: What about the competitive factor, the ego factor?

Allison: You've gotta be competitive. Boy, do I want to win. Not only do I want to win, I *don't* want to finish second. Second is great. Second pays a lot of money. But it's losing. First is winning, and second through last is losing. The other competition is always the gauge that you go by. When you're beating other people, then you've done good enough, and when you're not beating other people, then you gotta work harder. You've gotta get it from somewhere. Ego-wise? I've never been able to explain that. I had a guy ask me the other day if it was because I wanted all the girls to jump in bed with me. I almost took that as an insult. I felt like, really, it was an unfair question. In every man's ego there exists the idea, I think, that he wants all people to be impressed with him, but I don't see that I'd put it in those kind of terms. I like for people to like me—men, women, and children—and I get a special kick out of having young kids or young adults recognize me, admire me, and want to associate with me in some way or another. To me, that's a reward for hard work and a sign of success. Maybe that *is* my opinion of what ego is: to impress the girls. I don't know.

Question: What goes through your mind during a race?

Allison: That's one of the hardest things there is for me to explain. Let's say you're driving a big nail into a hard piece of wood. You're smacking that nail with that hammer—*bam, bam, bam*—and you're not really thinking anything else. You're looking at the head of the nail and you're swinging the hammer. This is kind of what you're doing in a race car. You're not thinking, *Boy, last year I won,* or, *Last year I lost,* or, *Last year I had a car that was unbelievable,* you're sitting there and you're driving that car. You're at a concentration level where all there's room for in your mind is to drive that car right to *this* point, or *that* point, or whatever. You come out on the back straightaway, and you have four or five seconds where you're just kind of sitting there, but you're straining, right on that straightaway. As a basic thing, that's all I've ever known.

Now, I've seen times when the car wasn't up to par, where I was in a much less than competitive situation, and you have a subconscious concern that everybody's coming from behind. In other words, I've found myself sitting there almost staring in the rearview mirror: *Who's coming? When are they coming? Where are they gonna be?* You're doing the best you can, but you're so bad off that you sit there and say, *Lord, I wish this thing was over.* I don't want to stop because that's not my way of playing the game, but I wish something would go wrong where I'd have to quit.

These things flash in your mind, but you don't dwell on 'em. You're still concentrating on driving that car around the race track.

Petty: You don't never think about nothing—I don't. I'm just out there blank, and everything I do and everything I see is a reflex. You think about what's going on. *Where's that damned Pearson at?* Or, *Where's Buddy? He was up there and I don't see him. Is he outrunning me now, or am I slowing down?* If you're having trouble with a particular corner, then you say, *Well, I'm going to try a* different lane or a different groove. You're involved in the race all the time as far as knowing what's going on, but as far as driving the car, I don't figure that when I get down yonder I gotta turn, or there's a car spinning and I gotta miss it. You just do it. It's like a boxer. When a cat throws a punch, he don't say, *Well, now. Here comes a punch. I gotta duck.* He ducks. And the more subconsciously he's doing it, the better fighter he is. The more he has to think, the slower he is, and the more he gets whupped.

Question: What is the ideal frame of mind for you to be in at the start of a race?

Allison: It's a lot of things. I could make some cute observations that come immediately to mind. The ideal frame of mind would be to know that my car was the best that day, and to know that Richard Petty is really upset.

Question: Why do you two guys dislike each other?

Petty: I don't dislike Bobby. Bobby's got a Richard Petty complex. Now, I can't help that. He doesn't mind getting beat by anybody but me. Don't get me wrong. He minds getting beat. But it don't bother him unless it's me, and that's the reason I said it's a Richard Petty complex. I don't know what Bobby's trouble is. I don't know what my trouble is with him. All I know is, after as many races as I've run, as many people as I've run with, as many people as I've run *over*—intentionally and unintentionally—and we ain't never had no cross words, why would it be Bobby Allison and me? Why should I pick on Bobby? He sure ain't got nothing I want. He's never done anything I wanted to do, and he's never accomplished anything I wanted to accomplish. So why should I hold anything against him?

Allison: Richard and I came from such totally different backgrounds that each of us captured a great amount of personal interest of the fans. See, I started out a kid with a pickup truck and a jalopy, and my early career was all in my own car and with my own work, rather than a lot of other people who got a factory ride in their early days. I never had a situation where I was totally funded, where

I didn't have to worry about where the next dollar was coming from. I hate to have it sound like sour grapes, and maybe it is and maybe it isn't. I don't think it's sour grapes, but just a natural reaction. I would like to have been like Richard Petty, where every time I sat down in a car, it was a factory-backed, totally funded race car. But then again, maybe I wouldn't have. When you look at it from the outside, the grass is always greener.

Question: Most other top drivers, it's been suggested, are a little jealous of you because from the beginning you've been in the best cars money can buy. Would you agree?

Petty: I don't know why, and I don't know that they are. I don't pay no attention whether they are or they're not. I get the feeling from time to time they are, but then they might get the feeling that I'm jealous of them. I don't know.

Question: Since you didn't come up through the modified and Sportsman ranks, though, do you feel you've paid your dues as much as those drivers who did?

Petty: I'll put it this way. I could take my car right now, just like it sits, and there's not but four or five could win races with it. The talent, or the experience, or the whole combination, is not there. I might have got in a winning car to begin with, but that didn't make me a winner. What made me a winner was learning to drive what I had. The only thing was, I learned to drive a Grand National car before they learned to drive a Grand National car. I had to take my last places and next-to-last places and tenths and fifteenths and wrecks and stuff just like they had to take 'em. I feel damned sure that Lee Petty could tell you I paid my dues because he paid it right out of his pocket. They was tearing up them modified and Sportsman cars, and I was tearing up a Grand National car. I was handed a winning car, but I wasn't handed my father's ability to drive it. I had to learn just like they had to learn. Some of 'em came from a lot of money and some of 'em came from dad-gum cabins, and they all had to learn how to walk the same way as we all had to learn to drive a race car. I just learned to drive a different kind of car than they did. I learned on a Grand National, and they had to learn on a modified and Sportsman because they didn't have the opportunity. I was very fortunate in being able to have the opportunity, but that didn't win 177 races [his total at the end of the 1975 season] for me, because a lot of other people's had opportunities just as good, or better, and they ain't won that many races.

Bobby come from the modifieds, where he blowed everybody's door off. I mean, he was king bee. And when he come to stock car racing, there was one cat to beat, and that was Richard Petty because he was winning everything in sight. So he set his sights for me, and he ain't never got there. That was a deal I couldn't help and he couldn't help. He really didn't mean it to happen.

It got started on the northern tour in '67. We had trouble at Islip [a short track on Long Island]. I was lapping him for something like the third time, and he wouldn't get out of the way. Me and him wound up running into each other, and I wound up on the short end of the stick and he went on to win the race. That didn't go over too good with my crowd, and the first thing you know, one thing led to another.

Then, at the end of the '67 season, we went to Asheville-Weaverville. He was leading the race and I was running second, and we come up on a lap car. He made a wrong move, and I went by both of 'em. He run a couple of laps and caught up. Going up the backstretch, he just run right in the back of me. Just . . . *bam.* And we run another lap or two, and he run into me again. Finally—there was about eight or ten laps to go—we went into the third corner and he just never let off. He just knocked the snot out of me and got me so far behind I never was able to catch up. He went on and won the race.

And then in '71, it so happened in that one year, it just seemed like me and him wound up racing at the end of every race. Or wound up hittin' each other. We wound up running a bunch of these little ol' short tracks and racing with each other all the time. The last place was Wilkesboro. We had them two cars, baby, they wouldn't even *move.* It looked like a Demolition Derby.

He wanted to win and I wanted to win. I wadn't taking nothin' off of him and he wadn't taking nothin' off of me. I ain't saying that I didn't run into him, but I'll truthfully say that I ain't never hit him first. Now, he'll tell you the same thing, but all you got to do is see anybody that was there, or see the films, and they'll show you.

Allison: When I came up through the modified and Sportsman, you had to win on a regular basis to make a living. If it took figuring out how to make the car go better, or figuring out how to drive *every* lap as hard as you drive the qualifying laps, this was just part of what it was gonna take me to be as professional as I wanted to be. And then, this carried over with me in the Grand National. They were used to running 250-mile or 500-mile races, where everybody would just kind of settle down into a pattern. Everybody'd kind of run their spot, and then this guy's engine would blow and that guy'd make a bad pit stop, and by and by everything would be weeded out. When it was one guy's turn to win, well, that was fine, and when it was another guy's turn to win, well, *that* was fine.

I know that I felt obligated to run Richard as hard as he could possibly be run every time I had a car good enough to run him that hard. I had kind of the underdog role, too, because once again, he always had the factory ride and I had such things as Chevelles, Plymouths, Dodges, Fords and Mercurys, and Chevrolets. I've been in the Matador since this particular thing passed. Richard could lose races to some other people, and it didn't seem to make any effect on him, but it seemed like he could not lose a race to me without really suffering. Pearson, let's say, could catch Richard and pass him—they could even bang fenders—and it wasn't all that big a deal. But I could catch him, and it would be, you know, no room on the track and bent fenders and all sorts of things. And whether he won or lost, hard feelings.

No one would dispute that he was king of racing over David Pearson. Everybody agreed that when it was him or David, in spite of the fact that David had won the championship three times, Richard was still king. But I was in a different situation. The fans really seemed to be behind me. I didn't win as many races as he did during that period of time [from 1967 through 1972], but I had just as many fans, or more. I've won the Most Popular Driver, like, four times. Because I won, or competed with him, in races that he had always won, I was kind of like an obstacle, like sort of a holdout keeping him from being all the way to the top.

Petty: Like I say, it's according to which side you're talking to. He's not all wrong, and I'm not all right. It takes two to make an argument, right? But, you know, I've run over Buddy Baker, and I've run over Cale Yarborough, and I've run over David Pearson—and they've run over me—and nothing like that's ever come out of it. It could have come from me, but if it would, it looks like I'da took it out on somebody before *he* got there. Or since.

Allison: Back when we were doing battle on the race tracks, I think I represented a personal threat to him. I feel like *he* felt like I was taking something away from him, and I never felt like he or anyone else was taking anything away from me. I felt like I raced everybody as hard as I raced him, but I don't feel that he ever raced anybody as hard as he raced me.

I think that someday when we both quit, we could probably be pretty good friends. He really is quite a person. He is a clean-cut, all-American boy, which I have a lot of sentiment toward, and he's a tough competitor. He's willing to put out the physical effort. I've always felt like a key to anybody's success is not the talent or the backing or the luck, but the effort. I really admire the guy. I don't feel he's as good a race car driver as I am, but I really admire him. He's had good opportunity, but he's done a tremendous job with it, both personally and professionally.

Petty: The only time we have trouble is when we get on the race track. As far as me and him settin' down talking or going out and eating together, or our families going out, we get along pretty good. My crowd just has a time with his crowd. Our wives get along. I don't guess they've ever had a cross word, even when we was at each other's throat. I try to get along with everybody. It's just that I couldn't never be fast friends with nobody in the racing business. You don't want to be so buddy-buddy that it'll cloud your way of thinking in a race sometimes. You know what I mean?

ON SATURDAY NIGHT THERE WAS A SPORTSMAN RACE AT a dirt track near Myrtle Beach, a honky-tonk resort on the South Carolina coast seventy miles east of Darlington. Nothing untoward happened. The Grand National stars in attendance—David Pearson, Bobby Allison, and Cale Yarborough—drew the crowd but were not real factors. Sam Sommers, a short-track specialist, won the race; Yarborough puked an engine.

Sunday morning was a time to rest and to wander through the town of Darlington. It was an unremarkable place, thrust into the limelight one weekend each year by the happenstance of Harold Brasington's long-ago dream. Although it was faintly distinguished by a score of lovely Old Colonial mansions and an equal number of marvelous, rambling, slightly shabby wood-frame houses of the sort you always wished your grandparents lived in, no one would have confused it with Monte Carlo or Daytona Beach or a host of other auto racing spas. It was basically just another quiet Southern county seat, where the mayor, Frank Wells, doubled as the town jeweler, and Joe Turner, the town barber, took into his home on race weekend four gentlemen from Virginia as he had done for years. The food was nothing to brag about unless you liked Southern home cooking, and the entertainment was nonexistent unless you brought your own. A brochure from the Darlington Historical Society reported that the area was explored by white men around 1730 and that the first settlers were Welsh Baptists from Pennsylvania and Delaware. Later came the English, the Scots-Irish, the French Huguenots, and the German Palatines, all of them attracted by the rich land and the nearby Pee Dee River, which would give that region of South Carolina its name. The Darlington Chamber of Commerce reported that Darlington sat 152 feet above sea level, that its average temperature was 64 degrees, and that its average rainfall was just under 43 inches. Darlington had been a pioneer in the culturing and marketing of tobacco and had the fourth largest tobacco auction in South Carolina. Rand McNally reported that the population of Darlington was 6,990, a figure disputed by the

Chamber, which claimed 7,000-plus. Whatever the correct number, it was one that would be swollen tenfold within the next twenty-four hours.

IF THE SOUTHERN 500 WAS WHY PEOPLE CAME TO Darlington, the Darlington Raceway infield was where they came first. By noon Sunday a multitudinous assortment of vehicles was lined up on the dirt road behind the track waiting for one o'clock, when the gates would be flung open to receive them. The garage area was deserted but for one security guard who stood watch over the forty cars that had made the race and two alternates. A concession stand offered a bag of ice for $1.25. A terry-cloth towel imprinted with the Stars and Bars of the Confederacy went for $3.50. A golf hat with a Purolator decal fetched $5. A Richard Petty throw rug brought an even $25. At 12:15 the price of cigarettes in the track cafeteria jumped a nickel to 65 cents a pack. At 12:24 the door to the field hospital, which would be the nerve center of the track until the race started, was unlocked. At 12:55 a cafeteria employee said to a coworker, "If you ain't ready now, you best go home." Precisely at one o'clock the first vehicles broke through two tunnels, beneath turn two and beneath turn three, and like insects suddenly exposed to harsh sunlight, they stopped, paused, and twitched before scurrying to their viewing spots.

Turns three and four drew the toughs. Two motorcycle gangs set up camp roughly midway between the turns beneath a huge, circular camouflage tent. Close by on either side, but not too close, were what could only be described as true Southern rednecks, good old boys of the first rank out to enjoy the weekend at all costs. In the first and second turns there were more couples and families, and they appeared to be more affluent, and more sedate, generally, than those spectators at the opposite end of the track. A plethora of tents unfurled: pup tents, Alpine tents, huge canvas tents that could easily sleep eight or ten. One family even pitched a little tiny tent for the purpose of keeping their firewood dry. The middle of the infield drew the biggest vehicles, including one 18-wheel diesel truck that on race day would be a sun deck aswarm with folks.

Also in the middle of the infield was a vast array of scaffoldings, some of them quite plain, others quite elaborate, even ingenious, in their construction.

Throughout the impromptu campground the conversations were hearty, boisterous, friendly. The air quickly filled with the savory smell of barbecue smoke. Several people passed out from the effects of the sun and the beer and the booze, or retired voluntarily. Although South Carolina law prohibited the Sunday sale of beer, it certainly didn't prohibit the drinking of it. Collegians out on their last free weekend of the summer chugged enormous quantities of the stuff, and the strains of "Dixie" could be heard as Confederate flags were hoisted everywhere. A van provided by the Alcohol Safety Action Program of the South Carolina Commission on Alcohol and Drug Abuse offered free Breathalyzer tests.

Two men in their early twenties worked a small concession stand that offered soft drinks, steamed hot dogs, and hamburgers. They said it was the first time either of them had worked the Darlington infield, and that they were both a little apprehensive.

"I thought about bringing a pistol," said one.

His friend was a pacifist. "If somebody hits me . . ." he said, and pointed to his other cheek.

They explained that they would work their stand for twenty-eight hours straight, fortified by four cases of beer, donated by the track, and a quart of Johnnie Walker Red. And pills.

"Yeah," said the first, "but not nearly enough."

ON SUNDAY NIGHT, A BANQUET HONORING THE SPORTS division of the American Broadcasting Company television network for its participation in automobile racing was held at the Florence Country Club. It was a lavish affair, the social highlight of the week. There were three open bars, and the cold shrimp was superb. Keith Jackson, the television broadcaster, accepted a trophy on behalf of ABC. The trophy consisted of several glistening ground lenses attached to an equal number of brilliant metal rods embedded in a walnut base, and it quivered impressively. Jackson revealed that he was a

Georgia boy who had entertained notions of being a stock car racer until he crashed at Lakewood one afternoon and woke up several hours later to hear his mother say, "That's it, son." The stock car scene, said Jackson, was "four whoops and hollers and five hot damns, and you've got a race." This, to much applause.

MIDNIGHT SUNDAY. WALTER D. "RED" TYLER HAD BEEN awake since early morning and would sleep only briefly until well past midnight Monday, being sustained during that time by nothing more than unusual stamina and home cooking. "Give me four soft-scrambled eggs, some country ham, and a quart of milk," he was fond of saying, "and I'll be all right." Tyler was a friendly man with a ruddy, freckled complexion who ran a plywood business in Florence. He was also a vice-president of the Darlington Raceway, and for twenty years it had been his responsibility to keep a semblance of order in the Darlington infield during the long night before the race. The infield campout was a Darlington tradition that had begun accidentally in 1950 when several thousand more people showed up for the first Southern 500 than were expected, and showed up a whole lot earlier. Stories from the Darlington infield over the years took on the aura of folk tales. There were stories of knifings and shootings; of gut-busting, knee-walking benders; of the woman who became so angry with her husband that she stripped off her clothes and made an informal tour of the oval on a motorcycle, a motorized Lady Godiva but not nearly so modest; of the local house of prostitution that brought hearses to the infield for the better servicing of its customers.

By the mid-1970s, however, the crowd had become more docile and was less openly imaginative than in the past. In recent years, Tyler said, tents, campers, and vans had come to outnumber cars in the infield. There was less opportunity for social intercourse, and that which did exist was not quite so exposed to public scrutiny and comment. Also, earlier in the evening a tremendous thunderstorm had made a direct hit on the track, knocking out the meager infield lights and flooding the two tunnels for five hours. Not a single vehicle could gain admittance until two divers were hastily recruited to unplug the tunnel drains.

Tyler met Barney Wallace, the track president, in Wallace's office. Both men were unusually tired and haggard. "We needed rain," said Wallace, "but not this much." Tyler said the infield was usually filled, 20,000 strong, by seven o'clock Monday morning, but that it appeared as though people would still be streaming in right until the start of the race.

The black night over the infield was frequently punctuated by the sudden staccato crack of a string of firecrackers or the whoosh of a Roman candle. Smoke from the scores of barbecue pits, as well as from the fireworks, hung layered in the still air, smoke so strong that it cleansed the nostrils and watered the eyes. People expended most of their energy trying to get dry or working to keep dry. Still, the mood was jovial, careless, loose. Ten dollars was not a bad price to pay for a party that would last for the better part of a day and a half.

JULIAN GRAHAM, A SLIGHT MAN WITH WISPY HAIR AND a pencil-thin moustache, was the Darlington Raceway's safety director, and like Tyler he had been a part of the race for twenty years and more. From his office at the field hospital, he explained that the track was under his control until the green flag dropped, that nobody in an official capacity moved except at his sufferance. He had a staff of 120 doctors, nurses, and other safety personnel, and there were fifteen ambulances scattered around the infield. But Graham also agreed that things had quieted down in recent years. A big problem now, he said, was burned feet caused by people stepping barefoot onto dark and smoldering barbecue pits. As he talked, a young boy came by with a cut foot. Another young boy staggered in on the shoulders of a companion, who told Graham, "My buddy couldn't take a knuckle sandwich."

During the race, Graham said, he would be stationed trackside in turn one. He remembered the 1958 Southern 500, when Bobby Myers was T-boned, and he, Graham, sat on Myers's stomach for forty minutes giving him artificial respiration until a doctor could be found to perform a tracheotomy.

Myers died, but Graham said he was still proud of the way he had responded that day.

IN THE DARKNESS, THE SQUAT SUPERSTRUCTURE OF THE Darlington Raceway appeared as if chiseled in black sandstone, somehow foreboding. Slowly the symbiotic sounds of the infield diminished, and the track was caught in a Gothic calm.

The first light of morning appeared from beyond the third turn and bathed the empty grandstand in pale whiteness. At precisely seven o'clock Monday morning, the crews began arriving to remove the tarpaulins from the sleek, brightly painted cars. The mechanical thoroughbreds, which had rested patiently through the cool, wet night, now seemed to tremble at the slightest touch.

Barbecue smoke again filled the air as the day's first meals were prepared. From ice chests and hip flasks came the stuff of the long weekend's second, third, perhaps fourth, hangover. The infield resembled the encampment of a medieval army, or that of Lee in the mountains, regrouping for one final grand, romantic attack. The grandstands, too, began to fill, slowly and cautiously, a patchwork of people brought together in yearly celebration. The spectators taking seats in the grandstand were generally more affluent than their infield counterparts, and were drawn in large measure from the white-collar managerial class of the New South. Still, it was easy to recall from not many years earlier a man in bib overalls, one of many, Carolina dirt worn timeless in his gnarled hands, his neck and face wrinkled by the Carolina sun, who had been seen giving up $60 for four tickets, four *good* tickets, for himself, the wife, and the two kids.

IN THE LAST HOUR BEFORE THE START, BUDDY BAKER walked through the garage area looking like a race driver. Richard Petty sipped a Coke. Bobby Allison was interviewed by Keith Jackson, who casually dangled a cigarette off camera. David Pearson talked with Glen Wood, his car owner. Maintenance crews swept still water off pit road.

Only in Cale Yarborough's garage stall was there any activity. He had been behind all week—all year—and it was not until moments before the pre-race introductions began that his crew finished installing his race engine and sent his car to the fourth turn to join the other thirty-nine starters.

As each driver was introduced to the cheering crowd, his car was driven from the turn and lined up, two-by-two, at the start-finish line. Pearson, Baker, and Yarborough chose to perform this little ritual task themselves. Petty and Allison did not, and received significantly less applause. Strom Thurmond, the senior senator from South Carolina, and a dozen lesser politicians, including Frank Wells, the mayor, were given their say. Since 1975 was not an election year, the speeches were short. Dale Inman, Richard Petty's crew chief and first cousin, chatted with a solemn, saddened Roger Penske, the owner of Bobby Allison's Matador, and of the Formula One car in which Mark Donohue had been killed two weeks and one day earlier. The invocation, ". . . grant that we have a good race, thrilling and exciting with no harm to anyone . . ." was lost in the general murmur. The National Anthem was played by the Fort Jackson Army Band. "Dixie" was not, though it used to be. Its official absence was more than made up by the many informal renditions offered by the infielders and grandstanders.

Rows of ruffian clouds, scraggly little pillows tinged with gray, filled the sky. The temperature was hot when the sun was out, cool when it was not. It was a perfect day, certainly compared with those of the week just past.

The public address announcer intoned, "Drivers, to your cars," and the 70,000 spectators stood and cheered.

Barney Wallace said, "Gentlemen . . ." and the "start your engines" part of his traditional speech was lost to the throbbing roar of the race cars.

Three civilian cars led the pack on the parade laps. In the first was the new Miss Southern 500, Terri Springs, enjoying her first full day on the job. In the second was Keith Jackson, who in addition to covering the race for ABC was also its Grand Marshal. The third car was the pace car. At the end of the first warm-up lap, Miss Southern 500 left the parade. At the end of the second, Keith Jackson did the same. On the third lap, the pace car pulled sharply ahead of the pack and swung off the track at the end of pit road just as the pack grumbled through turn four. The soft mumbling increased to a harsh roar as the forty cars, two-by-two in perfect formation, approached the flagstand. The starter eyed the cars carefully. Precisely at noon, just as Pearson and Baker in row one passed beneath him, he dramatically unfurled the green flag. All around the track the yellow caution lights blinked once and then went dark, signifying that the track was clear. The Southern 500 was under way.

BOBBY ALLISON SAID THAT AT THE START OF THE RACE there were only five drivers besides himself who had an honest chance to win it: Pearson, Petty, Baker, Benny Parsons and Dave Marcis. Upon further consideration, he added, he felt that only Petty and Marcis represented real threats. "And," he said, "I felt that if we did our homework right, we had a chance of beating both of them."

Petty's list of contenders was equally short. "You know Pearson runs good on that race track," he said. "Cale runs good on that race track. Buddy runs good on that race track. And Allison. The first thing you gotta do is to say who's won the races here. Them's the cats you gotta beat first." He dismissed all the other drivers out of hand. "It's such a daggone rough race track that no matter how good they run, you figure that if you can't beat 'em on the track, you're gonna beat 'em in the pits or you're gonna outfigure 'em somewhere," he said. "Marcis, for example, run real good in practice, but I still wadn't concerned with Marcis. He hadn't finished that good all year, and I didn't think he was going to start down there. So we just eliminated him completely for the race, as far as we was concerned."

Petty's quick analysis coincided with those of most other observers. Pearson, although he had never won the Southern 500, had won the spring Rebel race at Darlington four times. Petty was in the midst of the best year of his distinguished career. Baker, although his finishing record was not the best, had won both the Rebel and the Southern, and his daddy, Buck, had won the Southern in 1953, 1960, and 1964. Yarborough was a three-time Southern 500 winner. Allison was a two-time winner. Indeed, these five drivers had won fifteen of the last seventeen races at Darlington, either the Southern 500 or the Rebel 500. They appeared to be a cinch bet against the field, at Darlington and anywhere else.

A 500-MILE RACE USUALLY DIVIDED ITSELF NEATLY INTO three distinct phases. The first, which lasted no more than 100 miles, was a time for sorting things out. Inherent mechanical problems showed up quickly under the strain of flat-out competition, and because of heavy traffic, there was also a greater possibility of accidents than there would be later in the day. Any car that made it through the first 60 or so laps at a superspeedway was usually good for the rest of the afternoon. The second phase, which could last for 300 miles or longer, was a time for showing off as the cars strutted and pranced and showed their fine breeding and character. The final phase was the end game, the dash for the checkered flag.

THE FIRST 50 LAPS OF THE 367-LAP RACE WERE PREDICTABLY inconclusive. H. B. Bailey, who started last, finished last. He parked his Pontiac after one lap, citing carburetor problems. Jackie Rogers retired after 33 laps with a broken valve. Henley Gray was sidelined by a broken timing chain. Coo Coo Marlin blew an engine in turn one, bringing out the first caution flag of the afternoon. Walter Ballard crashed in turn two, and brought out the second.

"The way *I* drive the track is," said Ballard in explanation, "I wait until the cars string out. I kinda get me a gap because I can't afford to take any chances. Then, when the traffic clears out, I set me a good pace and I run it. I try to run by myself or with somebody I know has got good equipment and doesn't blow a lot of engines. I was running along pretty good and I was passing a slower car. What was it? Was that Dick Skillen? He was a rookie there, and this is what is really bad about a rookie. He had moved over to let me by on the outside of number three, so I passed him and I dove in the corner, and when I go in, he drove right on into my quarterpanel. He got me all crooked. I thought it got the back end of the car, but it got right into the left-rear tire and cut it. And the next lap, when I come off of number two, the tire blew and it spun me. And I spun around down there and hit the inside wall."

Ballard would be in and out of the race the rest of the afternoon, forced to patrol the apron of the track at an embarrassingly slow speed because of a faulty rear axle. His tenacity would allow him to finish eleven places higher and earn $365 more than he would have had he quit the race at the moment of his crash, but running so slowly was also such a humbling experience that he vowed never to repeat it. "I shouldn't have been on the race track with the car the way it was," he said. "It made me look like a damned idiot. To hand a little guy like me $300 or $400 is a lot of money, but I done made up my mind I'm not gonna do that anymore. I've got a lot of friends that come out and watch me run, and it isn't worth it to have them see me out there running really slow. People look at you and say, 'Darn, he's running awfully slow. He just can't get the job done.' They don't know you got a problem. They don't ever think about the car. Most of the fans, they're just concentrating on the driver."

UP FRONT, WHERE THE REAL RACE WAS, PEARSON LED most of the early going with Baker nipping at his bumper and Petty and Allison following easily. Yarborough improved his position only slightly, moving from thirteenth to ninth, and it was obvious that he would have to push his car and himself to the limit just to stay in sight of the leaders. He was even unable to significantly dominate a host of second-rank drivers whom he would normally have blown off the track.

ON THE RESTART FOLLOWING BALLARD'S ACCIDENT, THE fastest cars lined up to the outside of the track, the slowest to the inside—which lane a driver chose was up to him—and when the green flag came out to start the 48th lap, Richard Petty tried to steal the race.

It was not an easy task, stealing an automobile race, but Petty tried. At the first, it was hard to tell what he was up to. He opened a lead of a few car lengths, nothing, as the drivers behind him strung out and began to find their individual rhythms separate from those of the pack. But it was soon evident that Petty was building his lead at the rate of more than one-half second per lap, a prodigious accomplishment on the narrow, ancient, and dangerous track. By the 65th lap, Petty's lead was 15 seconds; by the 80th lap, Petty was right on the bumper of Bobby Allison, and Allison was ninth. Moments later he lapped Allison in turn one. He then knocked off Lennie Pond, Cale Yarborough, Richard Brooks, and Buddy Baker, just like that, and only three cars remained on the same lap with him—Marcis, Parsons, and Pearson.

TO TALK ABOUT A RACE DRIVER'S STYLE WAS A TRICKY business, for two reasons. First, while there certainly were imaginative and innovative drivers, when one did succeed with something new, he could be copied quickly and easily by every other driver in sight, in form if not always in result. Second, a stock car effectively hid a driver from sight. A spectator in the grandstand could see the result of certain actions, but not the actions themselves. He couldn't see a driver tap the brakes or feather the throttle—he could barely see a driver twitch his steering wheel—and because of the driver's bulky driving helmet and the mesh safety screen fastened over the driver's side window, the spectator could not even tell whether the driver was struggling or having an easy time of it. All but the most intimate observer could not even tell whether a driver was on a good lap except by noticing his position on the track relative to the competition. It was a bit like watching a basketball fly through the hoop without seeing the player who took the shot.

For all of this, each driver made a unique impression. Baker, his head held high, his left arm resting on his window panel, drove with sturdy determination, as though daring his steed to falter beneath him. Yarborough, curled up inside his car, gave the impression that he was transmitting his own personal tenacity to it. Allison, the fatalist, was wary but calm. Pearson, the natural, was merely there on a string, lap after lap. Petty was the most distinguishable. He had exceedingly long legs and sat hunched over his steering wheel with a distinct gap between him and the back of his seat, as though he were hurtling down some dark interstate in a driving rainstorm with bum windshield wipers. He was not "one with his car" in the same way, for example, that Willie Shoemaker, the jockey, was "one with his horse." It was easy to entertain the notion that Petty did not have his seat belt and shoulder harness fastened at all; that when he went through the next turn, he would suddenly be flung right out of his car.

PETTY'S STRIKING CHARGE, UNORTHODOX FOR SO EARLY in a race, was not made without careful thought. Petty was a desperately sick man. The day before, a head cold he had been nursing for several days turned into the twenty-four-hour flu. "I was up all Sunday night," he said, "and throwed up and all this good stuff. *Blaah!* Then I went over to the race track and laid down in the shower room there and stayed until race time. They got me up and put me in the car, and we took off and the car run good. I knew I couldn't make the whole race. Physically, I wasn't going to be able to make the whole race. So I run just as hard as I could just as long as I could. That was a deal that the strategy was just out the window. If I can get a lap on everybody, then I can get somebody else in the car, let them drive awhile, and even if we lose a lap, we're still going to be in good shape. So what I done, I run and run, and I lapped everybody but three cars. It wouldn'ta been long before we had them cats, too, because we was all in the same corner. Another 10–15 laps, I'da lapped everybody."

He did not get the chance. On the 102nd lap, Dean Dalton, a backmarker, blew an engine to bring out the third yellow flag of the day. It was a short caution, but devastating to Petty's chances. Instead of being a full lap ahead and in command, he had to settle for being merely the race leader, with Pearson, Parsons, and Marcis, all of whom had been allowed to catch up with Petty since they were on the same lap with him, and he did not have the stamina to mount a second effort. "That took a lot of starch out of me," he said. "I had really used myself up and hadn't accomplished what I'd set out to do."

THE CAUTION, HOWEVER, OFFERED WELCOME RELIEF FOR Bobby Allison, who had been plagued by a series of nagging problems, the most disconcerting of which was that his car had been filling up with the smell of burning rubber every time he went through a turn, suggesting to him that a fender was scraping one of his tires. "It really wasn't doing any serious damage," he said, "but the smoke was bothering me. I know if you blow a tire at Darlington, you're in deep trouble. I felt it was more important to keep the car in one piece until we got to a point in the race, a caution flag or something, where we could work on the car."

The two early cautions, for Coo-Coo Marlin's blown engine and Walter Ballard's wreck, had come and gone, but Allison's problem had remained. His car's communications system was not working well, and he had been obliged to explain to his crew what was wrong in person, just like in the old days before everybody started using two-way radios. But his crew could not *see* anything wrong, and twice it had sent him back out without touching the offending fender. "That was their choice," Allison said, "and I was willing to go along with it. Except that I still couldn't make myself drive that car as hard as it should be driven." The result was one lost lap, a combination of Petty's temerity and Allison's timidity.

The third time in the pits, Allison got his message across, and the offending fender was located and raised slightly. Allison wanted further action. He wanted his crew to beat the fender out away from the tire with a hammer. But owner Roger Penske, a fastidious sort, declined.

"He didn't want to do that because it makes the car look bad," said Allison.

ALTHOUGH THE CAST REMAINED THE SAME FROM WEEK to week and the arenas changed only in degree, each race of the Grand National season somehow emerged with a personality distinctly its own. It was already obvious that this race was not going to lend itself to the traditional tripartite analysis. After Petty's failure to establish clear dominance, the race entered a second phase, one that annoyed and frustrated nearly everybody. It lasted for 160 laps, or about 220 miles, and was the part of the race for which the 1975 Southern 500 would be remembered.

On the 128th lap, Benny Parsons spun and slid in turn two. Although he scared himself, he neither hit anything nor lost a lap. The brief yellow flag again bunched the field. Four laps later, with the race under green, David Pearson unexpectedly roared into the pits. He had brushed the wall slightly to avoid Parsons, and after a change of tires, he had brushed it again. The first mishap, and possibly both of them, had damaged his steering, and when he rejoined the race, he was no longer a contender. Allison lost a second lap to the lead cars when a soft tire forced him to the pits under green. Dave Marcis assumed the lead, with Petty close behind and Baker and Parsons strung out far behind, but on the same lap with the leader. Marcis was caught in the Darlington Trap and dived low off turn four to pass slower cars. Moments later, Baker did the same, although he waited until he was halfway down the front straight to begin the delicate maneuver. Marcis and Petty attempted to lap Bruce Jacobi in front of the pits, but Jacobi refused to move over, forcing Petty to quickly line up behind Marcis as they charged into turn one.

Suddenly, Buddy Baker blew an engine. There was no devious slide, no spin, and Baker was able to coast into the garage area without stopping. He emerged from his car terribly grim and angry, his face pocked with dust and rubber except for two pink, clean circles around his eyes. The yellow flag came out for the fifth time, allowing Allison to get back one of the two laps he had lost.

Benny Parsons pitted, also unexpectedly, amidst a storm of activity. Parsons climbed out of his car, a sick man, and Darrell Waltrip, a young driver whose car had failed earlier in the day, was hastily recruited to replace him. Were there gas or oil fumes in Parson's car, or did Parsons simply weaken from the heat? No one knew for sure, including Parsons, who walked unsteadily to the drivers' lounge.

"Hey," he shouted over his shoulder, "somebody tell Travis [Travis Carter, his chief mechanic] there ain't much brake in that car."

Looking very sheepish, like a kid who had been caught with his hand in the cookie jar, Parsons lay down on a hard, wood bench in the lounge, and a doctor from Julian Graham's field hospital wrapped his neck and face in cold towels. "I'm so damned sick to my stomach I cain't do it," he moaned. "Oh, shit. *Shit.*" It was hard to tell whether his expletives were due to his pain or because he had just been forced to climb out of a contending car.

Petty and Marcis continued their fight for the lead. Behind them on the same lap was Waltrip, driving Parsons's car. One lap down was Allison. Two laps down was Yarborough. Pearson slapped the wall again, in turn two, and after a change of tires, he made just two more laps and parked his car behind the pit wall. For sure, his Mercury was no longer competitive and perhaps even dangerous to drive, but whether he could have continued would remain an open question. Pearson was not known for staying on the track when he no longer had a chance to win.

The juggling continued. On lap 201 Allison passed Marcis and Petty to unwind himself and get back on the same lap with the leaders. On lap 208 Yarborough passed Marcis and Petty. On lap 210 Marcis's car quit the race, and the order was Petty, Waltrip, and Allison, all on the same lap. Yarborough was one lap down.

On lap 230 the sickly Petty knew he could no longer continue. His crew chief, Dale Inman, asked Baker to drive in relief, but Baker refused, pleading illness himself. Inman then recruited Marcis, and the transaction cost the Petty car one lap. On the 233rd lap, Waltrip, still driving Parsons's car, moved to the lead just as dark and ominous rain clouds began to form beyond the first turn. They threatened to add another messy element to a race that was already messy enough.

THE PRIMARY TROUBLE SPOT ON THE TRACK DURING THE first two-thirds of the race had been the exit of turn two. The reasons defied logic, except perhaps that the history of the third and fourth turns was imprinted on the minds of the drivers so strongly that they subconsciously had driven more carefully at that end of the track and had chosen to take the greater risks elsewhere. But in a flash, the three-four turn asserted itself with a powerful vengeance. James Hylton and Bruce Jacobi tangled at the entrance to the turn. Hylton spun high up on the banking and slid into the wall; Jacobi stayed low. Directly behind them were Marcis and Waltrip. Marcis spun and crunched the front end of the Petty car, but was able to keep moving. Waltrip was not so fortunate. He jammed Parsons's car into third gear and deliberately spun it to avoid Hylton, then shot backward up the banking and struck the wall a tremendous blow. Hylton walked to the field hospital to be checked out for possible broken ribs. The X-rays were negative, as was Hylton about Jacobi's driving. "Jacobi," he said, "flat run out of brains, if he had any to begin with." Jacobi denied all.

Under caution, Marcis and Waltrip returned their cars to their rightful drivers. Parsons's car, while ambulatory, was in shambles. Its battered rear end stuck up so high that Parsons could barely see through the rear window. But amazingly, there was nothing seriously wrong. The only real problem with the car was that Parsons's crew could not easily refuel it. The concrete wall had scored a direct hit on the car's left-rear quarterpanel, where the gas spout was. On each of eight yellow-flag laps, Parsons pitted and waited anxiously while his crew worked to free the spout with crowbars and sledgehammers. Parsons did not lose a lap. The Petty car did, however, and returned to action two laps in arrears. Allison was the leader.

The biggest benefactor of the shunt was the persistent Yarborough, who, although nearly a lap behind, had been ahead of Allison on the race track. Since the safety car always picked up the race leader during caution periods, the accident allowed Yarborough to move around the track and tuck in behind Allison. When racing resumed, with just over 100 laps to go, the order was: Allison in first, Yarborough in second, and Parsons in third, all on the same lap; a persistent journeyman named Lennie Pond in fourth, one lap down; a somewhat refreshed Petty in fifth, two laps down.

NOW IT WAS ALLISON'S TURN TO SHOW HIS COLORS, WHICH he did by building an 8-second lead over Yarborough during the next 13 laps. At which time it began to rain, lightly, and once again the cars were forced to trundle around the track at reduced speeds under the yellow. Four laps later, the sprinkle turned to a deluge and the race was red-flagged. The cars slogged to a stop at the start-finish line.

"If you've got any authority, pray for rain," said Allison. Half the laps had been completed, and Allison would be the winner if the race could not be resumed. But the weather report was reassuring. Although the showers continued heavily at times, they were local and would soon pass. Indeed, in the midst of the rain, a bright rainbow appeared to the north of the track.

Darrell Waltrip walked over to Parsons, the man whose chances for a Southern 500 victory he had probably destroyed, through no real fault of his own. He told Parsons that the lack of brakes really hadn't bothered him, but also said he'd had trouble breathing inside the car.

"Do you think you can make it?" Waltrip asked.

"I think so," said Parsons. "The car doesn't handle worth a shit, but I'm getting some bite."

"I'm ready to go," said Waltrip.

Waltrip wanted to get back in Parsons's car, but Parsons wasn't about to give him a second chance, although he knew Waltrip could not be held accountable for the accident. Still, neither driver looked the other in the eye. They stared vacantly over each other's shoulders, like political rivals invited by mistake to the same dinner party.

The race was delayed for 80 minutes. At 4:25 the drivers were called to their cars. Petty broke off an interview with Ned Jarrett, the 1966 winner who was covering the race in the pits for the Darlington radio network. Petty headed to his car to great cheers and a smattering of boos. At 4:30 the engines were restarted and the race was resumed, but because the track had not yet dried completely, the next 17 laps were run under caution. This final hiatus gave the crews, especially those of Yarborough and Parsons, a final chance to get their wounded cars in shape.

Yarborough's engine had begun to falter, not unexpectedly. It was running on no more than seven cylinders. On the off chance that the problem was nothing more serious than fouled spark plugs, crew chief Herb Nab decided to replace all of them. Replacing a set of spark plugs was not a difficult job when there was time, but Nab didn't have much. He had perhaps a little over one minute to work on Yarborough's car while the rest of the pack moved slowly around the track, and he had to get Yarborough back onto the track before the pack passed him by. Yarborough was second, and another lost lap would have been fatal to his already diminished chances. Each time Yarborough roared in, Nab dived under the hood and replaced one plug. Then Yarborough dashed out of the pits, drove around the damp track at nearly racing speed, and reentered the pits. This was done eight times in all. The public address announcer said, "The next time in, they'll wash the car, too." Nab was not amused.

Parsons likewise pitted frequently while his crew tried to hammer and bash his ugly racer into competitiveness. No doubt Parsons was thinking back to a similar drama two years before. Going into the last race of the 1973 season, at Rockingham, N.C., all Parsons had to do to clinch the Grand National driving championship was finish thirtieth. Although he had won but a single race that year, his persistence and the genius of his tutor, Ralph Moody, had brought him to the threshold of the title. Parsons was not a star. To the contrary, he was a symbol for all the other independents who had never quite been able to get things together. The championship would be one of the few worthy accomplishments in a career that might have taken a much different turn had Parsons not failed to impress Jacque Passino of the Ford Motor Company during that tryout against Cale Yarborough at Asheville-Weaverville ten years before.

Early in the Rockingham race, Parsons crashed and demolished his car, apparently beyond repair. But after his car had been towed to the garage area, mechanics and crew chiefs from a dozen different teams converged on the car and proceeded to literally rebuild it. Bobby Mausgrover, another journeyman, loaned Parsons a roll cage. The rear axle, the rear suspension, the steering system, the sway bars—all were replaced. The job took 75 minutes. When Parsons returned to the race, the wind buffeted him unmercifully because there was no sheet metal on the right side of his car. Parsons finished nearly 200 miles behind the winner, but in twenty-eighth position and the title was his.

BY LAP 287 THE TRACK WAS DRY. WITH 80 LAPS TO GO, the green flag was once again displayed. Lennie Pond, who had been fourth, retired with a burned-out wheel hub, and Parsons, Yarborough, and Allison, all on the same lap, were the race leaders. Directly in front of this trio, however, was Petty, almost two laps behind, an "almost" that would soon prove to be of great significance. Only two drivers, though, had a chance to win. They were Petty and Allison.

Petty was a purist. Some months later he was asked what went through his mind when a competitor dropped out of a race. He said he was always a little sad to see him go. But weren't there some afternoons when he didn't mind it when the competition had trouble?

"Well, yeah, sometimes," he said. "When they're outrunning you, you want to see 'em have trouble. But the deal is, when you win, you want to say you beat everybody, not that they had trouble and you won. The most satisfying wins is when some cats is racing you all day long, and you actually beat 'em. Not when they make a bad pit stop, or something happens to the car right at the last of the race. You know, you take the win and don't say nothing about it, but it's not as satisfying inwardly as it is when everybody runs hard all day, and then finishes."

For sure, Darlington was one of those "well, yeah, sometimes" days.

Allison felt that Petty was his only real challenger as the race neared its finish. He said of Parsons, "I had passed that car on the track. I really felt that that was a car I could pass." He said of Yarborough, "Cale was having all sorts of problems. I felt the only way he could win the race was if everybody else fell out. But if I fall out, I'm out of the picture anyway." He said of Petty, "His car was bent up quite a bit and maybe was down a little bit. But Petty's a tremendous competitor. In the very late stages of a race, he takes all kinds of chances when it comes down to winning."

So the stage was set for the end game. All that remained

was for the two minor players, Parsons and Yarborough, to make their exits, and this they did.

When the bunched cars charged into turn one on the restart, Allison easily passed Yarborough, just in time for him to get an excellent view of Parsons as he spun and hit the wall in turn two. Parsons's left-rear wheel was knocked cockeyed, and he was at last through.

The accident brought out the ninth caution flag of the enervating afternoon and allowed Petty to move around the track and creep up on the bumpers of Allison and Yarborough. He was just one lap behind.

Yarborough pitted during the yellow, his engine smoking. When the green flag dropped for the last time, on lap 297, 70 laps and less than 100 miles from home, he completed less than one lap at racing speed, then drove off the track and into the garage area, the rear end of his Chevrolet bathed in oil. Yarborough, the fastest driver in the world from Timmonsville, S.C., wasted no time in getting out of his car. His cheerful demeanor had turned to ice. Herb Nab, his chief mechanic, walked off in one direction; Junior Johnson, his car owner, in another. There was little to be said, certainly not among these three. All of them were thoroughly pissed.

SO AT LAST IT CAME DOWN TO ALLISON AND PETTY, THE two veteran antagonists who had raced each other so hard for so long, and so often with bitterness. Petty needed help. In order to win, he needed once more to unlap himself, get another caution flag that would let him move up directly behind Allison, and then beat Allison to the flag. Allison was having none of that. He increased his margin over Petty by perhaps two seconds. Then, with just under 50 laps to go, Petty moved up directly on Allison's bumper. Allison stretched his lead once again. It was clear that he did not want Petty to pass him until he was sure that there was no way for Petty to run him down. But with 21 laps to go, Petty suddenly moved by Allison on the low side of turn one. It was an uncontested pass. Or was it?

Allison said that he let Petty by. Petty said he wasn't sure whether Allison let him by or not. What was clear to Petty, however, was that he, Petty, was once again dreadfully sick and tired. What was clear to Allison was that something had broken on his, Allison's, car.

Petty said, "I was afraid of getting in a situation where I couldn't handle it. If there wasn't nobody on the race track, I could still run a bunch—run real fast. But when I was out in traffic, I was so conscious that I wasn't physically able to do what needed to be done that I'd back off. Mental was telling me, *Hey, you ain't strong enough. If that car in front of you gets sideways, you ain't strong enough to turn the steering wheel to miss him.* Bobby was throwing oil, and as quick as I caught up with him, he throwed oil all over my windshield and I couldn't see. And me being about two-thirds tired anyway, I was afraid to take any chances of getting too close because I didn't want to crash both of us. And then he kept getting slower and slower, and I said, *I gotta go.* So then I got out and got ahead of him."

Allison said, "Up until the point when he passed me, we were both running very hard. I kept holding him off until I felt we were at a point of the race where he could not beat me no matter what else happened, caution flags or anything. And I, by then, had a problem with my car. A piece of the rear suspension was broken. I didn't know what it was, but I knew whatever it was, it was very serious. I felt like it was a very strong possibility that I'd be out of the race at any moment, and maybe into the wall pretty hard, because the car would bounce and then just take a tremendous dart to the right. Going into one, it would do it real bad. Coming off of two, it would do it a little. And coming off of four, it would do it some. And for that reason, the last time he came up on me, which was then 20 laps to go, I moved over and let him go by."

From Allison's pits Roger Penske flashed a board that read, "L-20," confirming the remaining distance. With 15 laps to go, the board read, "+28," indicating to Allison that his lead was 28 seconds. Four laps later, the board read, "+26," telling Allison that Petty was gaining at the rate of one-half second per lap.

"At the end of any race you have all but won," said Allison, "you begin to almost pray, 'Don't let anything happen to this car.' Or, 'I hope we don't have a caution where everybody else catches up.' It's an inner fear, a mental strain. It's like you're hearing strange noises and everything. You don't really hear the noises, but you're keyed up to the point that you can almost hear something trying to go wrong."

What had gone wrong, although Allison did not know it at the time, was that a shock absorber had broken. While that added a certain excitement to his last few laps, it did not cause him any further trouble. He took the white flag, signifying one lap to go, and then he took the checkered flag. Petty was 25 seconds behind, thoroughly beaten.

As Allison drove triumphantly to Victory Lane to receive the rewards of his long labor, Petty drove into his garage stall. His windshield was covered with oil—from Allison's car and from every other car he had run near. Petty, on the verge of collapse a second time, wearily climbed from his car and stumbled past a gathering horde of autograph seekers toward the drivers' lounge. "I was really disgusted with myself as much as anything," he said, "knowing that the car was very capable of lapping everything down there—not only winning, but lapping them—and there I was running second. It was not the car's fault, or the crew, or anything. It was my fault. I could take 100 percent of the blame, and it's pretty tough."

Slowly, the sixteen other cars still running made their way to the garage area to join Petty's. They, and the others that had retired earlier, were no longer beautiful. They were battered and streaked with oil, and their worn drivers left them quickly. The postmortems were absent of emotion, and the celebrations few. The grandstand and the infield emptied, and the long journey home began.

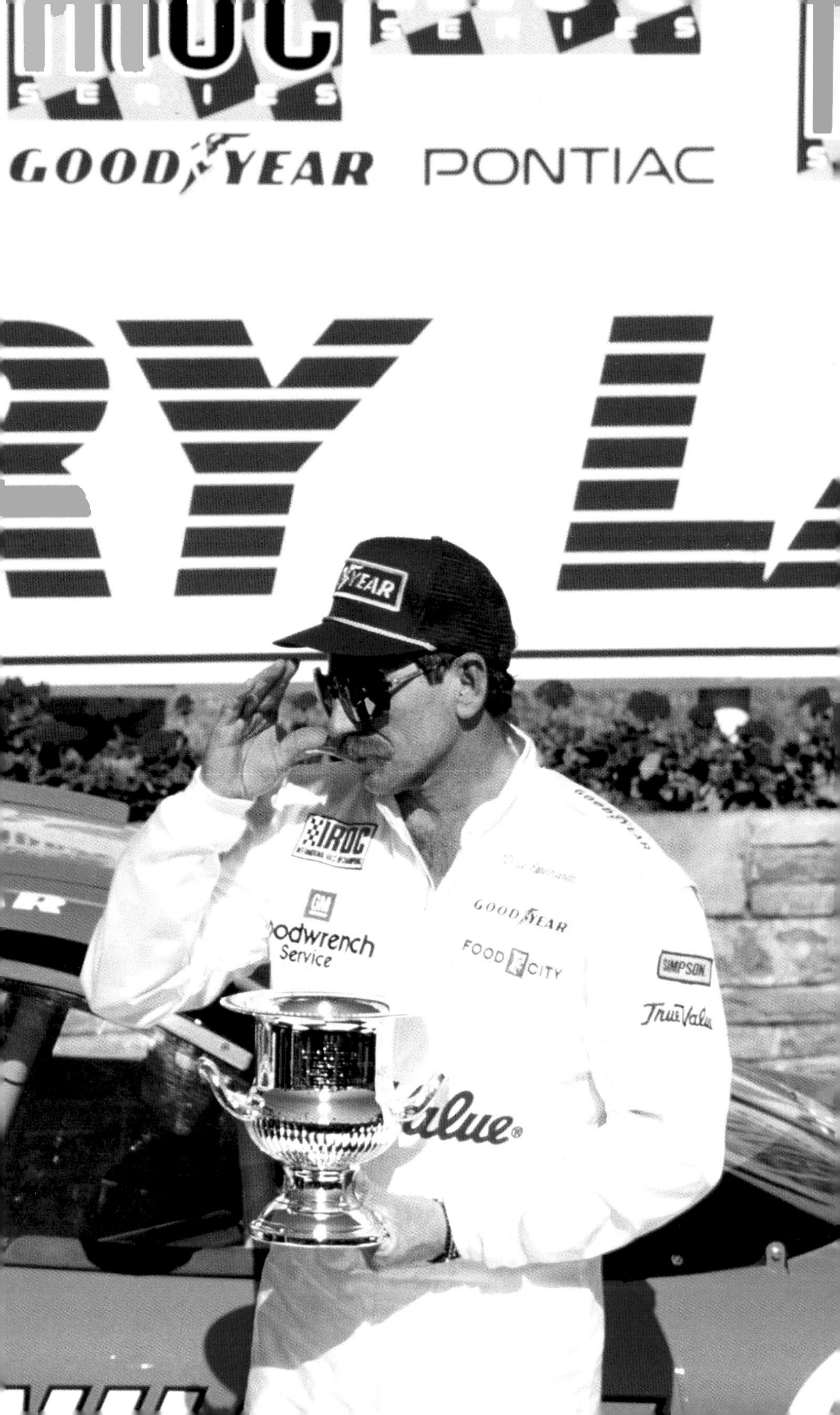

IROC
SERIES
GOODYEAR
PONTIAC
GOODYEAR
IROC
GM
oodwrench
Service
GOODYEAR
GOODYEAR
FOOD CITY
SIMPSON
True Value
alue®

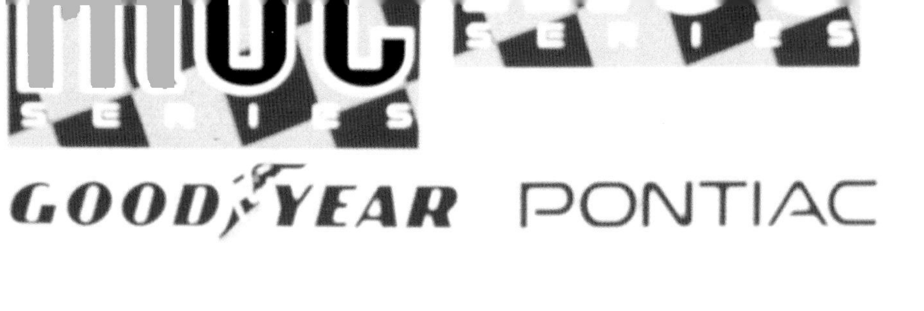

2. *Above:* Richard Petty, shown here in 1976 when he was at his absolute peak, won his record 200th race in 1984, then retired eight years later at the age of 55. *(Photo by John C. Meyers)*

1. *Previous page:* Dale Earnhardt, perhaps the best driver in NASCAR history, has won more races at Daytona than anybody else, but, through 1997, has never won the Daytona 500. *(Photo courtesy of Goodyear Tire and Rubber Company)*

3. *Top Left:* David Pearson is interviewed by Ken Squier moments after his famous victory over Richard Petty in the 1976 Daytona 500. The two future Hall of Fame drivers crashed on the last lap, and only Pearson was able to nurse his car to the finish line. *(Photo by John C. Meyers)*

4. *Top Right:* Darrell Waltrip won three championships in the 1980s while driving for Junior Johnson. *(Photo courtesy of RJR Photography)*

5. *Above:* Jeff Gordon, Rusty Wallace, and Geoff Bodine are interviewed prior to the running of the 1995 Daytona 500. *(Photo courtesy of Goodyear Tire and Rubber Company)*

6 & 7. The deep pockets of Bruton Smith (*ABOVE*) and the imaginative leadership of "Humpy" Wheeler (*BELOW*) have combined to invigorate racing throughout Smith's extensive empire. (*Photos courtesy of CMS Photography*)

8. *Above:* Roger Penske (*left*), shown with a top aide, Walt Zarnecki, has been a success in virtually all areas of motor sports for nearly forty years. *(Photo by Jon Soohoo for the California Speedway)*

9. *Below:* The France family has controlled NASCAR for a full half century. Shown here is the founder, William H. G. "Big Bill" France, flanked by his sons Bill Jr. (*left*), the current president, and Jim (*right*), the current executive vice-president. *(Photo courtesy of Goodyear Tire and Rubber Company)*

10. *Above Left:* Ernie Irvan, who returned to racing after a near-fatal crash at Michigan in 1994. *(Photo courtesy of RJR Photography)*

11. *Above Right:* Mark Martin, twice a runner-up to Dale Earnhardt for the Winston Cup driving championship. *(Photo courtesy of RJR Photography)*

12. *Below Left:* Dale Jarrett, the son of two-time driving champion Ned Jarrett. *(Photo courtesy of RJR Photography)*

13. *Below Right:* Rusty Wallace, one of three racing brothers from St. Louis. *(Photo courtesy of RJR Photography)*

14. *Above Left:* Sterling Marlin, son of the engaging veteran driver Coo Coo Marlin. *(Photo courtesy of CMS Photography)*

15. *Above Right:* Dale Jarrett after winning the 1995 Daytona 500. *(Photo courtesy of Goodyear Tire and Rubber Company)*

16. *Below:* The Goodyear drivers at the 1995 Daytona 500. *(Photo courtesy of Goodyear Tire and Rubber Company)*

17. *Above:* Jeff Gordon in 1995, before he switched brand loyalties and joined the Pepsi generation. *(Photo by KPC Photography for Goodyear Tire and Rubber Company)*

18. *Below:* Crew chief Ray Evernham, driver Jeff Gordon, and owner Rick Hendrick celebrate a short-track win at Bristol. *(Photo by Phil Cavali for Goodyear Tire and Rubber Company)*

Epilogue:

Lag Time

One of the unresolved mysteries of Southern stock car racing is its uncanny, almost unnatural ability to resist the winds of change that swept periodically over most other American sporting institutions. You could leave the South for a year or two, or even three or four, and return with the certain knowledge that things would be pretty much the way you had left them. At least that was my experience. I returned South after five years, in the spring and summer of 1980, for one final look, and what I found was as I expected. Stock car racing remained suspended in time, immutable. At one level, dry-slick clay bullrings such as the one at Summerville, S.C., still flourished, ongoing reminders of the sport's rude birthing, and there were even some slight indications that dirt-track racing was enjoying a mild resurgence. Grand National racing was doing just fine. The cars were smaller, more European, and most of them were Chevrolets, but individual race purses were at record levels, the Grand National division of NASCAR claimed more paying customers for its thirty or so annual races than any other automobile racing circuit in the world, and thanks to a pair of absolutely stunning races that were carried live to a disbelieving nationwide television audience, stock car racing was beginning to move beyond its parochial bounds and obtain a fair share of national recognition.

The first of these races, the 1976 Daytona 500, featured David Pearson and Richard Petty. At the beginning of the white-flag lap, Pearson led by a car length, but as their cars entered turn three for the last time, Petty edged even with his old rival. Throughout three and four they engaged in a delicate ballet, Pearson on the high side straining to keep his slender lead, Petty down low trying to wrest it away from him. He appeared to have succeeded, but when he pulled ahead and in front of Pearson as the cars exited the fourth turn not 600 yards from the finish line, he was over the edge. His car bobbled, as did Pearson's. Both slammed the outside wall and spun fearfully across the track into the infield grass. Both cars were badly battered. Petty, now no more than 50 feet from the flagstand, was unable to continue; Pearson, however, somehow managed to keep his engine running and sputtered across the finish line, the winner, at a speed of perhaps 25 mph.

That was a finish that could never be topped, but three years later, it was, and in the same race. In 1979 the Daytona combatants were Cale Yarborough and Donnie Allison, and, eventually, Donnie's brother, Bobby. Again the race came down to the last lap, this time with Donnie Allison holding a slight lead as he and Yarborough roared side by side into turn three. Yarborough attempted to pass Allison on the low side; Allison moved over and closed him off. The cars touched, and touched again, harder. Yarborough and Donnie spun into the wall—and a rather startled Richard Petty, who had long resigned himself to third place, motored on by to the checkers.

There was more to come. Bobby Allison finished his race and drove to where the two wrecked cars sat in turn three to check on the condition of his brother. In an instant, all three were at each other: Yarborough versus the two Allisons in a flurry of fisticuffs and flailing helmets. It was the sort of thing that Hollywood script writers would never dare pan off on their audiences, and although there were many official condemnations, both of the fight and of the accident that led to it, NASCAR executives and track promoters were secretly delighted, particularly since the fracas had been witnessed by 26 million people.

These and other less-publicized races also served to confirm that the hoary ancients who had been so dominant in 1975 were, as the new decade began, not any more inclined to yield their place at the top than they had been on my previous visit. For sure, certain other drivers had done right well for themselves, particularly Benny Parsons and Darrell Waltrip, the two men who had engaged in such a touching mini-drama in the 1975 Southern 500. Both had passed the $1 million mark in career earnings and were now among the favorites at any track they went to. Still . . . although four of the five drivers who had been front and center in 1975—Petty, Pearson, Yarborough, and Allison—were now well into their forties and the fifth, Buddy Baker, was 39, and although all five had suffered severe reversals during my five-year absence, none was yet ready to give up anything.

Buddy Baker remained an enigma, constructed of equal parts talent, courage, and bad racing luck, much of it of his own creation. In 1976 Baker had sixteen finishes in the top five but only one victory. Several drivers gave their cars nicknames that year. Petty called his Dodge "Old Blue." Yarborough called his Chevrolet "Old Yellow." Baker called his Ford "Old Grumpy." At the World 600 in Charlotte, Baker reluctantly agreed to car owner Bud Moore's request to lay off the pace for a change, save his car, and make a run for the checkers only at the end. Baker, however, more or less on his own, crashed on the front straightaway. He groggily exited his car, staggered across the track, and collapsed. "That shows you what strategy does," he fumed in the garage area. "They can kiss my backside. From now on, I'm going back to running like *I* want to run."

In 1977 Baker did not win even one race and parted company with Moore to drive for the M. C. Anderson racing team. In 1978 he was again shut out and parted company with M. C. Anderson to join W.I.N., Inc., a new outfit whose acronymic name stood for nothing more than what owner Harry Rainier hoped his car and new driver would one day do. "I feel like my career is starting all over again," Baker said, which was precisely what a race driver was supposed to say when he joined a new outfit.

In fact, 1979 turned out quite well for Baker. He won three races, the first of which ended a losing streak that had stretched to seventy-three races across all or parts of four seasons, and he sat on seven poles, more than any other driver. While it was not the kind of super season that Petty, Pearson, Yarborough, and Allison all had had with such astonishing frequency during their careers, for Baker it was enough, and he remained very much his own man. "I drive flat out and half turned over," he said, "but I don't apologize. You wouldn't ask Joe Frazier to fight like Ali, would you? There have been some low spots. Racing's broken my shoulder, my leg—my spirit—but I've been able to do things my way, and I'm proud of that. I've always managed to stay about one foot off the valley floor."

Likewise, Bobby Allison had two winless seasons, in 1976 and 1977. He also had one spectacular end-over-end crash at Rockingham, a less flashy but equally serious accident in a Sportsman race in Minnesota, and suffered a debilitating illness that even the Mayo Clinic could not explain. Still, he continued, full of his old mystery and grit. In 1978 he jumped into the Bud Moore car vacated by Baker, and that season and the next he won a total of ten races and over $700,000 in prize money.

Cale Yarborough forgot the tragedy and frustrations of 1975, and from 1976 through 1978 he reeled off the most brilliant three consecutive seasons in the history of the Grand National. He finished in the top five in seventy-nine of the ninety-one races that were held during those years and won twenty-eight of them, he won three straight driving titles and over $1.3 million in prize money, and he built a new mansion for himself and Betty Jo just down the road from his old one. But his crash with Donnie Allison at Daytona in early 1979 and its untoward aftermath signaled a year of bad fortune. He never did get the season squared away. Still, his pride and tenacity enabled him to win four races, a fair accomplishment by anyone's standards but his, and as the new decade began he was once again seeking to reach goals beyond the stars.

David Pearson parlayed his gutty victory over Richard Petty in the 1976 Daytona 500 into a marvelous season—ten wins in twenty-two starts—then began a downward slide that culminated at Darlington in the spring of 1979 when he was fired by car owner Glen Wood after he left the pits with only two of his four wheels securely fastened in the midst of the

Rebel 500. Wood turned his Mercury over to a relative youngster named Neil Bonnett, who responded by winning three races. Surely, Pearson would take the hint and gracefully slip into quiet retirement. He was, after all, 45, the oldest of the geriatrics.

Faint hope. Later that year a rookie, Dale Earnhardt, crashed his car and had to sit out four races. Pearson filled in for him, and in a strange car serviced by a strange crew, he finished second, fourth, seventh, and first, winning the Southern 500 at Darlington, the place where he had been so embarrassed five months before and still the most difficult race track on the circuit, by a comfortable two laps.

In 1978 Richard Petty, taking his cue from Baker and Allison before him, failed to win a race for the first time since his official rookie season of 1959, but after an off-season operation that cost him 40 percent of his ulcerated stomach, he bounced back to win the 1979 driving championship in spectacular fashion. Darrell Waltrip built an early lead in the points race, but midway through the season Petty began a dogged pursuit. He caught Waltrip with two races remaining; Waltrip caught him back with one race left. Going into the last race of the year, at Ontario, Calif., Waltrip, who was making his first serious run at the title, led by a mere two points. The title would be won by whichever driver finished ahead of the other. Nobody else was even a mathematical contender. The prerace gamesmanship was worthy of a textbook lesson in creative psychology. Waltrip, nervous and edgy, admitted that he only wanted to be ahead of Petty when the race ended; winning the race itself, he said, was not important to him. Petty, outwardly calm and unconcerned, said his only objective was to win the race; he would be content to let the championship chips fall where they may. Petty drove aggressively and Waltrip did not. When the afternoon was over, Petty was a solid fifth, one lap and three positions ahead of Waltrip, and the championship was his. It was his fifth title of the decade and the seventh of his career.

For all the success that Petty and his peers continued to enjoy, the last year of the decade was, in fact, a season of change, imperceptible though it might have been. However, if you looked closely at the record book, there were unmistakable signs that a younger generation of drivers, impatient with having had to sit on the sidelines for so long, was finally ready to make its move. Several of these drivers were the sons of Grand National veterans, and one, Kyle Petty—the son of Richard and the grandson of Lee—was so precocious as to win the very first automobile race he entered, the 1979 ARCA 200, a late-model preliminary to the Daytona 500.

Kyle Petty swore that he had never been behind the wheel of a race car before he took daddy's slightly used Dodge to Florida for some private practice the week before the ARCA race, although he did admit to having done some unofficial high-speed driving in a spiffy, 1969 Dodge Charger along the country roads near the Petty compound in Level Cross, N.C. "It would go 140 or 150 miles an hour," he said. "I knew what speed was."

He qualified second fastest for the ARCA race, and then, just like that, he won it. The date was February 11, 1979, and Kyle was 18 years, eight months, and nine days old.

While neither the ARCA drivers nor their cars were near Grand National caliber—ARCA (the Automobile Racing Club of America) was a lesser, Midwestern version of NASCAR—Kyle's performance absolutely stunned and enthralled the folks at the Beach. "I never seen racing people more excited," said Richard. "I don't necessarily mean the fans, but the racing crowd—the reporters, the other drivers, the people in the pits. Kyle was the coolest cat there."

Said Kyle to Richard after the race, "I just felt like I was supposed to win."

Said Richard to Kyle, quick to put matters in perspective, "You know what it's like to win, son. Now all you got to do is learn how to drive."

While Kyle Petty went off to learn how to drive, the 1979 race for Grand National Rookie of the Year honors, usually an amusing but meaningless piece of fluff of interest only to the involved drivers and their immediate families, took on nearly as much import as the contest for the driving championship itself. The three main contenders were Joe Millikan, a former employee of Petty Enterprises; Terry Labonte, a native of

Corpus Christi, Texas, who had moved to High Point, N.C., to be closer to the heart of the Grand National matter; and Dale Earnhardt of Kannapolis, N.C. All three finished in the top ten in overall championship points, as well as in money won, as race promoters, car owners, and fans alike looked carefully to see who would replace the old icons.

Earnhardt won, though the going was not easy. He began the season in splendid fashion and even led the Daytona 500, however briefly. On the eve of the Atlanta 500 in March, Jake Elder, a moody but wise crew chief, picked up his tools from Buddy Baker's stall and transported them to Earnhardt's. Elder had guided a host of young drivers through their Grand National apprenticeship, and whether it was coincidence or not, two weeks later, at Bristol, Tenn., Earnhardt became the first Grand National rookie in five years to win a race, and only the fourth in the entire history of NASCAR. "I couldn't believe it," said Earnhardt. "They give me the checkered flag, and it was just the most exciting time I've ever felt in my life."

Earnhardt put together a string of solid finishes that all but assured him of the rookie title by midseason, and he even climbed as high as fifth place in the overall championship points standings. But at Pocono in late July he slammed the wall viciously. He broke both his collarbones, and he did not wake up until several hours later, in a Pennsylvania hospital. "I can remember Jake in the hospital room," he said, "and that was about all I can remember that night. It was the next day before I could get my memory back of what was going on."

Car owner Rod Osterlund then hired David Pearson to drive the car in the absence of its regular chauffeur. "I've got to respect Pearson a lot," Earnhardt said, "because he got in and did the job and never tried to finagle and get the ride or do me any harm." Still, when Pearson took the lead at Talladega in his first start as Earnhardt's replacement, Dale, who was listening to the race from his home, abruptly turned off the radio and went fishing.

Earnhardt took back his ride in September, and although he needed relief help in several of the season's remaining races, strong finishes at Rockingham and Atlanta late in the year put him back into first place in the rookie standings, and a ninth-place finish at Ontario clinched the title for him.

Earnhardt was clearly the best of the rookies. More than that, his performance during the 1979 season indicated that he was on the cusp of greatness. It was not that he had won the rookie title. Plenty of drivers had done that and were never heard from again. Rather, he had a certain flair, a certain panache. He had returned from a bad crash and he had successfully challenged the best drivers around, trials by fire that had wilted the resolve of many veterans and neophytes before him. Save for tragedy or a failure of the will, it was all but certain that Dale Earnhardt would be the next Grand National star, the heir to the legacy of Tim Flock, Curtis Turner, Fireball Roberts, Freddy Lorenzen, Cale Yarborough, Richard Petty, and all the others who had preceded him.

In just four years of outlaw and NASCAR Sportsman racing on the handful of dirt and asphalt short tracks near his hometown of Kannapolis, Dale Earnhardt had established a reputation as a heady and aggressive professional, one whose sights were set firmly on the superspeedways of the Grand National circuit. In the occasional newspaper stories and program notes about him, he was usually identified as a sure-fire, can't-miss comer. It was an appellation with which he was usually quite comfortable. "I want to win a lot of races," he had said in 1975, then referring to the Grand Nationals, "and I want to win the points championship." Not that he was assured of Grand National stardom, or even of a good ride, but by the fall of that year, at age 24, he was on schedule and all the vital signs were good. Besides, there was the heritage.

Before his fatal heart attack in 1973, Ralph Earnhardt had been something of a legendary figure in the Carolinas. If son Dale was a classic example of the young driver who dreamed of the big time, father Ralph was an equally classic example of the older driver who chose to remain a big fish in a small pond. Ralph Earnhardt did run the Grand Nationals for several seasons, gaining a reputation as a hard-luck charger who led several races, finished few, and won none, but he preferred the short tracks of the Sportsman circuit near his home, where he won so often that even he had long ago lost track of the exact number of his victories. One year at the track in Hickory, N.C., he won seventeen straight features, a feat so devastating to the track's weekly attendance figures that near the end of his streak the angry promoter refused to present him with his trophies or let him kiss the beauty queen in Victory Circle.

Like his father, Dale Earnhardt loved racing with a passion. "I think about my car the last thing before I fall asleep and the first thing when I wake up," he said, which possibly explained why he had spent the night before I visited him sacked out on a couch in his mother's living room. It seemed there had been a marital spat. Dale said he hoped it would be temporary.

It was 1975. The house was a plain wooden structure on Sedan Street. Also in the neighborhood were V-8 Street and Coach Street, the raw avenues near the outskirts of the mill town having been named in honor of Ralph's racing accomplishments. Earnhardt was dressed for work, wearing loose-fitting mechanics' garb that accentuated his angular, broad-shouldered thinness. He gave a brief tour of the house where he had grown up and paused in front of his father's huge trophy room, which actually was one-half the living room. He said he wanted to partition off the trophy room some day and keep it climate controlled. Temperature changes were hard on the trophies; pieces of them kept breaking off. Out back was a garage where Earnhardt and his two brothers, Randy and Danny, worked on his Sportsman car, the spare parts and tires scattered about in predictable disarray. A gutted, cream-and-black Chevrolet Camaro, No. 8, sat in the backyard. Beneath the driver's window the name "Ralph" was painted in neat script. The Camaro was his father's last race car, Dale said, and someday he hoped to restore it to the way it was the last time Ralph drove it in competition.

In a voice that was at once painfully shy and full of quiet confidence, Earnhardt began to talk about his past and his then uncertain but promising future. A logical point of departure was a Sportsman race, the World Service Life 300, that had been run five days earlier, a Saturday, at the Charlotte Motor Speedway as a preliminary to the National 500. The race had attracted a fair number of Grand National regulars, both as observers and participants, and it had given Earnhardt a rather hair-raising bit of superspeedway experience.

Earnhardt: The only thing that makes you a good race driver, 90 percent, I feel like, is experience—knowing what to do when you get into a situation. Because you get to a situation on a race track, you got to do something. And you can't think about *what* to do, you got to *know* what to do. By the time you think about what to do, it's done happened.

Question: Is that what happened to you Saturday in the Sportsman race?

Earnhardt: Well, let's go back to Friday. It was before qualifying, and I was talking with David Pearson about drafting. We was talking about the little cars, the Novas. I had a Nova.

Question: Had you driven on a superspeedway before?

Earnhardt: Yes. I drove the previous World Service Life, the Sportsman race, and I drove the World 600. Charlotte's the only two, and they were both in big Chrysler cars, a '69 Plymouth Roadrunner and a '73 Dodge Charger, and so we was talking about these little cars in the draft. Pearson told me don't never follow a man in the corner too low or start in a corner under a man, 'cause a draft would tend to make your car loose in the rear. Then we was talking about staying in behind a feller, up above him in the corners, and your car would really work. I listened to every word he said, and then I went and done it—exactly what he told me not to do. During the race I was working with the draft—drafting on Bobby Allison and filling it and testing it myself—and I thought I'd worked it out pretty well. Well, there at the end of the race I was running fifth behind Sam Sommers. There's three laps to go, and if I pass Sam it'd of been fourth place. But I got too anxious. I drafted up on Sam down the front straightaway and started in the corner under him. When I did, that draft broke the car loose and it started up. I had always been taught on short tracks never to lock the car up if you haven't completely lost control, which I didn't feel like I had. I just feathered out of the gas. The car caught traction again, and it started to crawl back down across the race track. It leveled out and hit the grass down there in the apron, and I straightened on up and come back onto the race track. After the race, Allison, who had been right behind me at that point, come over and congratulated me on handling the car pretty well. He said most guys would have locked it up or froze, and I hadn't thought about what I did until Allison said something. I just was there. I can remember feathering out of the gas, and the car done just exactly what it ought to have done, I reckon. It was really something that don't usually happen. You don't usually straighten a car up like that on a superspeedway. When you're out of control, you're out of control. I was out of control, really, but yet, the car wadn't completely gone.

Question: Does something like that scare you?

Earnhardt: No, only it was a disappointment. I was wanting to get by Sam for fourth place, and that was the only thing I was thinking about. I finished up sixth, but I just marked it down as experience. I don't think about getting hurt. When I crashed up at Hickory awhile back, that's the first time I ever been . . . I wadn't knocked unconscious, but I was dazed for a couple of minutes. I can remember the car hitting the wall and everything was sorta starred-like, and the next time I remember was my brother Danny talking to me. He come all the way from the pits and was talking to me at the car before I realized where I was at. Nobody likes to get hurt. Everybody's got a fear of getting hurt. When daddy was driving, I was always scared that he was going to get hurt, but it's never crossed *my* mind, especially when I'm racing. If I wreck and get hurt, I wreck and get hurt. But I cain't remember ever thinking about it from the time I started.

Question: Was the car you raced at Charlotte built as a superspeedway car, or was it a converted short-track car?

Earnhardt: Let me explain that to you. I was intending on driving the car I drove last year, the '69 Roadrunner, but the man who owned it sold it about a month before the race, and that left me without a ride. We started building the Nova, a short-track car, last winter, and my brothers and I, we got to talking about running the car on the superspeedways ourselves. A number of people have helped us put it all together here and there with just odds and ends. We didn't change that much on it. The car basically is still like it was for a short track, the chassis and all. When you're building a superspeedway car, you put more rake in when you're building it, and we didn't put none at all in this car. It set level. We got a little help from sponsors here and there: Henson's Construction, Reed Motors, Miller's Plumbing, and Hot Rod Barn. It was like $200 and $300 a sponsor. Howard Furniture helped out a great deal. It seems like a bunch, and you think, *Where do you have room to put the names all on?* But we got 'em on there and it all worked out. It ended up the best thing to do because now we've got a race car built, we done real good the first race with it, and it's a good short-track car yet.

Question: You started off on dirt. How did you learn to drive dirt?

Earnhardt: I've always felt like I could drive on dirt. When I was younger, I watched my father drive, so when I started driving, in the middle of '71, it seemed like it was all natural. It just seemed like I knew what was happening, like I'd been through the situation before. And I'd never drove a race car. I was superior on dirt. I started about midseason. At the end of the year, the last race I run I was second. The next year, I got a better ride with a better car. We won the point championship in Charlotte, at the Fairgrounds, and Concord, a dirt outlaw track. Then the next year I won it again. And then my father died in September of that year; my father died in September of '73.

Question: What kind of a driver was your father?

Earnhardt: I think him and the Pettys were the same-type people. He was always a levelheaded type of person. He always thought things out before he done 'em. He was always ready when he was at the race track. He always respected the other man. He always controlled his temper real well. He's got in scrapes with people, but he always wanted to leave the racing on the track. I seen daddy and Tiny Lund battling down at Hickory, just frammin' and knockin' in every corner, and after the race—down there at the restaurant?—cut up and go on like nothing ever happened. When he got out of the race car, that was it. It was over.

Question: Was he an aggressive driver?

Earnhardt: In his day he was. He could win every race he run, as far as I was concerned. His driving ability was superior to everyone else's. He enjoyed superspeedway racing, but I don't think that's what he wanted to do. I think he loved the short-track racing more. It was his living to race. He took care of his equipment real well. He would rather finish second to a man than take a chance of tearing his car up. On the last lap, say, if he and this guy were running close, probably knowing he could nudge the other feller out—rough him up a little and get by him?—nine times out of ten, he wouldn't do that. He would go ahead and finish second to him. But daddy, he won 60 percent of the races he run a year, on the average, up until the last year when he had heart problems. He didn't run that many races then, and he didn't run that hard. That hurt me a lot to see my daddy running fourth and fifth, back in there, knowing all the time he weren't feeling up to it. But he was still driving. He felt that's what he wanted to do.

He was, all around, a pretty decent fellow. He looked after his family real well. There's three things, I think, he always wanted in life. He wanted a good wife, a good family, and he wanted to be a good race-car driver. And I sort of set my goals to have pride in what I got, whether it be a good family or be a good race-car driver. I want to take pride in it. I don't want to be halfway at it. If I'm going to do something, I'd like to go all the way at it.

Question: What kinds of things did he talk with you about, as far as your driving?

Earnhardt: My father never really sat down and told me how to drive a race car. He was always talking respect for other drivers. He taught me to always expect the unexpected and to be on my guard. Once I got into a scrape with a boy. Harry Galloway. I spun him out one night, and the next night in the heat race he started messing with me. Well, I was out in front of him and I got to trying to stay away from him and I wadn't keeping the car in control completely. I was getting wild with the car, and he caught me and spun me out. A couple of days later, after it was all over, daddy—we'd set down working here in the shop—he said, "You know what you done wrong Saturday night?" And I said, "He spun me out, is all I know." He said, "No, you could of kept him from spinning you out. When he hit you, you was completely off guard. You didn't have the car under control or nothing. You was running from him. Anytime a man's trying to wreck you or mess with you, or if you're running with a man in the corners, save a little gas. When he does hit you, you got some power to play with, to work the car with." See, I was going in there flatfooted and wide open, and I didn't have nothing.

He taught me a few things like that. Or, when I was trying to pass somebody, he told me the best time, how to wait for the best advantage.

Question: Was your father always a full-time racer?

Earnhardt: He worked out here in the shop during the winter and all, on people's cars as a mechanic, but he was a full-time racer. From the time I can remember, that's all we done but race. A couple of times—a number of times—when my father would be lying in bed at night, all of a sudden he'd get up and put his clothes on. And my mother would ask him where he was going. "I'm going out to the shop." Why? "I just thought of something I want to change." And he'd go out and work while he had it on his mind, fresh.

Question: Did you ever *not* consider driving a race car? For example, did you play other sports in high school?

Earnhardt: No. I'll tell you, I never even really dated that much or went out much at night at all. I was always here working on the race car helping daddy. When I turned 16, I quit school. It's something now I wished I'd never done, for my daddy's sake alone, because he never did want me to quit. He begged me—well, he didn't beg me, but he did everything but beg me—not to, and offered me a car and just anything I wanted. But I thought I wanted to work on race cars full time like daddy was doing. He didn't accept it for a while, but then a couple of months later he finally accepted it and we got real close.

And when I was 17, I started dating my first wife. I ended up marrying her when I was 18—just turned 18. My father didn't want me to do *that.* Well, me and my father drove further apart, as far as our racing. I had a little boy. I was working at Charlotte at Great Dane Trailer during the day, and I'd come over here a few nights a week. But I wasn't around that much, and when you're not around every day, you feel like a stranger to what's going on. When I was married to my first wife, living with her, I never thought about driving, myself, as much as I thought about it before. Well, about a year and a half after I got married, we separated. I moved back home, and I was back into racing again. About a month after I got my divorce from my first wife, I turned around and got married to my second wife. She'd been around racing and all—her father worked for the K&K Insurance racing team—and she enjoyed it.

I had two good years [of dirt-track racing] and then I started racing on asphalt and doing it all myself after daddy died. And it's been harder—money and time and everything. It's like when I was working on the car here night and day. A woman thinks, *Why does he have to work on it all the time?* My wife's sister cain't see it. A lot of my friends think, *Why don't you do an eight-hour-a-day job and work on that race car a little bit in the night?* Well, you cain't do it that way if you want to go where I'm going. Or, I cain't. Because I'm my-type person. This is what I live for. Racing is my business and my profession. Hell, if I wanted to go work in a cotton mill, I would have done that when I was 16 years old. I'm not putting a cotton mill down, or a job. A job's fine for who likes it, but I don't. Not me. I worked up at Great Dane Trailer. I enjoyed that pretty good. I done a good day's work for people. But I didn't have no desire to go anywhere or get any better or anything. I didn't care whether I got a raise or not. When quittin' time came, I was gone home. Where racing, working on these cars, I can work on them day and night and don't never get tired or never fail my mind. A man ought to do what he wants to, if there's any way, if that's what he's going to be happy at. I know there's a majority of times a man can't do what he wants to because of financial problems or whatever, but I don't think a man should work all of his life for nothing, and that's what he'd be doing if he didn't enjoy it.

The only time I ever thought about not racing was when I was married to my first wife, because I had a family, I knew the expenses, and I just felt like I'd never have the chance, never get the opportunity to start. But once I did start, I did pretty good from then on. I've always wanted to race, I'm enjoying it, and I'm wanting to be good at it some day. I've had it rough and I'll have it rough in years to come. It's not over with. The tough part will always be tough.

Question: When you made the transition from dirt to asphalt in 1974, what adjustments did you have to make?

Earnhardt: It was hard in a way, and it wadn't in a way. Like I said, my father died in September of '73 and I finished out the year on dirt. We had all this racing stuff here, and my brothers and I, we'd been talking about me going to asphalt—or me going to NASCAR, is what it was. I was wanting to go somewhere from where I was at. I didn't want to stay at Concord and outlaw on dirt all my life. I love dirt racing; dirt racing isn't why I changed to asphalt. It was NASCAR, your organization and going somewhere. So when we changed over to asphalt, I bought Harry Gant's car—he'd won a bunch of races with the car—and I started driving.

The only difference I found on asphalt is, you've got to be smoother. You can't be radical with a car; you can't jack a car around. You've got to run every lap as quick as you can, the closest to every lap the same. On dirt, I can make a mistake and correct it and go on; on asphalt, you can't make too many mistakes. They've been drivers who say that it's best to start on dirt because your reflexes are so much quicker. Nine times out of ten you're driving a car hung out, sideways in the corner and everything, and you can control the car with your gas. On asphalt, you're used to driving it with the steering wheel.

It was hard for me to calm myself down to running beside someone on asphalt and not beatin' and bangin' as much as I did on dirt. Down there at Concord there weren't a race that went by that you didn't fram and beat with somebody, or get into somebody. But on asphalt, you got to respect the other guy a little more. You got to be more cautious to running with him.

Different people . . . It's hard to explain how the difference was. The people seemed more relaxed around the race track than what I'd been used to. They weren't all excited about this and that and about people doing things. Like I say, asphalt racing is a lot smoother than dirt.

The first of the year, in '74, our expectations was to run in the top ten. That would have been super. We started to running, and it weren't ten races and we was running second to Tommy Houston over at Metrolina Speedway in Charlotte, and running in the top three and four and five at Hickory. We kept on doing better and better, and finally, we won a race, in Charlotte. And then the very next night we won at Hickory. Well, that just throwed us all off.

The first race I won, I was back in fourth at the first of the race, and I come from fourth to second and I was running second to Tommy Houston. Ten races I run second to him there, and I was running behind him again. I'd been watching him every race, and I just about knew where I could beat him. I got to beating him a little more and more every corner, right from the middle of the corner off, and finally I got up beside of him and got by him. Well, here I was leading the race, and I hadn't never been in this position; this was something new to me. I won it. There wadn't about five laps to go when I passed him, and I won it by four car lengths. The next night at Hickory, I beat Bob Pressley by the same thing. There at the end I passed Bob Pressley and beat him by five or six car lengths.

So it weren't hard for me as far as my driving part, but like I said, my daddy just died, and I was starting something that I'd never, never been without his advice. He hadn't run on asphalt that much in the year before he died, but he knew things to do in a situation—handling problems, when your car's not working well. He'd always been around to help me out with them. He really helped me on that more than the driving. It was hard for him not being around. It was a great loss to me, my daddy was, and now that we've got things going purty good—I'm up another stage from where I was; a great deal better than what I was—I'd like for him to be around to see where I'm at, and for us all to be right there like it was.

Question: How much money do you have to take in from various sources to break even on the year?

Earnhardt: I got no idea, this year. Last year we made $13,000 at Hickory and Charlotte. That was total money at those two tracks, and we come out about even. Paying my salary and everything, we spent about $14,000 and had a little bit of sponsor help that made the difference. This year, I haven't made a salary. They haven't had the money to pay me. We've made something like $6,000 so far, and I think we've spent $8,000. We've had sponsor help that probably evened us up.

Question: There don't seem to be very many young Grand National drivers around. A lot of drivers seem to be content to stay in Sportsman racing.

Earnhardt: They've made a living there.

Question: Yes, but is it your inclination just to make a living in Sportsman, or . . . ?

Earnhardt: No. Like I said, that's why I started running NASCAR—to go somewhere. I'm going to eventually go to Grand National. I ain't saying I'll never come back to Sportsman, or never run dirt again. I ain't saying I'll never come back and run around home, just outlaw, and not be satisfied with that. That's what my father done. He got up in age and fell back to making real good money here around home. And I can do it now—make a living at it. But I'm wanting to go somewhere in racing. I don't want to run Sportsman all my life. I want to go to Grand National, and if I do real well, I'd like to stay there and be a top Grand National driver.

You can't do it without money. You got fellers that would probably be one helluva driver, or they are—

really, they are—that probably could have made it with the money. But they never did. Just like you take a lot of the Grand National independent guys. They're just there to survive. They want to run good, but they won't really get in there and go hard. They want to finish the race and make a dollar because what they're racing on is what they make. They ain't racing on the sponsor. Now, that scares me right there. What if I don't have the backing and I don't make it? I hope one of these days I can get a good sponsor that will give me the chance to show what I can do.

Question: What tells you that you've got the ability?

Earnhardt: Nothing don't tell me that. I just feel that way. I feel like one of these days I can be a good driver on a superspeedway. I'd like to think I'm a purty decent driver. You'll never be the best until maybe you're in Petty's shoes, which I don't think you'll see another feller superior to Petty as far as wins and everything, but I like to think . . . Ned Jarrett and everybody up there at Hickory rates me as in the top five drivers, on a short track. My name's always been pretty high up there in the top five or six when you're naming all the drivers that does well.

When I started driving, I felt like I could drive dirt. Well, I accomplished it, to a certain extent. Then I wanted to go to asphalt. Well, we went to asphalt on the short tracks, and I feel like I've accomplished a good bit and can drive a short track pretty well to everybody else's ability. And now I'm looking ahead to the Grand National superspeedway races.

Question: At your age and with your experience, can you pick out other drivers around you who you feel could also succeed in Grand National?

Earnhardt: I don't like to call names or nothing, but there's people that's driving Grand National now that you can look at and say he'll make a good driver, and then there's some of them that you know'll never make a good driver. You can run Grand National all your life and never win a race, you know. You've got to meet what the race track demands. There's limitations to what a man can do. If you can't run 150 miles an hour and you've got to run

154, you'll never win the race because you're not running fast enough. Right? And you've got to want to do it. Let's say you got a feller out here driving a race car and he won't go as hard as he needs to go. You can't *make* him go hard; you can't make him do something he don't want to do. But you can take somebody that just goes ass-busting as hard as he can go, and even though he's doing it wrong, you can work with him and gear him down a little bit and get his mind working right—and then make him a good race driver.

Question: A curious question, perhaps, but what kind of standing do you have in your community—in Kannapolis—being a race driver?

Earnhardt: All these people that's here, the older people, been around when daddy was around, and the ones that have moved here knows what's happening up here. We're on good terms, but I haven't really talked to them as far as what do they think about me racing. Like I said, there's a lot of them that wouldn't understand why I've devoted so much time to it or how I can stay out there and work in the garage all the time. They don't understand why you ain't got a job that works eight hours a day and come home and be done with it; why you do something that takes so much of your time.

Well, one of these days, this is going to slack off. And if I get good enough, get the money behind me, get a good crew, I'll have time. Right now, I'm more or less the one-man band. My brothers help me all they can, and they help me full time at the race track. But *I'm* the one that's worrying about the car getting to the race track. And *I'm* the one that's worrying about loading the truck and seeing everything's there. And *I'm* the one that's worrying about the engine: Is it ready? And *I'm* the one that's worrying about the car: Is it set up? Is the tires all changed and on the car right?

But a driver needs to stay fresh in his mind when he's driving. I get out there and work on the car all day long, and then get in and practice and practice, and drive it, and work on it, and stay up late at night thinking about it, and worrying with it. And when the race time comes, you're wore out. Even though you slept the night before, you're wore out.

You take the Pettys. They work during the day. They're off at night. Their garage lights aren't on over there unless something out of the ordinary happens. They can go home, Maurice and all of them, and they get up the next morning and go back to work. Richard's got more time than anybody else because Maurice and them won't let him around the race car until it's time to drive it, and that's the only time. At a race track, do you ever watch Richard? He sets somewhere at the truck, don't he? He talks to the press, he walks around the pits and talks to the people, and the rest of them's there working on the car. When it's time to drive it, he comes, gets in it, and that's it. Then he gets out of it, tells Maurice what the car done, and he'll walk away from the car. Maurice will tell him, "Don't work on this car. It ain't your place to. Stay away from my car." Petty and Pearson and Baker and all the guys up there that's got the crews to do it, they can relax. Relax their mind.

I'm hoping one of these days that's how it'll turn out for me. You've got to work hard and start at the bottom and go up. Just like I said to my wife, nobody's going to walk over and give it to me: "I got $200,000 behind you. Let's go. Get me a $30,000 race car, and all I want you to do is drive it." They ain't nobody going to do that. You've got to work, and build your reputation and abilities up, and get the experience on your own.

Question: So how far away are you from Grand National?

Earnhardt: I've got no idea, really. This next year I'm wanting to run Sportsman, and if I can get a good ride, I'd like to run a few Grand National races. I'd like to go in it hard, wide open, possibly the next year, which would be 1977.

He missed by two years.

I talked with Earnhardt again in July 1980, at the headquarters of the Rod Osterlund Racing Team, a collection of beige, concrete-block buildings on North Carolina Highway 115 just north of Charlotte whose plain exteriors successfully concealed the big-bucks Grand National operation inside. Rod

Osterlund was a relative newcomer to Grand National racing, a wealthy California industrialist who had plucked Earnhardt from the Sportsman ranks at the end of the 1978 season. It was a gamble, as those things always were, but one that paid off handsomely, and midway through the 1980 season Earnhardt had already proven that his magnificent 1979 run, as Tim Flock might have said, was no flukey. Certainly, his mind was relaxed. He had already won two races, at Bristol and Atlanta (and before the week was over he would win a third, at Nashville), he was the year's leading money winner, and he was caught up in a tantalizing duel for the driving championship with Richard Petty, who seemed determined to put one more whippersnapper in his place, as he had Darrell Waltrip in 1979, before turning over the Petty Enterprises shop to son Kyle. *Sports Illustrated, People,* and *The New York Times* were all preparing articles on him, and he had recently signed a five-year contract with Osterlund that would guarantee him financial security for years to come. Clearly, he had grabbed the brass ring.

Earnhardt no longer slept on his mother's couch. The week following his accident at Pocono he had moved from Kannapolis to a bachelor pad—he was divorced—on Lake Norman, a pleasant recreational spot not far from the Osterlund shop. When we met he had on a pair of cowboy boots made from rattlesnake skin and a matching belt. But for all his recent success, Earnhardt had changed little. At 29 he was still lean and wiry, he wore a moustache, and he slouched a lot. Also, he limped slightly. He had, he said, recently broken a toe while kicking a bedpost. He declined to elaborate. Except for a slight settling about the stomach, an occupational hazard of anybody who earned their living sitting down, even at 200 mph, he looked much as he had in 1975. He was polite but nervous; uncomfortable at rest. He would rather have been fishing.

Until the Osterlund ride came along, Earnhardt said, his career had been pretty uneventful. "Just a lot of Saturday night Sportsman racing," he said. "It's not really all that interesting. They's a lot of what I would call lag time in there."

Still, it served the purpose of allowing him to complete his apprenticeship. That part of his career was over, though the learning process most assuredly was not. Unlike many young drivers, Earnhardt was not afraid to seek advice from his elders, nor was he unwilling to confront a driver after an altercation on the race track to make sure that the incident did not carry over to future races. Early in the 1980 season, for example, he and Petty and several other drivers got tangled up at the start of a race at Martinsville. "It was a situation where it really wadn't my fault," said Earnhardt. "I got into another car and had a tire go down and went into Richard. At the next race I went over and talked to him, and we straightened it all out. We talked about it. I told him what I thought, and he talked to me, and it was all over with. It didn't carry on. If I hadn't of been smart enough, or man enough—or whatever it was—to go over to Richard, and just stayed away from him and kept to myself, it would have just built up."

No second-year driver since the earliest days of NASCAR had ever challenged for the Grand National driving championship, but Earnhardt was almost lethargic when he talked about his championship duel with Petty. "You think about it," he said, "but what can you do about it? I feel like he feels the same way. I don't think there'll be any pressure on Richard or me, either one, if it comes down to us at the end—as opposed to how it was last year between him and Waltrip. Richard knows I'm going to go out there to race to win, no matter what, and that's the way he's going to do. If there is any pressure from the points, it'll come when there's one or two or three races left and I'm either ahead of him or behind. And I hope I hear his footsteps instead of him hearing mine."

Earnhardt heard footsteps the rest of the year. He won the 1980 driving title—and well over $500,000 in prize money—by holding off a late-season rush by Cale Yarborough. Richard Petty finished a distant fourth. Earnhardt, he was a throwback—hell, all of them were.

Afterword

The Money Tree

BACK IN 1981, WHEN *FAST AS WHITE LIGHTNING* WAS FIRST PUBlished, Gerald Martin wrote in the *Southern Motorsports Journal,* "The time will come when new men with the new ideas, more money, less compassion, and different roots will change the good ol' boy image of the sport. . . . So enjoy it while you can, folks. Grab for a star while you can. Chat awhile. Get an autograph. Racing's changing. The monster's coming. Progress they call it. The good ol' days are now, but they won't be here for long."

Martin was right of course. To find out for myself whether the soul of stock car racing had been compromised by these changes or merely altered by them, nearly a generation after the publication of this book I again set off to report on a sport that continues to amaze and entertain me nearly as much as it did when I wrote about it regularly. I wanted to describe the change Martin rightly predicted would occur and see whether it was for the better or the worse or was simply . . . change.

The most significant difference between the stock car racing of the early 1980s and that of the late 1990s was to be found neither in the drivers nor their cars. The drivers, with rare exception, remained rural good ol' boys with few pretentions and little formal education beyond high school. Certainly the cars they drove were more sophisticated than those of nearly two decades earlier, but not by a whole lot. In the overall scheme of things, the NASCAR Winston Cup circuit was the

Jurassic Park of the motorsports world, a place where mechanical progress was the least significant element in the racing equation and was, indeed, frowned upon.

What had changed, and remarkably so, was the degree of American corporate involvement in this, the most American of motor sports. Stock cars had always been a form of high-speed, low-flying advertisements, with decals and brilliant paint jobs covering virtually every available inch of the metallic billboards. Now, not just the individual teams received gobs of money to go racing in exchange for some pretty high visibility, but the individual races, as well as the series themselves, had obtained corporate sponsorship.

To the business of racing one could also add NASCAR Thunder, a chain of retail stores selling officially licensed products; the NASCAR Cafe in Myrtle Beach, S.C., with more to follow, identified in press releases as "NASCAR's interactive eating experience"; and a NASCAR SpeedPark in Las Vegas that featured go-carts resembling Winston Cup cars and Craftsman trucks—truck-racing having made its successful debut in 1995. One early conclusion was obvious: in the new world of NASCAR, money ruled. Babbittry was in its ascendancy. "The Americanization of Dixie," to cite the title of the prescient 1974 book by John Egerton, was complete—in the form of the book's subtitle: "the Southernization of America."

In 1972, the first year of the downsized schedule that eliminated all but a handful of the short-track events that the sport had been reared upon, just one of the thirty-two surviving races went by anything except local, indigenous names such as the Southern 500, the Motor State 400, the Mason-Dixon 500, and so on. The one exception was to be found at the new track near Talladega, Ala., where the second race of the 1972 season was changed from the Alabama 500 to the Winston 500 in deference to the brand of cigarettes that had taken over sponsorship of the entire Grand National series the year before. The Grand National series—make that the Busch Grand National series—was now the exclusive property of the second-tier cars formerly called Grand American.

By 1980, fourteen of the thirty-one Winston Cup Grand National races, as the series was now formally known, had found corporate sponsorships; by 1997, fully twenty-seven of the thirty-two races were corporately sponsored, the only holdouts being the Daytona 500, the Brickyard 400 at the Indianapolis Motor Speedway, one of the two races at Louden, N.H., and the pair of races at Pocono, in Pennsylvania. Even these last three events had had corporate sponsorship the year before and surely will in the future.

Now everything is for sale, including Victory Lane, which at some races boasts an official McDonald's Drive-Thru interview conducted within an official Purolator winner's circle. There are approximately a dozen top-drawer sponsorships in Winston Cup racing, companies whose wares are allowed to be identified as "official" NASCAR products. Pepsi-Cola is the official soft drink of NASCAR; Raybestos is the official brakes of NASCAR; MAXX is the official trading card of NASCAR; Gatorade is the official sports beverage of NASCAR; DieHard is the official battery of NASCAR; Du Pont is the official automotive finish of NASCAR; Western Auto is the official parts and service store of NASCAR; and on and on.

The creativity displayed by the corporate connectives is mind-boggling. Having run out of first-line products to offer potential sponsors, yet not wishing to turn down any sponsorship money whatsoever, the Winston Cup series has found myriad semilegitimate ways to enhance the flow of cash, most prominent among them being the proliferation of corporate-sponsored awards. The Plasti-Kote winning and Quality Finish award—Plasti-Kote being the official spray paint of NASCAR—honors the crew chief of the winning car in each of the thirty-two series races; the AE Clevite Engine Parts award honors the series's top engine builder. Some of the awards are stretches, such as the Goody's Headache Award, given to the driver who suffers the worst luck in a race, or the RCA Pit Strategy award. Others are just plain outrageous: consider the UAW-GM Teamwork of Excellence award given to the crew, driver, and car that demonstrate the best teamwork during each of the series races; the AP Parts Meet the Challenge award, given to the driver who makes up the most positions from the start to the finish of a race. (This is a particularly meaningless accomplishment. Since cars are allowed to close up under the yellow caution flag, and since passing at nearly all of the race tracks is relatively easy, a car's position at the start of the race counts virtually for nothing.)

This corporate flag-waving has resulted in plenty of cutthroat counterprogramming. That Pepsi is the official soft drink of NASCAR does not preclude the Charlotte Motor Speedway from gaining sponsorship for its World 600 from—Coca-Cola. DieHard's being the official battery does not prevent Interstate from signing on as Bobby Labonte's prime sponsor. McDonald's status as the official NASCAR hamburger can't stop Burger King from sponsoring Joe Nemechek. Busch beer's sponsorship of the Grand National series cannot prevent a Coors Light or a Miller's Lite car from obtaining equal billing, and even Winston's sponsorship of the entire series cannot legally dissuade a Joe Camel car or a Skoal Bandit racer from showing up.

All of this makes things particularly tough for Bill Brodrick, known on the Winston Cup circuit as the "hatman." Brodrick is employed by Union 76, the official gas of the series (though this does not dissuade Ernie Irvan from driving a car sponsored by Texaco), and his sole professional task in life is to exert absolute control over the postrace ceremonies in Victory Lane by making sure the winner of the race is photographed and seen on television wearing the hats, one at a time, of his various sponsors. It is Brodrick's job first to make sure the driver wears all the proper hats, and second to make sure the driver wears all the proper hats in order of sponsor involvement. Brodrick has been doing this job forever, since the days when Linda Vaughn, an extraordinarily statuesque and voluptuous blonde, graced Victory Lane in the employ of one sponsor or another.

As the winning car approaches Victory Lane, Brodrick, hats at the ready, escorts it and its driver through the assembled hordes of press photographers, sponsor photographers, and television crews to its proper place. Once the driver—who is usually in a fairly good mood after winning the race, but who is also pooped—unhooks his safety harness, unplugs his radio communications, and lowers the mesh safety net from his window, Brodrick gives him a drink and then, one-two-three-four, begins popping hats on the poor guy's head. Brodrick has to be both quick and careful.

In June 1997, Jeff Gordon won the inaugural California 500 (sponsored by NAPA) at Roger Penske's new two-mile oval track at Fontana. Immediately upon entering Victory Lane, he was given a great big glass of Pepsi with a great big Pepsi logo on it. After Gordon took off his helmet, Brodrick popped on the Du Pont hat in honor of Gordon's primary sponsor while Gordon was interviewed live on national television. Once the interview ended and the cameras were presumed to be down, Gordon gave his Pepsi to a bystander and switched to a liquid that might have been fizzy water or just plain tap water. Whatever it was, it was clear, and clearly not a Pepsi.

NOW, IN THE LATE 1990S, WINSTON CUP RACING HAS BECOME the preeminent motorsports attraction in the country, and perhaps the world. Virtually all its vital signs have blown through the top of the charts, and the aura of gushy, feel-good optimism that touches every corner of the empire, from the boardrooms across corporate America and the soundproofed executive suites high above the steep-banked ovals to the Featherlite trailers in the garage areas behind pit road, continues unimpeded. While all this has happened rather suddenly, the key elements of the equation are apparent to everybody.

Absolutely central to the success of Winston Cup racing was the decision to take track ownerships public. Historically, race-track ownership was a true entrepreneurial venture. A single individual or, at most, a small group of partners were responsible for building and running virtually every race track in America, from the storied big boys such as the Indianapolis Motor Speedway, which opened for business in 1909, and Daytona, where they'd been running on the hard beach sands long before Bill France senior built his speedway in 1959, to the small-track bullrings that provided the venues for most of the racing until the downsizing of the schedule in 1972.

Bruton Smith and Humpy Wheeler took their group of race tracks, Speedway Motorsports, Inc., public in 1990; Billy France junior's International Speedway Corporation followed two years later; Roger Penske's group of tracks jumped on board in 1994. While none of these three offerings outperformed the leading market indicators in the years of the raging bull market that followed, they did okay nonetheless and infused the sport with millions of investment dollars that would otherwise have stayed on the sidelines.

On March 20, 1997, Montgomery Securities, an investment brokerage house based in San Francisco, held a "Motorsports Conference" at the Essex House in New York City to help new investors understand exactly what was going on in the sport. The presentation was enlightening on several fronts, but the main thrust was to show how thoroughly NASCAR racing in general (which includes the Busch Grand National series and the Craftsman Truck Series) and Winston Cup racing in particular had risen to the top of the motorsports heap. A sampling of the numbers bandied about at the Montgomery Securities presentation tell the story:

- Attendance at all three NASCAR series—Winston Cup, Busch Grand National, and Craftsman Trucks—in 1996 exceeded 8 million people and represented 52 percent of the total attendance at all forms of motorsports events in the United States. The thirty-four Winston Cup dates (including the thirty-two regular races and two special events) alone accounted for 36 percent of the total.
- Winston Cup fans have a median income of $39,280. Further, 39 percent are college educated, a whopping 50 percent are between 25 and 44 years old, and 71 percent are considered loyal to Winston Cup products—that is, they buy the products advertised on the sides and tops of the race cars.
- There is a Winston Cup track within 200 miles of seventeen of the top twenty-five advertising markets in the United States; major league race tracks are in place or in the planning stages for all save three of the missing eight.
- Winston Cup events have a profit margin (total revenues minus total expenses) of 60 percent.

For the most part, the report showed a nice, though not spectacular, bottom line for investors. For Bruton Smith's Speedway Motorsports, the earnings had steadily climbed from $0.16 per share in 1990, the year it went public, to $0.53 for 1995, and were projected at $1.02 for 1998. For Penske Motorsports, the climb was from an actual $0.80 for 1994 to a projected $1.35 in 1998. For the International Speedway Corporation, earnings were $0.34 per share in 1992, $0.53 per share in 1995, and were estimated to reach $0.80 per share for fiscal 1998.

IT WAS NOT SURPRISING, THEN, THAT AS THE 1997 SEASON progressed, by far the most significant offtrack battle was to be found in the three-cornered fight for the ownership of the race tracks, because control of the venues was coming to be seen as the key to control of the sport itself.

Bruton Smith and Humpy Wheeler regularly and rigorously denied that their lengthy agendas included the pursuit of NASCAR itself, at least the late-model Winston Cup part of it, either from within the organization or without. However, rumors surfaced regularly of a new racing circuit to rival the one that had remained in the control of the France family for nearly a half century. These rumors, in combination with the furious track-acquisition wars of 1996 and 1997, gave Smith's and Wheeler's denials a somewhat hollow and disingenuous tone. The only reasonable conclusion was that Roger Penske, the third heavyweight in the NASCAR track wars, probably was not out to form a new racing organization, having already created one racing circuit in his own image.

As noted, NASCAR's modern era dates from the 1972 downsizing of what is now known as the Winston Cup circuit. At that time, stock car racing was still perceived as a Southern regional sport. This did not present a serious problem until the 1980s, when the advent of new television networks, particularly ESPN and TNN, made it possible for every race to be sold to a national television audience. But with a majority of the races still located in the Southeast, national advertisers were stuck with regional audiences, which meant low ratings—and which in turn meant unhappy advertisers. Clearly, the sport had to expand.

And Winston Cup racing did expand, primarily through its awarding of valuable race dates to new tracks or to existing tracks in those top twenty-five market areas in the United States that didn't yet have any. Pocono Raceway, in Long Pond, Pa., joined the circuit in 1974 to embrace the Philadelphia market, eighty miles away. The road course at Watkins Glen, N.Y., for years the home of the United States Grand Prix, returned to the

Winston Cup circuit in 1986 after an absence of twenty-one years. The fast mile track at Phoenix, heretofore the preserve of open-wheel racers, came on board in 1988. Sears Point, a road course in northern California, joined in 1989 to nail down the San Francisco market. Loudon, N.H., just up the road from Boston, signed up in 1993. In the most dramatic marketing coup of its long history, NASCAR added the fabled Indianapolis Motor Speedway to its roster in 1994. For over eight decades, the only race ever run on the distinctive flat-banked, 2.5-mile course was the Indianapolis 500, on Memorial Day. Traditionalists were horrified; sponsors and advertisers were not. Finally, in the spring of 1997, came the new track near Dallas–Fort Worth and another in southern California at Fontana, a hellishly hot town just to the west of San Bernardino.

Bruton Smith's Texas Motor Speedway replaced a speedway near Bryan, Texas, that opened for business in 1969 but lost its Winston Cup race date twelve years later due to a lack of customers. The track was in the middle of nowhere, too far away from anybody to get to in a reasonable time. Roger Penske's California Speedway was perceived as a clone of the Michigan International Speedway, the track near Jackson along the heavily populated Detroit-Chicago corridor that Penske had owned for over two decades, but it was not. Wider than Michigan and with a two-tiered racing groove, similar to the one at Texas, it, too, was designed to accommodate both the heavy, 3,400-pound stock cars and the lighter, open-wheel, open-cockpit race cars that would also compete there. However, the California track had a smooth seamlessness to it that stood in stark contrast to the tight, pinched turns at Texas, which were an immediate source of controversy.

There was no controversy at California, and in the early laps of the inaugural California 500 in June, fans were treated to the delicious sight of their favorites careening along three, four, and sometimes five abreast before they got themselves sorted out and found the racing groove. Whether this was good or bad or merely different was something longtime followers of the sport began to debate almost immediately. Sometimes race tracks built by the seat of the pants had more character than their younger, sleeker counterparts.

My favorite would always be Darlington. The news, in early 1997, that the start-finish line would be moved from the middle of the extant front straight to the middle of the back straight, so that more luxury boxes could be constructed along the "front" straight (a major highway runs directly behind the original front straight, precluding further grandstand expansion) didn't bother me at all. As the drivers pointed out, they still had to negotiate the turns. It was just that now they'd be barreling through the old one-two turn at the west end of the track en route to the finish line instead of three and four.

The big-bucks ownership fight for control of the tracks came about because there are only fifty-two weeks in a year, and because a Winston Cup automobile race is a very site-intensive event. Thanks to the heavy merchandising push, a Winston Cup race date generated revenues far in excess of mere ticket sales. Concessions and souvenirs added significantly to the monies obtained at the gate. Other on-site extravaganzas throughout the year add significantly to the take. At Smith and Wheeler's Charlotte Motor Speedway, for example, in 1997 there were seven World Karting Association races, a series of Legends races for five-eighths-scale replicas of pioneer race cars from the thirties and forties, and a pair of monster car shows. All this was in addition to the various mainstream race dates. NASCAR race dates, however, are central.

In 1997 there were thirty-two Winston Cup races. Add to that the two special events, The Winston, an event at Charlotte limited to the previous season's race winners, and the Busch Clash, an event at Daytona limited to the previous year's pole winners; toss in a nonpoints race in Japan after the regular season was over; include the demands of increasingly sophisticated testing programs; and consider also the request of sponsors for advertising shoots and personal appearances—and pretty soon it's time to go to Daytona for the start of another season.

Winston Cup race dates, then, are limited and precious, and if you own a race track and want one—or if you've just built a track and need two dates instead of the one you've been allocated—you have to be creative.

An owner of a race track could obtain additional Winston Cup dates merely by buying another race track that already had one or two. The prized race dates were included in the selling price. Thus began the race-date cannibalization of small tracks in the already saturated Carolinas market, and not surprisingly, the central player was Bruton Smith.

As noted, at the start of the 1996 season, Smith's enterprise, Speedway Motorsports, Inc., already owned, in addition to Charlotte, the race tracks at Atlanta, Bristol (Tenn.), and Sears Point: four tracks and seven dates. The France family enterprise, the International Speedway Corporation, weighed in with Daytona, Darlington, Talladega, and Watkins Glen: four tracks and seven dates.

But Bruton was completing this new track in Texas and did not yet have a race date for it. His solution was to approach the owners of North Wilkesboro, a storied venue but vulnerable because its seating capacity was just 45,000 and its cramped infield could hold only 9,000 more.

North Wilkesboro was owned equally by two families, including the heirs of the man who had built it nearly a half century before, Enoc Staley. Smith got an agreement from the Staley heirs for their half of the track, but at the last minute was blindsided by Robert Bahre, who just happened to own the track at Loudon, N.H. Bahre's track had just one date; he wanted two. He went after the remaining 50 percent of North Wilkesboro and was successful. The track was closed down and the race dates parsed out: one to Smith, which he transferred to his new Texas track, and one to Bahre, which became a second Loudon race date.

A similar venture occurred involving Smith and Roger Penske.

Smith, having received one race date for his new Texas track through his purchase of half of North Wilkesboro, then went after the North Carolina Motor Speedway, a spiffy mile track vulnerable for the same reasons as North Wilkesboro: its small seating capacity and its proximity to the crowded Charlotte marketplace.

Enter Roger Penske, whose Penske Motorsports, Inc., had obtained Michigan International Raceway in 1973 in a bankruptcy proceeding and was building the California track. He'd already gotten one date from NASCAR for the southern-

California location, but needed another. He, too, went after the Rock, as the North Carolina Motor Speedway is known, and in short order, Penske and Smith sued each other.

Finally, in July of 1997 the France family again added to its own bulging race-track portfolio by buying Phoenix outright from its owner, Buddy Jobe. The move was correctly seen as a ploy by the France family to prevent Smith, who was now in danger of losing Rockingham to Penske, from going after Phoenix himself.

At the end of 1997, pending the outcome of the inevitable legal challenges, this is how the updated scorecard read for the Big Three of NASCAR's Winston Cup ownership:

• The International Speedway Corporation (ISC), run by the France family, which also ran NASCAR, the sanctioning body, owned five Winston Cup race tracks and controlled eight race dates.

• Speedway Motorsports, Inc. (SMI), controlled by Bruton Smith, owned five tracks and eight race dates.

• Penske Motorsports, Inc. (PMI), operated by Roger Penske, owned three tracks and five dates.

The early line said that Penske would quickly transfer one of the Rockingham dates to his new California facility, and—this was the lesser possibility—that Smith, who had not hesitated to participate in the dismantling of North Wilkesboro, would strip tiny Bristol of one of its dates and transfer it to his Texas facility.

THE 1.5-MILE TEXAS MOTOR SPEEDWAY, LOCATED NORTHWEST of Fort Worth roughly at the junction of State Roads 114 and 156, is huge. With seating for 154,000 people, including ninety-four luxury boxes, it is the second-largest sports stadium in the United States, behind the Indianapolis Motor Speedway and its estimated 265,000 seats. Anxious to see the new kid on the motorsports block for myself, I made the 650-mile drive from Santa Fe, N.M., where I now live, to Dallas–Fort Worth for the inaugural event, scheduled for April 6, 1997.

Four flags flew over the Texas Motor Speedway, those of the United States, the State of Texas, Interstate Batteries, and Coca-Cola, the last two being the weekend's main race sponsors.

I arrived shortly after noon on the Thursday of race week. Although the racing surface and pits had been finished for some time—there had been prerace testing one month earlier—workmen were still putting finishing touches on the place less than twenty-four hours before official practice was scheduled to begin.

I met Bruton Smith in his office at the Speedway approximately two hours after his $120-million race track opened for business. Sleek, polished, and benignly modest, at 69 he had the satisfied air of a man whose outright ownership of five race tracks—Charlotte, Atlanta, Bristol, and Sears Point in addition to Texas—and thus control of eight of the thirty-two Winston Cup dates, made him perhaps the single most powerful person in stock car racing, even more powerful than the France family, which had controlled and nurtured the sport since its inception exactly fifty years earlier. Before the week was out, it would be revealed that Smith and Penske were, in fact, engaged in their dingdong fight for control of the North Carolina Motor Speedway, at Rockingham.

It was crazy to try to converse in any depth. The weather was lousy, the place was still under construction, and minions from here and there popped in with dozens of questions and concerns. While Smith is a facile businessman, he is not necessarily quotable. "Interviewing Bruton is like talking to cardboard," others had said of him.

I hadn't found this true the first time around, twenty-two years earlier. Still, my questions regarding the reasons for stock car racing's tremendous current popularity and the direction it might take in the near future would have to wait. Smith did, however, make some significant observations on the state of the sport and mentioned how amazed he was at the level of attention given to the sport in the media. He wryly remembered his earliest days as a promoter in the Carolinas when television was a novelty and how he had had to beg newspaper sports editors to cover his events.

The race track was open for just a couple of hours that Thursday. Ricky Craven, the number three driver for the Rick Hendrick superteam that included the boyish wunderkind Jeff Gordon, the 1995 Winston Cup champion, and his avuncular teammate, Terry Labonte, the titlist in 1984 and 1996, might have wished the track never opened at all. At 10:44 A.M., less than an hour after the track went green for practice, Craven slammed the outside wall of turn four hard in his Chevrolet Monte Carlo. The reason for the crash was not immediately clear, although early speculation centered on the possibility that Craven had strayed below the white line at the bottom of the track and lost traction on the flat apron before careening back up to the outside wall.

Craven's accident was the most serious of three incidents on Day One. He was taken to Parkland Hospital in Dallas with a broken right shoulder blade and a brain contusion. His condition was listed as serious, and he would, in fact, miss four races before returning to action.

As predicted, at around 2:30 in the afternoon, showers turned to rain and washed out the rest of practice—and the first day's qualifying as well.

BACK AT MY HOTEL, QUITE BY ACCIDENT I RAN ACROSS A meeting of the Jeff Gordon Fan Club. A man from Williams, Ariz., by the name of Russ Harris and his wife started the club in 1991, when Gordon was still driving open-wheel race cars with little thought of NASCAR. Now, said Harris, there were more than 14,000 members nationwide. An individual membership, good for twelve months, cost $19.95 and included admission to Fan Club events and the opportunity to meet Jeff in person. (A double asterisk, however, warned that "Fan Club events will be subject to a room or food charge. Jeff's appearance is based upon availability and not guaranteed.")

The fee for this particular event was $15. The room, with seating for perhaps 250 people, filled up quickly. A sign warned, "One autographed item per person only." Nearly everybody did, in fact, bring something for Gordon to sign. Several people brought in entire tires, big fat slicks each weighing fifty pounds.

The meeting, emceed by Region IV coordinator Kim Miller, began precisely at 7 P.M. Gordon walked in, accompanied by his wife, Brooke, and spoke briefly. "This is a Texas crowd," he said, "and Bruton's hoping to fill 150,000 seats come Sunday."

He mentioned Ricky Craven's accident: "We'll all be praying for him, and y'all be prayin' for him, too."

During a question-and-answer session, a fan commended Gordon because "you never forget to thank the Lord."

A question concerned the health of Rick Hendrick, Gordon's team owner, who earlier in the year had been diagnosed with leukemia. "He's on interferon, on chemo," said Gordon, "but there's no hair loss. He does get sick, with flu symptoms, and he will need a bone marrow transplant."

Then Gordon and Brooke moved on to the autographs, each occupying a space at opposite ends of a long table. Mainly, Jeff signed autographs while Brooke, a former beauty queen and quite stunning, had her picture taken.

Bob Brannon, who serves both as Gordon's business agent and public relations person, said Gordon did perhaps a half dozen of these Fan Club appearances each year.

At exactly 8:15, Gordon and his wife left the room. "God bless each and every one of you," Gordon said.

The rain ended around midnight, but by Friday morning, Day Two, the showers had cranked up again in earnest, continuing to turn 900 acres of prime parking lot into a sea of churned mud.

I took the opportunity to make another pass along the extensive commercial midway behind the main grandstand. It was mind-boggling—trailer after trailer after trailer of food, licensed products, and hands-on entertainment to rival any halfway decent county fair. Earplugs, a necessity, went for $2 per pair. Dale Earnhardt earrings sold for $18 to $38 per pair. Hats went for $15 to $25, depending on the driver. A picture of Richard Petty, now a car owner, and his driver, Bobby Hamilton, signed by the artist, Jeanette Law, sold for $75; autographed by Petty and Hamilton, the price jumped to $175. Framing was $90 additional. An Ernie Irvan 14-karat gold pin could be had for $66. Race scanners that allowed you to listen in on conversations between drivers and their pit crews and spotters sold for $110 to $245, or you could rent a ten-channel scanner for $35. For $5 additional, frequencies could be updated daily. Hooters girls, more or less scantily clad, bounced up and down the midway pasting "I ❤ Hooters" on willing passers-by. For $25 you could buy the top part of a checkered-flag bikini; the bottom cost an additional $15. Two pieces of Williams fried chicken sold for $4; you could have the entire bird for $14. Inside the gate at the end of the main straightaway, near the entrance to turn one, Somerset Catering offered turkey legs for $5, a small bag of potato chips for $1, and bottled water for $2. At Bubba's, the track cafeteria, a sign politely asked folks to please use the small plastic cups when filling up with water; the water was free.

At the entrance to the elevators that took you to the luxury suites, a sign read:

> Attire
> Business Casual Recommended
> Please—no tank tops, halter tops
> swim suits, athletic shorts or
> underwear-style tee shirts allowed

At the Thunder Theater, sponsored by Winston, you could review the history of stock car racing in five-year increments beginning in 1971, the year Winston became the major series sponsor. The film featured close racing and a lot of spectacular crashes, none of them life-threatening or even injury-inducing. The 1991–95 segment highlighted the great 1992 points race among Alan Kulwicki, Davey Allison, and Bill Elliott, won by Kulwicki in the last race of the season. It was great stuff. No mention was made of the following year's airplane crash that killed Kulwicki and the helicopter crash that killed Allison.

A Bank of America VersaTeller stood at the ready to pounce on any temporarily empty wallets.

All of this was extraordinarily upbeat and feel-good, but I felt slightly uneasy in its midst for no good reason I could immediately identify.

Three more inches of rain fell on the speedway Friday. On radio 1310, an all-sports talk station, there was a prototypical reference to the stock car racing crowd trying to congregate at the speedway as "the tubeless and topless" set.

On Channel 4, driver Kenny Wallace said, "Bruton Smith has built these cats one helluva race track. It's fast as lightning, that's for sure."

The first race weekend ever at the new Texas Motor Speedway proved highly entertaining, although the weather and the newness of the track kept the frustration level tantalizingly high.

The precursor to the main event was Saturday's 300-mile Busch Grand National event—the Busch series being to the Winston Cup what Triple A baseball is to the major leagues. Ken Squier, the veteran CBS motorsports anchor, referred to the five inches of rain that the track had received in the previous twenty-four hours and made a brief reference to the 90-minute traffic jams on the roads leading to the track.

A crack, no doubt water-induced, had appeared overnight in turn one and was quickly repaired. At the start of the Saturday telecast, water stains were clearly visible on the racing surface, but high up against the wall, and certainly they would present no untoward difficulties for the drivers. The clearing wind was a rather spiffy 18 to 25 miles per hour, and the track was very green, the series of deluges having washed off what little rubber had been ground into the racing groove.

The quick summary of the preliminary race showed eight cautions in 300 miles of racing, and a race average of 122.9 mph. Six of the eight cautions were for incidents that began in turn four, leading to the front double-dogleg.

The Busch cars made it through seven laps before the first yellow; the Winston Cup guys didn't make the first turn, Johnny Benson of Grand Rapids, Mich., a 33-year-old sophomore, tangling with Darrell Waltrip, the 50-year-old, three-time driving champion celebrating his silver-anniversary—and final—year in Winston Cup racing. This began a melee that ultimately collected Morgan Shepherd, Jeremy Mayfield, Dale Earnhardt, Todd Bodine, and Kyle Petty, among others, prompting Kyle to tell the nationwide television audience, "A bunch of the world's greatest drivers got together for a little mishap in turn one."

The fun continued. A total of ten cautions occupied 78 of the race's 334 laps, slowed the race to a 125.105 mph average, and took out or damaged most of the favorites. The race was won by Jeff Burton, the first Winston Cup victory of his career.

Before the race, Kenny Wallace had praised the track. Brother Rusty, however, after he blew an engine and hit the wall on lap 165, told reporters the track would need "a total reconstruction to get it right." After the race, he elaborated, "Ain't no way to run here again without changes."

The rap against the new track was that it didn't behave very much like the track it was seen to be patterned after—the D-shaped, 1.5-mile Charlotte Motor Speedway. Drivers complained that the contours of the track left just one racing lane at the exit to turn four, and that the unique, two-tiered banking in both turns—a steep twenty-four degrees near the outside wall for stock cars and a relatively flat eight degrees at the inside for open-wheel race cars—pretty much eliminated side-by-side racing, and passing, anywhere. Stock car racing's decade-long romance with the press was temporarily derailed. Moaned *Sports Illustrated,* "Everything is deluxe at the new Texas Motor Speedway—except the track." *The New York Times* described Smith's efforts to replicate the Charlotte track as "beastly."

My opinion is that TMS got a bad rap. Certainly automobile racing ought to be reasonably safe, but nothing in the good book says it has to be easy. If a race track suddenly pinched down from two fast lanes to one, so what? Darlington, for the most part a single-groove race track if there ever was one, turned out the way it did because of a minnow pond and remains the most challenging and interesting track on the Winston Cup circuit.

Nor could the drivers use the newness of the Texas track as an excuse. The very next Sunday, at Bristol, a .533-mile bullring that has been part of the circuit since 1961, the world's best taxi drivers, as stock car racers are sometimes called, caused twenty cautions, a NASCAR record, before Jeff Gordon pushed Rusty Wallace aside on the last turn of the last lap to take the checkers.

FOLLOWING THE PUBLIC STOCK OFFERINGS AND THE INFUSION of money they generated, a second factor contributing to the success of Winston Cup racing in the 1990s was the chaotic state of competing motorsports series. The most unfortunate dispute was to be found in the world of open-wheel racing, where two rival philosophies engaged in a death-grip struggle for control of the most sacred of American racing institutions, the Indianapolis 500.

In a nutshell, the Indianapolis 500, held on Memorial Day, or close to it, every year from 1911 on except for the war years, was the single most significant race on the motorsports calendar. But its organization, which basically meant the late Tony Hulman and his heirs, was also the most arteriosclerotic in the entire world of sports. Mainly, it lacked vision.

Into the fray many years ago came Roger Penske, a key figure in motor sports since his days as a sports car racer in the 1950s and 1960s, and then as a car owner. As an owner, he campaigned everything from hot-wheel, Trans Am sports cars to Formula One machines. The death of Mark Donohue, his dear friend and most accomplished driver, during a practice session for the 1975 Austrian Grand Prix, took Penske away from Europe forever, and he turned to IndyCar racing full-time. Between 1972 and 1994 his drivers, often racing cars that were not only owned by Penske but built by him as well, won the Indy 500 a record ten times.

Tony George, Tony Hulman's grandson, took over the Indianapolis organization in 1989, and a philosophical rift over what IndyCar racing should be soon developed between George and Penske. In short, George favored rules changes that would drastically reduce the exorbitant cost of fielding a car for the Indy 500 and the racing series of which it was the overbearing centerpiece. Penske and the majority of car owners did not agree with this philosophy, and in relatively short order the divide was complete. On one side was CART, the sanctioning organization dominated by Penske and including most of the marquee drivers and owners. On the other side was the Indy Racing League. Its only real marquee names were the legendary A. J. Foyt, whose loyalties had always been to the Hulman family, and—the biggest marquee name of them all—the Indianapolis 500-mile race itself. George's IRL drew the rules for the 500 in such a way as to include the less expensive IRL cars and exclude the more exotic CART vehicles.

Bruton Smith aligned himself with the Indy Racing League and, in so doing, quickly got IRL races scheduled for his showpiece track at Charlotte and also for his new track in Texas. And not incidentally, NASCAR's support of the IRL was a huge contributing factor in the Brickyard's suddenly becoming available to the Winston Cup stock car set.

Formula One racing, while it never had the cachet in this country that it did in Europe and most of the rest of the world, simply disappeared from American sight after the 1991 United States Grand Prix–West, held in Phoenix, and never resurfaced. Money and talent that might once have found a home in what was still the most romantic form of racing on the face of the globe went elsewhere. Logic and history dictated that "elsewhere" would have meant open-wheel IndyCar racing, but because of the disarray there, it now meant stock car racing, which was able to corral the most awesome young talent around: Jeff Gordon.

In the not-too-distant past, it was possible for an auto-racing junkie who lived in the United States to wake up early on Memorial Day and catch the running of the Monaco Grand Prix on ABC television, then switch over to the Indianapolis 500 in time to catch its late-morning start (11 A.M., central daylight time), and then tweak the radio dial and maybe find the last few hundred miles of the World 600 in Charlotte. In 1997, however, more dexterity was required, plus a six-pack of Demerol. Thanks to organizational chaos, some weird rules, and a couple of storm cells, what used to be one day of neatly packaged, flat-out racing stretched into a chaotic four.

On Saturday, May 24, the Championship Auto Racing Teams gathered at a brand-new oval at the motorsports complex in Madison, Ill., called Gateway International Raceway, for the inaugural Motorola 300. The track was an odd 1.27-miles around, generating a race of an odd 237 laps. (To some, the 237-lap Motorola 300 did not have the same ring to it as the 200-lap Indianapolis 500.) Its gentle uniqueness came from the one-two turn's being banked eleven degrees and the three-four turn's being banked nine degrees. Its geography was noteworthy for being exactly five miles east of the splendid Gateway Arch in downtown St. Louis, the nation's twentieth largest market.

The race was okay, nothing special. Paul Tracy won, his third in a row for car-owner Penske, on some careful fuel calculations that allowed him to finish the race without the splash-and-dash gas stop required by his rivals to make it through the last few laps.

The next day, at 5:45 A.M. Santa Fe time, was the Grand Prix of . . . Spain. Monte Carlo, one learned, had years before been pushed to an earlier slot on the Formula One calendar. Spain, too, was an okay race, but nothing out of the ordinary.

The Indianapolis 500 was also scheduled to be run that day, but a massive storm postponed it for twenty-four hours. Just as well. Indy fans could use the time to absorb the information that *The New York Times* had recently concluded that the Indianapolis 500 had been exceeded in importance by the Daytona 500.

The Coca-Cola 600, once known as the World 600, was run under the lights at the 1.5-mile Charlotte Motor Speedway, nighttime racing being one of the many bracing innovations that Humpy Wheeler had brought to stock car racing in general and CMS in particular. Indeed, a compelling argument could be made that under Wheeler's management, Charlotte was the true epicenter of stock car racing, no matter what the folks at NASCAR headquarters in Daytona Beach might say.

The race, shown on TBS, was anchored by Ken Squier, the omniscient motorsports guru who also anchored motorsports telecasts on CBS. Rain from the fringes of the same storm that clobbered Indianapolis delayed the start of the Charlotte event, but the minor slowdown at the track did not ease the gushing from the telecast booth.

Dale Earnhardt, driving the first Richard Childress team car, in a prerace interview made a reference to having just wiped off his Nikes. Reporter Patty Moise conducted an emotional interview with Joe Nemechek, whose brother, John, had been killed not long before in a Craftsman truck race at the new track near Homestead, Fla. A reference was made to the EconoLodge starting grid, and to the Brut blimp, which Squier identified as "the best-smelling blimp in the air." It was noted that Superteam boss Rick Hendrick, whose drivers were Jeff Gordon, Terry Labonte, and Ricky Craven, was still home, battling his leukemia.

After a fleet of service trucks had lapped the track several times in an effort to dry it, the race began, but under heavy skies. By lap 4 (of a scheduled 400), Gordon had charged into the lead under the glistening lights that made the cars look as if they were lathered in Vaseline. Car owner Mike Beam reported that his driver, Bill Elliott, was "pumped." We were told that Mike Skinner, Childress's number two driver, was "having a great run." By lap 16, Squier had intoned, "It just doesn't get any better than this: unbelievable racing."

The first yellow was displayed on lap 54 for "debris on the track." When the cars resumed under green, Squier again noted the "wide-open, tremendous racing."

The race continued in fits and jerks, and as it neared the halfway point, an approaching storm put team crew chiefs squarely on the spot: Should their drivers pit under green and risk losing track position permanently in the event the race was declared official after just 200 laps, or should they stay out on the track and risk running out of gas?

More rain, described with understatement as a "frog swallower," hit on lap 194, 6 short of the 200 necessary for the race to become official. After a two-and-a-half-hour delay, the race resumed, first under yellow and then green, at 11:44. Squier, noting that Darrell Waltrip was wearing a silver driving suit and helmet in honor of his twenty-fifth, and final, season of Winston Cup racing, commented, "He looks like a baked potato."

At 12:45 A.M., NASCAR decreed there would be 20 more laps of racing, and that would be it—a race called on account of lateness. (NASCAR could do this. The year before, an afternoon race at Talladega that had run late was called on account of excessive sunshine. The lowering sun, said NASCAR director Gary Nelson, "was directly in the drivers' eyes" and blinding them.)

With 18 laps remaining, Jeff Gordon, who had once appeared to be pretty much out of the chase, passed Rusty Wallace for the lead. That's the way it ended.

Rusty Wallace said his Miller Lite car "really hauled ass," then explained that some loose lug nuts had caused him to slow at the end and be passed by Gordon.

Gordon, in the Purolator Victory Circle, said, "I want to thank Pepsi. I know it's a Coca-Cola race, but . . ."

The Indy 500 tried again on Monday, the 26th, threatened by a green blob of bad weather on the radar west of the Speedway. For the first time in thirty years, the cars ran normally aspirated engines, an Indy Racing League tweak of the rules book that had knocked 20 mph off the top speeds of the Indy cars. That, plus a blustery wind and cold air and the presence of thirteen rookies in the starting lineup, offered a recipe for disaster. As the drivers in the starting field of thirty-three swerved left and right to heat up their tires, three cars crashed on the last yellow warm-up lap, knocking out the entire fifth row even before the race began. Then a car parked on the back straight, and another steamed into the pits, smoking.

The next try at a start was ragged, but safe. But then the rains came yet again, and again everybody went home, determined to try again on Tuesday.

It didn't get much better. Robby Gordon, who had run at Charlotte, suffered car failure on the first green lap, bringing out the first yellow. On the restart, Steve Kinser hit something. Finally, they got the race going for real, and eventually Arie Luyendyk won it. On balance, however, it was more or less an aesthetic disaster, with just thirteen of the thirty-three starters running at the end of the race, only five of them on the lead lap. Yuck.

AFTER PUBLIC TRACK OWNERSHIP AND THE CHAOS IN RIVAL racing organizations, the third element contributing to the success of Winston Cup racing was the drive toward parity. In the ideal Winston Cup scenario, it seemed, forty cars would start the race and forty would finish it, all of them on the same lap and preferably all within a half second or so of each other. A technical advantage achieved by a team was simply not allowed to stand if there was any way at all to nullify it. The task of moderating this parity fell to Gary Nelson, the Winston Cup series director, who had once been Bobby Allison's crew chief, and also Darrell Waltrip's, and knew his way around the rule book as well as he did the innards of a high-performance engine.

The rules were changed weekly, and in seemingly arcane areas. There was, for example, the "sag" rule, which meant a car could not droop excessively when four 50-pound weights were attached to each of its four corners. The purpose was to prevent a car from dropping too low at speed and thus gaining an unfair aerodynamic advantage. Similarly, radio aerials and rooftop television mini-cams came under scrutiny because it was felt they affected aerodynamics, especially at the faster tracks. Roof lines and air dams were modified constantly.

Yet this tight rules enforcement did not necessarily ensure parity among the manufacturers. In a supreme irony of this most American of sporting events involving the most American of products, the kind of car a driver drove was increasingly irrelevant. In 1972, seven makes of cars were entered in Winston Cup races; in 1981 there were eight. But by 1996 the number had dropped to three: Ford, Chevrolet, and Pontiac. NASCAR had long ago stopped pretending that its racing series for late-model stock cars bore any more than a cosmetic resemblance to the cars that rolled off Detroit assembly lines. They were, in fact, one-of-a-kind formula cars, and the kind of engines to be found under the hood or the shape of the sheet metal that covered the roll cage was not nearly as significant as the sponsors' decals that now covered virtually every inch of the car.

That Jeff Gordon drove the Du Pont car serviced by Rainbow Warriors was infinitely more noteworthy than the happenstance of its being a Chevrolet; that Ricky Rudd drove the Tide car was most significant, not that it was a Ford. When it was announced midway through 1997 that Ford was discontinuing the Thunderbird and that the Ford stable of drivers would be driving Tauruses from 1998 on, nobody blanched (except, perhaps, the civilian Thunderbird owners). The power plant, for better or worse, would be the same, and that's what mattered most. The vehicles in the Craftsman Truck series, remember, were nothing more than Winston Cup cars with truck bodies instead of car bodies.

Chrysler, the third of Detroit's Big Three automobile manufacturers, and the company that had once provided the sleek Plymouths that Richard Petty drove to most of his 200 career victories and the terrifying Dodges once driven by the likes of Buddy Baker, was on the sidelines completely. Its chairman, Francoise Destange, was reported to have explained away his company's absence with the probably apocryphal remark, "NASCAR is a primitive form—also, we don't have a good V-8 engine except for trucks."

All of these developments meant closer racing and, on balance, better racing. Some statistical comparisons between the 1974, 1981, and 1996 seasons show exactly how Winston Cup racing has changed over nearly a quarter of a century:

	1974	**1981**	**1996**
Races	30	31	31
Cautions per race	6.0	7.1	6.0
Percentage of laps run under green per race	85.4	86.9	89.0
Lead changes per race	*	24.9	20.1
Different leaders per race	*	8.3	9.5
Finishers on lead lap per race	2.3	4.3	12.4

The one set of numbers that stands out, of course, has to do with cars still running on the lead lap. Thanks to the push for mechanical parity, a fairly recent development, as well as to the close-up rule under cautions, which had been around forever, more and more teams remain in contention deeper and deeper into a race.

Logic dictated that this has to produce more race winners, and it did. Consider: In 1972, the first year of the downsized schedule, six drivers won thirty-one races; in 1981 nine drivers won thirty-one races; in 1996 eleven drivers won thirty-one races; and in 1997 eleven drivers won thirty-two races (although Jeff Gordon had won ten).

(Ironically, two of the winningest drivers in history, Richard Petty and Cale Yarborough, both went more than a decade without wins as car owners. Bobby Hamilton's victory for Petty Enterprises at Phoenix late in 1996 came thirteen years after Richard Petty's last wins as a driver for the family concern, in

1983. Similarly, Cale Yarborough went almost eleven years without a victory as an owner before John Andretti ended the drought at Daytona in July of 1997.)

Gone forever were the days when a stout car could cover the field. Since 1994, only once in well over one hundred races did a driver lap the field. Geoff Bodine, driving for Junior Johnson on Johnson's home track of North Wilkesboro, won the 1994 Tyson Holly Farms 400 by a lap over a thoroughly whupped Terry Labonte. And on only five occasions during those four seasons did fewer than four cars finish on the lead lap. Indeed, at the squirrelly road courses, where passing is difficult anyway, or at the superspeedway races—assuming they are relatively clean—it was not uncommon to find twenty or more cars, half the field, hurtling toward the finish line on the same lap.

Numbers such as these suggest that the time is past when a single driver, possessed of decent talent and with a potful of money and technical support behind him, can dominate the sport for more than a season or two. With more and more corporate sponsorships available, which in turn brings more and more technical expertise into the arena, the gap between the race winners and the back markers has closed to virtually nothing. It is all the more remarkable, then, that during this very period of equalizing corporate largess, Dale Earnhardt was able to establish himself not only as the finest driver of his era but as the best driver ever to sit behind the wheel of a late-model stock car.

I don't make this statement casually, particularly since it comes at the expense of Richard Petty, who, more than any other single individual, had come to epitomize what stock car racing was all about. He—Petty—was loyal to his clan, his sponsors, his fans, and his sport.

If Petty was the apotheosis of what the public wanted its race car heroes to be like, Earnhardt, from the beginning, was his opposite. Where Petty won with finesse—although, as we have already seen, he was not above stepping into the muck, if that was required—Earnhardt won with brute force and intimidation. Where Petty was easy with his fans and with the small number of journalistic regulars who covered the circuit during his best years, Earnhardt was uncomfortable with stardom from the beginning. Where Petty was seen as the homey family man devoted to his Randleman roots, Earnhardt was portrayed as a distant loner whose loyalties were short-term and ultimately self-serving.

Still, when the first issue of the glossy, self-serving magazine *Inside NASCAR* hit the streets in January 1997, the one article of substance dealt interestingly with the question of whether Earnhardt, who had won seven championships in fifteen years beginning with the 1980 title that had conveniently provided the finale for the first edition of this book, or Petty, whose seven championship seasons began in 1964 and ended in 1979, deserved the title of best ever.

Earnhardt won, hands down, and I could not have agreed more.

It was reasonably clear from the moment Earnhardt entered Winston Cup competition that he was capable of winning races, but for several seasons the main question was whether he knew how to finish them. His first championship year was with owner Rod Osterlund, but when Osterlund left racing midway through 1981, Earnhardt flirted with Jim Stacy and Richard Childress, the latter a journeyman driver of little distinction who was getting his feet wet as an owner. In 1982 and 1983, Earnhardt, from an old-school racing family, hooked up with "Big Bud" Moore, another old-schooler. The results were disastrous. He won just three of sixty races and was listed DNF—Did Not Finish—thirty-one times.

Now, there are DNFs and there are DNFs. Sometimes they are caused by mechanical things—blown engines, a mismatched set of tires, and the like—and sometimes they are caused by the driver running out of brains. During his two years with Bud Moore Engineering, there were plenty of both kinds. It was not until 1984, when Earnhardt reforged an alliance with Childress, now committed to owning race cars and not driving them, that Earnhardt began to soar—and to change his image from the raucous "Ironhead" of his early years to that of the "Intimidator."

In 1986, Earnhardt began an extraordinary run of six championships in nine seasons, and it is significant that while he won approximately one race in five during this halcyon period, his DNF rate was a paltry 8 percent. By comparison, in his 216 races before 1986, Earnhardt won just 15 (a 7 percent success rate) while falling out of 63 (29 percent).

Earnhardt fans can recite the stories of their favorite Earnhardt races at the drop of a lug nut.

They begin with the litany of his Daytona 500 defeats. Although he had won a total of twenty-eight races of one sort or another at the track, his losses in the 500 were legendary. Through 1997, he was zero for nineteen in the most prestigious race on the NASCAR calendar. In the 1990s he has lost to Dale Jarrett by .16 of a second in 1993, to Sterling Marlin by .61 of a second in 1995, and to Jarrett again in 1996, this time by .12 of a second. At 180 miles per hour, you travel 264 feet per second. Thus, Earnhardt lost just these three races by the cumulative distance of a touch under 235 feet.

There was the fall race at Bristol in 1995 when Earnhardt more or less drop-kicked Terry Labonte across the finish line, with Labonte winning the race by .13 of a second.

There were any number of noteworthy wins at Talladega, the track that would nail him in 1996. In 1984, he won the summer race at the monster in a photo finish with Buddy Baker and Terry Labonte that wasn't decided officially for an hour. In 1994, he won the spring race there over Ernie Irvan, Michael Waltrip, Jimmy Spencer, and Ken Schrader in another photo finish so close that you could literally have thrown a blanket over those five cars.

And there was the spring race at Richmond in 1986, his first championship year with Childress, when he crashed Darrell Waltrip, who was leading, so overtly that NASCAR fined him $5,000 and put him on probation. The fine was later reduced and the probation rescinded—NASCAR has always been reluctant to sit down a star for long—after an appeal by Childress. But Bill Gazaway, the competition director for the Winston Cup series, told the press, "There is a fine line between hard racing and reckless driving, and Earnhardt clearly stepped over that line Sunday. We simply cannot tolerate or condone such actions. We must preserve the integrity of our sport."

In 1986, the *Southern Motorsports Journal,* now defunct but once one of the grittier racing journals, compiled a partial list of Earnhardt's racing sins. For 1985 alone, they included driving into Tim Richmond at Richmond, a practice crash with Kyle Petty, taking Ricky Rudd sideways at Bristol, and forcing Waltrip, his antagonist for much of the 1980s, onto the grass at Charlotte.

The reasons for Earnhardt's grim tenacity were the subject of psychological second-guessing by virtually everybody along pit road. Earnhardt, a shy person who appeared quite happy to hide behind his dark sunglasses and his manufactured image as "the Man in Black," was rarely forthcoming, but in the new climate surrounding NASCAR and Winston Cup racing, he didn't particularly have to be. Humpy Wheeler, president of the Charlotte Motor Speedway, explained Earnhardt's attitude, and the attitude of most other drivers as well, this way: "They want to make as much as they can as quickly as they can because they all know it can end for them this weekend."

The one member of the press—a former member, at least—close to Earnhardt was a reporter by the name of Joe Whitlock, a garrulous good ol' boy from South Carolina who had been around stock car racing forever. Whitlock covered racing for *The State,* a newspaper in Columbia, S.C., then worked for NASCAR as the head of its news bureau, and finally, in the late 1970s, became a confidant of Earnhardt's and his semiofficial public relations person. This was about the time the face of racing was changing. The big bucks were starting to pour in, and the kid from the scruffy mill town of Kannapolis, N.C., would soon be among the first to tap the money tree. Whitlock and Earnhardt were reasonably close friends, and over several years, Earnhardt gave Whitlock information for what everybody assumed would be the definitive Dale Earnhardt book.

But it would never happen. Whitlock, it turned out, was fighting hidden battles of his own, and on May 6, 1991, he took a shotgun and committed suicide.

Ed Hinton, a motorsports writer for *Sports Illustrated,* reported all of this four years later in a fine article about Earnhardt's climb to the financial mountaintop. The piece intimated that once he became a megastar, Earnhardt ousted Whitlock from the inner circle and cast him adrift, indirectly contributing to his death. The result was to push Earnhardt deeper into his reclusiveness.

In 1995, Earnhardt lost the driving title fairly decisively to the new kid on the block, Jeff Gordon, but entered 1996 with his optimism intact. However, while leading a wild freight train of cars down the front straight at the season's second Talladega race, on July 28, Earnhardt's black No. 3 Chevrolet Monte Carlo was apparently tapped in the rear by Ernie Irvan. The next thing the horrified Alabama crowd saw was the sight of Earnhardt's car standing on its nose against the outside wall. It tumbled onto the driver's side, and in the eleven-car melee that followed, was clobbered at least three times, including a nearly direct shot in the roof.

It was the worst accident of Earnhardt's career since a similar mishap at Pocono in his official rookie season of 1979 sidelined him for four races. He broke his sternum and left collarbone, and any hopes of an eighth driving championship were shattered. Going into Talladega, he had trailed leader Terry Labonte by just 12 points; the injury, however, traumatized his title chances. Although he foolishly did not miss a single race—he was in the car at the start the following week at Indianapolis, then amazingly led 54 of the first 64 laps the following week at the tortuous Watkins Glen road course—by season's end he had slipped to fourth in the points behind Terry Labonte, Gordon, and Dale Jarrett.

As the 1997 season moved beyond its midpoint, the question that was starting to surface was whether the Earnhardt era might finally be drawing to a close, or even if it might already have ended. Heresy, to be sure. But at the Brickyard 400 on August 2, Earnhardt's personal winless streak stretched to 46, by far the longest in his storied career. A scary episode one month later at the Southern 500 only added fuel to the fire. At the start of the race, Earnhardt banged the wall hard in turn one and again in turn two. He kept his car moving, but radioed to Childress that he could not find the entrance to the pits. He circled the track slowly for two laps before coming in. The first ghastly thought was that he had suffered a heart attack, or perhaps a stroke or some disorienting neurological event. But a battery of doctors gave him a medical okay the next week, and after a so-so run at Richmond, he ran near the lead all afternoon at New Hampshire before fading to sixth, then finished a strong second at Dover and Martinsville.

But at the age of 46, he was beyond the time when any of the heroic champions of the previous generation had won their last driving title. Bobby Allison won his final race, the 1988 Daytona 500, at the age of 50, just four months before the crash at Pocono that ended his career, but his only title year was 1983, when he was 45. Similarly, David Pearson won the third of his three championships, all of them before the downsizing of the schedule, in 1969. He was 34. Petty was 42 when he won his seventh title. He kept winning for five more years, then went zip for an amazing eight seasons before he got out of the car at the end of 1992, at the age of 55. Cale Yarborough raced through 1988, when he was 49, but he'd stopped winning three years earlier and had picked up the third of his three driving titles back in 1978, when he was a youthful 39.

Still, Earnhardt's tenacity remains exciting. He went to Florida in February 1997 to try again for the Daytona 500, the race that continues to elude him, with a new mechanic, Larry McReynolds, whom Childress had hired away from the powerful big-track Robert Yates team, and a demeanor that was, for him, positively cheery. Indeed, he led, or challenged for the lead, for virtually the entire race before apparently coming afoul of his own aggressiveness just over twelve laps from the finish. He had gotten loose coming off turn two while challenging Bill Elliott for the lead in front of him and holding off Jeff Gordon behind him. Then he got airborne and landed, roof to roof, on top of Ernie Irvan while also collecting Irvan's teammate, Dale Jarrett, before things calmed down. Stunned, he was taken to an ambulance as a precautionary measure. Then, as he later told the press, he noted that his car still had wheels. Leaping from the ambulance and without consulting Childress, his owner, or McReynolds, his new chief wrench, both of whom had only the vaguest idea of what was going on, he fired up the black No. 3 Monte Carlo and returned to the race, five laps in arrears. Even though he could no longer win the race, the few points he might pick up by reentering the fray could perhaps serve him well at the end of the season.

As it turned out, Earnhardt's gesture earned him nothing. He finished 31st, exactly where he would have finished without the gallant effort. All that was gained was another not unsubstantial couple of pages in the Earnhardt legend.*

Through all of this, Dale Earnhardt has become a rich middle-aged man. *Forbes* magazine, in its annual ratings of rich athletes, in December 1996 reported that Earnhardt's total income for the year was approximately $10.5 million—$2.5

---

*This episode demonstrated yet again that the Winston Cup scoring system is nonsensical. It awards 175 points for a race win, plus an additional 5 points for leading at least one lap and an additional 5 points more for leading the most laps. Thus, the winner of the race is guaranteed 180 points. However, if the second-place driver leads the most laps, you have the silly circumstance where two drivers end up with an equal amount of points in a race won by just one of them. It is also common that further down the charts where the points differential becomes 4 per position and then 3, the absurd situation develops where, because of the bonus system, a driver earns more points than the fellow who finishes immediately ahead of him on the race track.

Thus, the acceptable goal of many teams in any given Winston Cup race is to finish acceptably high up; winning the race, while nice, is not necessary because the penalty for losing it is so slight.

Occasionally, this results in a false champion, most recently in 1996 when Terry Labonte, winner of just two races in thirty-one starts, took the driving title while Jeff Gordon, despite winning a whopping ten races, finished 37 points in arrears.

If, for example, NASCAR adopted a scoring system that really did reward the winner of the race by, let's say, doling out points for first through ten this way—100, 75, 60, 50, 40, 30, 20, 15, 10, 5—the top seven placings for 1996 would have looked like this:

Driver	**Wins**	**Points**	**Pos.**	**Winston Pts.**	**Winston Pos.**
Jeff Gordon	10	1720	1	4620	2
Dale Jarrett	4	1420	2	4568	3
Terry Labonte	2	1380	3	4657	1
Mark Martin	0	975	4	4278	5
Dale Earnhardt	2	835	5	4327	4
Rusty Wallace	5	815	6	3717	7
Ricky Rudd	1	530	7	3845	6

You're welcome, Jeff.

million from actual race-track earnings and the whopping rest from his long list of endorsements and merchandising ventures presided over by his third wife, Teresa, and his agent, a former fundamentalist preacher by the name of Don Hawk. The same article reported that Earnhardt had recently sold his souvenir licensing company for $30 million but would retain royalty rights for the next fifteen years. While these numbers pale by comparison with the stratospheric figures compiled by the likes of basketball's Michael Jordan and boxing's Mike Tyson, and while the last estimates of NASCAR's licensed sales were just about one-eighth those of the National Football League, which more or less invented the process, they represent a quantum leap in the world of stock car racing. To illustrate this point further, here is a list of some prize money figures for the three milestone seasons of 1972 (the first of the downsized schedule), 1980 (the last full season covered by this book the first time around and Earnhardt's first championship year), and 1996:

1972

Points Position	Name	Money Won
1.	Richard Petty	$240,515
2.	Bobby Allison	274,995
3.	James Hylton	96,655
10.	Ben Arnold	31,115
15.	Dave Marcis	34,421
25.	Coo Coo Marlin	28,124

1980

Points Position	Name	Money Won
1.	Dale Earnhardt	$588,926
2.	Cale Yarborough	537,358
3.	Benny Parsons	385,140
10.	Richard Childress	157,420
15.	Cecil Gordon	83,300
25.	Bobby Wawak	21,080

1996

1.	Terry Labonte	$4,030,648
2.	Jeff Gordon	3,428,485
3.	Dale Jarrett	2,985,418
10.	Ernie Irvan	1,683,313
15.	Jimmy Spencer	1,090,876
25.	Wally Dallenbach	837,001

In 1996, thirty-four drivers earned more on the race track than did Earnhardt in his first championship year. By the end of 1996, thirteen active drivers had exceeded Richard Petty's career winnings of $7.755 million, including his son, Kyle, and a whole bunch of others were closing in. The 1997 champion, Jeff Gordon, all by himself raked in more than $6.3 million.

AMIDST THE GLITZ AND THE GLITTER AND THE RELENTLESS proactive commercialism that had come to drive the sport during these halcyon years, inevitable episodes of tragedy reminded the troops that stock car racing remained a dangerous enterprise. The very fact that stock car racing was one of the safer forms of motor sports made the occasional instances, as always, stand out in stark contrast to the norm.

The irony of the eighties and nineties was that the three most critical fatalities, to drivers whose continued presence would almost certainly have resulted in a very different Winston Cup record book, all occurred away from the race track.

Tim Richmond was the first. A supreme talent from the northern Ohio town of Ashland, he was, during his brief and meteoric career, a talisman of sorts, both in the route he took to NASCAR and the way he died. Northern Ohio was not a hotbed of stock car activity—certainly not of the NASCAR variety. Its racing loyalties were to the Midwestern associations, such as ARCA, and to USAC. The goal was the Indianapolis 500, and the path to that goal led through open-wheel midget racers and sprint cars.

Richmond took that route, and his climb was sensational.

By 1980 he was driving for Roger Penske, in his ascendancy as a car owner. At the Indianapolis 500 that year, Richmond was not only sensational, he was spectacular and dramatic as well. On the day before pole qualifying, he set the fastest practice time of the month. On the morning of pole qualifying, he crashed heavily and could not take his four-lap qualifying run until the second weekend. Still, he qualified fifth fastest overall. In the race itself, he started nineteenth on the grid, ran third most of the day, and actually led one lap, then ran out of gas after he'd completed the race, in eighth place, and came to a stop in turn four. No problem. The winner was Johnny Rutherford, and after Rutherford took the checkered flag, he stopped and picked up Richmond and gave him a ride to his pit en route to Victory Lane.

That Indianapolis 500, however, was just one of two finishes Richmond managed in nine IndyCar races in 1980, and late that year he headed south, for NASCAR. If this didn't actually start a trend, it certainly encouraged a defection to NASCAR by drivers who might have stayed with what had once been the more glamorous IndyCar circuit. Several years later John Andretti, nephew to the great Mario Andretti and cousin to Mario's equally accomplished son, Michael, eschewed the logic of IndyCar racing in favor of the Winston Cup. Jeff Gordon found his way from California to North Carolina by the same process. In a different era, he, too, might well have stayed with the IndyCar circuit.

Writing in *Southern Motorsports Journal,* Gerald Martin said of Richmond in 1983, "He is perhaps the most marketable of the new breed in a sport that is being drowned in Madison Avenue soap. . . . But he's no phony."

In a later column, Martin asked Richmond about his reputation as a woman chaser. "Well, I darn sure don't chase men," he told Martin. "I don't see anything wrong with me looking at the ladies. That's just a natural phenomenon. . . . When I meet someone, I try to get to know her in ways other than just having a cup of coffee."

Richmond was as dramatically spectacular in the South as he'd been up North. In April 1984, his crew chief pled guilty to three counts of receiving stolen property; later that same season, Richmond himself got into a fight in the garage area with the legendary David Pearson. In mid-1986, a crash with Richard Petty in the tunnel turn at Pocono prompted an unabashed Richmond to tell reporters, "I'm a little stirred right now with people who call themselves racecar drivers and can't drive any better than I can."

At that time, he could afford to be cocky. From 1982 through 1985 he'd won just four races and five poles and had finished 18th, 11th, 13th, and 11th in the money standings. *SMJ* reported in 1985 that Richmond had embarked on a rigorous training schedule that included aerobic dancing, exercise classes, and a diet of brown rice, bananas, steamed potatoes, and vegetables. Coincidence or not, in 1986 Richmond had one of those career seasons that every driver fantasizes about. In a midseason stretch that began at Pocono on June 8 and ended at Richmond on September 7, he won six of ten races and finished second in three of the others. His season-ending tally showed seven wins, eight poles, earnings of $973,221, and a third-place finish in the points race behind Earnhardt and Waltrip.

Less than three years later he was dead, of AIDS.

Richmond maintained he got the disease through promiscuous heterosexual contact. After winning two more races early in the 1987 season, and after rumors that he had AIDS had been confirmed, Richmond was banned from NASCAR garage areas following a protest by nervous and outraged drivers, and he never raced again.

Alan Kulwicki was a different sort. A mild-mannered, well-educated journeyman from Wisconsin, he came South in 1985 from the American Speed Association, a regional organization, at the age of 30 for a brief look at Winston Cup racing. In 1986 he came down to stay and earned Rookie of the Year honors, a designation that was often an entrée to a ride with an established, well-heeled team.

At a time when multicar teams were seen as the wave of the future—a coal-mine owner named J. D. Stacy once fielded a seven-car stable—Kulwicki stubbornly decided to remain an independent owner-driver despite a rumored offer, around 1990, of $1 million to drive for Junior Johnson. His success was limited going into the 1992 season—single victories in 1988, 1990, and 1991—but he ingratiated himself with stock car fans by introducing the "Polish Victory Lap," in which he would spin his car 180 degrees after taking the checkered flag and then tour the track backward. Kulwicki partisans or not, the crowd loved it.

During the 1992 season—Richard Petty's last as a driver and the first, for a single race, by an unknown Californian named Jeff Gordon—Kulwicki won just two races—compared with five each by Bill Elliott in a car prepared by Junior Johnson and by Davey Allison in a car owned by Robert Yates—but because the NASCAR scoring system, as we've seen, rewards consistency over performance, the points race came down to the final event of the season, at Atlanta. Allison led Kulwicki by 30 points and Elliott by 40 going in, and the championship was his to lose—which he did two-thirds of the way through the race when Ernie Irvan lost a tire and got sideways directly in front of Allison and Rusty Wallace. Wallace avoided Irvan; Allison T-boned him and was out of the race. Now the driving championship would be decided by Kulwicki and Elliott, running one-two on the track. With 27 laps to go, Kulwicki pitted for gas while leading, knowing that he had already led 103 laps and would gain the 5 bonus points that went to the driver who led the most laps. This cost him his chance to win the race, but no matter. While Elliott took the checkers, Kulwicki won the title by just 10 points, and Davey Allison no doubt won the Goody's headache award.

Within a year, both Kulwicki and Allison were dead.

Kulwicki and three others died on April 2, 1993, in the crash of a private plane as it left the race track at Bristol, Tennessee.

His death was of course mourned, but when Davey Allison was killed four months later, the stock car racing community was stunned into numbness. It was difficult to believe that yet another Allison—another member of the fabled "Alabama Gang"—had come to a tragic and violent end.

The Allisons and the Alabama Gang included brothers Bobby and Donnie, Bobby's sons, Clifford and Davey, and various other drivers, most notably Neil Bonnett and Red Farmer, who were from the same Birmingham, Ala., suburb of Hueytown or nearby. By and large they did things right, and yet, through the 1980s and well into the 1990s, terrible things kept happening to them.

Donnie Allison began the 1981 racing season with high hopes, but in the World 600 at Charlotte in late May, he had a horrific accident with Dick Brooks and missed virtually all the rest of the season. His team disbanded at the end of the year, and he never got a quality ride after that.

Bobby Allison won his third Daytona 500 in 1988 after a ferocious, end-of-race duel with his oldest son, Davey. But at the first Pocono race that year, Bobby crashed hard on the back straight and suffered life-threatening injuries. He made a remarkable recovery, but the accident clearly diminished his mental capacities. He never raced again. Two seasons later, he formed his own racing team, but from 1990 through 1996 his various drivers could not win a race. Indeed, in 207 starts, Bobby Allison Racing cars mustered just 13 top-five finishes. This in itself was no crime. As mentioned, Petty Enterprises went twelve full seasons without a victory until Bobby Hamilton pulled one off in 1996, and Cale Yarborough Motorsports was zip for ten seasons until John Andretti won in 1997; through 1997, cars owned by Butch Mock had gone twenty years with just four victories; through 1997 owner Junie Donlavey Jr. was one win for twenty-seven seasons despite entering 770 cars driven by fifty-one different drivers in 747 races.

So far, the mishaps, while brutal, might have been called acceptable under the general category of "That's Racing."

But the demons emerged at Michigan in August of 1992 when Clifford Allison, Bobby's youngest son, the third of his and his wife Judy's four children, was killed in a practice accident—barely days after Bobby had confided to reporters that Michigan was his favorite race track because you could easily run there three abreast.

The crusher was Davey, who clearly had the talent to challenge the dominance of the older Earnhardt and most certainly would have been an equal match for Jeff Gordon. A competent pilot of fixed-wing aircraft (NASCAR drivers like to fly; Ricky Rudd has flown with the Blue Angels, albeit as a passenger), Davey then undertook learning to fly helicopters. On July 12, 1993, he was at the controls of his latest toy, a jet helicopter, with Red Farmer, a longtime friend of the Allison clan, as his only passenger. Davey tried to set the craft down in a small, fenced-in area in the middle of the Talladega race track. He lost control, and the helicopter rolled and crashed to the ground on its side. Farmer suffered a lot of broken bones, but survived. Davey died early the next morning at a hospital in Birmingham.

These tragedies were made all the sadder by the fact that the Allisons were universally understood to be good people. They were God-fearing, churchgoing folks who did not parade their religion on their driving suits. ("God was on our side today." "The Good Lord wanted us to win out there." "God guided us through that carnage out in turn four, and He found a little extra fuel for us—don't know where.") They behaved well. They were nice, except occasionally on the race track, where their tenacity and unwillingness to bend even an inch, anywhere, at any time, under any circumstance, gave them the reputation, especially Bobby, as drivers who would not quit or yield for anything.

And just when one was beginning to think the fates had certainly run out of bodies, Neil Bonnett, 47 and nearing the end of his career, was killed on February 11, 1994, during a practice session for the Daytona 500.

For a final parenthetical twist, the first president of the Alan Kulwicki Fan Club was Carrie Allison, the smitten youngest daughter of Bobby and Judy.

DESPITE THESE VERY REAL TRAGEDIES, WINSTON CUP RACING could boast of an acceptable safety record. The newer race tracks, were, by and large, wider than their first- and second-generation counterparts—witness the sight of cars racing four and five abreast at Roger Penske's new California Speedway—yet this did not seem to take the edge off the racing. It was historically true that the safer racing became, in the form of improvements in track design or race car construction, the braver the drivers got—thus keeping a taut balance between unwanted carnage and undesirable blandness. On this score, incidentally, I gave an early marginal victory to Bruton Smith's Texas Motor Speedway in the arena of new track construction.

Once he added a touch more room to take the pinch out of a couple of turns, particularly the fourth, he would have a more interesting track than Penske's California gem. In time, it would be seen as its generation's Darlington, just as California would be viewed as the new Daytona.

As the nineties drew to a close, stock car racing's main concern was the federal government's frontal assault on the tobacco industry. The tentative agreement announced in June of 1997 between big government and big tobacco appears to mean the end of visible sponsorships by companies such as R. J. Reynolds and Philip Morris of racing teams such as Ken Schrader's Skoal Bandit Chevrolet and Jimmy Spencer's Joe Camel Ford, and of races such as the Winston 500 at Talladega, and, of course, the entire Winston Cup series. But no one, except perhaps some tobacco executives, is concerned for the future of the sport should the agreement be implemented. For better or worse, Winston Cup racing had long ago become bigger than any single sponsor, no matter how large, and corporate America stands anxiously in a queue ready at the drop of a match to replace the cancer sticks with other indispensable products. Coca-Cola, which sponsored two major races, the Coca-Cola 600 (formerly the World 600) at Charlotte and the Mountain Dew Southern 500 (formerly the Southern 500) at Darlington, would love, one thinks, to jump in and give Pepsi, the official drink of NASCAR, a tweak on its corporate nose. McDonald's, which sponsors just one race car and no races, is perhaps another candidate to be a series sponsor.

The Budweiser Cup? The Miller Cup? The Interstate Batteries Cup? The Spam Cup? The list of possible replacements is virtually endless.

NASCAR's biggest problem, really, as 1997 drew to a close, was where to go next. Japan was scheduled to open a $300-million oval race track in 1998, at Suzuka. In Europe, which invented the road race and turned down its nose at circle-track racing, Grand Touring cars were starting to race on oval tracks. Megamergers and acquisitions will soon make it possible to equalize V-6, V-8, and V-10 power plants so that stock car racing can be truly global—once the Europeans bite the bullet and build a big, superspeedway-type oval track. This could only be of commercial benefit to the core Winston Cup sponsors, many of which are part of multinational corporations anyway.

As 1997 neared its end, the first winner was the Las Vegas Motor Speedway, a 1.5-mile track purchased earlier in the year by the same family that operates the New Hampshire track. It was awarded a Winston Cup date for 1998, upping the number of races to 33.

A lesser problem for NASCAR was what on earth to do about Jeff Gordon in particular and the Rick Hendrick superteam in general, which threatened to dominate the circuit to the point of boredom. Gordon was the Rookie of the Year in 1993, eighth in points in 1994, Winston Cup champion in 1995, second to teammate Terry Labonte in 1996; in 1997, he won ten of the first twenty-five races and held on to win his second title. At this pace, Gordon, who turned 26 on August 4, 1997, would break Richard Petty's seemingly unsurpassable record of 200 career victories before he hits 45.

He is truly a wunderkind, a prodigy in a sport that generally prefers its champions to mature a little before they win consistently. Born in California, he began racing go-carts and quarter-midgets at the age of 5. His stepfather moved the family to Indiana when Jeff was 13 to enhance his racing career; California wouldn't allow him an adult competitor's license. In the Midwest he was the 1990 USAC Midget champion, but then, like Tim Richmond and Alan Kulwicki before him, he decided to abandon open-wheel racing in favor of the increasingly more prestigious NASCAR circuits.

He drove one race for Ray Hendrick in the watershed year of 1992 and never looked back.

Good-looking, in a Michael J. Fox sort of way, he secretly courted Brooke Sealey, one of the several 1993 Miss Winston models, and married her in November 1994 and appeared more or less to be leading the perfect life even as he prepared to carry Winston Cup racing into the next millennium. As reported in *Wheels,* the excellent 1997 book on stock car racing by Paul Hemphill, Darrell Waltrip gave this assessment of Gordon: "He's the prototype of the future driver, groomed for it since he was a kid. He doesn't throw his helmet and cuss NASCAR when something goes wrong, he just goes back to work. The guy's a great driver." Examples of his tenacity and his ability to create victory are already endless. Consider the 1997 Daytona 500, in which on four occasions Gordon did things on the track that were absolutely essential to his win.

The first was early in the race when a cut tire forced him to pit under the green; he then had to fight mightily once he was back on the track to avoid being lapped and put hopelessly in arrears by the angry pack bearing down on him.

The second was late in the race when a fortuitous caution allowed him to close behind the lead pack. Gordon then clawed his way to third, behind Bill Elliott and Dale Earnhardt, and positioned himself for a run to the checkers.

The third came when he maneuvered alongside Earnhardt in the one-two turn and held his position while Earnhardt lost control and crashed dramatically on the back straight.

Finally, when the green flag came out after the Earnhardt caution, Gordon had to run hard to ensure he'd be in first place if the race ended under yellow—which, in fact, it did due to a twelve-car brawl three laps from the end.

Gordon led teammates Labonte and Craven to a one-two-three finish for the Rick Hendrick entry, but Hendrick was not there to enjoy the sweep. He was in a Charlotte hospital fighting leukemia and did not make an appearance at a race track all season.

Hendrick was also under the gun on another front throughout 1997, having been indicted by the federal government the previous year for a scam involving his myriad automobile dealerships, over five and one-half dozen in all. In late August 1997, he entered a guilty plea to a single count of mail fraud, and in exchange, federal prosecutors dropped thirteen charges of money laundering and one of conspiracy.

ONE OF THE PLEASURES OF DOING THE RESEARCH FOR THE reissue of this book was to catch up on what had become of the people who had been generous with their time, and their scrapbooks, some twenty years before.

Some, inevitably, were dead. Darel Dieringer, the transplanted Indianan who drove so well and so spectacularly, particularly at Darlington, died of cancer in 1989. John Holman, the no-nonsense business half of the brilliant Holman-Moody partnership, suffered a fatal heart attack in 1976, even before "Fast As White Lightning" was published the first time.

Most of "my people" were doing just fine. Richard Petty, whom I'd talked with at his family shop in Randleman, N.C., interrupted once or twice in a two-hour session by his son, Kyle, then a gangly quarterback for his high school football team, had made the transition from king-of-the-hill race car driver to one-of-the-pack race car owner with reasonable good grace. Similarly, Cale Yarborough, a three-time driving champion for Junior Johnson, had made an apparently comfortable transition after his relatively early retirement at the age of 48 in 1988, although as noted, he, like Petty, found that owning a race car was a whole lot more difficult than driving one.

Ned Jarrett, the patriarch of a truly nice family, now operated from behind a microphone—and in front of the television cameras—as easily as he ever did at the wheel of a car. He was the first ex-driver to carve a broadcasting career for himself and was later joined by the likes of Buddy Baker and Benny Parsons.

Bruton Smith, of course, had built all sorts of empires for himself since his return to racing after his years in the desert, as had Humpy Wheeler, the most innovative of racing executives. Smith's money and Wheeler's ideas had combined—along with the powerful growth of the city of Charlotte, which in the nineties surpassed its longtime snobbish rival, Atlanta, in population and, it could be argued, influence—to change the face of stock car racing and return its epicenter from the hard sands of Daytona Beach to the red clay of the Carolina Piedmont. And Jim Hunter, a former sportswriter who had previously served as a public relations gadfly for Gene White, an Atlanta car owner, and as the executive editor of the *NASCAR Press Guide and Record Book*, now found himself in stock car racing's dream job as the head of the Darlington Raceway.

There were the inevitable tragedies. Butch Lindley, the Sportsman driver from South Carolina who never had the inclination to race Winston Cup cars, crashed badly at Bradenton, Fla., on April 13, 1985, in something called an All-Pro event, went into an irreversible coma, and died five years later. And as noted, a series of tragedies befell the Alabama Gang in defiance of any actuarial table. One of my fondest memories remains of the time I met Bobby Allison, tape recorder at the ready, at his home in Hueytown, Ala., fully intending to begin my interview in a comfortable setting at ground level. Instead, we drove to the airport, popped into his private plane, and flew to Cincinnati so he could make a personal appearance at one of his fan clubs. My interview was conducted at 8,000 feet. I asked my questions and Allison answered them as we both warily scanned the Ohio River Valley for signs of air traffic.

One key person I didn't talk with the first time around was Junior Johnson. There was no particular reason for this omission, except perhaps that he was a somewhat intimidating subject given that the definitive piece on him had been done some time before in *Esquire* magazine by Tom Wolfe. But an omission it certainly was. More than any other single person, Johnson represented the NASCAR continuum. He was an ex-bootlegger—he had been pardoned by President Reagan for his long-ago white-lightning transgressions on December 26, 1986—and then a storied driver of the factory era who defied the odds in the most extraordinary fashion to become the most successful car owner of the modern era. It is only a mild stretch to suggest that Johnson might, in fact, be responsible for the modern era. For it was he, so went the stories, who visited R. J. Reynolds in the early 1970s and suggested the company take over the series sponsorship.

So, it was nice to get a call from *AutoWeek* in the spring of 1996 asking if I'd like to do a profile of Johnson on the occasion of his rather abrupt retirement from racing.

He and his wife, Flossie Clark, had been fixtures at NASCAR races for nearly four decades. Now he had separated from Flossie to marry a much younger woman by whom he'd fathered two boys. He had also sold his racing operation to his most recent driver, Geoff Bodine. Coincidentally, the sale occurred at just about the time Johnson's home track at North Wilkesboro, a place where they'd been running Grand National, and now, Winston Cup, races since 1952, was being closed down. Bruton Smith and Robert Bahre, the acrimonious co-owners of the .625-mile bullring, were darkening the place so that its two dates could be divvied up between Smith's new Texas Motor Speedway and Bahre's 1.058-mile oval at Loudon, N.H.

Johnson, then a couple of months shy of 66, who needed no introduction to *AutoWeek* readers, and his wife, the former Lisa Day, 30, who most certainly did, lived in what was more or less a palace, a brand-new, double-winged Georgian thing that rested grandly atop a North Carolina hill not far from the junction of Old U.S. Highway 421 and Interstate 77. The house was set on 200 acres, upon which grazed 200 head of Santa Gertrudis beef cattle, part of Johnson's herd of 600—the other 400 being scattered in various nearby pastures. Three barbecue grills stood at the ready on the back porch; in the yard was a huge sandbox for the kids, Robert Glen Johnson III, and Meredith, the baby. By the front door were two bricks etched with the names *Junior* and *Lisa,* a nice touch. In all, Lisa said, the place had 14,000 square feet on two stories. Johnson and his new family had lived there less than a year.

The interior was tastefully decorated. Dominating one wall was a classic, black-and-white photograph of Junior in his early driving days that showed him wearing a T-shirt, a helmet, and a wraparound visor that reflected the stands in front of him. Beyond the photo, however, there were few signs of Johnson's 43-year racing career. A wine rack was filled with some of Sonoma Valley's finest, obtained the year before during the race weekend at Sears Point, Calif.

On the day of qualifying for the First Union 400, the spring race at North Wilkesboro, Johnson was found in a pair of bib overalls and a work cap atop a small front-loader, rearranging dirt. He and four friends were preparing a large patch of the yard for seeding. Philip Pardue was one of these friends, Alvin Cheeks was another, and Bud Holloman was the third. Somebody remarked that the fourth man, the one on the far bulldozer, was 78 years old.

"That's Mr. Burgess," Junior said. "I'm not sure what Mr. Burgess's first name is. I always just call him Mr. Burgess."

Johnson got off his front-loader. He rearranged himself on the ground and leaned back against a pyramid of seed bags. It was less than four months since his surprising announcement that he had sold his No. 11 race car and his share in the No. 27 team car and was, in fact, retired from racing. Since then, he had been host to a constant parade of friends, and of journalists anxious to reprise his fabled career as North Carolina's most storied bootlegger, NASCAR's most folkloric driver, and the modern era of Winston Cup racing's most accomplished car owner.

Johnson confirmed once again that he had not been to a race since The Announcement at the end of the 1995 season and that he had no plans to go to one anytime soon. (However, the night before, he had exchanged bons mots with Darrell Waltrip, his former driver, and Ned Jarrett, his former driving rival, while taping a segment of *This Week in NASCAR*. Later in the spring, he would implant his hands in the Court of Legends walkway at the Charlotte Motor Speedway.) He said he hadn't really been tempted, but then he mischievously added that three people not now in racing, whose names, he said, people would recognize if he said them, had approached him about forming a team if only he'd run it.

But he'd told all of them he wouldn't.

"I don't miss it," he said in his Brushy Mountains vernacular, whose wonderful nuances even a tape recorder could not accurately convey. "My reason for not missing it is because I've already done about everything you can do in the sport anyway."

Johnson, who had had a shock of white hair since his late teens, appeared to be in great shape. He seemed thinner than in his driving days, although he claimed his weight was about the same: 220 pounds, give or take. It was, he said, just better distributed. Lisa said she'd been trying to feed him more pasta and Caesar salads and fewer of the traditional six-course meals, heavy on the fat and don't hold the gravy, that remain a staple of country life in the South.

Johnson appeared at ease. "I'm very, very relaxed and happy with my life," he said. "I don't know anything I'd change about it. I'm basically right now doing my will and making sure my children is going to be taken care of—college, private school—and that my wife is well taken care of before her death, and that the children wind up with all their assets. Once I get all that in place, the future'll take care of itself."

His new digs, in Yadkin County, are but a long shout from the Wilkes County line and the famous Ingle Hollow address of his past. While it would have lent a pleasant poetic note if it were true, no matter how hard you tried, you could not hear the guttural roar from the ancient North Wilkesboro Speedway, some fifteen miles to the west, where cars were still being raced by the heirs and descendants of Johnson's own particular Thunder Road.

Not even when the wind was right?

"No," Junior Johnson said firmly. And this, he swore, was gospel.

The truth about Johnson, like much of his legendary craftiness, was not at all complicated and had only to do with simple numbers. On June 28, 1995, Johnson turned 65; Lisa, his wife of less than four years, was just 30; Robert Glen Johnson III—nobody dared call him Junior Junior, or Junior Squared—was not yet three; Meredith, the baby, would turn one in midsummer.

While Johnson was not as reticent as he once was, he still remains the most private of individuals. This is high irony, given that over the past five years or so his private life had taken more twists and turns than a poorly crafted Russian novel. He is one of those rare public figures whose true-to-life sagas exceeded the mythology, more often than not.

Information about Junior had tended to arrive in bunches. The first bundle was the article by Tom Wolfe, the writer and social commentator, in the February 1965 issue of *Esquire* magazine. It was titled "The Last American Hero Is Junior Johnson. Yes!" It ensured Johnson's fame well beyond the insular world of NASCAR, and the memory of its appearance still causes sportswriters, national and regional alike, to twitch with envy.

The second was a three-part series of articles by Robert Zeller, a journalist, that appeared in three Southern newspapers in 1993. These thoroughly researched stories laid bare the less romantic aspects of Johnson's whiskey-running past as well as the details of his separation and divorce from Flossie Clark, his companion in and out of marriage for nearly forty years, and his subsequent marriage to Lisa Day.

Johnson either confirmed or did not deny the major points contained in the articles by Zeller: Yes, he'd been married before Flossie, briefly, in 1949, when he was still a teenager; yes, he had continued to run whiskey following his release from federal prison in October 1957, after he'd served an eleven-month, three-day sentence stemming from being found at the Johnson family still (the crime for which President Reagan had pardoned him); yes, he'd fallen asleep at the wheel of a whiskey car in 1958 and slammed into another car, killing a woman passenger in the other vehicle. (Johnson pled guilty to manslaughter. He was fined $300 and given a five-year suspended sentence.)

However, it was the sequence of his separation and divorce from Flossie, and his relationship with Lisa, that became the talk of NASCAR. Junior and Flossie's divorce was in many ways a tragic event for stock car racing insiders. As one of the inner circle said, "Johnson was liked, but Flossie was beloved." The short of it, as Zeller reported, was that Junior and Flossie, having drifted apart, were on the verge of a reasonably amicable financial settlement regarding their considerable holdings when Flossie received a phone call suggesting that Johnson had taken up with another woman.

"I thought he was done with that sort of thing," Flossie told Zeller. A property settlement was not reached until nearly a year after the divorce, and it's safe to conclude that the phone call made a big difference in the final balance.

Lisa Day Johnson is an attractive strawberry blonde who grew up in Ingle Hollow, a close neighbor of the Johnsons. Both she and Junior gave practiced responses to the inevitable question of how they met, and when. "Lisa growed up and lived not two-three miles from me," Junior said. "I've known her all her life. We've always been friends, and our friendship just turned into more than being just friends."

Junior and Flossie did not have children. They were divorced in October 1992. Junior and Lisa were married two months later, at the Ritz-Carlton in Atlanta. Robert III was born on August 24, 1993; Meredith arrived on July 13, 1995. "We have no plans for more," Lisa said, "but I don't know what the Lord has in mind."

In the midst of this soap opera, Johnson had triple-bypass, open-heart surgery, at the Duke University Medical Center in Durham. (Coincidentally, Lisa was a registered nurse with a specialty in cardiology.)

Possibly the most significant event, as it related to Johnson's retirement, occurred in 1991 when a North Carolina State student named Brent Kauthen was killed in an automobile accident. Kauthen was the son of a woman named Mary Ellen Kauthen, who in 1990 had married Herb Fishel, the executive director of General Motors Motorsports.

Kauthen had begun visiting the Johnsons when he was just eight years old, and following his graduation from high school, he moved in with Junior and Flossie. By all accounts, he was an electronics genius.

"He was the guy I was intending to take over the whole operation," Johnson explained. "I kindly groomed him in the things I wanted him to be able to do in the racing operation, basically computers."

Johnson financed Kauthen's college education at Raleigh and purchased some expensive computers for the school, ones that would also help Johnson and Kauthen with valuable race-car-engine telemetry.

After a long pause and with some reluctance, Johnson then added, "He was my key to setting my race team away from everybody and beyond them in the future. And of course when he got killed, it all went with him."

Johnson had always been his own person, unafraid to take on authority at every turn and NASCAR's in particular. He got wiser and smarter as he got older, and certainly obtained maturity, but he got no less stubborn. In what turned out to be his farewell appearance at the Daytona 500, in 1995, Johnson was fined a record $45,000 (reduced to $40,000 on appeal) for an illegal intake manifold; at the 1990 Winston, the special event for the previous season's race winners, he was suspended for twelve races (reduced to three on appeal) for using an oversize engine.

His most significant run-in took place in 1992 over Bill Elliott's rear end. Elliott began the season, his first with Johnson, with a furious early run of four straight victories—at Rockingham, Richmond, Atlanta, and Darlington—and nobody could quite figure out why. The answer was a cambered rear end, with the wheels offset three degrees from the vertical, which allowed Elliott's car to work better on banking. Once the trick was brought to NASCAR's attention (Johnson believed one of his crew members had loose lips), NASCAR wrote a rule limiting the camber to 1.8 degrees. NASCAR maintained it made the change in the interest of safety—too many broken rear axles resulted when other teams tried to catch up—but this almost certainly cost Johnson and Elliott a championship. In the closest points race in Winston Cup history, Elliott lost the title to Alan Kulwicki by just those 10 points.

Still, Johnson's final totals as a car owner were hefty enough. His drivers won 139 races, $22,133,785 in prize money, and six championships. The driving titles, three each by Yarborough and Darrell Waltrip, tied Johnson with Richard Childress for the most by an owner in NASCAR's modern era. Johnson's 127 wins from 1972 through 1995 are far and away the most by an owner in this period; his final earnings placed him third behind Rick Hendrick and Childress, both of whom have amassed their winnings largely during the lucrative eighties and nineties.

Through success and controversy, Johnson was never short of opinions.

• On his success: "I've always had a pretty good mind for seeing beyond what I'm looking at, and I've always been lucky enough to figure out about anything that came along that I was messing with. And, I don't do it the hard way. I do it the easy way. I see a lot of people try to overpower the method of physics by having a little education."

• On NASCAR: "When I kept passing the rule book up, and passing it up with better ideas, as quick as they'd see what I had and was beating everybody with, they'd either make it illegal, or make it legal and tell everybody what it was, by announcing you can run so-and-so at the next race. You might as well just go having a meeting and say, 'Hey, guys, Junior's got this here, and if you don't got it, you need to be gettin' it.'"

• On Bobby Allison, who drove only one season for him, in 1972: "You've got to do things Bobby Allison's way or you just can't get along with him. He'd win races—he was good enough to win a race in nearly anything—but money wasn't a part of it. I couldn't race with him because I'd go in it to win races and make money, too. So we couldn't have never stayed together anyway."

• On Cale Yarborough, his driver from 1973 through 1980: "I've seen him drive cars that I've said there ain't no dad-gum way. He'd wreck 'em, and the dad-gum wheels would be everywhere on 'em, and he'd still drive the shit out of 'em. I've never seen him give up. Or give out."

• On Darrell Waltrip, his driver from 1981 through 1986: "I've seen Darrell give up and give out, too."

• To Darrell Waltrip in 1981 (as reported by Waltrip on *This Week in NASCAR*) after Waltrip all but promised Johnson he'd win the driving championship if he got the Junior Johnson ride: "Well, if you do, you'd better." (He did.)

Despite his disclaimer that he sought easy solutions, Johnson was a workaholic throughout his career. "Until about six-seven years ago," he said, "I'd spend nights in the shop when everybody's gone home. I'd go eat supper, come back, work to two-three o'clock, get four-five hours' sleep, and be right back in that shop the next morning. They didn't nothing move that I didn't know what it was. If it was right, I left it alone; if it was wrong, I made 'em fix it, and that's the way it has to be done."

Inevitably, speculation arose that what ultimately pushed Johnson into retirement was either dissatisfaction with his most recent drivers, none of whom had won a driving title since Waltrip achieved his third, in 1985, or terminal annoyance, finally, with his old adversary, NASCAR.

Jim Hunter, the former journalist who had become the president and general manager of Darlington Raceway, offered this scenario:

"Johnson was one of the most knowledgeable people around, but the playing fields changed. Instead of five and six teams to beat, there were fifteen to twenty, then twenty to thirty, and Junior's relationship with these other teams changed. People used to go to him for advice and he'd help out. But Junior had to quit telling them things. Junior trained a lot of people, and now these people were beating him. Maybe that affected him—Junior often said that things ain't the same."

One reaches a similar conclusion when one looks at Johnson's function as an owner. At the height of Johnson's career, it was assumed that he was part of an informal board of owners and crew chiefs that included the likes of Glen Wood, Banjo

Matthews, Bud Moore, John Holman, and Ralph Moody. This "board" would pass on technical matters in closed session, as it were, and then make informal, but persuasive, recommendations to NASCAR. But when the present generation of extremely well-heeled owners began to take over the garage area, Johnson and the old guard were, in effect, gently eased from their positions of influence in favor of no-nonsense rules enforcers such as Gary Nelson. The fun was soon gone.

Johnson said the explanation was not nearly that convoluted. He said he'd started to think about his retirement only a couple of years before, "especially when my little first boy come along. And then when my little girl come along, I got real serious about it. I felt it was time to get out and get on with my life and family and enjoy the rest of my days doing things I wanted to do."

Which was exactly what he was doing that fine spring day in 1996.

The next day, on the very eve of the North Wilkesboro race, Jimmy Spencer, who in 1994 earned the only two Winston Cup victories of his career driving for Johnson, had dinner with Junior and Lisa, and afterward, longtime car-owner Junie Donlavey stopped by and visited for a while. Down the road a bit, Flossie hosted Bill Elliott for breakfast, then entertained Darrell Waltrip and his wife, Stevie, for dinner.

However, what seemed to matter most was not this mild appearance of divided loyalties but rather some gentle horseplay between Johnson and Robert III that had taken place next to the recently moved earth and in full view of those 200 head of cattle.

Robert and his dog roamed the field and played in the dirt next to where Junior sat.

"Get out of there!" Johnson shouted. "Ye'll black yer shoes up, boy."

Robert took heed, but only briefly. He maneuvered among the bags of seed, then began hitting on his old man.

"What have you done?" Johnson said in mock protest. "Oh, you hit me! You hit me! Well . . . I hit you right back."

Then the 65-year-old patriarch and his 3-year-old namesake tumbled into each other's arms and rolled laughing on the ground.

Index

B

C

R

Z

About the Author

Kim Chapin worked as a reporter for the *Atlanta Journal* and as a staff writer for *Sports Illustrated*. He is now a writer and freelance journalist and lives in Santa Fe, New Mexico, with his wife, Anne Constable, and their two children, Alexander and Nicholas. His previous books include *Tennis to Win* and *Billie Jean* (both with Billie Jean King), *The Beauty of Running* (with Gayle Barron), *Dogwood Afternoons,* and *The Road to Wembley.*